LEGO® MINIFIGURE
A VISUAL HISTORY

UPDATED AND EXPANDED

Written by
Simon Hugo with Gregory Farshtey and Daniel Lipkowitz

Senior Editor Helen Murray
Project Editor Lisa Stock
Editor Kathryn Hill
US Senior Editor Kayla Dugger
US Executive Editor Lori Cates Hand
Project Art Editor Jenny Edwards
Designers Rosamund Bird, Thelma-Jane Robb
Senior Production Editor Jennifer Murray
Senior Production Controller Lloyd Robertson
Managing Editor Tori Kosara
Managing Art Editor Jo Connor
Publisher Paula Regan
Art Director Charlotte Coulais
Managing Director Mark Searle

Additional photography Gary Ombler,
Thomas Baunsgaard Pedersen, Tim Trøjborg

This American Edition, 2025
First American Edition, 2013
Published in the United States by DK Publishing,
a division of Penguin Random House LLC
1745 Broadway, 20th Floor, New York, NY 10019

Page design copyright © 2013, 2021, 2025 Dorling Kindersley Limited
A Penguin Random House Company

Published in Great Britain by Dorling Kindersley Limited
ISBN 979-8-2171-2604-0 (trade edition)
979-8-2171-2605-7 (library edition)

Printed and bound in China

www.dk.com
www.LEGO.com

LEGO® MINIFIGURE
A VISUAL HISTORY

UPDATED AND EXPANDED

CONTENTS

BRINGING LEGO® PLAY TO LIFE   6

WHAT'S A MINIFIGURE?   8

HOW IS A MINIFIGURE MADE?   10

TIMELINE   12

1970s

16

1978 18

1979 20

1980s

22

1980 24

1981 26

1982 28

1983 30

1984 32

1985 34

1986 36

HATS AMAZING!   38

1987 40

1988 42

1989 44

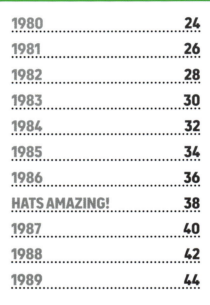

1990s

46

1990 48

1991 50

1992 52

1993 54

1994 56

1995 58

1996 60

A CUT ABOVE   64

1997 66

1998 70

1999 74

2000s

80

2000	82
2001	88
2002	94
2003	100
2004	106
HEADS UP, EVERYONE!	112
2005	114
2006	120
2007	126
2008	132
2009	140

2010s

146

2010	148
2011	156
2012	164
MINI GEAR	174
2013	176
2014	186
2015	194
2016	202
GO WILD!	210
2017	212
2018	220
2019	228

2020s

236

2020	238
2021	248
2022	258
2023	268
MEGA MINIFIGURES	280
2024	282
2025	294
INDEX	300
ACKNOWLEDGMENTS	304

BRINGING LEGO® PLAY TO LIFE

IN THE 1960S and early 1970s, the focus in LEGO® building was on constructing models like houses, cars, and trains. But something important was missing: people to live in the houses, drive the cars, and run the trains! If children wanted characters to play in their LEGO creations, they had to make them out of bricks themselves. To address this need for role-play and storytelling, the company first created large, buildable family figures, and later shrank them down to a size that would fit in better with smaller LEGO models. In 1975, a figure was launched with a blank yellow head; a torso with arm-shaped bumps; and a single, solid leg piece. In 1978, this forerunner to the minifigure was updated with moving arms and legs, hands that could hold accessories, and a face painted with two dots for eyes and a friendly smile. The famous LEGO minifigure was ready to play!

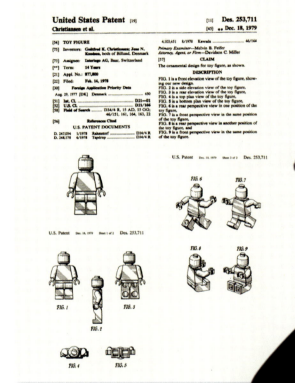

Minifigure patent The 1979 US patent for the LEGO minifigure design demonstrated its iconic shape, the brick-compatible holes on its feet and legs, and the way its limbs could move.

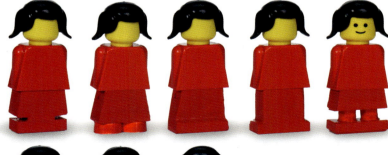

Step-by-step The female minifigure went through many concept stages before it was decided that it would share the same standard legs as male minifigures.

BIRTH OF A LEGEND

To create the prototype for the first minifigure, designer Jens Nygård Knudsen and a team of colleagues sawed and filed LEGO bricks into a miniature human form. Three years and 50 additional prototypes carved in plastic and cast in tin later, he produced the updated modern-style minifigure. Among the sets it debuted in was set 600, featuring a police officer and a buildable brick patrol car.

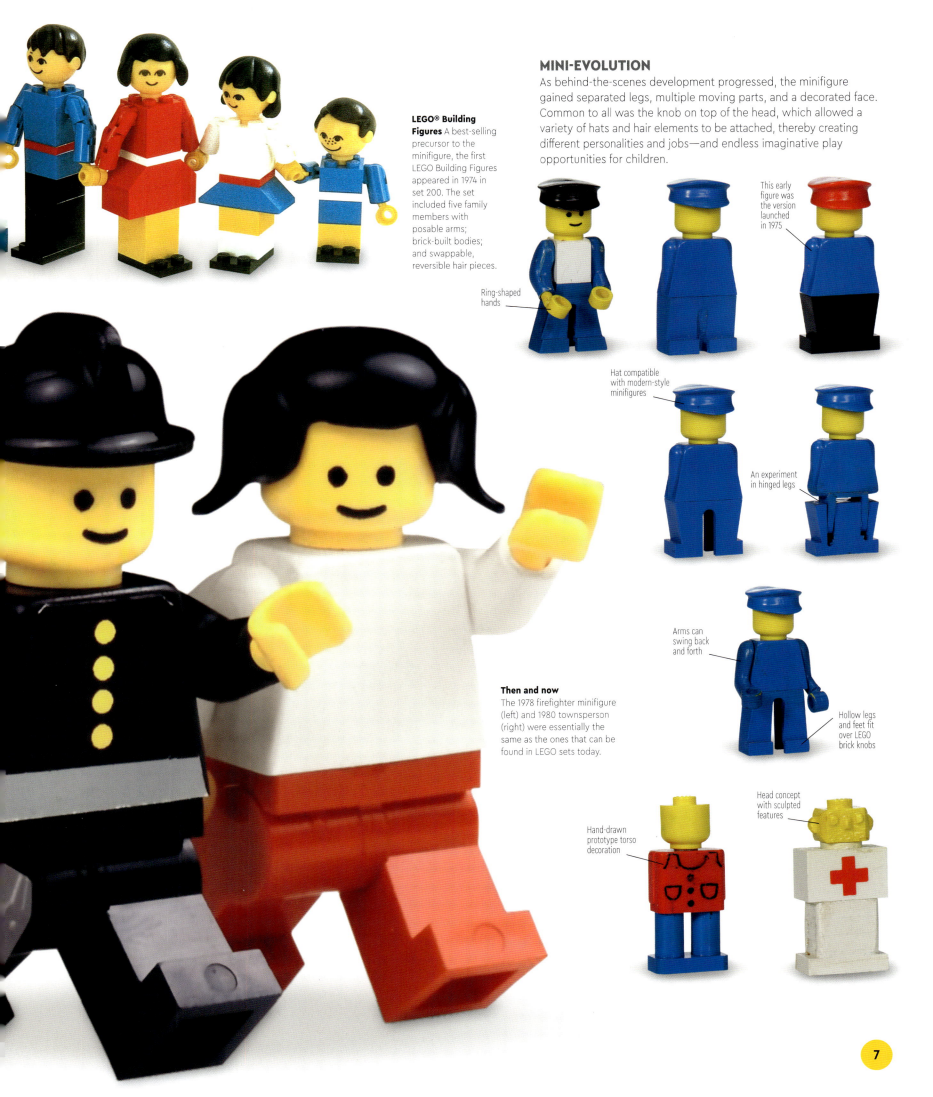

LEGO® Building Figures A best-selling precursor to the minifigure, the first LEGO Building Figures appeared in 1974 in set 200. The set included five family members with posable arms; brick-built bodies; and swappable, reversible hair pieces.

MINI-EVOLUTION

As behind-the-scenes development progressed, the minifigure gained separated legs, multiple moving parts, and a decorated face. Common to all was the knob on top of the head, which allowed a variety of hats and hair elements to be attached, thereby creating different personalities and jobs—and endless imaginative play opportunities for children.

This early figure was the version launched in 1975

Ring-shaped hands

Hat compatible with modern-style minifigures

An experiment in hinged legs

Arms can swing back and forth

Hollow legs and feet fit over LEGO brick knobs

Then and now
The 1978 firefighter minifigure (left) and 1980 townsperson (right) were essentially the same as the ones that can be found in LEGO sets today.

Hand-drawn prototype torso decoration

Head concept with sculpted features

WHAT'S A MINIFIGURE?

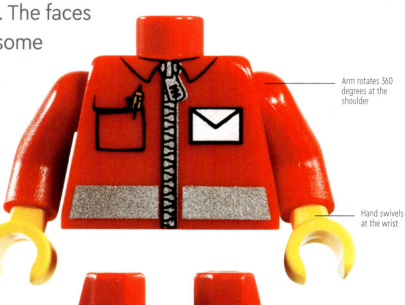

Size matters Without a hat or hair piece, a minifigure stands exactly four LEGO bricks high. This precise measurement makes it easy to construct LEGO buildings and vehicles that can fit minifigures inside.

A LEGO® MINIFIGURE is a small, posable figure of a person or being. Most minifigures have rotating arms, legs, hands, and heads. They have connectors on their bodies that are compatible with LEGO bricks and other elements. They often represent archetypes, such as firefighters, astronauts, and knights. A minifigure can be disassembled and combined with parts from other minifigures to create an entirely new character. The faces of many minifigures carry a friendly smile, but some have other expressions—even multiple ones! Minifigures drive cars, live in castles, fly spaceships, and fill the world of construction with endless possibilities for fun, role-play, and imagination.

Knob on top of head can connect to headgear and other LEGO pieces

Build a minifigure A standard LEGO minifigure comes in three sections when you open a new LEGO set: the head, the torso with arms and hands, and the waist and legs.

Arm rotates 360 degrees at the shoulder

Hand swivels at the wrist

MINIFIGURES AT WORK

LEGO minifigures hail from many different places and times, including the past, present, and future, as well as worlds of fantasy and science fiction. You can tell where a minifigure comes from and what kind of job it has by looking at the details of its printed clothing and its accessories.

Legs swing back and forth for sitting and walking poses

Holes on backs of legs and bottoms of feet attach to LEGO brick knobs

A uniform with reflective stripes and a special helmet makes it clear that this is a firefighter.

With his overalls, cap, and shovel, what else could this hardworking fellow be but a farmer?

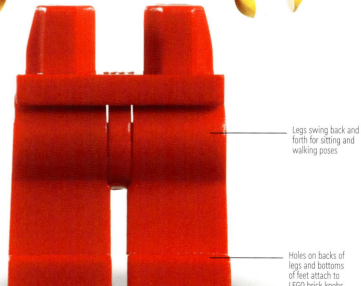

An ancient gladiator carries a sword and shield and wears a protective helmet and leather armor.

8

MEET THE MINIFIGURES ...

A minifigure must have a number of essential key minifigure characteristics in order to be considered a true LEGO minifigure. Although all the characters shown here have different faces, clothes, accessories, and even some body parts, each one is still a minifigure because it is based around the same basic LEGO minifigure design.

This alien hybrid has an extra arm, nonmatching legs, and a unique printed face.

A stylish crook is made taller with a striking hairstyle and detachable headphones around her neck.

This fiery monster has transparent flames over her printed head piece and a ghostly lower body in place of legs.

Minifigures can represent anybody from any country or culture.

The Spider Queen's webbed dress design is printed on her torso and a sloping skirt piece.

This costumed character has a tail piece between his torso and legs and wings instead of arms!

Two artificial limbs help propel this medal-winning sprinter to victory.

This youngster has a printed hearing aid. His short legs show that he is a child.

Python Dynamite is one of many characters with a specially shaped head piece.

Handy A zookeeper holds a banana in one hand and a hungry baby chimpanzee in the other.

HAIR, HATS, AND GEAR

The minifigure's head knob lets you attach and swap hundreds of different hair pieces, hats, and helmets. Their hands can hold a wide variety of accessories, and backpacks and armor can be attached to their bodies.

Armor This knight wears a helmet and an armor piece fitted over his torso.

MEET THE NONMINIFIGURES ...

Not every LEGO figure is a minifigure! Many other colorful characters inhabit the universe of LEGO building. The LEGO® *Star Wars*™ droid and the LEGO® Friends mini doll are not minifigures because they are not made up of any standard minifigure parts. The skeleton does not have enough standard parts to count as a true minifigure.

LEGO skeleton

LEGO *Star Wars* battle droid

LEGO Friends mini doll

HOW TO USE THIS BOOK

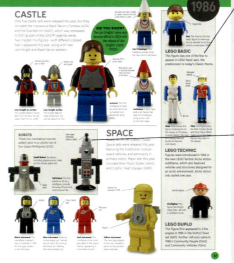

Some themes have a style of figure that is all their own, such as LEGO® DUPLO® figures and LEGO Friends mini dolls. These nonminifigure themes appear in gray boxes throughout the book.

Some nonminifigures are designed to fit in and interact with minifigures in their themes; these include LEGO *Star Wars* droids, LEGO® Castle skeletons, and LEGO® Space aliens. They appear in gray boxes, too.

HOW IS A MINIFIGURE MADE?

CREATING A NEW LEGO® MINIFIGURE doesn't happen overnight! It can take more than a year from the time an idea is first sketched out to the moment a brand-new character is picked off the LEGO production line to be packed up and sent to stores all around the world. Lots of talented LEGO team members contribute to the making of a minifigure, from designers and graphic artists to engineers. Then there are the amazing machines that make each design a reality, and the quality assurance experts that oversee their super-fast operation. Here's how 2025's LEGO® Minifigures Jetpack Racer rocketed into being.

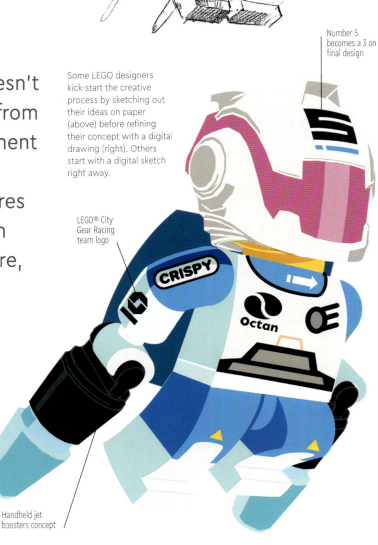

New helmet concept with fin but no front airscoop

Jetpack and flames are not drawn to resemble LEGO elements at this stage

Number 5 becomes a 3 on final design

Some LEGO designers kick-start the creative process by sketching out their ideas on paper (above) before refining their concept with a digital drawing (right). Others start with a digital sketch right away.

LEGO® City Gear Racing team logo

Handheld jet boosters concept

The LEGO Minifigures team hold brainstorming sessions at the LEGO offices in Billund, Denmark.

BRAINSTORMING

No one knows more about minifigures than the team behind the collectible LEGO Minifigures theme! When they start work on a new character, they share their most recent ideas in a brainstorming session. They may be inspired by a current trend or something from ancient history. Some see possibilities in nature, while others draw on their love of sports or popular culture. Together, they work to develop their favorite ideas into detailed character concepts.

DESIGN

In larger LEGO sets, the design of a minifigure helps tell a bigger story. In the LEGO Minifigures theme, one single character has to tell the whole story! To make sure a new minifigure's design is clear and easily understood, a dedicated designer will spend plenty of time refining their character concept and accessories. Together with a graphic designer, they work on a screen to draw the decorations that will be printed on the minifigure. And when entirely new parts are needed (such as the Jetpack Racer's helmet), they will turn to an element designer. These technically minded creatives use their know-how and a range of software to design new pieces that fit perfectly with all those that already exist. Element designers also work with mechanical engineers to make new elements safe, strong, and suitable for many years of mass production.

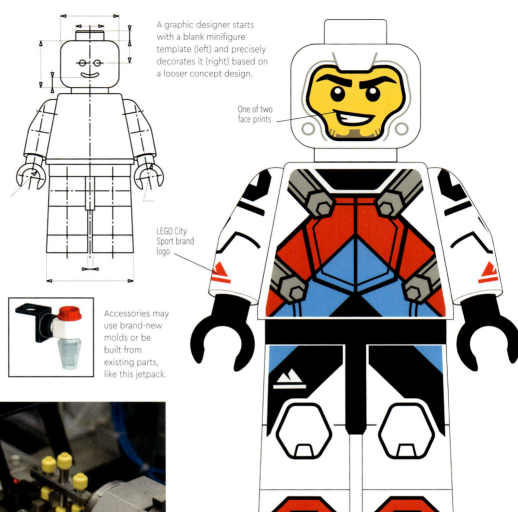

A graphic designer starts with a blank minifigure template (left) and precisely decorates it (right) based on a looser concept design.

One of two face prints

LEGO City Sport brand logo

Accessories may use brand-new molds or be built from existing parts, like this jetpack.

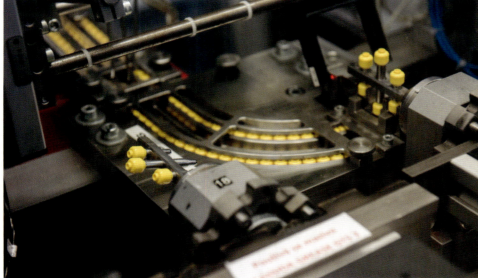

MANUFACTURE

Like most LEGO elements, minifigure parts start out as a material called granulate, which looks a bit like rice. Granulate is heated until it melts into a thick soup, then pumped into high-pressure metal molds to create the familiar shapes of minifigure heads, legs, hair pieces, and so on. When a molding machine ejects its freshly made elements, some are hand-selected for quality testing, while the rest are taken away by big blue robots for printing, assembly, or storage. Finally, the various parts are sorted into boxes to make full LEGO sets, precisely weighed to make sure nothing is missing, and sent out into the world!

The finished minifigure has lots in common with the initial concept, but has also changed in many ways. Several familiar logos link the character to a wider LEGO world.

New helmet molded in separate parts and assembled in factory

NOW MY STORY REALLY BEGINS ... GOTTA FLY!

Octan branding first seen in 1990s LEGO® Town sets

SUSTAINABLE STYLE

Many of today's minifigure accessories are made from a plant-based material called Bio-PE. Some of the 200-plus Bio-PE elements currently in production include minifigure suitcases, headgear, musical instruments, backpacks, and oxygen tanks.

TIMELINE

EVEN THOUGH their fundamental design has remained the same for more than 50 years, minifigures have gone through many changes over the decades. This timeline chronicles some of the most important events in minifigure history, including the first new facial expressions and new body parts and the first licensed characters from the big screen, as well as the debuts of classic minifigure elements, accessories, and other LEGO® figures.

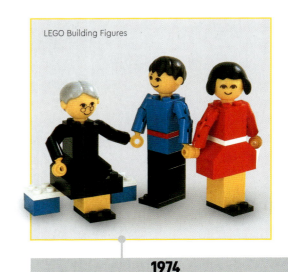
LEGO Building Figures

1974
● The first LEGO figures—LEGO Building Figures— have round heads with painted expressions, posable arms, and bodies built out of LEGO bricks.

Lucy Lamb
LEGO FABULAND figure

Freddy Fox
LEGO FABULAND figure

LEGO Technic figure

1979
● Animal-headed LEGO® FABULAND™ figures are launched.

1986
● The LEGO® Technic figure is launched.

1989
● LEGO® Pirates introduces the first minifigures with different face prints and body parts, such as wooden legs and hook-hands. ● The first monkey figure uses minifigure arms for all four limbs.

LEGO Island video game

LEGO SCALA figure Emma

1995
● First minifigure with glasses.
● First skeleton figure. ● Flippers are the first minifigure footwear.

1997
● First minifigure with a printed sloped skirt piece.
● LEGO® Island is the first video game to star (digital) minifigures. ● LEGO® SCALA™ figures are launched.

Early three-piece figure with red hat

LEGO DUPLO figures

1975

- Small and simple three-piece LEGO figures are released, with an unpainted face and no separate limbs. ● First minifigure-compatible headgear.

1976

- LEGO® DUPLO® figures are launched.

1978

- The first true LEGO minifigure, with posable arms and legs and the classic smile expression. ● The LEGOLAND® themes Town, Castle, and Space launch with new minifigure accessories and wearable gear.

LEGO BELVILLE figures

1990

- The first LEGO ghost minifigure has a glow-in-the-dark shroud element. ● First time a slope is used instead of legs for a minifigure's dress.

1993

- First separate beard piece. ● First minifigure headgear with printing. ● First fabric minifigure cape.

1994

- First printed minifigure legs. ● LEGO® BELVILLE™ figures are launched.

1998

- LEGO® Adventurers is the first theme to give all its minifigures names. ● LEGO® Castle launches the first ninja minifigures.

1999

- LEGO® Star Wars™ introduces many new minifigure parts and accessories. ● Jar Jar Binks is the first minifigure to have a specially sculpted head piece.

2001

- LEGO® Harry Potter™ launches. ● Professor Quirrell is the first minifigure to have a double-sided head print. ● Professor Snape is the first to have a glow-in-the-dark head.

2002

- LEGO® Spider-Man™ is the first Super Hero minifigure.

Astrobot image on a data disc sent to Mars

2003

● Minifigures debut with special arms and spring-loaded legs for holding and throwing basketballs. ● First minifigures based on famous people. ● First minifigures with human skin tones. ● First minifigure with arm printing. ● Pictures of minifigure astronauts land on Mars aboard a pair of NASA rovers.

2005

● Minifigures with built-in batteries carry light-up lightsabers and police flashlights. ● A magnetic accessory lets LEGO Harry Potter grab a golden dragon egg. ● A mermaid is the first minifigure with a tail instead of legs. ● First LEGO Vikings.

2006

● LEGO® EXO-FORCE™ stars minifigures with faces and hair pieces inspired by Japanese animation, as well as robot figures with new body, arm, and leg pieces. ● First printed hair piece.

2007

● Gold-colored C-3PO minifigures feature in 10,000 LEGO sets and two 14-carat gold versions are given away to mark 30 years of *Star Wars*™. ● LEGO® Mars Mission introduces new glow-in-the-dark alien figures. ● First minifigures with soft plastic heads.

Meet mini doll Nicole from LEGO Friends

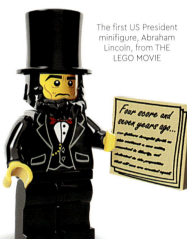

The first US President minifigure, Abraham Lincoln, from THE LEGO MOVIE

2011

● Metal minifigures of the Roman gods Jupiter and Juno and the astronomer Galileo are launched into space on the Juno space probe. ● LEGO® NINJAGO® launches, with many new minifigure accessories and new-look skeleton figures. ● First hair piece with ears.

2012

● The mini doll debuts in LEGO® Friends. ● LEGO NINJAGO introduces snake head and tail pieces and a torso extender with extra arms. ● LEGO® *The Lord of the Rings*™ features many new minifigure parts. ● LEGO® Monster Fighters stars minifigures with bat wing arms and mechanical legs.

2013

● The minifigure tribes that make up LEGO® Legends of Chima™ feature all-new, animal-shaped head accessories. ● LEGO® Teenage Mutant Ninja Turtles™ introduces new turtle shell and head pieces. ● The LEGO® Minifigures Chicken Suit Guy is the first without hands.

2014

● THE LEGO® MOVIE™ makes minifigures into film stars. ● LEGO® MINECRAFT® minifigures come with new block-shaped heads. ● LEGO® *Disney Princess*™ is the second mini doll theme. ● LEGO® The Simpsons™ features all-new head molds for TV's most famous family.

Sweet Mayhem from THE LEGO MOVIE 2

LEGO *Disney* Mulan micro doll

2019

● Sets based on THE LEGO® MOVIE 2™ are the first to combine minifigures and mini dolls. ● Anniversary minifigures mark 20 years of the LEGO *Star Wars* range. ● LEGO® Hidden Side™ sets include minifigures with interchangeable normal and haunted heads.

2020

● LEGO® Monkie Kid™ launches with lots of new minifigure parts. ● LEGO Hidden Side unleashes the first two-headed minifigure. ● Micro dolls debut in LEGO *Disney* storybook sets. ● The LEGO® Super Mario™ theme stars a new kind of large, battery-powered LEGO figure.

2021

● LEGO® City features the first minifigure with a guide dog trained to assist people with visual impairment, plus a harness accessory. ● The Everyone Is Awesome set celebrates diversity with a full spectrum of monochrome minifigures. ● Gold-colored minifigures mark 20 years of LEGO Harry Potter and 10 years of LEGO NINJAGO.

Giant Troll figure

2008
● A special event celebrates 30 years of the LEGO minifigure. ● LEGO® Agents introduces a minifigure cyborg arm piece and lots of new named characters. ● LEGO Castle debuts dwarf and troll minifigures and a Giant Troll figure.

2009
● New LEGO® Games figures are much smaller than minifigures and are used as playing pieces in brick-built board games. ● LEGO® Space Police launches new minifigure alien heads. ● First hair piece with a hole for attaching hats and other accessories.

2010
● The collectible LEGO Minifigures range launches. ● A new minifigure trophy accessory doubles as a microfigure—a tiny representation of a minifigure for microscale builds. ● LEGO® Atlantis introduces lots of new minifigure pieces, such as shark heads and squid tentacles. ● LEGO® Toy Story™ sets include Woody and Jessie figures with extra-long arms and legs.

2015
● Minifigures from many different fictional worlds join forces in the LEGO® DIMENSIONS video game and play sets. Placing real minifigures on a special Toy Pad element brings them to life in the game. ● Mini dolls are more magical than ever with the launch of LEGO® Elves.

2016
● LEGO® NEXO KNIGHTS™ features new minifigure armor and monster figures. ● LEGO City debuts a new baby figure and a minifigure wheelchair piece. ● LEGO® Disney sets feature minifigures for the first time. ● LEGO® BrickHeadz introduces a new kind of brick-built LEGO character.

2017
● Sets based on THE LEGO® BATMAN MOVIE introduce new characters and a new Utility Belt piece. ● The ninja get new looks in THE LEGO® NINJAGO® MOVIE™ and associated sets. ● Mini dolls gain new powers in the LEGO® DC Super Hero Girls theme.

2018
● Seventeen collectible Minifigures in party gear mark the 40th anniversary of the LEGO minifigure. ● LEGO® Wizarding World™ sets see the return of Harry Potter and his pals after a seven-year break. ● New medium-length leg pieces.

LEGO Minifigure with male head

2022
● A LEGO City shopper is the first to wear a modern prosthetic leg. ● The LEGO® Ideas Table Football set comes with 44 heads and 43 hair pieces for customizing its 22 minifigure players. ● LEGO® Avatar sets reintroduce the long arms and legs first seen in LEGO Toy Story.

2023
● LEGO® DREAMZzz™ launches new dream creature figures. ● A mini doll with a limb difference is one of many new faces in LEGO Friends. ● New minifigures mark the Disney 100 anniversary. ● LEGO The Lord of the Rings characters return in a LEGO® Icons set after a 10-year break.

2024
● Minifigures with animal heads star in LEGO® Animal Crossing™. ● The 51 minifigure heads in the Over the Moon with Pharrell Williams set have the widest range of skin tones ever seen in a LEGO product. ● Collectible LEGO Minifigures in the Dungeons & Dragons Series are the first to come with a choice of male and female heads.

2025
● Formula 1 racecar driver minifigures feature in LEGO City, LEGO Icons, and LEGO® Speed Champions sets. ● The collectible LEGO Minifigures theme introduces a new prosthetic hand piece. ● A LEGO Friends mini doll is one of first three LEGO characters to feature a Hidden Disabilities Sunflower lanyard.

1970s

The 1970s were when it all began. First, there were big, buildable people with round yellow heads. Then came mini-sized, solid-bodied figures with swappable hats and expressionless faces. Finally, in 1978, the best parts of both were combined to create a smiling little character with movable arms and legs. The LEGO® minifigure was born, and with it came three new lines—Town, Castle, and Space—creating an entire world of constructible vehicles and accessories to bring it to life.

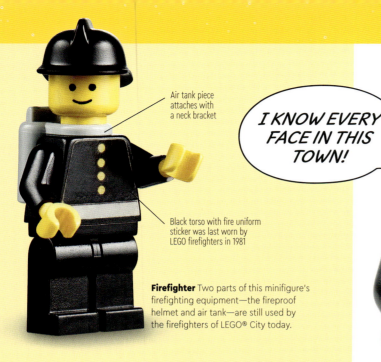

Air tank piece attaches with a neck bracket

Black torso with fire uniform sticker was last worn by LEGO firefighters in 1981

Firefighter Two parts of this minifigure's firefighting equipment—the fireproof helmet and air tank—are still used by the firefighters of LEGO® City today.

1978

THE MODERN MINIFIGURE as we know it was born in 1978, making it one of the biggest years ever for LEGO® building. The new LEGO characters were vastly different from their precursors, released in 1975, which were static, unprinted, and made from bricks. Made up of nine separate pieces (a head, a torso, hips, two arms, two hands, and two legs), minifigures now had cheery printed faces and arms and legs that moved to make them posable for play. You might think that would be enough excitement for one year, but there was more! Three new themes were introduced—Town, Castle, and Space— as part of the LEGOLAND® play theme.

I KNOW EVERY FACE IN THIS TOWN!

TOWN

One of the first LEGO minifigures ever produced was a police officer minifigure for the LEGOLAND Town theme. The year 1978 would bring much more than law and order, though—fire officers, construction workers, medics, street sweepers, and more would begin populating Town, bringing life to a place that builders would return to again and again.

LEGOLAND Town Police badge

Buttoned-up jacket

Police Officer This minifigure is one of only two minifigures to have worn the original police uniform, featuring a stickered torso.

Most of Town's civilian minifigures have plain torsos

Woman About Town This simply dressed minifigure appears in seven sets between 1978 and 1983.

Comfortable white tunic

Company uniform

Passenger This minifigure is dressed in plain traveling clothes for her debut on the Passenger Coach (164).

Service Station Worker This oil company worker keeps the citizens of Town on the move.

Nurse The first-ever female minifigure works as a nurse in Town. Only this minifigure has ever worn this white stickered torso piece.

Hairstyle first designed for 1975's static LEGO figures

White sailing hat

Star Coast Guard symbol

Coast Guard Captain The head of sea security only appears at the Coast Guard Station (575).

Medical symbol

Blue hat

Red torso with shirt-pattern sticker is unique to this minifigure

Street Sweeper Town is kept pristine by this busy minifigure in Town Square (1589).

Worker's cap protects their head

Red hat makes them visible on the tracks

Plain clothes for heavy manual work

Cargo Worker One of the first ordinary minifigure citizens of Town, this minifigure works at the Cargo Station (165).

Dressed professionally in a jacket over a shirt and tie

Train Conductor This minifigure was the first to feature a torso that was printed instead of stickered.

Town House With Garden Two minifigures live in this delightful house (376), complete with flowers and sun lounger.

Black cowboy hat matches the sharp suit

Unique stickered torso features a black jacket and red tie

Red briefcase

High Roller This well-dressed character appears in just one set, a bustling street scene called Main Street (1589).

Helmet with chinstrap

Red Astronaut Like his white-clad counterpart, this trailblazer wears a style of helmet found in LEGO® Space (and Town) sets until 1988.

Printed torso features the LEGO Space logo

Classic, all-white space suit

Protective space suit covers the hands, too

White Astronaut He's set for an out-of-this-world adventure! This excited astronaut appeared in 37 sets from 1978 to 1987.

SPACE

It was time for minifigures to blast off into Space in 1978, when the theme's first three sets were launched. The Rocket Launcher (462), Space Cruiser (487), and Space Command Center (493) all featured astronaut minifigures. Each intrepid space adventurer wore a full-body space suit in white or red—with the classic yellow face peering out from the helmet.

LEGO® DUPLO®

The earliest DUPLO figures predate the modern minifigure, having first appeared in 1976. They had a head and a one-piece body with no arms or legs—a design that would change in the years that followed.

Blue sailor hat identifies them as a seafaring figure

DUPLO Sailor With a wide smile and freckled face, this happy sailor popped up in five nautical-themed DUPLO sets from 1978 to 1990.

CASTLE

Only this knight has ever worn this visor in light gray

Defending soldiers wear a purple tabard with a crown

The very first Castle set charged onto the LEGO building scene in 1978. It would go on to become a bestseller for the next six years. Castle (375)—nicknamed the "Yellow Castle"—featured a working, crank-raised drawbridge and contained 14 knight minifigures and four brick-built horses, making it great for endless play.

Visor with plume fits over the classic LEGO helmet worn by the astronauts (above)

Shield emblem of the attacking army

Plume Helmet Knight Part of the blue cavalry that protects the Yellow Castle, only one knight of this kind appears in the set.

Black Cavalry Knight Dressed in black and ready to attack, this Black Cavalry Knight has a foreboding appearance.

I LOVE THE YELLOW CASTLE. THE KNIGHT LIFE IS GREAT!

Helmet with neck guard was first worn by this knight

Stickered tabard with neck bracket fits over the knight's torso

Blue Knight An army of seven of these minifigures defends the Yellow Castle from the invading army.

Helmet for protection against flying arrows

Torso with a royal crest

YOU RANG, SIR?

Knight Modeling a new helmet for the Castle theme, this minifigure appears in Knight's Procession (677).

1979

THE MINIFIGURE CELEBRATED

its first birthday in grand style in 1979, with new sets for LEGOLAND® Castle, Space, and Town. In other nonminifigure news: LEGO® SCALA™, a jewelry and accessories line for girls, was introduced; LEGO® DUPLO® expanded with two new subthemes, Playhouse and Farm; and LEGO® FABULAND™ was launched, which was seen as a bridge theme for children growing out of LEGO DUPLO. But for many fans, this was the year that showed the minifigure was here to stay.

CASTLE

The second and third Castle sets in history came out in 1979: Knights' Tournament (383) and Knight's Procession (677). They were both released in Europe this year, but would not reach US shelves until 1981. Knights' Tournament came with six minifigures, but no horse figures as we know them today—the horses had to be built using bricks.

Helmet in light gray

Red torso with crest

Procession Knight This knight has a helmet with neck and nose guards for maximum protection.

CAN YOU ATTACH A HAIRDRYER TO MY THRONE?

Short, red hair piece

Gold necklace

Male hair piece new to this year

Tricolor crest

Prince This regal prince sports a new hair piece, which has since become an iconic LEGO element.

Princess With her bright red hair, this is the first female minifigure in the Castle theme, paving the way for many more.

DID YOU KNOW?
The Prince's brown hair piece has been used in more than 130 sets.

A yellow helmet matches their head color

SPACE

1979 was a huge year for Space, with a dozen sets released, plus building plates resembling a lunar landscape, and minifigure packs. Unlike later Space subthemes, these sets were free of any kind of conflict or aliens. Astronaut minifigures explored the galaxy with smiles on their faces in spaceships and are still remembered with fondness by many adult fans.

Gold space logo

Yellow Astronaut This minifigure is bright yellow— a new color for an astronaut in the Space theme.

Landing Plates This set (454) comes with a circular landing pad and a section of spaceport roadway.

Chef Wearing a new hat, the first chef minifigure is ready to work in Snack Bar (675), a new set for 1979.

Iconic chef's hat

I'M VERY PROUD OF MY NEW HAT!

DID YOU KNOW?
The Baby's set, Kitchen (269), also featured larger, brick-built parents and an older sibling.

Peaked cap

Red shirt under blazer

Hard hat for working on site

Torso with vest print

Bright red neckerchief

Taxi Driver This remarkably well-dressed taxi driver comes in one set: Taxi (608).

Construction Worker
The printed torso on this minifigure is one of many that is new to this year.

Gray hips and legs

The same peaked cap as on the taxi driver

Same hair piece as seen on the LEGOLAND Castle Prince

Button-up pockets

Blue sweater

Same helmet worn by LEGO astronauts

Short, black hair piece

Torso with badge and zipper details

Traffic Police Officer
Biker gear and a police badge must mean this minifigure is a traffic cop.

Baby Part of the short-lived LEGO Building Figure theme, this baby has an outfit with bib detail.

LEGO FABULAND
With colorful, easy-to-build models and fun animal characters, LEGO FABULAND was introduced to fill the niche between DUPLO and LEGO System models. The popular play theme would last until 1989.

Oversized molded fox head

Red, chunky legs

Freddy Fox Wide-eyed and bushy-tailed, this fox appears in six FABULAND sets, including Town Hall (140).

Bear face with printed snout

Bernard Bear
This friendly bear comes with his own pick-up truck in one set (329).

Red peaked cap

Exxon Worker
Sporting a torso with an Exxon sticker, this minifigure is in the Exxon Fuel Pumper set (554).

Sticker with Exxon logo

EXXON

Distinctive feline features

Charlie Cat This smiling cat works at FABULAND's Doc David's Hospital (34 and 137).

Mechanic This helpful minifigure comes with a wrench in the Auto Service Truck set (646).

Boy This young man is part of a Homemaker set: Family Room (268).

Head molded to look woolly

Torso with yellow top

Lucy Lamb This lamb comes with long ears and printed eyelashes.

TOWN

LEGO builders looking to create their own town layout had lots to work with in 1979, with many new sets and updated minifigures. There was a Taxi (608) and a Bus Station (379) so minifigures could get around, a Snack Bar (675) for hungry minifigures, and many more. Only a small number of minifigures were new this year; most were variations on ones released in 1978.

1980s

The 1980s were a golden age for LEGO® minifigures, as many young builders were discovering them for the first time. Although the beloved minifigure's clothes and headgear might be switched around from set to set, the basic style remained the same—until 1989, when the arrival of the swashbuckling new LEGO® Pirates theme changed everything. Suddenly, minifigures could have printed beards, bangs, and eyepatches, not to mention all-new hand and leg pieces. The possibilities were endless!

HEY, I'VE GOT AN IDEA!

Striped blue T-shirt

Bill This clever minifigure came with the LEGO *Idea Book*, which followed the adventures of Bill and Mary.

1980

THIS YEAR SAW the LEGO Group continuing to expand, with new factories being built and the brick establishing itself in more and more homes. No new themes were introduced this year, but the LEGOLAND® Town theme saw significant expansion. The latest in a line of LEGO® *Idea Books* would also come out, with a story centered on Bill and Mary, the two minifigures packaged with it. But inventive LEGO fans were already coming up with great ideas of their own and experimenting with their new sets and minifigures!

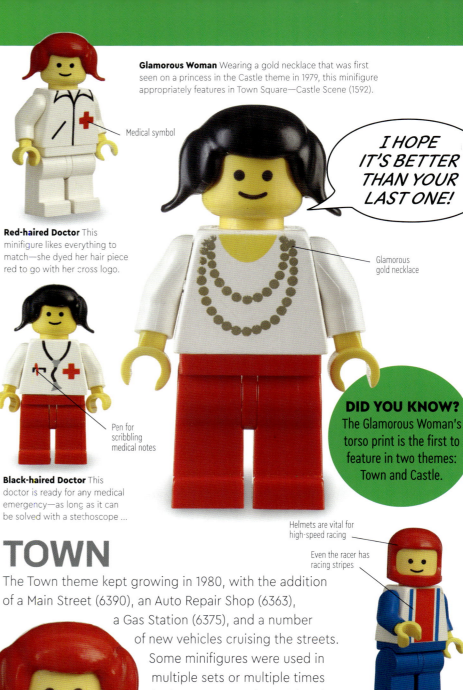

Glamorous Woman Wearing a gold necklace that was first seen on a princess in the Castle theme in 1979, this minifigure appropriately features in Town Square—Castle Scene (1592).

Medical symbol

Red-haired Doctor This minifigure likes everything to match—she dyed her hair piece red to go with her cross logo.

Glamorous gold necklace

Pen for scribbling medical notes

Black-haired Doctor This doctor is ready for any medical emergency—as long as it can be solved with a stethoscope ...

I HOPE IT'S BETTER THAN YOUR LAST ONE!

DID YOU KNOW? The Glamorous Woman's torso print is the first to feature in two themes: Town and Castle.

Helmets are vital for high-speed racing

Even the racer has racing stripes

Racecar Driver This speed-lover drives a Race Car (6609) with its own stylish blue and red stripes.

TOWN

The Town theme kept growing in 1980, with the addition of a Main Street (6390), an Auto Repair Shop (6363), a Gas Station (6375), and a number of new vehicles cruising the streets. Some minifigures were used in multiple sets or multiple times in the same set, often with only minor variations.

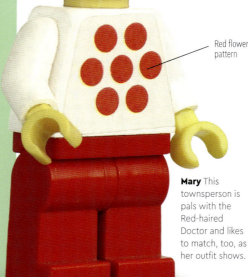

Red flower pattern

Mary This townsperson is pals with the Red-haired Doctor and likes to match, too, as her outfit shows.

Top hat

GOT MY TOP HAT This all-black figure represents a statue in the Town Square (1592). Nobody seems to know just who it is supposed to be a statue of, but they had a very nice hat!

Statue This statue figure is the last to use the static LEGO figure parts introduced in 1975.

Torso with shirt detail

Builder Unlike other construction workers introduced this year, this one insists on wearing black pants to work!

Exxon logo

Exxon Worker Run out of gas? This helpful worker will be at your service in Exxon Gas Station (6375).

Red hard hat

Blue button-down shirt

Construction Worker Appearing in more than 20 sets, this minifigure has been catching up on their sleep for the past 10 years.

Same shirt as the Builder and Construction Worker

Engine Driver This LEGO Trains minifigure ruled the rails until 1985, with occasional visits to LEGOLAND Town.

Mærsk Line Worker This minifigure works for a real-life container shipping company in the promotional set Mærsk Line Container Truck (1651).

Sky-blue hard hat

I'M SO EXCITED, I JUST CAN'T CONTAIN MYSELF.

Black fire helmet

Fire Chief This minifigure is the first of many to wear this smart uniform but one of the last to wear the original fire helmet in black.

Rare white hair piece

Police badge

Police Officer This townsperson was part of a LEGO set made especially for schools.

Fancy top hat

Domed medieval-style helmet

CASTLE GUARD

This Guard comes from a LEGOLAND Town set rather than a Castle one. It was called Town Square (1592) and depicted a modern-day carnival passing an ancient castle. Variants of the set were released in several countries, with different national flags and food stalls.

1592   LEGO

Town Square The UK version of this set (1592, pictured) comes with a union flag, a fish-and-chip shop, and 11 minifigures.

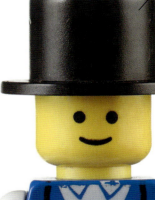

Lion with two hearts

Blue vest with shirt underneath

Castle Guard This minifigure has a distinctive torso design, perhaps inspired by English King Richard the Lionheart.

DID YOU KNOW?
The LEGO top hat piece has been worn by around 40 minifigures.

Dignitary This Town Square carnival attendee has a similar style to the same set's top-hatted statue.

ANYONE NEED A HAND?

Plain blue top

Black pants, in case of job interviews

Blue Top Townsperson Ready to do any job at any time, this minifigure keeps their full range of talents under a fetching red cap.

1981

THE JOURNEY OF the minifigure soared onward and upward this year. The LEGOLAND® Town and Space themes continued to expand, bringing with them new and exciting places for LEGO® fans to build and play. New police, fire, and medical minifigures joined the ever-growing cast of LEGO characters as Town continued to base imaginative play on real-world places and the heroes who work in them.

TOWN

You never know what may happen in Town. You could be relaxing in a Summer Cottage (6365), while firefighters race from the Fire Station (6382) to save the day. Got a medical emergency? The LEGO ambulance or the minifigures from the Red Cross Helicopter (6691) may help out. Real life was the key theme this year, and this would continue for years to come.

Vest print

Red Top Woman There's plenty to see from her front garden, so the Red Top Woman spends her time sipping tea and watching her neighbors.

Officer's hat

All-weather jacket

Precinct badge

Police Officer It's quite safe in Town, so the Police Officer spends all day greeting visitors and directing traffic.

6365

LEGOLAND

LEGO

Summer Cottage The Red Top Woman has spent a lot of time perfecting the front garden of Summer Cottage (6365) so she can entertain her guests.

Neatly combed hair

MY FACE HURTS FROM SMILING SO MUCH.

DID YOU KNOW? The Red Cross Helicopter (6691) was the first minifigure-compatible helicopter to be released.

Always smiling

Red Top Man This minifigure can always be found in some kind of scrape, waiting to be rescued. But he seems quite cheerful about it!

White Top Townsperson Closely related to Blue Top Townsperson, this minifigure is careful to wash their shirts separately.

Hard hat protects from falling debris

Neat sweater vest

Fire Station Manager This minifigure is a vital part of the Town's firefighting team.

Firefighter's uniform

Firefighter Just one lucky minifigure gets to wear this helmet in white during 1981.

6382

Fire Station This station (6382) is very busy. There is always something to do, whether it is polishing the engine or manning the radios.

Service Station Worker This minifigure makes sure all the vehicles in Town are full of gas and ready to roll.

Blue overalls are perfect for any task

DID YOU KNOW? The first LEGO firefighter to wear a white hat was introduced this year.

Warm pants for working outdoors

Blue Top Woman Changing tires or fighting fires, this minifigure lends a hand wherever she is needed.

Red hat stands out in a crowd

Medic When there is not an emergency, the Medic drives an ambulance around the town. He greets people and offers lifts.

Pocket holds bandages and treats

I THINK YOUR HEAD NEEDS TO BE REPLACED.

Symbol indicates a medical professional

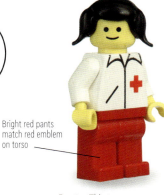

Bright red pants match red emblem on torso

Doctor This torso, with broad collars and a medical symbol, has featured in 13 sets.

Standard white medical uniform

All of this year's medics share this torso print

Surgeon The Surgeon is always spotless—she hates getting anything on her crisp white uniform.

Pilot's helmet

Helicopter Pilot This flying ace always wears a helmet for taking to the sky at a moment's notice.

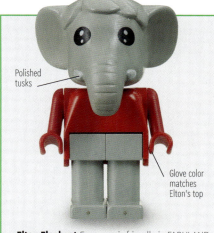

Polished tusks

Glove color matches Elton's top

Elton Elephant Everyone is friendly in FABULAND, but Elton is also known for his stylish outfits and polite nature. He appears in three sets.

LEGO® FABULAND™

The gentle fun of FABULAND continued this year, with the introduction of cute new characters Elton Elephant, Bonnie Bunny, Boris Bulldog, and Barney Bear, who all showed up to play.

LEGO® BASIC

LEGO Basic introduced figures in this year—these colorful finger puppet figures would be a part of LEGO Basic Building sets for decades. These sets were designed to promote creative play and focused solely on building instead of a specific model.

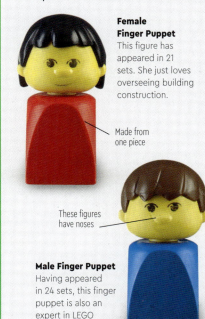

Female Finger Puppet This figure has appeared in 21 sets. She just loves overseeing building construction.

Made from one piece

These figures have noses

Male Finger Puppet Having appeared in 24 sets, this finger puppet is also an expert in LEGO architecture.

> **RED ALERT! SUPER-COOL BIKER COMING THROUGH!**

Classic helmet in red

Red torso with zipper details

Red-suited Biker This minifigure comes with 35 friends as part of Little People with Accessories (1066). The bumper set was made just for schools.

1982

TOWN AND SPACE were the big stories this year. Three new Space sets rocketed into the universe in 1982, bringing with them four astronaut minifigures. Meanwhile, Town fans could explore everywhere from the local post office to the highways and byways of the city. Also released this year was a set featuring an amazing 36 minifigures, including a chef, a doctor, a firefighter, and a police officer.

> **MINIFIGURES SURE GET LOTS OF FAN MAIL!**

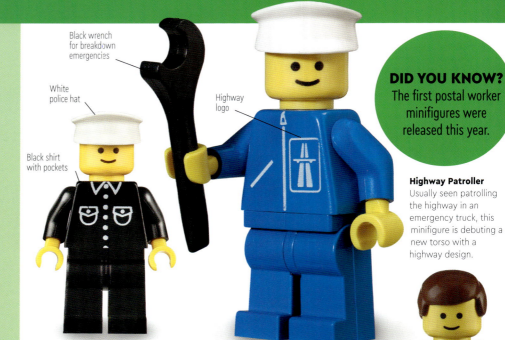

Black wrench for breakdown emergencies

White police hat

Highway logo

Black shirt with pockets

DID YOU KNOW? The first postal worker minifigures were released this year.

Highway Patroller Usually seen patrolling the highway in an emergency truck, this minifigure is debuting a new torso with a highway design.

Breakdown Responder Smartly dressed and mechanically minded, this minifigure comes to the rescue in Breakdown Assistance (1590).

TOWN

Town went postal this year! Although there had been other sets in the past with the word "Mail" on a brick, 1982's Mail Truck (6651) and Post Office (6362) models were the first ones to really focus on the postal delivery service. This would later be expanded into the Cargo subtheme.

Torso also seen on Lord Sam Sinister from the LEGO® Adventurers theme in 1998

Driver On his way to the office, this minifigure's car breaks down. Luckily, the Breakdown Responder is on the case in Breakdown Assistance (1590).

Postal Worker Proudly wearing a new shirt with the post office logo, this minifigure always delivers the mail with a smile.

Post office logo

Mail Truck Driver This worker looks happy, but really wants a shirt with the Town post office bugle on it, too.

Blue shirt with pocket detail

Mail Van This set (6651) features a truck, a mailbox, and a postal worker minifigure.

I CAN FACE ANY PERIL DRESSED IN MY FANCY UNIFORM.

Medical red cross logo

Doctor With a stethoscope around her neck and a pen in her top pocket, this doctor is ready to take someone's stats.

All-black uniform is set off by gold details and red belt

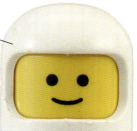

White helmet with chin guard

Firefighter This firefighter gets to the scene of a fire in super-fast time in their helicopter, from Fire Patrol Copter (6657).

Gold lapel detail on torso

Red belt with gold buckle

Fire Captain Unfortunately, this Fire Captain suffers from terrible seasickness, and so only features in one set, Fire Boat (4025).

Final appearance for this white hair piece

Red Triplet Three identical copies of this minifigure feature in one special set for schools.

Utility gray helmet

DID YOU KNOW?
Yellow was chosen for minifigures from the original LEGO color palette as an ethnically neutral color—to represent all races and ethnicities.

Monochrome Triplet Three of these minifigures with rare gray helmets feature in the same set as the Red Triplets.

Oversized molded bear head

Billy Bear This bear works at the service station in FABULAND and comes in three sets.

Big, yellow beak for gnawing

Patrick Parrot Say cheese! This colorful parrot prefers to be behind the camera in Photographer Patrick Parrot (3782).

LEGO® FABULAND™
FABULAND roared ahead in 1982, releasing 24 figures, more than any other theme. Eleven new sets were added, including a FABULAND House complete with a car.

DON'T I LOOK GREAT IN STRIPES? BE HONEST.

Striped sweater

Little People with Accessories This LEGO® Dacta™ set (1066) holds the record for the most minifigures in a single set! The 36 characters come in 12 different designs.

Striped Person This minifigure is extremely proud of their home—in fact, they love their Town House (6372) so much, they never leave it.

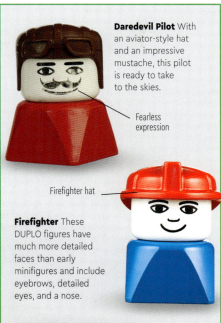

Daredevil Pilot With an aviator-style hat and an impressive mustache, this pilot is ready to take to the skies.

Fearless expression

Firefighter hat

Firefighter These DUPLO figures have much more detailed faces than early minifigures and include eyebrows, detailed eyes, and a nose.

LEGO® DUPLO®
Little builders got the chance to have some adventures of their own as a fire engine and a plane joined the assortment, complete with Firefighter and Daredevil Pilot figures.

Helmet also seen on the Space astronauts from 1978

I'M SURE MY RED STRIPE MAKES ME GO FASTER!

Striped torso also paired with red arms this year

Biker This minifigure originally came with a wrench, but no motorcycle to use it on!

1983

THIS YEAR, TOWN provided a lot of action and fun with new sets and minifigures, while Space hit the stratosphere with five exciting sets. Castle released only one set, but it was a minifigure collection—so definitely worth getting excited about! It all added up to new police, fire, and knight minifigures, plus some new townspeople to populate a playscape. Many of these minifigures became highly collectible in later years.

TOWN

Town offered a varied mix of sets this year, including a new Police Station (6384) and Police Car (6623); two construction-themed sets; and a forerunner of the Cargo subtheme, the Delivery Van (6624). There was a new Railway Station (7824), complete with nine new minifigures, and four firefighters appeared in a minifigure-only set.

Air tank is full of oxygen

Firefighter Classic firefighter to the rescue! This torso was first seen in 1980, and it still looks pristine!

Plain white torso has been worn by more than 100 other minifigures

Motorcycle Rider A new LEGO motorcycle made its debut this year, and this minifigure was among the first to ride it.

DID YOU KNOW?
The Railway Station (7824) would be the last Railway Station released for eight years.

Classic cowboy hat worn by more than 30 other minifigures

Torso seen on more than 10 other minifigures

Red hair piece worn by just 12 other minifigures

Gold necklace

Dapper Passenger This minifigure is one of several to carry new, opening suitcase pieces in Railway Station (set 7824).

Elegant Passenger This minifigure waits for a train in the same set as the Dapper Passenger and the Patient Cowpoke.

Train Station Worker The passengers better have their train tickets ready—this worker is just about to inspect them.

Patient Cowpoke Like the other passengers in Railway Station (7824), the cowpoke is resigned to the lack of a train in the set!

7824

Railway Station Nine minifigures, a ticket booth, and a food stand for hungry commuters are included in this set (7824).

Vacationer This tourist is staying at her new Holiday Home (6374). She is most excited about her sliding patio roof.

Red arms used with this torso print for the first time

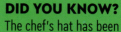

HEY, CENTER PARTS ARE JUST SO COOL RIGHT NOW.

Parted hair piece

Striped torso is new this year

Striped Top Person This trendsetting minifigure is the first of hundreds to wear their hair long!

DID YOU KNOW?
The chef's hat has been in production for 45 years and features in more than 100 sets.

Cap features in just one 1983 set

There are no ketchup stains on this chef's whites!

Chef Serving the hungry townspeople hamburgers always puts a smile on this chef's face.

Zip-up jacket on torso is identical to Service Station Customer and Freight Operator

Hungry Person This minifigure wants a hamburger and wants it NOW, in Burger Stand (6683).

Service Station Attendant This motorhead's all-new cap is worn by more than 400 minifigures in 14 colors.

Helmet has protected more than 30 other minifigure heads

Service Station Customer This customer always gets speedy service at the Service Station (6371).

Visor with grille clips onto helmet

Standard black hair piece

Red police hat

Red Top Person First seen in this year's Police Station (6384), this colorful character joined a TV Camera Crew in 1986.

Freight Operator A job at the Freight Loading Depot (7838) keeps this minifigure smiling.

Freight Train Operator Wearing a blue uniform and yellow cap, this figure keeps all the DUPLO trains running smoothly.

Blue train uniform

Classic Castle shield emblem

Black Knight This brave knight's torso was first worn by a knight in 1978, and has only been seen on five other knight minifigures.

CASTLE

Only one Castle set was released in 1983—Castle Minifigures (6002), a collection of four knight minifigures. The two pairs of knights had different helmets and torso designs, marking them as belonging to different royal factions.

LEGO® DUPLO®

This DUPLO figure appeared in two DUPLO Train sets this year—Freight Train (2700) and Passenger Train (2705). The smiling worker also made an appearance in later years in DUPLO Gas Station (2639) and DUPLO Farm sets.

YAY! SOMEONE TO JOUST AGAINST!

Affixed face grille helmet

Armored breastplate print is new this year

Yellow Plume Knight This brave knight helps protect the King's castle with his lance and shield.

1984

IN THE EARLY DAYS, LEGO® minifigures rarely ran into conflict or encountered anything that would wipe the big grins off their faces. Space explorers didn't clash with aliens, everything ran smoothly in Town, and the Castle knights only had gentle adventures. However, the peace was disrupted in 1984, as Castle introduced two new opposing groups—the Lion Knights and the Black Falcons—complete with their own castles, catapults, and siege towers.

CASTLE

The Lion Knights and the Black Falcons were the first of several groups that would make up the Castle mythos. They arrived with two fortresses, the Knight's Castle (6073) and King's Castle (6080), plus an impressive Siege Tower (6061).

Black plume

Blue Knight This armored ace loves 1984's new knights' helmets and new plume pieces, which can be worn forward, backward, or sideways.

Plume element introduced this year

Black Knight This accomplished rider shows some serious skills in Knight's Challenge (1584).

Gray grille helmet

Red Knight This knight looks friendly, but just try escaping from the Siege Tower (6061) and see what happens!

Black Falcon Archer This foot soldier proudly wears their faction's new crest and a brand-new quiver of arrows piece.

The Black Falcons typically wear black helmets with chinstraps

Helmet with neck protector

Black Falcon Guard This soldier loves their new nose guard helmet almost as much as banquets and battles!

New cowl element keeps minifigure's head warm

Tie shirt also comes in blue and green in later years

Peasant This Peasant is debuting a new torso with printed pouch and a farmer's cowl.

DID YOU KNOW? Horses became sturdier this year—now made of one piece instead of being brick-built.

Siege Tower This set (6061) includes one of the year's new horse figures, which were available in black and white.

Blacksmith Being a Blacksmith is a messy job. Luckily, this minifigure wears an apron to keep his otherwise bare torso clean.

Brown apron exclusive to this minifigure

Sailor The last time this figure went fishing, all they caught was a cold! They hope to be more successful on their next trip.

Life jacket

Lion Knight Guard This warrior wields a spear, despite having battle-axes on their livery.

Lion Knight crest

WHO'S GONNA ATTACK A BLACKSMITH'S SHOP?

Diver This deep sea diver is determined not to get stranded at sea, so is attached to a safety reel.

Diving helmet

DID YOU KNOW? The Blacksmith's apron piece is also worn by knights as a cape in red, blue, and black.

Bow and arrow piece is new this year

Lion Knight Archer While some Lion Knights wear a crossed ax emblem, most favor this rampant lion.

LEGO® DUPLO®

LEGO DUPLO sailed the ocean blue this year with sets including Deep Sea Diver (2618) and Sea Explorer (2649). New figures sported diving gear and life jackets as they adventured on and beneath the waves.

SPACE

Space returned with eight new sets in 1984, including the Intergalactic Command Base (6971) and the Robot Command Center (6951). Astronaut minifigures appeared in two new colors as they explored the universe and searched for precious uranium.

Same suit favored by Benny in 2014's THE LEGO® MOVIE™

Classic Space logo

Black Astronaut Black is a new color for the Space astronauts this year.

Blue Astronaut This interplanetary explorer is hoping to find blue moons in the one-seater Space Dart-I (6824).

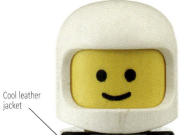

Cool leather jacket

Cap is blue for the first time this year

Helmet and torso combination exclusive to this minifigure

Helicopter Pilot This pilot looks a lot like a Town traffic cop until you notice they don't have a badge.

Overalls are new this year

Mechanic This minifigure fixes motorcycles and cars in this year's sets.

Motorcycle Courier The post is never late when this biker is on the beat.

TOWN

Seventeen new sets hit the shelves in 1984, with the most significant being the first Cargo Center (6391). The subject of letter and package delivery had only been seen once before, in a 1982 Post Office set (6362). This set was followed up with a Delivery Center (6377) in 1985. Cargo later appeared as a subtheme of its own, in 2007.

I'M ALL A-QUIVER ABOUT MY QUIVER!

Helmet with chin guard

Lion Knight Archer This minifigure is a tiny bit taller than the Lion Knight Guard, thanks to a quiver of arrows accessory.

1985

THE LEGO® SYSTEM in play with its endless possibilities celebrated its 30th birthday in 1985—with a record number of new minifigures released and the launch of Airport as part of the Town theme. Both Town and Space saw strong assortments this year, while Castle took a bit of a back seat before making a comeback in 1986. This year offered further proof that the dynamic world of LEGO building and LEGO minifigures would continue to change and grow every year.

CASTLE

This year, Castle only released two sets and a minifigure collection. These added to the Black Falcon and Lion Knight factions, but were smaller models. Prisoner Convoy (6055) featured five horses and four minifigures and was the only Castle carriage to be drawn by four horses. Black Knight's Treasure (6011) featured only one Black Falcon knight minifigure.

Black Falcon emblem

Black Falcon Guard This soldier defends the Prisoner Convoy against Lion Knights and robber peasants!

Lion Knights' emblem

Lion Knight Guard This guard likes being shorter than the Lion Knight Archer. It makes dodging arrows easier.

DID YOU KNOW? The 1985 Castle sets were released in Europe and other parts of the world, but not the United States.

Jetpack also seen in gray in 1986 and black in 1990

White Astronaut with Jetpack This year's new jetpack element has knobs for building on the front and back.

Solar panel

Lever piece

Blue Robot This brick-built helper's head is made from a brick with knobs on five sides.

Black Robot Just five pieces make up the smaller of this year's two techno buddies.

ROBOTS ROCK

These two robots appeared in Space sets this year. Although neither is officially classed as a minifigure, they represent some of the earlier robots and androids in a LEGO theme.

SPACE

Thirteen new Space sets were released in 1985, most of them consisting of a small vehicle with one astronaut minifigure. The larger sets, including the Solar Power Transporter (6952) and FX-Star Patroller (6931), continued the tradition of Space models being modular, with features such as detachable cockpits.

Forklift Driver This driver hopes to be a car mechanic one day and has already invested in the hat.

Overalls with a handy pocket

Caring face

Overalls are black for the first time

Car Mechanic Black overalls make their debut this year. They're perfect for masking this mechanic's oil stains.

Bright red hair

Community Worker This minifigure rides one of the first LEGO bicycles in a set made for schools.

DO I GET FREQUENT BUILDER MILES?

Same zipper detail as Helicopter Pilot

Hat worn by more than 200 minifigures

Horn emblem

Biker This Biker's torso is new this year—it probably won't stay pristine white for long!

Postal Worker Like the Community Worker and the Biker, this minifigure is exclusive to Community Workers (1063).

TOWN

Town set a record this year, with an impressive 49 new minifigures released. The big story, however, was the chance to fly the buildable skies of LEGO air as the first ever Airport set (6392) made its appearance.

Torso with airplane detail introduced this year

Ground Crew Directing minifigure vacationers to their planes is a hard job when you spend all day on the ground!

Gold buttons

Airplane logo

Pressed black pants

Pilot The frequent flyer is about to take to the skies wearing the Pilot's uniform, introduced this year.

Stripes are in this era's core LEGO colors

Red helmet is also popular with Classic Space astronauts

Red neckerchief

Hat design debuted in 1975

Luggage Cart Driver This minifigure thinks that driving across the runway is as much fun as taking off from it!

Helicopter Pilot This pilot would like to know why no one at the airport wears a helicopter logo.

Ice Cream Vendor Can't make it to the airport? Visit the Ice Cream Cart (6601) instead!

Container Truck Driver A stetson hat makes this minifigure feel like he's driving cattle, not a truck.

Airport Tower Operator Responsible for directing all the LEGO planes, this minifigure is always calm—even when she sees another minifigure wearing her hair piece.

Hair piece seen on more than 100 minifigures

Airport LEGO building finally took to the skies from this airport (6392), which included eight minifigures, a control tower, a plane, a helicopter, and even a restaurant for hungry passengers.

Only one other minifigure wears this top with red pants

THIS CAP GIVES ME HAT HAIR.

Plain white cap

Plain red torso also used on Classic Castle knights between 1978 and 1981 (underneath their breastplates)

Speedboat Driver Exclusive to set RV with Speedboat (6698), this minifigure can't wait to get out on the water.

1986

ANOTHER BRILLIANT YEAR for fun and imagination, 1986 saw a wide variety of Town sets, new Lion Knight and Black Falcon sets in Castle, and more Classic Space sets. Town and Space also got the first Light and Sound kits, an electronic system that used light and sound bricks powered by a 9V battery box, bringing even more excitement to the LEGO® play experience. Minifigures were joined by new LEGO® DUPLO®, LEGO® Basic, and LEGO® Technic figures as the world of LEGO building continued to expand.

Townsperson with hat This minifigure is new this year but is wearing a striped T-shirt, first introduced in 1985.

I HAVE NO HAIR TO GET HAT HAIR.

Perhaps the "S" logo stands for speed?

Motorcycle Racer This speedster comes in Motocross Racing (6677) and is wearing a new torso this year.

Torso used only on Town minifigures

Hair piece later used in 2001 for Professor Snape from the LEGO® Harry Potter™ theme

Blue undershirt

TOWN

Twenty-eight sets appeared in 1986, including the first police station in three years, Police Command Base (6386); a new RV with a Speedboat (6698); and a detailed Riding Stable (6379).

Townsperson with necklace She lives in the Town, not Castle, but this minifigure has the same torso as the female minifigures from the Castle theme.

Protective hard hat

Black variant of construction helmet is new this year

Only two Town minifigures have this torso

Showjumper Giddy-up! This horse rider is well-prepared for a day jumping over brick hurdles wearing a fancy new riding jacket.

New torso design this year

White-gloved hands

Stable Hand Practical blue overalls are necessary when it comes to mucking out stables and cleaning horses all day.

Jockey With the same torso print as the Motorcycle Racer but in different colors, this horse rider looks more modern than the Showjumper.

Riding Stable Two horses have plenty of exercise and a luxurious stable in this set (6379), which also comes with a horse rider, stable boy, and hay cart.

CASTLE

Only five Castle sets were released this year, but they included the impressive Black Falcon's Fortress (6074) and the Guarded Inn (6067), which was rereleased in 2001 as part of the LEGO® Legends series. Two maiden minifigures—with different-colored hats—appeared this year, along with new Lion Knight and Black Falcon soldiers.

DID YOU KNOW?
The Lion Knights' name only became official in 2022 with the release of Lion Knights' Castle (10305).

Hat piece also seen in black on Queen Leonora from the Castle theme in 2000

Helmets are either gray or black

Helmet with neck guard

Lion Knight Ax Archer This soldier doesn't shoot axes from his bow, he just wears them on his outfit!

Lion Knight Archer This knight likes his nose protection, but worries about his chin.

Showing off his armor wares

Armorer This first minifigure to have an armor print but no helmet runs the Armor Shop (6041).

Cart Passenger This medieval woman loves her new hennin hat piece.

Blue plastic cape is attached between neck and torso at the back

Innkeeper A blue cape and a red hennin hat help this minifigure bring some color to the Dark Ages!

Huge smile

Boy This may be the first Basic figure to have legs, but he decides to sit down and fly a Helicopter (390).

LEGO BASIC

This figure was one of the few to appear in LEGO Basic sets, the predecessor to today's Classic theme.

Helicopter helmet

Warm, zip-up jacket

Ski suit

Skier One minute this figure is having fun on the slopes on his Snow Scooter (8620), the next he is being rescued by the Air Rescue Unit (8660).

Pilot This figure pilots his Polar Copter (8640) and Prop Plane (8855), making sure the Skier figures stay safe on the slopes.

LEGO TECHNIC

Figures were introduced in 1986 in the new LEGO Technic Arctic Action subtheme, which also featured vehicles and structures designed for an arctic environment. Arctic Action only lasted one year.

Red fire helmet

Firefighter This figure has fought many fires—all with a confident smile.

LEGO DUPLO

This figure first appeared in a fire engine in 1985 in the DUPLO Town set (2611). Further call-outs came in 1986's Community People (1042) and Community Vehicles (1044).

ROBOTS

These two mechanical marvels added value to a colorful set of four Space Minifigures (6702).

Lever piece commonly used on robots

Small Robot Six pieces, including gripping arms, make up this simple space-bot.

Robot claws

Tall Robot This bot stands as tall as a minifigure, proudly showing off a printed control panel tile.

SPACE

Ready for lift-off! Sixteen Classic Space sets were released this year, featuring the traditional modular space vehicles and astronauts in primary colors. Major sets this year included Alien Moon Stalker (6940) and Cosmic Fleet Voyager (6985).

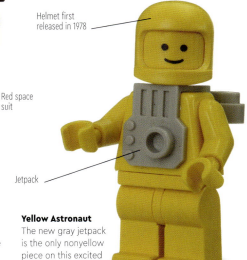

Jetpack

Classic Space logo

Red space suit

Helmet first released in 1978

Jetpack

Black Astronaut The spacefarer's jetpack was introduced in 1985, but the gray variant is new this year.

Blue Astronaut Wearing a blue space suit, helmet, and air tank, this smiling astronaut isn't feeling blue about exploring!

Red Astronaut This minifigure is the most abundant in the Space theme, appearing in more than 40 sets.

Yellow Astronaut The new gray jetpack is the only nonyellow piece on this excited space explorer.

Classic astronaut helmet • 1978
• Red Astronaut • LEGOLAND Space

Peaked cap • 1978 • Coast Guard
Captain • LEGOLAND Town

Black fire helmet • 1978
• Firefighter • LEGOLAND Town

Black stetson • 1978 • High Roller
• LEGOLAND Town

Helmet with nose guard • 1978
• Blue Cavalry Knight
• LEGOLAND Castle

Yellow helmet with blue visor
• 1987 • Yellow Futuron Astronaut
• LEGOLAND Space

**Pointed hat with brim and
yellow feather** • 1987 • Forester
with Pouch • LEGOLAND Castle

Bicorn with crossbones • 1989
• Captain Redbeard • LEGO Pirates

Red bandana • 1989 • Blue Pirate
• LEGO Pirates

Tricorn • 1989 • Pirate Blue Shirt
• LEGO Pirates

Pith helmet • 1998 • Baron Von
Barron • LEGO Adventurers

Ninja mask • 2000 • Ninja
• LEGO Castle

Jester's hat • 2008 • Jester
• LEGO Castle

Gold crown tiara • 2009
• Crown Queen • LEGO Castle

Beret • 2010 • Mime
• LEGO Minifigures

Kasa hat • 2011 • Master Wu
• LEGO NINJAGO

Santa hat • 2012
• Santa Claus • LEGO Minifigures

Elf hat with ears • 2013
• Holiday Elf • LEGO Minifigures

Red crested helmet
• 2013 • Roman Commander
• LEGO Minifigures

Winter hood • 2014
• Arctic Explorer • LEGO City

Bandages • 2016
• Clumsy Guy • LEGO Minifigures

Hard hat with lamp • 2018
• Miner • LEGO City

Hoodie over baseball cap • 2019
• Jack Davids • LEGO Hidden Side

Sou'wester • 2019
• Captain Jonas • LEGO Hidden Side

Hard hat with ponytail • 2022
• Horse Rider • LEGO City

Hard hat • 1979 • Construction Worker • LEGOLAND Town

Chef's hat • 1979 • Chef • LEGOLAND Town

Top hat • 1980 • Dignitary • LEGOLAND Town

Grille helmet with black plume • 1984 • Blue Knight • LEGOLAND Castle

Hennin • 1986 • Innkeeper • LEGOLAND Castle

Fusilier hat • 1989 • Imperial Soldier • LEGO Pirates

Wizard's hat • 1993 • Majisto Wizard • LEGO Castle

Gold crown with white plume • 1995 • The King • LEGO Castle

Helmet with nose guard and bat wings • 1997 • Basil the Bat Lord • LEGO Castle

Transparent bubble helmet • 1998 • Gypsy Moth • LEGO Space

Bearskin • 2011 • Royal Guard • LEGO Minifigures

Domed sailor's hat • 2011 • Sailor • LEGO Minifigures

Witch's hat with hair • 2015 • Wacky Witch • LEGO Minifigures

Hard hat with ear protectors • 2015 • Construction Worker • LEGO City

Year of the Rabbit hat • 2023 • Lunar New Year Celebrant • LEGO seasonal

Mushroom hat • 2024 • Mushroom Sprite • LEGO Minifigures

HATS AMAZING!

LEGO® HEADGEAR has been around longer than the modern minifigure. The precursors to the LEGO minifigure, released in 1975, may have had blank faces, but they were also wearing hats! LEGO hats fit onto a knob on the top of the standard minifigure head. They not only look stylish, but also help establish a minifigure's identity and suggest story ideas during play. Some hats (and helmets) are common, while others are made especially for just one character. All of them are endlessly interchangeable, so there is no limit to the different hats a standard minifigure can wear!

Helmet with blue visor element is new this year

Gold zipper

Red Futuron Astronaut
Updating the classic astronauts of 1978, the Futuron faction have new helmets and zip-up space suits.

1987

NO MATTER WHERE a minifigure went in 1987, they were sure to run into adventure. Deep in the woods of Castle, Forester minifigures made an appearance for the first time. Beyond the stars, Futuron and Blacktron were about to have a galaxy-shaking encounter. Closer to home, a new LEGO® Club was founded in this year and would eventually bring minifigure fun into the homes of millions of LEGO fans. Buckle up your rocket belt and get ready to blast off into 1987!

FUTURON

Premiering with six sets, Futuron centers on peaceful minifigures based on Earth's moon. They have fun exploring the galaxy, but they have to constantly contend with the wicked Blacktron Astronauts.

Air tank

Blue Futuron Astronaut Every Futuron explorer has a blue, lift-up visor. This one likes the color most of all.

Classic Space logo

DID YOU KNOW?
Faces are printed onto LEGO minifigures using a mechanized process called Tampo printing.

Yellow Futuron Astronaut The busiest minifigure in the Futuron range had featured in 12 sets by 1990.

Monorail Transport System This set (6990) features a battery-operated monorail plus five Futuron minifigures.

SPACE

Space introduced its first two competing factions in 1987—the Futuron explorers and the mysterious Blacktron Astronauts. Design of the minifigures, particularly on Blacktron, was a huge advance from Classic Space and helped cement Space as a much-loved LEGO line.

BLACKTRON BUDDY
The Blacktron Astronauts don't carry out all their missions alone—they need the help of this robot figure. The Blacktron Robot was only available in one set, Invader (6894).

Robot arm

Blacktron Robot
This bot is all black apart from one transparent red piece, indicating it is switched on!

BLACKTRON
The Blacktron Astronauts made their debut in three sets, including their starship, Renegade (6954). This faction has its own agenda, so friendship with a Futuron is not guaranteed.

Opaque visor can hide face entirely

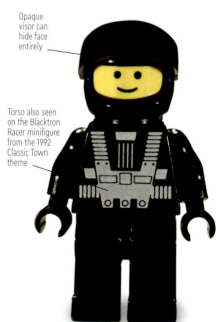

Torso also seen on the Blacktron Racer minifigure from the 1992 Classic Town theme

Blacktron Astronaut Wearing a new torso with a silver power pack design, this Blacktron Astronaut looks sleek and striking.

Black Falcon Knight A grilled helmet and armored breastplate should be enough to protect this knight in battle!

Affixed grille helmet

Silver armor

KNIGHT CLASH

The Lion Knight and Black Falcon minifigures squared off in sets including Battering Ram (6062) this year, with the Lion Knights laying siege to Black Falcon strongholds.

Helmet with chin guard

Gold lion symbol

Lion Knight This courageous minifigure shows no fear in the face of the Black Falcons' battering ram!

Blue plume

Blue Forester This skilled archer loves bows, arrows, and this all-new pointed hat design!

Green hat matches tunic and pants

Red Forester This minifigure likes to hang out with the other outlaws in their Camouflaged Outpost.

FORESTERS

The Forester minifigures made their first appearance in the Camouflaged Outpost set (6066), identifiable by their distinctive hats.

Basket element is new for 1987

Black Forester Not every forester gets a quiver of arrows. This one has a basket on their back instead.

CASTLE

New characters joined the medieval scene in 1987, as the Forester minifigures joined the Castle cast. They appeared in only one set this year, but their arrows would continue to fly until 1990. Elsewhere, the Lion Knights battled the Black Falcons and would clash with the Foresters, too, in future sets.

Tie shirt

Red plume

Forester with Pouch The printed pouch on this outlaw's belt is full of coins for the needy.

Lead Forester How do we know this forester is in charge? They chose everyone else's code names!

White hat most usually seen on Police minifigures

Double-breasted suit jacket

LOW BRIDGE! EVERYONE TAKE OFF THEIR HEADS!

Ship's Captain A new uniform with shiny gold buttons and an anchor badge marks this minifigure out as a first-class sailor.

TOWN

Cargo had to be transported, and the Town minifigures were on the job! The Cargo Carrier (4030) appeared this year, complete with a captain and crew. But it wasn't all work in Town—the 4-Wheelin' Truck (6641) tore down the roads, looking for adventure!

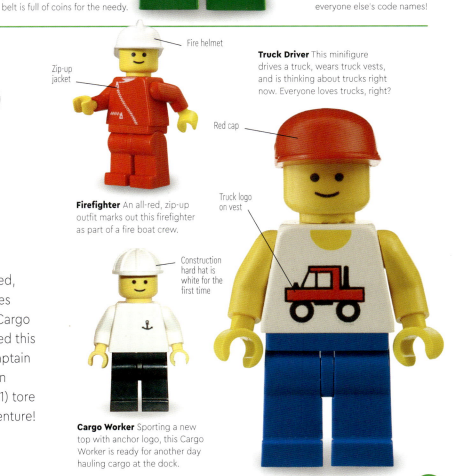

Fire helmet

Zip-up jacket

Firefighter An all-red, zip-up outfit marks out this firefighter as part of a fire boat crew.

Construction hard hat is white for the first time

Cargo Worker Sporting a new top with anchor logo, this Cargo Worker is ready for another day hauling cargo at the dock.

Truck Driver This minifigure drives a truck, wears truck vests, and is thinking about trucks right now. Everyone loves trucks, right?

Red cap

Truck logo on vest

Standard black male hair piece

Pocket for essential tools

WE ONLY TAKE PLASTIC.

Mechanic This Mechanic's new red overalls are only seen on Classic Town minifigures.

1988

IT WAS ANOTHER exciting year for LEGO® builders. Town was back with the biggest race-themed set produced to date. Castle introduced the brutish Black Knights, and Futuron and Blacktron continued to clash in the far reaches of the Space theme. No matter what the situation, though, minifigures were always smiling. The minifigures from the three LEGOLAND® themes (Town, Castle, and Space) seemed content to carry on as they were. However, little did they know that this time next year, what it meant to be a minifigure would change forever ...

TOWN

It was all about cars and keeping them well-serviced and on the LEGO roads in Town this year. Victory Lap Raceway (6395), with a whopping 13 minifigures—including mechanics, spectators, and four racers—left the starting line, as did the Metro Park & Service Tower (6394).

Town Driver This minifigure can't get enough of the car wash in Metro Park & Service Tower (6394).

Striped T-shirt

DID YOU KNOW? Metro Park & Service Tower (6394) is the first set to feature car wash brushes.

Metro Park & Service Tower Keeping all the Town cars running, this set (6394) includes a service station, multistory parking garage, and six minifigures.

Standard helmet with visor

WHY AM I SMILING? I'M LOST!

Motorcycle Driver This Motorcycle Driver has the same torso as the Jockey from 1986.

Baton for signaling to pilots

Blue cap matches pants

Airplane logo

Aircraft Controller There's no mistaking where this minifigure works, thanks to a striking airport uniform.

Torso also seen on the Truck Driver from 1987

Pit Crew This motorsports fan has a dream job working at the Victory Lap Raceway (6395).

Lead Forester This outlaw has totally changed their look since 1987. Now their hat has a yellow plume!

Red collar

FORESTERS

Only one set, Forestmen's Hideout (6054), marked the second year of the Forester faction. With vines to climb up and targets to shoot at, the Foresters would be ready to take on any naughty knights.

Plume also fits into knights' helmets

Pouch is full to bursting

Shield piece is brown for the first time

CASTLE

The Black Knights arrived this year, with their powerful fortress, the Black Monarch's Castle (6085). Guarded by 12 knight minifigures, it was the first of two castles for this popular Castle faction. Beyond the gates, the Black Knights and the Lion Knights would oppose each other in the Knight's Challenge joust before the eyes of two spectator minifigures.

Dark gray helmet with chin guard

Scale mail armor over blue torso

Bow and arrow are perfect for scaring off intruders

Forester with Shield The Foresters get their own shield design this year, depicting a majestic stag.

Black Knight Guard Wearing new armor with scale mail, this knight stands guard outside the Black Monarch's Castle (6085).

Blue torso matches blue pants

Final appearance for this torso in an all-new set

Black Knight When they're not clashing with their forest foes, the knights are busy jousting in sets such as Knight's Challenge (1584).

Lion Knight Squire In a year full of Black Knights, this brave Lion Knight doesn't stop smiling for a second!

Knight's Challenge Let the games begin! Depicting a jousting tournament, this set (1584) includes an audience stand, a weapons' rack, and a tapped keg, as well as eight minifigures.

1584

LEGO
LEGOLAND

Circus Ringmaster Keeping the Circus Clowns in line, as well as making sure his mustache is neatly trimmed, is no laughing matter for the Ringmaster.

Bow tie

Aviator helmet

Blue Clown This Clown has guts—he is blasted out of a cannon every night, much to the DUPLO audience's amusement.

Big bow tie

Red Clown Luckily for this Clown, he just has to ride an elephant while carrying an umbrella in the DUPLO Town Circus Caravan (2652).

LEGO® DUPLO®

LEGO DUPLO was off to see a show with the Circus Caravan set, one of seven sets released this year. This was the first appearance of the Circus Ringmaster figure.

Dragon Shield Black Knight The red torso with scale mail pattern that adorns this knight is new this year.

Long pole with ax attachment

Helmet is seen on many LEGO knights

Purse pouch

Black helmet with neck protector

Peasant The humble Peasant is attending a jousting tournament—just as a spectator, however.

Black Knight The Black Knight's armor was first seen in 1984, but it still looks just as shiny this year.

SHIVER ME LEGO BRICK TIMBERS!

Eyepatch seen for the first time

Striped top underneath jacket

Blue Jacket Pirate This pirate is proud to be the first of his pals to wear the new pirate torso and tricorn hat.

1989

NOT SINCE 1978 had there been such an exciting year for the LEGO® minifigure. LEGO® Pirates was launched and was an immediate hit. Suddenly, minifigures had moved on from the traditional simple smile to having multiple facial expressions. Many new elements also arrived as the minifigure took a quantum leap toward the minifigure of today. Meanwhile, on the other side of the law-and-order fence, the Space Police arrived to keep an eye on Blacktron Astronauts and recruit a new generation of fans to LEGO® Space!

Shako hat

Backpack

Epaulettes are new this year

Hat same as Captain Redbeard's, minus skull and crossbones print

Imperial Soldier uniform

Imperial Soldier This soldier likes his home comforts—he keeps his bedding in his backpack.

Governor Broadside With his fancy hat and blue coat, there's no doubting that this soldier is in charge.

Lt. de Martinet The courageous Lieutenant often leads the charge into battle—and he never loses his head.

Imperial Officer The Officer has the same head as the Lieutenant, but a different hat.

PIRATES

No one had ever seen anything like it before: a bunch of minifigures with scruffy beards and thick mustaches, with wooden legs and hook-hands, and carrying flintlock pistols and muskets. The pirates had arrived in a big way, sailing the Black Seas Barracuda (6285) against the forces of the Imperials. The seas—and the world of LEGO minifigures—would never be the same again.

First time a minifigure has had red lips

New red corset matches ruby necklace

Female Pirate This pirate risks her life every day sailing the seas—she is always looking for a new adventure.

DID YOU KNOW?
A comic book called *The Golden Medallion* was released in 1989 to promote the LEGO Pirates theme.

Captain Redbeard Ahoy, me hearties! With all-new elements, Captain Redbeard is ready to sail the seas on the lookout for treasure.

New bandana protects minifigure head from bracing sea winds

Young Pirate Striped vests are a favorite with pirates. This sea dog's red bandana matches perfectly.

Ominous skull and crossbones bicorn hat

Blue-and-white striped vest

Blue Pirate This rascally fellow's stubbled face, with its droopy mustache, is new this year.

Red-and-white striped vest

Blue Bandana Pirate This pirate is sporting the same vest as his pal, but he has chosen white pants instead.

Wooden leg

Hook-hand

Forester This outlaw's hideout is the River Fortress (6077). Shh! Don't tell anyone.

Forester hat

Yellow plume

I'M JUST A SIMPLE HAY HAULER.

Farmer's cowl also seen on the LEGO® Castle Wolfpack gang in 1992

Blue collar

Leather belt

Blue Forester An expert at camouflage, this forester can be found in just one set!

Torso is the same as the Forester, but in gray

CASTLE

The Foresters returned with their largest set to date, River Fortress (6077), which they fought hard to protect from the Lion Knights. Another set released this year was Smuggler's Hayride (1974), which featured a treasure chest hidden under brick hay bales. Law and order was restored soon after, as the Foresters were phased out in 1990.

Smuggler This minifigure uses a hay cart to sneak contraband from castle to castle.

LEGO® DUPLO®

These two LEGO DUPLO figures were part of an 18-figure set for schools, designed to make the play theme more representative.

Red necklace

Tie matches pants

Man with Tie This figure makes an appearance in the LEGO DUPLO Figures International set (9159), and he's dressed for the occasion!

Woman with Necklace This figure also appears in 1992's World People (9980).

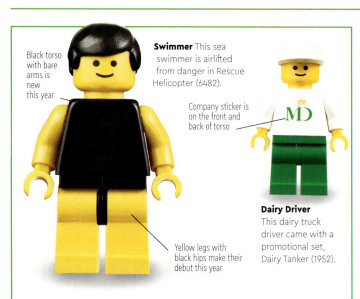

Black torso with bare arms is new this year

Swimmer This sea swimmer is airlifted from danger in Rescue Helicopter (6482).

Company sticker is on the front and back of torso

Dairy Driver This dairy truck driver came with a promotional set, Dairy Tanker (1952).

Yellow legs with black hips make their debut this year

TOWN

Town was at sea this year, with a new Coast Guard Base (6387) and a Rescue Helicopter (6482). This was the first time a new LEGO Coast Guard logo was used in a set, and the last Coast Guard base produced until 1995. This year's Rescue Helicopter was the largest LEGO System chopper to date. 1989 also saw the release of a Dairy Tanker (1952) promotional set, featuring a friendly minifigure driver.

SPACE

The Space Police, one of the best-loved Space lines, arrived this year to serve and protect the law-abiding Futuron citizens from Blacktron bad apples. This was the first of three Space subthemes based around intergalactic law enforcement.

Visor is red for the first time

Gold logo

Antenna

FUTURON FRIEND

Appearing exclusively in Lunar MPV Vehicle (1621), this brick-built figure accompanied Futuron Astronauts on another daring space mission. But was the bot a secret spy for the Blacktron faction ...?

Futuron Robot A hinged brick base lets this robot bend forward like a minifigure.

Torso design is the same as the Futuron Astronauts from 1987

Space Police Officer This friendly star cop rarely sees red—only when he puts down his visor!

1990s

LEGO® mania! The '90s saw an explosion of wild new LEGO play themes, and with them came an even wilder array of new minifigures. Ghosts, cowboys, robots, aliens, witches, and wizards abounded. Minifigures traveled through time, blasted off to futuristic frozen planets, explored ancient pyramids, and went diving to the bottom of the sea. Capping it all off at the decade's end was the biggest news in minifigure history: a famous licensed theme of truly galactic proportions!

TIME TO BLAST OFF INTO THE '90S!

Helmet with visor is vital for space walks

NASA sticker on torso

Shuttle Astronaut This NASA minifigure appears in only one set: Space Launch Shuttle (1682).

1990

AS A NEW DECADE dawned, LEGO® Town, LEGO® Space, and LEGO® Castle became play themes in their own right, and their minifigures were getting ready for many new adventures. Far up in LEGO Space, M:Tron joined the line-up, while the Foresters said farewell in LEGO Castle. Over in LEGO Town, everyone was getting ready to travel on a jet plane to visit far-off lands. LEGO® DUPLO® also continued to grow, adding new subthemes this year. With new minifigures in space, on land, and even a new minifigure haunting a medieval castle, it was a year of action and adventure for builders young and old.

LEGO TOWN

Builders visiting LEGO Town in 1990 had lots to choose from. They could take off from the airport, visit the Breezeway Café (6376) for lunch, or ride with the police from the Pursuit Squad (6354). LEGO Town continued its tradition of presenting a fun variety of places to play.

Classic hair piece

Red neckerchief offsets the chef's whites

Not a hair out of place

New torso with vest and bow tie

Showjumper With a sharp-suited torso and white gloves, this minifigure is competition-ready!

Chef This minifigure works at the Breezeway Café, serving delicious food to all the minifigure patrons.

Waiter Sporting formal attire and a slick hairdo, this waiter works in a classy establishment.

Helmet protects head in rough seas

Bright yellow life jacket makes Coast Guard visible at sea

Torso with fancy gold trim and buttons

Fire Helicopter Pilot This airborne firefighter is exclusive to Fire Control Center (6389).

Coast Guard Wearing a new life jacket accessory, this minifigure is ready for action.

M:Tron Astronaut With a new torso and visor color, this minifigure is ready to blast off into space.

LEGO SPACE

The M:Tron subtheme replaced Futuron this year, introducing gravity-defying magnets to LEGO Space. It was the first space subtheme to feature vehicles only, with no ground base for the faction. Elsewhere, Futuron-style astronauts explored a new frontier: LEGO® Education sets for schools.

Air tanks for a space walk

M:Tron logo

A classic smiling face under the visor

Red and Green Astronaut This is the first LEGO astronaut to wear green.

Black and Yellow Astronaut This explorer is found in just one set for schools.

Air tank attaches to back with neck bracket

Ghost Underneath the Ghost's new shroud piece is a white torso and a plain black head.

Ghoulish face, but still smiling

White minifigure arms

BOO!

The first LEGO ghost minifigure mysteriously appeared this year, glowing in the dark in the King's Mountain Fortress (6081). This smiling spirit would be around for the next five years.

King's Mountain Fortress This stone fort (6081) comes with eight minifigures, including knights, guards, and a Medieval Woman.

Female Zookeeper This figure came in two LEGO DUPLO Zoo sets (2669, 2666) and a LEGO DUPLO People set (9979).

Green zookeeper's uniform

Red Knight The Black Falcons had better watch out—this knight is armored and ready for battle.

Helmet with covered visor and red plume

LEGO CASTLE

There was plenty of excitement in the world of LEGO Castle in 1990, with the introduction of the first minifigure skirt piece and the Foresters' final adventures for many years. The year also saw the first castle built on a raised baseplate. It was a merry medieval time for all!

Breastplate armor

Scale mail torso provides protection

Blue Knight This year's new visor and armor pieces are a big hit, but this knight doesn't feel a thing!

Traditional Forester hat

Quiver full of arrows

Lead Forester Two Lion Knights are poised to catch this outlaw in Dungeon Hunters (6042).

Yellow hat for all weathers

Zoo logo on torso

Male Zookeeper This figure is seen in many places, from safaris to zoo trains—he's a busy guy!

LEGO DUPLO

Preschool toys were made even more fun this year with the introduction of sets based on Zoo and Race. Little builders had plenty to see and do with these new worlds!

IS IT A HAT OR A ROCKET NOSE CONE? YOU DECIDE!

Red hennin worn by four other minifigures

Red feather plume

Visor to protect face

Black Knight This year's knights may tremble at ghosts, but their new armor does a great job of hiding it!

New torso with necklace detail

Medieval Woman This minifigure is the first to wear a sloped skirt piece in place of legs. Now that's history!

Hat style first worn by LEGO® Pirates

Same face print as Medieval Woman

Green Forester This forester has the same torso print as the Medieval Woman, but in forest green.

All Forester minifigures have plain green legs

Motorcycle Racer This figure appeared in Racer (2609) with a blue LEGO DUPLO car with "2" on it.

Number helps identify racer on the course.

Red hat matches tie

Railway logo

TICKETS, PLEASE!

Station Manager A smart new uniform with a railway logo helps this minifigure look and feel important.

1991

THE BIGGEST NEWS of 1991 came from the high seas. After the massive success of LEGO® Pirates in 1989, the line had effectively taken a year off in 1990. It came back with the roar of cannon fire this year, and with sets that are still fondly remembered to this day. An old LEGO® Space friend returned, too, as Blacktron was updated and turned into Blacktron II. In LEGO® Town, the Firefighters dispatched a new unit—RSQ911—to save the day.

White hard hat

Chevron-style design on torso

Hair piece seen on more than 125 other minifigures

Same torso as Railway Worker

Trackside Staff You can't miss this railworker's bold new high-vis torso print. It keeps them safe as they work trackside.

Onboard Staff This minifigure is most impressed with the new railway uniform, especially the bright red neckerchief.

Maintenance Staff The railway tracks don't repair themselves— this worker fixes them, in Road and Rail Maintenance (4546).

Same red hat as the Station Manager's

Railway logo printed on torso

I NEED A TIMETABLE ACCESSORY!

Railway Worker Whether at the Metro Station (4554) or aboard the Metroliner (4558), this minifigure is always ready to help passengers.

LEGO® TRAIN

LEGO Train entered a new era in 1991, as 9V train sets took over from 12V and 4.5V. Six new sets appeared this year, including the Metroliner (4558) and the Metro Station (4554), with 19 minifigures between them. These included conductors, railway workers, and passengers. 9V dominated LEGO Train until 2006.

LEGO PIRATES

The second major wave of Pirates sets came out this year, including Rock Island Refuge (6273) and Lagoon Lock-Up (6267). Five sets sailed the Spanish Main, featuring pirate and Imperial Soldier minifigures. Hoist the sails!

Red bandana

Orange belt

Gray Pirate This scruffy guy wears gray pants instead of blue. This is the only difference between him and his 1989 variant.

New torso with neon green logo

Jetpack for freestyle flying

Blacktron II Astronaut
This minifigure thinks the new Blacktron logo is simply out of this world.

M:Tron Astronaut
A classic LEGO Space jetpack gives this minifigure a real boost.

DID YOU KNOW?
More than 600 minifigures have worn the standard helmet since its redesign in 1987.

Blacktron II Commander
Wearing new bodywear, the jetpack with twin handles, this minifigure is ready for a mission.

Transparent neon green visor to protect their grin

Jetpack with twin handles

Blacktron II logo

LEGO SPACE

Blacktron II rocketed into the stratosphere in 1991, with a dozen sets. This was a remake of the original Blacktron from 1987, and many of the sets were similar to those released previously. The major change was in the look of the minifigures, who all received new uniforms with a black octagon logo. An M:Tron minifigure was also released—the first minifigure from the M:Tron subtheme to feature a jetpack.

LEGO® DUPLO®

Police became a part of DUPLO Town in 1991, with the release of a new Police Station (2672) and a Police Emergency Unit (2654). New figures included police officers and a crook.

Prisoner number matches set number

Silver police badge

Jailbreak Joe This stubble-faced figure came in one set: Police Set (2672).

Policeman Part of six sets, this figure was a familiar face on the beat in 1991.

Black cap

Police Chief
If there was a minifigure emergency, this guy would be there, in Emergency Unit (2654).

LEGO TOWN

RSQ911, part of the Fire subtheme, came out this year, along with some new nautical-themed sets like Cabin Cruiser (4011) and Coastal Cutter (6353). Minifigures learned to love the life jacket, as a total of 10 minifigures wore this accessory in 1991.

Cap to combat glare from water

Boater Part of the Cabin Cruiser set (4011), this minifigure came with a new accessory: a fishing rod.

LEGO® CASTLE

Only one new Castle set was released this year: King's Catapult (1480). Launched as part of the Lion Knights subtheme, it featured pieces to build a catapult and one new Lion Knight soldier. It was a lonely year for this minifigure, but Castle would return in 1992.

Knight There are no new parts on this minifigure, but it is a new combination of parts.

Scale mail decoration on torso

Yellow life jacket

Coast Guard The life jacket had only been worn by one minifigure in 1990. The Coast Guard thinks that safety is always in fashion!

I NEED COFFEE, NOW!

Classic hair piece

Business suit

Commuter This minifigure is always rushing to work, clutching a smart suitcase accessory.

Last appearance for this torso print

Airport Firefighter
Two of these runway responders feature in Jetport Fire Squad (6440).

Broad-brimmed tricorn hat

Frilled shirt

Blue Pirate A new head piece with shaggy hair, a mustache, and a beard is exclusive to this rugged minifigure.

> ARRRR! NEW LANDS TO PLUNDER!

1992

THIS YEAR SAW SOME NEW FACES

and the return of some old ones. Both LEGO® Space and LEGO® Castle followed the lead of LEGO® Pirates and upgraded their minifigure heads to the more modern look that is visible today. The Space Police subtheme returned (nicknamed Space Police II), while Castle got a brand-new bunch of bad guys, and Pirates faced a new military foe. For those minifigures who just wanted to get away from it all, new subtheme LEGO® Paradisa offered up a variety of tropical delights.

LEGO PIRATES

The Pirates got a new enemy this year, the Imperial Guard, as nine new sets appeared. The Imperial Guard minifigures were very similar to Imperial Soldiers, which featured from 1989 to 1991, with only a change of uniform. They would battle the Pirates for four years before being replaced by the Imperial Armada in 1997.

Brimmed hat keeps rainwater at bay

New torso with striped vest

Striped Pirate Protocol requires this pirate to maintain a rugged appearance.

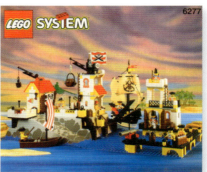

Imperial Trading Post One of the largest Imperial Guard sets, this set (6277) comes with a merchant ship, a row boat, and cannons.

Elaborate black bicorn hat

White triple feather plume

Printed sideburns

Ornamental shoulder decorations

Shaggy beard

New torso with crossbelts

Gray hook replaces hand

Black Pirate A new torso for this minifigure has a black knife tucked into his crossbelt—so the pirate's one hand can be free.

Officer A new head piece with an unkempt hairstyle shows this Imperial Guard focuses on keeping his robes tidy rather than his hair.

Admiral This very important Imperial Guard minifigure has a dashing new head piece and torso.

LEGO SPACE

It was Space Police's turn to get revamped in 1992, with new uniforms and new ships—but no permanent base. Pitted against their enemies, Blacktron II, Space Police II would protect civilian space explorers for the next year.

Neck bracket connects air tanks to back

Radio for contacting the base

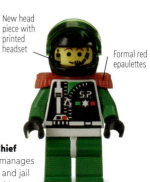

Space Police Officer This Officer proudly bears the Space Police logo on a brand-new torso.

New head piece with printed headset

Formal red epaulettes

Space Police Chief This minifigure manages a police station and jail aboard a spaceship.

LEGO CASTLE

LEGO Castle was inspired by Pirates this year, premiering the same kind of printed head pieces as Pirates debuted in 1989. Robbers and renegades the Wolfpack made their presence known in two sets before skulking back into the shadows at the end of 1993.

A farmer's cowl covers unkempt hair

Wolfpack motif

New decorative wings on helmet sides

Shaggy appearance

Strong breastplate armor

Red belt to hold up pants

Knight The biggest challenge for this armored minifigure is getting around without making too much noise.

Eyepatch Bandit The new brown torso worn by this minifigure helps him hide among the trees in the forest.

Mustachioed Bandit This outlaw can afford to smile because the wolf emblem on his chest does the glaring for him!

Reading glasses

Sideswept hairstyle

Sweet, frilly shirt

LEGO DUPLO Grandma This bespectacled pensioner appears only in Grandma's Kitchen (2551).

LEGO DUPLO Grandpa This figure is featured in two sets: Supermarket (9167) and Grandma's Kitchen (2551).

LEGO® DUPLO®

These two figures were cooking up something delicious in Grandma's Kitchen set (2551). Although LEGO DUPLO had no new themes this year, it continued to provide plenty of fun for young builders.

Poolside Paradise This vacation dream home (6416) is built on a raised baseplate with a sunken pool area.

Rare convex, transparent panels

Open-top sports car

Unique baseplate with inground pool

The sunglasses print was new this year

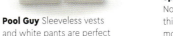

THIS PLACE IS A MINIFIGURE'S PARADISE ...

Life jacket

Nautical striped vest

Black swimming trunks

Speedboat Driver Nothing pleases this minifigure more than feeling the wind in his hair piece as he sails.

Pool Guy Sleeveless vests and white pants are perfect attire for a casual sun-lover.

Hard riding hat

Vest for hot days

Stable Hand This minifigure's head piece and torso were introduced this year.

Swimmer This minifigure has a new torso design and appears in Poolside Paradise (6416).

Palm tree motif on new torso

Polka-dot swimming costume

Vendor This is the first minifigure to feature freckles. They wear a cap to shield their face from the sun.

LEGO PARADISA

This bright and breezy new LEGO Town subtheme launched with four sets in 1992. It focused on vacations and leisure and used plenty of pastel-colored bricks. New minifigures designed for the range included men with sunglasses and smartly trimmed mustaches, and women with long ponytails. The subtheme lasted for six sun-soaked years.

New pointed hat piece

Pouch for carrying potions

ADMIT IT, YOU LOVE THE HAT.

Majisto As the first wizard minifigure, Majisto is as proud of his wizard's hat as he is of his brand-new separate beard piece.

1993

THE STRENGTH OF LEGO® minifigures as a concept rested on the idea that each minifigure could be customized and used in a variety of settings. The ability to add to new and old sets would help keep long-standing themes looking fresh and current. Both the LEGO® Castle and LEGO® Space themes got new factions and new places to explore this year. From the scorched plains ruled by the Dragon Masters to the frigid wasteland of the Ice Planet, LEGO fans and their minifigures were given plenty of exciting and innovative ways to stir their imagination in 1993.

Helmet with chin guard

Brave Knight A new head piece and torso were introduced this year for this minifigure.

Dragon emblem on chest

DID YOU KNOW? Majisto was the first Castle minifigure to be given an official name.

Blue Dragon Knight This minifigure is only featured in Majisto's Magical Workshop (6048).

Fancy upturned mustache

Chest plate armor

Black visor is hinged at the sides

New face print with red hair

Fabric cape is introduced this year

Red Dragon Master The plume and decorative wings worn by this knight were first seen in 1992's Black Knight's Castle (6009).

LEGO CASTLE

The beat of huge, leathery wings announced the arrival of Dragon Masters, the newest Castle subtheme. The wizard Majisto sent his dragons into battle in a line that introduced several new minifigures, cloth pieces, and the now famous flame piece to LEGO building. The dragons roared only until 1995.

HA! NOW THIS IS WHAT I CALL A HAT!

New shoulder armor printing

Fire Breathing Fortress Featuring six minifigures, this set (6082) has a trapdoor that dumps intruders into a pit.

Blue Dragon Master Almost identical to the Red Dragon Master, this knight also has mismatched arms and legs—an eye-catching design first for minifigures.

Large dragon figures were new this year

LEGO® TOWN

1993 proved to be a big year for LEGO Town, starting with the move of all Police and Fire sets to a new subtheme, Rescue. Airport and Race both had new sets, but the highlight had to be the new Central Precinct HQ (6398), the first police station in two years, following Pier Police in 1991 (6540).

Helmet protects in high-speed pursuits

Thick, weatherproof jacket

Patrol Officer Found in two sets this year, this minifigure has a new torso and helmet.

Prisoner number

Jailbreak Joe The printed torso on this crook has been featured on four minifigures in total.

DID YOU KNOW?
Central Police HQ (6398) was the first set to have a crook minifigure—Jailbreak Joe.

Helmet is essential

Stubbled cheeks and chin

Red Stunt Pilot The new flight jacket torso print on this minifigure appears for the first time this year.

Fur collar for warmth

Peaked cap is official Police uniform

Police Officer This cop has a new mustache and a big new badge on his uniform.

Helmet printed with stripes

Green vest

Stunt Pilot This is the first year in which printing is featured on a minifigure's helmet.

Standard ponytail hair piece

Jogging suit

Spectator A new torso with all-weather gear shows this minifigure is ready to watch the pilots' air show.

New police baseball cap

ID card clipped to chest

Police Sheriff The sheriff only appears in Central Precinct HQ (6398) and is the first minifigure to feature this new torso.

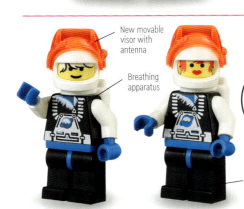

New movable visor with antenna

Breathing apparatus

Heavy-duty space boots

Ice Planet Man Clearly pleased to be heading into space, this minifigure has the first face print with messy white-blond bangs.

Ice Planet Woman Wearing a focused expression, this minifigure checks her breathing apparatus is secure.

Ice Planet Chief The chief features a new torso with a formal jacket print—fitting for a high-ranking minifigure.

IT'S SO COLD, MY MUSTACHE HAS FROZEN!

Shaggy eyebrows

Ice Planet insignia

LEGO SPACE

Another new faction joined the LEGO Space saga with Ice Planet 2002. It charted the adventures of ice saw–wielding scientists exploring a frozen world in the distant future of 2002! They featured in six sets during 1993 and three more the following year, alongside new subthemes Unitron and Spyrius.

Peaked pilot's hat

Airline logo

Jetliner Pilot This pilot only appears this year and is seen in three sets. His eager expression and wide eyes show that he is ready to take to the air.

Pilot with Helmet This pilot is seen in two sets alongside the Jetliner Pilot: Airport (2679) and LEGO DUPLO Airport (9163). He has a headset to listen to ground control.

LEGO® DUPLO®

For the first time in eight years, LEGO DUPLO figures took to the air with the release of the LEGO DUPLO Airport sets. The Airport subtheme would be up and away until 2005.

Standard LEGO helmet is completely clear for the first time

HI, I'M RUSTY ... WHAT'S SO FUNNY?

Head can also be seen in 1996 on a robot in the Time Cruisers theme

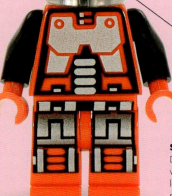

Spyrius Droid The Spyrius Droid minifigure is all new, with exclusive torso and legs. This is the first time a minifigure has printed legs!

1994

THIS YEAR SAW a combination of venturing into new areas and building on what already worked. LEGO® Pirates and LEGO® Space were both back with new subthemes, while LEGO® BELVILLE™, a nonminifigure line blending building with realistic dolls, began a 15-year run. LEGO® Town was in the air with a new aircraft and stunt chopper, on land with new Fire and Police sets, and at sea with the Coastal Patrol. There were many adventures to be had for LEGO minifigure fans in 1994.

Exclusive blue-and-silver Spyrius printing on helmet

Breathing tubes printed on torso

Spyrius Chief The leader of this year's Space villains has a unique rugged head piece and printed helmet.

LEGO SPACE

Good fought against bad beyond the stars in 1994 as two new subthemes of LEGO Space were launched. Unitron took over from Space Police II as the new heroes of LEGO Space, battling the villains of Spyrius. From their Lunar Launch site, this team of spies carried out their devious plans in five sets this year.

DID YOU KNOW?
Spyrius was the first LEGO subtheme to feature robot minifigures.

Dark gray uniform is a new LEGO color in the Space theme

Unitron Chief Although the head piece, helmet, and torso are new for this year, only the helmet is exclusive to the Unitron Chief.

Pirate hat has space for a feather

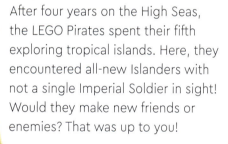

LEGO PIRATES

After four years on the High Seas, the LEGO Pirates spent their fifth exploring tropical islands. Here, they encountered all-new Islanders with not a single Imperial Soldier in sight! Would they make new friends or enemies? That was up to you!

Ragged clothes from a hard life at sea

Captain Ironhook This salty sea dog is much less smartly dressed than his rival, Captain Redbeard!

Shirt shared with seven other pirates—yuck!

Striped Pirate This rare rogue was exclusive to one North American set.

Construction helmet

LEGO® TRAIN

In 1994, Freight Rail Runner (4564) was the largest of the three LEGO Train sets released. The set included three minifigures, a Conductor, and two railway workers.

Torso exclusive to this Conductor and the 1991 variant

Conductor This minifigure is a variant of a 1991 Conductor who wears black pants.

Construction worker This minifigure is exclusive to set 4564, but the torso can be seen on five others.

LEGO TOWN

LEGO Town had something for everyone this year: five sets were released in the Rescue subtheme, including Flame Fighters (6571), which featured a fire station, fire engine, and helicopter. Car fans had three Race sets to build, while those in need of a vacation could take a jet plane from the busy Century Skyway airport (6597).

Helmet is exclusive to this minifigure

Gold badges

Fire Chief Town firefighters get new uniforms this year, but only the chief gets a badge on his helmet!

Cool sunglasses

Pen clipped into pocket

Blue EMT Star of Life pattern

BRUISED BRICK? I'M HERE TO HELP.

Paramedic This medical minifigure has a fresh look this year thanks to all-new torso and hat prints.

Plain white fire helmet worn by more than 130 minifigures

Printed gauge shows safe level of oxygen

OKAY, WHO BURNED THE TOAST?

Black gloves

Firefighter This minifigure wears a fire proximity suit with a gauge for his detachable oxygen supply.

Exclusive torso

Neatly tied scarf

Flight Attendant This minifigure knows where all the safety exits are, and she never has a LEGO hair out of place.

Smiling head piece with eyebrows is new in 1994

Leather jacket torso is also new this year

Hot Rod Driver This cool minifigure is exclusive to Hot Rod Club (6561) in the Race subtheme. The set also features a hot rod workshop, two hot rod cars, and a motorcycle.

Townsperson Variants of this minifigure were released in 1996 with red pants, and in 1998 with green pants.

Shirt torso is new this year

Adult Man This posable male appeared in Pretty Wishes Playhouse (5890) with a woman, a girl, and a baby boy.

Young Girl Three variants of this figure were released between 1994 and 1996, wearing pink shorts (above), a pink skirt, and a yellow skirt.

LEGO BELVILLE

A combination of traditional LEGO bricks and new pink and purple elements, BELVILLE also featured larger, doll-like figures with more joints for greater posability. Early sets were themed around everyday family life.

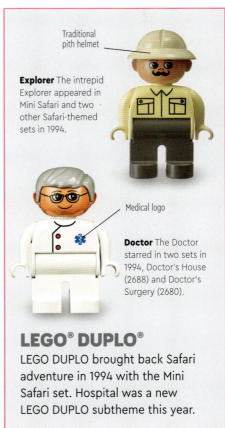

Traditional pith helmet

Explorer The intrepid Explorer appeared in Mini Safari and two other Safari-themed sets in 1994.

Medical logo

Doctor The Doctor starred in two sets in 1994, Doctor's House (2688) and Doctor's Surgery (2680).

LEGO® DUPLO®

LEGO DUPLO brought back Safari adventure in 1994 with the Mini Safari set. Hospital was a new LEGO DUPLO subtheme this year.

Blue visor

White helmet piece covers the shoulders

All the Aquanauts wear the same blue suits

I THOUGHT THIS WAS GOING TO BE A POOL PARTY…

Aquanaut Commander This minifigure's job is to drive the submarine. Their head with freckles and a red headband with a "C" in the middle is new this year.

1995

ANOTHER LANDMARK YEAR, 1995 saw the 40th anniversary of LEGO® System building sets. To celebrate, the next big play theme was introduced: Aquazone, along with a new version of Castle. Over in LEGO® Space, Unitron was discontinued after only one year and two sets. However, 1995 was a year with far-ranging effects, sparking a trend for underwater play themes and introducing one iconic bony figure who would appear in almost 50 sets over the next 18 years. Can you guess who it is?

Mærsk logo

Mærsk Truck Driver Mærsk is a real-world company based in Copenhagen, Denmark. This minifigure is exclusive to the two 1995 sets.

LEGO® AQUAZONE

Adventure lurked beneath the waves in Aquazone, a new play theme set in the depths of the ocean. The Aquanauts were undersea miners searching for crystals. However, the villainous Aquashark miners were out to steal whatever the Aquanauts dug up!

Aquashark This villain's black diving suit is decorated with a grinning shark logo. The black helmet with shoulder protection is new this year.

Torso is exclusive to the 1995 Aquasharks

Black-gloved hands

Head piece was first seen on the Space Police Chief in 1992

Black visor

Aquanaut diving suit

Jock Clouseau Radio expert Jock Clouseau has two variants in 1995—one with flippers and one without.

5…4…3…2…1… GET READY FOR BLAST-OFF!

LAUNCH COMMAND

Five sets blasted off this year as LEGO Town explored space in a big way. Unlike LEGO Space, Launch Command focused on real-world space exploration, including space shuttles and moon walkers.

Gold chrome visor, new this year

It's vital to stay in radio contact with Earth

New torso, also seen on another astronaut minifigure in 1995

Astronaut Thanks to the hard work of the minifigures on the ground, this astronaut makes it to space in Moon Walker (6516).

ID badge

Unique head

Scientist Exclusive to Shuttle Launch Pad (6339), the smart scientist has two unique parts—his head and his torso.

LEGO® TOWN

It was a year of excitement and variety for LEGO Town. Hurricane Harbor (6338), the first Coast Guard base set in six years, kept watch over the waves. Two special Mærsk cargo truck sets appeared, but were sold only in Denmark. LEGO Town even went into space with the new Launch Command models.

LEGO® CASTLE

The Royal Knights arrived this year in five sets, including a castle of their own. This Castle subtheme is best known for introducing the skeleton figure and the first king minifigure to wear an actual crown. The Royal Knights would reign supreme through 1995 and 1996.

Royal Archer A variant without a quiver was also released in 1996.

Helmet with chin guard

Lion's head shield is exclusive to this minifigure

HELLO BONES

The skeleton figure made its first appearance in 1995 in three sets—two from LEGO Castle and one from LEGO® Pirates. Including variants with hats, it has appeared in more than 50 sets.

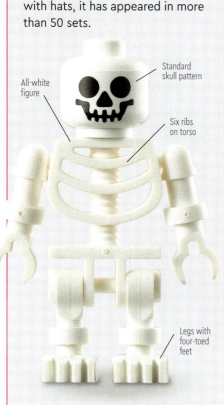

All-white figure

Standard skull pattern

Six ribs on torso

Legs with four-toed feet

Detachable plume of white feathers

The gold crown makes its debut in 1995

The King Three variants of this king were released in 1995, each with a new torso featuring a lion's head design.

THIS CROWN IS REALLY HEAVY!

New torso with fearsome lion crest

Cape

Two variants have blue pants; one has white

Mustache Knight This noble knight is distinguished by his impressive mustache.

Gray helmet with neck and nose protectors

Dark brown hair

Dungarees Kid This figure of a child appears in 12 LEGO Primo sets between 1995 and 2001.

Red shirt with blue dungarees

LEGO® PRIMO®

Aimed at the youngest builders, PRIMO replaced LEGO® Baby in 1995. It featured colorful toys intended for children from 6 to 24 months, and single-piece figures that were perfect for little hands.

I'M THE COOLEST CRANE OPERATOR YOU'LL SEE.

Torso with red safety bib print is new this year

Crane Operator It takes a steady hand to operate a huge cargo crane, but this calm minifigure is up to the job in Cargo Crane (4552).

Torso with a sunset and dolphin print vest is new this year

Dolphin Fan Set 6414 featured a dolphin and this minifigure, who was eager to swim with it.

Dolphin Point Hungry minifigures can climb the pink stairs to the ice cream parlor for a treat in this Paradisa set (6414).

DID YOU KNOW? Paradisa sets were the first to feature pink, dark pink, and medium green colors.

LEGO® PARADISA

Once again, Paradisa was the place to be with the new Dolphin Point set (6414) featuring four minifigures. This elaborate model included a two-story lighthouse complete with a lantern and an ice cream shop.

LEGO® TRAIN

Two new sets roared down the tracks in 1995, all of them dealing with cargo hauling. Five minifigures worked the rails, making sure that LEGO freight got where it needed to go. The new Cargo Station (4555) was the first one produced since 1978, and the first Cargo set using the battery-operated 9V power system.

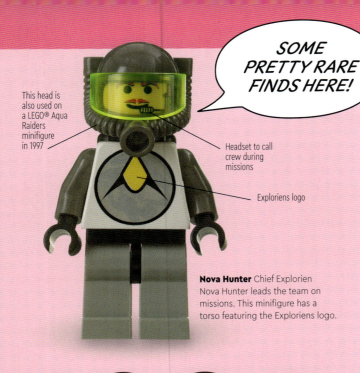

This head is also used on a LEGO® Aqua Raiders minifigure in 1997

SOME PRETTY RARE FINDS HERE!

Headset to call crew during missions

Exploriens logo

Nova Hunter Chief Explorien Nova Hunter leads the team on missions. This minifigure has a torso featuring the Exploriens logo.

1996

PERHAPS THE BIGGEST news for LEGO® minifigures this year was the introduction of LEGO.com. For the first time, fans could go online to access information, games, and activities, and also to shop for their favorite minifigures and sets. And there was plenty for LEGO fans to see online this year, as new themes LEGO® Western and LEGO® Time Cruisers were introduced, along with the Castle Dark Forest and Space Exploriens subthemes. From the distant past to the far future, LEGO building was everywhere in 1996!

WHERE TO GO NEXT ... HOW ABOUT A TRIP TO ANCIENT EGYPT?

LEGO® SPACE

The Exploriens were new space travelers introduced in nine sets in 1996. They searched the galaxy for fossils, accompanied by their robot Ann Droid—the second robot in the history of LEGO Space. Operating out of Android Base (6958) as well as the smaller Nebula Outpost (6899), the Exploriens hung up their space helmets in 1996.

Breathing apparatus

Hosepipe attached to helmet

Headset printed on face

Helmet

Transparent green light 1×1 piece

Android face print

Armor protects internal mechanics

Ann Droid The LEGO Exploriens team's robot features a unique transparent head piece. Her name is a play on the word "android."

Explorien This minifigure has an Explorien torso—he's thankful that it has oxygen controls.

LEGO TIME CRUISERS

The first and so far only LEGO theme focused on time travel featured a team—Dr. Cyber, Tim (his assistant), a robot, and a monkey—that traveled through time on various missions. It lasted two years.

Head piece also seen on Spyrius Robot from LEGO Space in 1994

Dr. Cyber's Robot This robot is designed and built by inventive Dr. Cyber.

Time Cruisers minifigures were the first to have eye whites

Nose print debuted this year, but it is rarely used as a feature

"T" for Tim print on torso

Tim Dr. Cyber's assistant, Tim, travels with him on all trips through time.

Dr. Cyber This genius invented the time-traveling Hypno Cruiser, powered by historic hats!

Unique face print

Pencil tied to bow tie

Pocket watch

LEGO® PIRATES

LEGO Pirates underwent a major redesign in 1996, as the Pirates and Islanders were joined by a new faction. The Imperial Armada was out to hunt down the pesky Pirates, but even their Flagship (6280) was no match for the Pirates' dreaded Skull's Eye Schooner (6286).

Plume fits into helmet hole

Pirate hat

Pirate Captain A clash with the soldiers has cost the captain his right leg—he wears a wooden one instead.

Admiral Head of the Armada flagship, the Admiral minifigure is always seen with his armor plate on—hunting pirates is a risky business.

Officer This elaborately dressed minifigure wears a triple plume piece, which fits into his hat.

Silver button print on jacket

Silver breastplate guards against attacks

Shirt collar print

Decorative gold medal

Wooden leg

DID YOU KNOW?
The style of the Armada crew is based on Conquistadors from the 1600s.

Tattooed Pirate The bandana piece is also seen on more than 80 minifigures, including the 2009 Hondo Ohnaka minifigure from the LEGO® Star Wars™ theme.

Striped uniform design

White Shirt Pirate No pirate would be complete without a bandana accessory. This minifigure's bandana is hiding a bald patch on his head!

Green vest

Anchor tattoo

Leather belt print

Red Soldier Clad in red, this soldier is the most common minifigure in the sets from the Imperial Armada theme.

Armada Flagship This set (6280) comes with a twin-mast ship and three Imperial Armada minifigures.

LEGO® CASTLE

Castle fans ventured into the Dark Forest this year, with three sets produced for this short-lived subtheme. In a reimagining of the Foresters subtheme from the late 1980s, green-clad bandits hid in the hollow trees of the woods, clashing with Royal Knights, Black Knights, and Dragon Masters. Led by Rob N. Hood, they stole from the rich, but who they gave the treasure to was never clear.

Blue Outlaw This bandit isn't a fan of green. His blue-and-brown outfit helps him hide among the blueberry bushes.

Studded shirt pattern on torso

HAND OVER YOUR GOLD BRICKS!

Stylized mustache and goatee

Bangs hair pattern

Scraggly hair visible under cowl

Drooping mustache

Pouch to carry supplies

Rob N. Hood Rob's plume accessory also came in black, yellow, blue, and white.

Red leather belt

Forest Archer This cheery archer has a new head with choppy bangs and can't stop smiling about it.

Forest Bandit The forest can be dangerous. This bandit wears a brown cowl around his neck to try to blend in.

LEGO WESTERN

It was all about lawmen and outlaws in 1996, with plenty of new pieces and fun for young cowpokes. It was the first LEGO play theme to focus on the Wild West, and it lasted into 1997. In 2013, the LEGO Group returned to the Wild West with LEGO® *The Lone Ranger*™, based on the Disney movie.

Pencil for quick calculations

NEW TO THESE PARTS, STRANGER?

Unique detailed torso

Banker Carrying a stash of $100 bills, a pocket watch, and gold-rimmed glasses, this banker minifigure is asking for trouble ...

HOWDY! ANYBODY KNOW WHERE I CAN GET A HAIRCUT?

Messy blond hair partially covers eyes

Zack Dandy cowboy Zack dons a fringed vest over a red shirt to stand out from the cowboy crowd.

Sheriff is smiling— for now

Sheriff's badge

Watch fob

Sheriff The brave Sheriff looks good, with a unique torso and new star-printed cowboy hat.

Emblem of two crossed sabers

Stars indicate rank

Cavalry Colonel The printed cowboy hat is new and the Western Cavalry torso is exclusive to this minifigure.

Imperial Soldiers from the LEGO Pirates theme and knights from the LEGO Castle theme also have this head

Belt has "US" initials

Pouch for storage

Cavalry Lieutenant The Lieutenant's neckerchief accessory is a new element introduced this year.

Cavalry Soldier The Calvary Soldier is debuting a new cap design for this year.

Gold tooth

Playing cards pattern on vest

Gold chain

Dewey Cheatum Cheatum is his name, and cheating is his game. Although judging from his angry expression, he must have just lost a card game!

Missing teeth

Removable neckerchief

Belt carries bullets

Flatfoot Thompson This nasty outlaw minifigure features a unique realistic nose and scowling eyes pattern.

Six-shooter tucked into belt for easy access

Reversed neckerchief piece

Black Bart Bart is always ready to blow things up at the drop of a 10-gallon hat.

Sheriff's Lock-up Accessories in this set (6755) include a wanted poster, printed dynamite, and four minifigures.

Sheriff

Jail cell

Zack's up to no good again

Sheriff station

Flatfoot Thompson

Dewey Cheatum

SHERIFF

Cat. No. 1, JE 96912C*. Overview of the recto (A) and verso (B). The textile reinforcement is a recent conservation intervention. The black discolouration at the recto is due to the deterioration of the leather.*

Cat. No. 1, JE 96912C*. C-E) Details of the outer two rows of the enhanced edge of the recto. The arrow in figure D points to the knot in the thread; the arrow in figure E points to the painted decoration that was covered by the innermost set of appliqué. Scale bars are 10 mm.*

Cat. No. 1, JE 96912B. Overview of the recto (A) and verso (B). The textile reinforcement is a recent conservation intervention. The black discolouration at the recto is due to the deterioration of the leather.

C

Cat. No. 1, JE 96912B. C) Detail of the enhanced edge of the recto. Scale bar is 10 mm.

proximately 4-5.8 mm). Since the edge is much more complete than in fragments A and B, described above, one can better understand its construction (figure C-G). The entire edge consists of three sets of applied strips of leather that are secured by means of running stitching as well as, probably, glue (figure H). The innermost one (width: 6.1 mm) is far from complete, but its attachment by means of sinew thread in running stitching lengthwise down the centre remains visible. The colour of the strip is not clear, although there is one bit that looks green. Small scraps are visible of a much narrower green strip that is added lengthwise down the centre to the first strip. In turn, an even narrower red strip was attached on top of this. Of this, again, only small scraps remain. Note that this set of strips is placed over a band with dots (arrow in figure E). Then, going outwards, a strip of the red foundation is exposed (width: 4.2 mm). Beyond this is another band that consists of a white strip (width: 6.5 mm) which might have been secured on either side with close, equally spaced running stitches. However, no thread is preserved and the rows of stitching are, in most of its length, not covered with the white strip (anymore?). Upon this wider strip is a narrower green strip (width: 3 mm), which is affixed with sinew thread in

LEGO® TOWN

It was back to the racetrack with awesome sets like Indy Transport (6335), complete with three new minifigures, a truck, and three racecars. The truck carried the cars to the track, where the mechanics readied them for the race. Several new airplanes were also released this year.

WINDOW FITTER
This minifigure was included in House with Roof-Windows (1854). The house featured a dining room and a bedroom on the top floor.

Velux sticker on torso

Window Fitter The minifigure in some countries wears the logo of Danish manufacturer Velux.

As well as this cap, the driver came with a race helmet

Black sunglasses

Zipped jumpsuit

Jet Pilot This pilot minifigure is ready for some thrills in a star-patterned jumpsuit and helmet.

Turbo Charger This racecar driver minifigure is wearing a new torso, printed with the Octan logo.

Red belt

Indy Transport Three racetrack minifigures are included in this set (6335), ready to battle it out on the racetrack.

Pointed mustache print

NOW BOARDING FOR LEGO TOWN AND DARK FOREST.

Ponytail hair piece

Railway logo

Railway Employee This minifigure's head is also used on the LEGO® Star Wars™ Biggs Darklighter minifigure released in 1999.

Torso with palm tree and horse detail is new for this year

Passenger Although this minifigure is wearing clothes from the LEGO Paradisa subtheme, she actually appears in the LEGO Train set Cargo Railway (4559).

DID YOU KNOW?
The Train Station set (2150) was largely based on 1991's Metro Station (4554).

Train Engineer This important-looking train engineer maintains the tracks for the LEGO DUPLO trains.

Curly mustache

LEGO® TRAIN

Passengers were ready to board the LEGO Train, thanks to a new Train Station set (2150) featuring eight minifigures. The station was complete with a waiting room, a snack bar, and a platform for boarding. This was the first train station set in five years and the last until 1999.

LEGO® DUPLO®

This engineer was ready to take little builders to new adventures! LEGO DUPLO Train returned with six sets, following a two-year absence. Both battery-operated trains and push-along trains were available.

A CUT ABOVE

THE FIRST MINIFIGURES had very simple hairstyles, but as time has passed, hair pieces have got more varied and downright daring! As with hats and other headgear, hair pieces attach to the knob on top of the head piece. Hair can help identify a character—for example, hair can reflect the style of a theme, such as the LEGO® EXO-FORCE™ anime-inspired hair pieces. Some hair pieces include facial hair, such as the Caveman's bushy beard, while others, such as Grandpa's comb-over, feature very little hair at all! From braids to quiffs and even mohawks—minifigures have had them all.

Braids • 1978 • Doctor • LEGOLAND Town

Short back and sides • 1979 • Boy • LEGOLAND Town

Flowing, swept-back long hair • 2007 • Crown Princess • LEGO Castle

Severe bob with straight bangs • 2008 • Claw-Dette • LEGO Agents

Mohawk • 2011 • Punk Rocker • LEGO Minifigures

Slick bob with gold hairband • 2011 • Egyptian Queen • LEGO Minifigures

Swept bangs with headphones • 2012 • DJ • LEGO Minifigures

Combed short hair with gold leaves • 2013 • Roman Emperor • LEGO Minifigures

Hair braided with strips of bark • 2013 • Forest Woman • LEGO Minifigures

Wavy retro bob • 2013 • Hollywood Starlet • LEGO Minifigures

Comb-over • 2013 • Grandpa • LEGO Minifigures

Undercut • 2018 • Nails • LEGO NINJAGO

Topknot • 2018 • Cole • LEGO NINJAGO

1950s quiff • 2018 • Rock Star • LEGO Creator Expert

Messy bun • 2019 • Programmer • LEGO Minifigures

Twin buns • 2021 • Stuntz Driver • LEGO City

Short bob cut with swept bangs •
1983 • Striped Top Person
• LEGOLAND Town

Ponytail • 1992
• Horse Rider • LEGO Town

Crew cut • 2001
• Dash Justice • LEGO Alpha Team

Combed widow's peak • 2002
• Vampire • LEGO Studios

Floppy hair in angular sections
• 2006 • Takeshi • LEGO EXO-FORCE

Striped spikes • 2008 • Dr. Inferno
• LEGO Agents

Bubble perm • 2010 • Circus Clown
• LEGO Minifigures

Shoulder-length, tousled
• 2010 • Caveman • LEGO Minifigures

Messy updo with bone hairband
• 2011 • Cave Woman
• LEGO Minifigures

Upswept hair with bun
• 2011 • Ice Skater
• LEGO Minifigures

Long hair with flower • 2011
• Hula Dancer • LEGO Minifigures

High ponytail with pink stripe
• 2012 • Skater Girl
• LEGO Minifigures

Long, layered bob • 2012
• Rocker Girl • LEGO Minifigures

**Extra-long, straight hair with
hairband** • 2012 • Hippie
• LEGO Minifigures

Messed-up bed hair • 2012
• Sleepyhead • LEGO Minifigures

Tangled snakes • 2013 • Medusa
• LEGO Minifigures

Sleek, layered hair • 2013
• Trendsetter • LEGO Minifigures

Long hair and bushy beard
• 2015 • Classic King
• LEGO Minifigures

Mullet • 2016
• Wrestling Champion
• LEGO Minifigures

Bald with handlebar mustache
• 2017 • Circus Strong Man
• LEGO Minifigures

Natural curls • 2022
• Picnicker • LEGO City

Side sweep • 2023
• Arctic Explorer • LEGO City

Tied-back braids • 2023
• Pilot • LEGO City

Flat top and goatee • 2023
• Bass Player • LEGO Icons

Rococo wig • 2023
• Rococo Aristocrat
• LEGO Minifigures

Quiver holds arrows

Drooping mustache print

Cape has a spider printed on the back

Fleur-de-lis pattern on torso

DON'T CALL ME CONE HEAD!

Helmet Knight A new torso design adorns this minifigure. His conical helmet also has a chin guard.

1997

IT WAS ALL ABOUT weird and wild villains this year. Witches, bats, and dragons appeared in Fright Knights, the new LEGO® Castle subtheme, while the heroic LEGO® Time Cruisers met their match in the fiendish Time Twisters. Meanwhile, in LEGO® Space, strange aliens from the UFO subtheme battled the robots of Roboforce. For those who preferred more peaceful play, LEGO® Town offered wilderness exploration in the Outback subtheme or a trip beneath the sea with the Divers.

Single tooth printed on mouth

Spider emblem

Willa the Witch This is the first (but not the last) witch minifigure. The sloped skirt piece is printed for the first time.

LEGO CASTLE

Things took a sinister turn with the introduction of Fright Knights, a new Castle subtheme featuring creepy knights led by Basil the Bat Lord. Black dragons, witches, crystal balls, and flying broomsticks figured in the 10 seriously supernatural sets. Fright Knights lasted for two years before disappearing into the shadows.

Bat wings are attached to helmet

Basil the Bat Lord Ghoulish leader of the Fright Knights, this minifigure appears in sets with and without his cape.

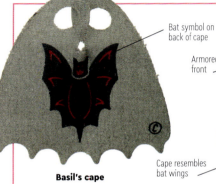

Bat symbol on back of cape

Armored front

Basil's cape

Cape resembles bat wings

Knight's plume on helmet

Halberd

Helmet with neck protector

I'M ACTUALLY REALLY SCARED OF BATS.

Bushy beard

Studded armor-printed torso

Shield with bat print

Air supply

Suit mechanics printed on torso

Green hook replaces left hand

Aquaraider with Hook With a green hook to aid him, this Aquaraider is sure to find some precious minerals on the seabed.

Red Plume Fright Knight This knight is clad in a new armored torso, also seen on Professor Millennium in 1997, from the LEGO Time Cruisers theme.

Armored Knight This minifigure is proudly wearing an armored torso introduced this year.

LEGO® AQUAZONE

The Aquaraiders appeared in 1997, with three ships and plans to mine valuable minerals from the sea floor. Although they were part of the Aquazone universe, no Aquanauts or Aquasharks appeared in their sets. This was to be their only year beneath the sea.

LEGO SPACE

Up to 1997, LEGO Space focused primarily on human astronauts, with a few robots thrown in. This year, aliens showed up in a big way in the UFO subtheme, the first characters in what was a long and colorful line-up of LEGO extraterrestrials.

Blue Alien Traveling in the Cyber Saucer (6999) makes this alien minifigure green around the gills.

Techdroid II When this robot minifigure malfunctions, it takes a space age to figure out which circuit has broken.

Gray mask

Chest armor also seen on Insectoids, in 1998

Rectangular visor serves as eyes

Circuit pattern extends to legs

Unique torso with intricate circuit detail

Wire pattern on helmet

Golden wires on legs

UFO

The first UFO minifigure was released as a key chain in 1996, serving as the advance guard for this year's full alien fleet. Thirteen sets included all-alien characters, with no human friends or foes.

Alpha Draconis This alien leader is terrified of his own reflection, so he wears his helmet at all times.

Red Alien This alien might look like it's smiling, but it definitely doesn't come in peace.

Transparent orange head piece

Large blue eye shield

Golden circuitry on torso

Techdroid I The concept of walking is alien to this android minifigure—it can usually be seen on its Cyber Blaster (6818).

Head piece also worn by Unitron Chief from the Unitron subtheme in 1994

ROBOFORCE

Fighting for justice in the galaxy, the astronauts of Roboforce pilot big robots equipped for battle or to rescue space explorers.

Chip Nebula As leader of Roboforce, Chip feels it's only right that he gets to wear super-cool silver shades.

Roboforce logo

Printed red bandana

Roboforce Astronaut Nothing makes this astronaut happier than controlling their Robo Stalker (2153).

LEGO TIME CRUISERS

The second year of Time Cruisers introduced the villainous Time Twisters. Professor Millennium and his twin brother, Tony, traveled to the past to loot ancient treasures, pursued by the Time Cruisers. A ghost and a skeleton also came along for the ride as the Time Twisters meddled with history.

Skeleton From the Time Cruisers board game, this is the first time a skull head was featured on a regular torso.

Top hat

Biker-style leather jacket

Black cap worn by more than 80 other minifigures

Tony Twister This mean-looking minifigure features removable yellow epaulettes worn over the torso.

I'M STEALING THE PYRAMIDS NEXT!

Epaulette

Silver striped armor

Professor Millennium The scheming Professor's torso is also seen on the Fright Knight minifigures in 1997.

DID YOU KNOW? This precise ghost shroud piece appears in more than a dozen sets.

Ghost A long, glow-in-the-dark shroud piece covers a standard LEGO minifigure to create the updated iconic ghost.

Blank head piece

Beneath the shroud

White minifigure legs are new for the ghost this year

Camera Operator This TV professional captures all the racing action in the Outback, but dreams of a life in front of the camera.

Cap to shield face from sun

LEGO TOWN

Town traveled from the arid desert to the depths of the ocean in 1997, launching two new subthemes: Divers and Outback. The Race subtheme entered its final year, but there was still lots of action with exciting sets such as Crisis News Crew (6553). This year also saw the launch of Town Jr., which had simpler sets for younger builders.

Camera-ready face

News channel logo

News Anchor Unfortunately, this News Anchor had a short-lived career, appearing in only one set: Crisis News Crew (6553).

CLASSIC
A total of 48 new Town sets came out this year, as Town minifigures explored the wilderness and traveled the sea, looking for adventure wherever they went.

LEGO® SCALA
LEGO SCALA began life as a range of brick-built jewelry in 1979 and 1980. In 1997, the name was revived for a collection of dolls with fabric clothes and brushable hair. This version of LEGO SCALA ran until 2001.

Voluminous blonde hair

Posable arms

Kate This SCALA figure appears only once, in Nursery (3241), where she looks after the baby.

Shoe pieces are separate

Happy but hungry

Baby This happy, red-hatted toddler is waiting for her feed.

White lace top

Blue floral skirt

Emma This doll has every self-care product at her disposal in Beauty Studio (3200).

"i" for Infomaniac

LEGO® ISLAND
This promotional minifigure came with the LEGO Island video game—the first to feature minifigures. The game was released only in the United States.

Infomaniac The Infomaniac's head is full to bursting with all sorts of information about LEGO Island—well, he did create it!

Plain green torso

DUCK PILOT
This jolly minifigure was part of a chocolate promotion in the Netherlands, and was also used for an Easter egg promotion in the UK in 1999.

Pilot The minifigure flies a giant duck in a 17-piece set called ... Flying Duck (1824)!

TOWN JR.
The sirens were blaring as Town Jr. launched with new Fire sets, including the Blaze Brigade (6554) and a Fire Engine (6486). The Town also got a new Bank (6566) to keep the townspeople's LEGO money safe, and the police were in hot pursuit of a robber in Roadblock Runners (6549).

Only four police minifigures have ever worn this police hat

THAT'S SOME BIG POLICEMAN!

Police badge

Police Officer The robber's definitely not going to get away with *this* police minifigure in pursuit in Roadblock Runners (6549).

Bank uniform torso is exclusive to this minifigure

Guard The townspeople trust this man with their hard-earned dollars in Bank (6566).

ID card

Gray bank uniform

Bank Driver Looking cool in shades, this minifigure drives an armored car full of cash in Bank (6566).

Diving mask element is new this year

Diving suit

DIVER? NO, I ALWAYS DRESS LIKE THIS.

Blue Diver Equipped with a scuba tank and flippers, this diver is all geared up to explore life under the sea.

Sunglasses

Sleeveless top

Boat Skipper This minifigure assists the divers in their underwater explorations and is determined to look cool doing it!

DIVERS

A brand-new LEGO Town subtheme, Divers made a splash this year with 12 sets. Unlike Aquazone, Divers was a realistic line, focusing on real-world undersea exploration.

Deep Reef Refuge This underwater lab (6441) comes with sea animals and five diver minifigures who long to explore the mysteries of the deep blue sea.

Headset for communicating with divers

Treasure Pilot Part of a treasure-hunting party, this pilot assists the divers from a submersible.

DID YOU KNOW?
This is the only underwater subtheme to include real-world diver down flags (flags placed on the water to indicate that there is a diver below).

LEGO® DUPLO® DINO

Dino combined cave people with dinosaurs for junior-aged fun. The dinosaurs and figures roamed the Earth for three years before the subtheme went extinct.

Female hair piece

Eyelashes add a feminine touch

Cave Woman A tooth necklace adorns the torso of the Cave Woman. It's not her tooth, but that of a fierce animal!

Same head piece as Crewperson

Red flippers

Treasure Hunter This diver discovers treasure in Sea Hunter (6555), along with a new sawfish figure!

Cap covers blond hair pattern

Hair peeks out from under cap

Printed headset for communicating with crew

LEGO Divers submarine logo

Air gauge on diving suit

Chopper Pilot Four diver minifigures have the same head piece with headset and shaggy brown hair.

Crewperson This minifigure works on a research ship, but he hopes to become a diver one day.

Red diving helmet

DIVER AND SHARK

This happy explorer might not be happy for much longer—he encounters a nasty shark in a promotional set (2871). This minifigure was also used for a restaurant promotion in 1998.

Red Diver Nothing will distract this Diver on his hunt for sea treasure—not even a scary shark!

Black scuba gloves

Lace collar

LEGO® PARADISA

Paradisa ended its five-year run this year with the release of four sets, bringing the island vacation to a close. The figures and ponies have not reappeared (so far), and many of the building pieces are rare.

Paradisa Woman This resort worker runs a spinning wheel game at the Fun Fair (6547).

I'M HARRY. COME FLY WITH ME!

Wool lining to keep warm

Bomber jacket torso is exclusive to Harry Cane

Harry Cane The brave pilot dons an aviator cap and goggles, both new elements this year.

1998

IT WAS A BUSY and rewarding year for LEGO® minifigure fans. LEGO® Space fans ran into a swarm of Insectoids, while ninja snuck into the LEGO® Castle theme. The LEGO® Adventurers headed for Egypt to battle a nasty mummy; the Hydronauts challenged the Stingrays beneath the waves; and LEGO® Technic launched CyberSlam, which featured more LEGO Technic figures. This was the final year in which a licensed play theme was not part of the assortment. Times were about to change ...

Pinned-up slouch hat

Accessories can be slotted into the sides of the backpack

Neckerchief knotted around neck

Johnny Thunder The fearless adventurer minifigure makes his debut in a desert safari jacket and brand-new slouch hat.

LEGO ADVENTURERS

New this year, Adventurers launched with 21 sets, centered on the search for the Re-Gou Ruby by a group of daring heroes. The ruby was guarded by undead Pharaoh Hotep and pursued by wicked treasure hunters like Baron Von Barron. Johnny Thunder, Pippin Reed, and Professor Lightning were the theme's heroes, appearing repeatedly in its five-year run under various names in various countries.

Pharaoh's Forbidden Ruins The 10 minifigures included in this set (5988) have much to keep them busy on this adventure, including a temple, hot air balloon, and truck.

Pith helmet

Helmet identical to Charles Lightning's

Backpack

Backpack element is new this year

Bow tie

Compass

Pen for jotting down notes

Pippin Reed Traveling the world with her friend Johnny Thunder, reporter Pippin takes her trusty compass everywhere.

Charles Lightning The archaeologist minifigure is wearing a pith helmet, a new element this year.

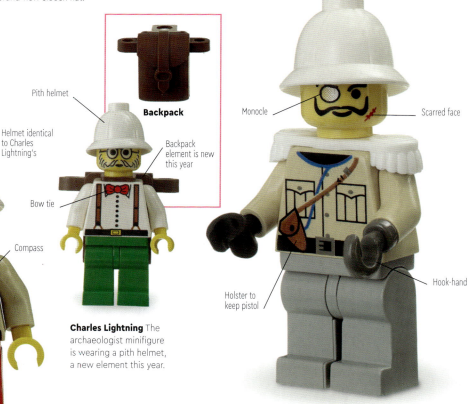

Monocle

Scarred face

Holster to keep pistol

Hook-hand

Baron Von Barron Johnny Thunder's main enemy, the Baron, sports a unique torso and head piece.

LEGO® AQUAZONE

Deep beneath the sea, the Hydronaut miners were locked in battle with the aquatic mutant Stingrays, in what was to be the final Aquazone subtheme. This was the last year of underwater adventures until Alpha Team's Mission Deep Sea in 2002.

Intense red eyes

Helmet is unique to the Stingrays

Power supply

Raven Ray Despite his high-tech suit and wicked mind, the cunning Raven Ray is often captured by the Hydronauts.

Visor also seen on Aquaraiders from LEGO® Aquazone in 1997

Captain Hank Hydro Leader of the Hydronaut missions, Hank is well respected by the other Hydronauts.

Chrome rebreather

Diving instrument

Red diving gloves

Head piece

Gills for breathing underwater

Wide, fish-like mouth

Protective underwater helmet

Mutant, fish-like armor

Manta Ray The chief of the villainous Stingrays, this minifigure feels most comfortable when he's in charge of the Stingray Stormer (6198).

Bulbous alien design

Helmet

Tough armor protects torso

Armor

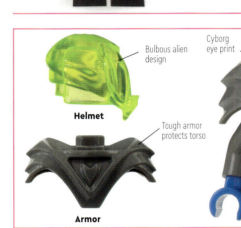

Cyborg eye print

PHEW! THIS ARMOR IS HEAVY!

Cybernetic power circuits

Gypsy Moth The Queen of the Zotaxians, Gypsy Moth commands mining operations on Holox—their home in exile.

LEGO SPACE

Fleeing their home planet, the Zotaxians crash-landed on a planet populated by large insects in this new Insectoid subtheme. They disguised their armor and vehicles to look insectlike to try to fool the hostile wildlife (not altogether successfully). The Insectoid minifigures were designed to look like cyborgs, with lots of circuitry printing on their legs and torsos.

DID YOU KNOW?
This was the last Space subtheme to have only one faction.

Transparent-clear helmet

Data storage unit in head

Emblem shows Insectoid affiliation

Gigabot This robot minifigure is made of a bronze-printed head, torso, and legs—all exclusive to the helpful Gigabot.

Transparent helmet

Power connector lines on torso

Danny Longlegs A communications expert and leader of the Arachnoid Star Base, this minifigure appears in Cosmic Creeper (6837) only.

Armor protects from bug attacks

Dark Zotaxian This Zotaxian hunts for crystals in Arachnoid Star Base (6977).

Transparent-neon green helmet

Power gauge

Circuit pattern on leg

Zotaxian This alien minifigure is seen only once, in Celestial Stinger (6969).

Instrument panel

Green Zotaxian Not every Zotaxian wears fancy armor. This one favors a Classic Space oxygen tank.

LEGO TECHNIC

LEGO Technic released more figures in 1998, with the Cyber Strikers (8257)—twin combat vehicles, each with a figure, and CyberMaster (8483), which included a model with a programmable brick that worked with a software program.

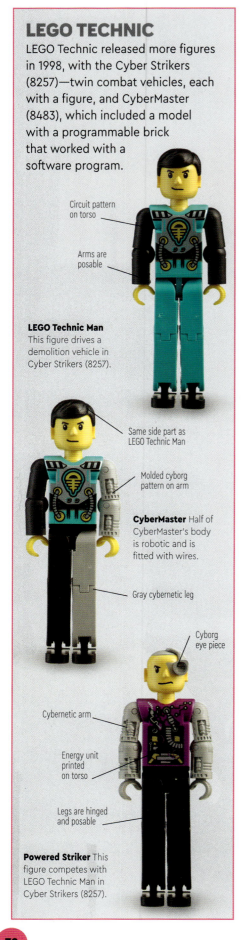

Circuit pattern on torso

Arms are posable

LEGO Technic Man This figure drives a demolition vehicle in Cyber Strikers (8257).

Same side part as LEGO Technic Man

Molded cyborg pattern on arm

CyberMaster Half of CyberMaster's body is robotic and is fitted with wires.

Gray cybernetic leg

Cyborg eye piece

Cybernetic arm

Energy unit printed on torso

Legs are hinged and posable

Powered Striker This figure competes with LEGO Technic Man in Cyber Strikers (8257).

LEGO CASTLE

LEGO Castle looked beyond Europe for inspiration in 1998 and launched a Ninja subtheme set in feudal Japan. Shogun Gi-Dan and his friend Ito, the gray ninja, battled the bandit Kendo, his henchmen, and the black ninja Bonsai for an ancient treasure. The ninja were in action until 2000.

Flying Ninja Fortress With 687 pieces and nine minifigures, this set (6093) has three ninja treasures as well as a number of traps to be discovered.

Ragged head wrap

Tattered armor

Kendo The chief crook has an exclusive face and torso print.

Thin mustache

Knife tucked under belt

Patchwork on vest

Crook With his tattered vest, it looks like this robber has encountered the ninja warriors recently!

DID YOU KNOW?
The Ninja subtheme introduced the samurai helmet and ninja hood elements.

Head wrap piece includes sheath for sword on back

Face print includes headband and sideburns

Katana sword is new this year

Ito The only ninja to wear a gray ninja wrap, Ito makes his debut in the Flying Ninja Fortress (6093).

I WEAR THIS TO COCKTAIL PARTIES.

Head wrap hides identity

Protective scale mail armor underneath wrap

Ninja throwing star

Bonsai This stealthy ninja wears an all-black ninja wrap so he can hide in the shadows undetected.

LEGO® TOWN

Two new subthemes were introduced in 1998—Res-Q and Extreme Team. Res-Q in particular made an impact on future themes, and emergency vehicles are still a popular part of the LEGO® City assortment. Classic Town was also well represented, including a new Truck Stop (6329). An exciting new Cargo Center (6330) arrived, including a forklift and a helicopter!

> UM, HELLO? I CAN'T SEE!

Movable visor

Extreme Racer An action junkie, this minifigure flies a plane in the Daredevil Flight Squad (6582).

Double pockets

EXTREME TEAM

Town went extreme with this subtheme, which focused on wild sports such as hang gliding, drag racing, and whitewater rafting. The Extreme Team screeched to a halt after 1999.

Printed air gauge

Gray crew uniform

Ground Crew Assistant for Team Extreme, this guy prefers to keep his minifigure feet firmly on the ground.

Transparent visor attaches to helmet

Res-Q logo

> ROGER AND OUT? BUT I'M BOB!

RES-Q

Res-Q launched as a new Town subtheme in 1998 with eight sets, the largest being the Emergency Response Center (6479). The line ended in 1999, but the organization continued to come to the rescue in the Studios, Soccer, and Jack Stone themes.

Covered pocket flaps

Lifeguard Featuring only in the Res-Q Lifeguard (2962), this helmeted hero keeps minifigures safe at the beach.

Res-Q Responder This all-around rescuer drives a truck, rides a motorcycle, and flies a helicopter across three sets.

The Postal Worker's favorite color is red

Striped shirt under jacket

Reflective silver shades

Cargo logo

Thick zipper pattern

Pants match tie

Mechanic Seen only once, in Truck Stop (6329), this minifigure is an expert in vehicle repair.

Biker Bob The head and torso pieces of this speed-loving minifigure are unique—and cool dude Bob knows it!

Cargo Staff An expert in handling cargo, this staffer is exclusive to the Cargo Center set (6330).

Postal Worker A newly designed LEGO Post logo adorns this minifigure's torso.

LEGO® *LOCO*

One of the highlights of 1998 was the release of LEGO *Loco*, a town-building video game with an emphasis on trains. These two minifigures were from a promotional Handcar set (2585) given out with the CD-ROM.

Cool Kid Exclusive to the Handcar set (2585), this minifigure has a unique white torso with a LEGO brick design on it.

Rare nose printing

2×4 LEGO brick element printed on torso

Red mask hides identity

Cape fits over neck

LEGO Train logo

Super Station Master Looking more super hero than station master, this minifigure's masked head piece is unique.

LEGO SEASONAL

This festive Santa Claus appeared in the 1998 and 1999 Advent Calendars, then reappeared in 2010 as part of the Vintage Minifigure Collection.

Molded beard piece

The 1995 Santa variant has red hips

Santa Claus Despite wearing a bandana commonly seen on Pirate minifigures, Santa still prefers sleighing to sailing.

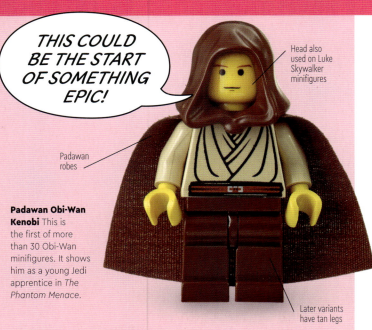

THIS COULD BE THE START OF SOMETHING EPIC!

Head also used on Luke Skywalker minifigures

Padawan robes

Padawan Obi-Wan Kenobi This is the first of more than 30 Obi-Wan minifigures. It shows him as a young Jedi apprentice in *The Phantom Menace*.

Later variants have tan legs

1999

THE WORLD OF LEGO® minifigures changed forever in 1999, with the release of the first LEGO® *Star Wars*™ sets. It was the first licensed minifigure theme ever produced by the LEGO Group and would prove to be a massive success, spawning LEGO video games, animated shorts, books, and more in years to come. Other big news this year included the opening of LEGOLAND® California in Carlsbad, US, and the release of the LEGO® Rock Raiders, LEGO® Adventurers: Jungle, and LEGO® DUPLO® Winnie the Pooh™ themes.

Maul's Zabrak horns are missing from this version

Unique torso

Darth Maul The Sith apprentice featured a regular head piece with unique facial tattoos.

LEGO STAR WARS

It was a great experiment—could sets based on the classic *Star Wars* films and the newest movie, *The Phantom Menace*, be a hit? Could a licensed play theme bring in legions of new fans for LEGO building? The answer to both was a resounding yes, producing one of the greatest success stories in the history of the LEGO Group. And it's still going strong over 25 years later!

Pulled-back hair piece and head piece are exclusive to Qui-Gon

Qui-Gon Jinn Appearing in four sets in 1999 alone, the LEGO version of the doomed Jedi Master has lasted much longer than the movie version!

Long hair piece with top braid also seen on Padmé's daughter Princess Leia

Torso is unique to this variant

Standard black pants

Padmé Naberrie The Queen of Naboo s in disguise. Padmé wasn't seen in her royal robes until 2012.

Gray helmet and matching goggles

Head piece also used on a female soccer player in the Soccer theme in 2001

Boy Anakin Skywalker This young minifigure saves the galaxy in one set—Naboo Fighter (7141).

This variant appears in two sets in 1999—Anakin's Podracer (7131) and Mos Espa (7171)

Boy Anakin Skywalker variant The only difference between the two 1999 Anakin variants is the helmet color.

THE PHANTOM MENACE

As the biggest movie event of 1999, Episode I—*The Phantom Menace* dominated the first year of LEGO *Star Wars* sets. Tatooine podracers, Gungan submarines, and Royal Naboo N-1 starfighters all featured in the early line-up.

Head piece also used on a Gungan soldier in 2001

Jar Jar's clothing is simple

Jar Jar Binks This Gungan was the first minifigure not to have a round head piece. His untidy torso is also unique.

Dark gray legs can be seen on more than 45 minifigures

Sith Infiltrator Darth Maul's Sith Infiltrator stealth ship (7151), known as the *Scimitar*, was released in 1999 and updated in 2007, 2011, 2015, and 2024.

DROIDS AND PODRACERS

The famous Boonta Eve Classic podracing scene came to life with figures of Anakin's rival drivers and a pit droid. The first battle droid also debuted this year.

Gasgano wears the same helmet and goggles as Anakin Skywalker

Gasgano Only appearing in one set, this rare podracing figure has unique head and torso pieces.

Sebulba This unusual figure is made of a single LEGO piece and is only found in Mos Espa Podrace (7171).

Later versions had more detail and colors

Pit Droid Three pit droid variants were released in 1999, ready to fix any malfunctions. This version belongs to Anakin Skywalker.

Yellow photoreceptor

Head piece specially created for the battle droids

Later versions do not have a backpack

Battle Droid The first version of the B1 battle droid is easy to defeat—it can't even hold a blaster properly!

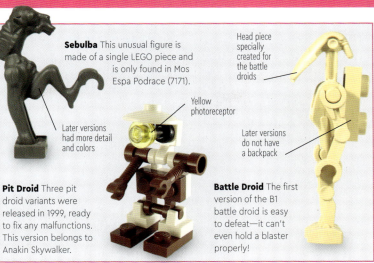

Hair piece also seen on Draco Malfoy from the LEGO® Harry Potter™ theme

Unique torso with simple white tunic

Young Luke Skywalker The future Jedi's early life as a Tatooine farm boy is the inspiration for his first LEGO minifigure.

Tan leg wraps

ORIGINAL TRILOGY

The first five classic LEGO *Star Wars* sets also came out this year, with minifigures of favorite characters such as Luke Skywalker, Darth Vader, and Obi-Wan Kenobi and models of the X-wing and TIE fighter.

Head piece also seen on more than 15 pirate minifigures

Rebel Technician The tan uniform is worn only by this hardworking minifigure and a Rebel Engineer in 2000.

Obi-Wan "Ben" Kenobi This older version of the exiled Jedi Knight has a unique head and torso and is exclusive to Landspeeder (7110).

2011 version has a buckle detail on the belt

Brown visor

Torso is unique to this variant

Hoth Rebel Trooper Warmly dressed for the ice planet Hoth, this rebel minifigure appears in Snowspeeder (7130).

Rebel pilot helmet

Dak Ralter Also in set 7130, this rebel pilot operates the snowspeeder's guns for Luke Skywalker, who flies the craft.

Rebel g-suit worn by 12 minifigures

Helmet is exclusive to four Luke pilot variants

Luke Skywalker Pilot Tatooine is a distant memory for this minifigure as he makes his debut as a rebel pilot in two sets this year.

Unique torso— the back is plain khaki

Camouflage Luke This minifigure is designed to blend in on the forest moon of Endor, but his chin dimple and cybernetic hand reveal his identity.

ASTROMECH DROIDS

The most famous astromech droid of all is R2-D2. The first LEGO version of this iconic character was released this year, and at least one version of him has been produced every year since.

R2-D2 Each of R2-D2's three parts were created specially for his figure, then refined on later versions.

R2-D2's legs are joined to his body with LEGO Technic pins

Head piece pattern is slightly different to R2's

R5-D4 This red astromech droid uses the same torso design as R2 but has red printing instead of blue.

Helmet is exclusive to Biggs

Biggs wears the same suit as his friend Luke Skywalker

Biggs Darklighter This minifigure did not survive the rebels' attack on the first Death Star. He appears in the X-Wing Fighter set (7140).

G-suit is worn by X- and Y-wing pilots

Darth Vader The Sith warrior's minifigure debut is just as menacing as his on-screen counterpart.

Standard LEGO cloak completes the Sith lord's look

Vader has a scarred gray head piece underneath his helmet

Dutch Vander This brave rebel minifigure flies a Y-wing fighter in set 7150, but he perishes in the Battle of Yavin.

AAARRRGH— WHERE'S THE BRAKE?!!!

Imperial Scout Trooper Wearing lighter armor than a normal stormtrooper, this minifigure often undertakes dangerous solo missions.

Head piece

Unique torso

Scout helmet fits over head so that only the black visor shows

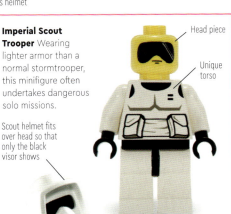

Scientist Featuring an updated torso, this variant of the Scientist is exclusive to a single 1999 set—Test Shuttle (3067).

Popular head piece, seen on more than 20 minifigures

Pristine white lab coat

Space Port logo

Same head, hat, and torso as other variant

LEGO® TOWN

LEGO Town continued to push the boundaries in 1999, flying high with Space Port and diving deep with the Coast Guard. The former was a subtheme in its own right, building on the success of earlier Launch Command sets. The latter was part of the new City Center line, which was geared toward 5- to 10-year-olds.

Scientist Variant Wearing black pants instead of white, this Scientist variant appears in three sets in 1999.

Shuttle Security Guard This serious minifigure patrols the Space Port in his helicopter, checking that everything is in order.

Head piece seen on more than 10 other minifigures

Exclusive torso with ID badge, Space Port logo, and Security insignia

The first variant has a construction helmet, the second a white cap, and the third has a red cap

Ground Controller Variant Three very similar variants of the Ground Controller minifigure are released in 1999. The only differences are their hats!

Torso is exclusive to three Ground Controller variants

Ground Controller Exclusive to Mission Control (6456), this minifigure is the vital link between Earth and the astronauts out in space.

Standard red pants

Black visor is attached to breathing gear

Air pressure gauge

Firefighter with Breathing Apparatus This Firefighter has an identical head, torso, and legs to the Fire Mechanic released in 1994, but has a specialist helmet, breathing apparatus, and air tanks.

SPACE PORT

Space Port was the successor to 1995's Launch Command, and it featured more sets and a greater variety of vehicles and minifigures than the previous theme. Minifigures included astronauts, scientists, and ground crew.

Head piece also used on the Aquanaut Jock Clouseau in 1995

Jetpack previously seen in the 1991 Blacktron II Space theme

Gold visor is down to protect the Moon Explorer's eyes from the sun's rays

Shuttle Pilot The only female astronaut in the line-up has a unique new torso featuring the Space Port logo and breathing pipes.

Female head piece with radio set is new this year

Helmet first seen on the Aquazone Hydronauts in 1998

Torso is new this year

Same head and torso as the Satellite Repair Guy

Satellite Repair Guy This repair man has a tough job to do—he has to fix a satellite in space! He's got his space suit and jetpack on, but where has his wrench floated off to?

Moon Explorer This intrepid minifigure travels all the way to the moon and explores it in his Lunar Rover (6463).

White helmet is also used on the Moon Explorer

LEGO® TOWN JR. AND CITY CENTER

LEGO Town Jr. was phased out in 1999 and was replaced by City Center. The sets continued to feature more simplified building for younger fans and included Coast Guard, Fire, and Police models.

IT'S A GOOD THING MY HAT IS WATERPROOF!

Another variant has a ponytail instead of a cap

Detachable life jacket

Coast Guard One of two female minifigures in Coast Guard HQ (6435), this variant does her job at sea, while the other variant rides to the rescue on land using an all-terrain trike.

Headset ensures that the Coast Guard can radio for backup if he needs it

Rapid Responder If the Coast Guard has to travel a short distance fast, this Rapid Responder minifigure uses a small motor-powered inflatable boat to take them.

Beach Patrol Appearing in his own set, Beach Buggy (6437), this Coast Guard patrols the beach checking for sharks or swimmers in distress.

Coast Guard HQ This set (6435) includes six minifigures, a speedboat, small boat, helicopter, beach buggy, and trike.

DID YOU KNOW?
LEGO Town's first and only Milk Delivery Truck (1029) was released in 1999—available exclusively in Norway!

IT'S A GOOD THING MY MUSTACHE IS WATERPROOF!

New torso is unique to this minifigure

Coast Guard logo

ID badge

Coast Guard Chief The Chief is in charge of all the Coast Guard minifigures. During a mission, he has to think quickly and tell everyone else what to do.

Head piece with blue sunglasses is new this year

Standard Coast Guard torso with white arms

PROMOTIONAL

Special licensed minifigures also appeared this year, including a Shell racecar driver, a McDonald's worker, and a Boston Red Sox baseball player. The latter was available only through a promotion at Fenway Park (the Red Sox's home stadium).

Red helmet with black visor

Racecar Driver This minifigure appears in three sets this year—Dragster (1250), Shell Service Station (1256), and Race Car (1253).

The torso is the only new element

Standard baseball cap

Standard red LEGO cap

Unique stickered torso with the McDonald's logo

All-white uniform with Red Sox logo

Matching red pants complete the uniform

Red Sox Baseball Player This promotional minifigure has a unique torso in white with the official Red Sox logo on the front.

McDonald's Worker This minifigure came with LEGO McDonald's Restaurant (3438), which was only available in the US via the LEGO online store.

Mechanic One of five minifigures in Roadside Repair (6434), the Mechanic can fix any vehicle in record time.

Torso used on four Mechanic minifigure variants

> NO SLIMY SPACE SLUG IS GOING TO STOP ME!

LEGO ROCK RAIDERS

In 1999, a crack team of space miner minifigures found themselves trapped on an alien world. The good news was that there were energy crystals to mine, but the bad news was that there were some pretty nasty monsters there, too. This first visit to the LEGO underground had an impressive multimedia life with a video game and in-box comics, as well as traditional sets.

Axel Appearing in four sets in 1999, Axel has a new head piece that is exclusive to his two variants and a 2001 Boat Driver in the Studios theme.

Transparent neon green visor

In 2000, Axel wears a black visor instead

New torso with overalls and goggles printing

Underwater helmet first seen on the Explorien Chief in 1996

Torso is new and unique to Jet

Jet The sole female member of the Rock Raiders team has new head and torso prints, used only by her 1999 and 2000 variants.

Printed bandana keeps sweat out of Bandit's eyes when he's mining

DID YOU KNOW?
The construction helmet has been worn by more than 220 minifigures since 1978.

Torso with red sweater and overalls is unique to this minifigure

Standard-issue blue pants

Bandit This tough minifigure has a unique head with angry brown eyebrows, a bushy beard and mustache, and a cool blue bandana. Don't mess with him!

Head piece is new this year

Torso is exclusive to three variants of Docs

Docs This miner minifigure has an unusual look—he wears his glasses on his forehead and a black neckerchief knotted around his neck.

Rock Raiders This set (4930) features Axel, Sparks, Docs, Bandit, and Jet, plus a rock for them to raid for crystals.

Goggles were first introduced in 1998

Head piece is new this year

Sparks is the miners' mechanic, so he always keeps a wrench handy

LEGO® SCALA™

This year's 15 LEGO SCALA sets included eight sets with stylishly dressed dolls, six with additional outfits, and one with a horse and stable accessories.

Polka-dot halter top with jeans and extra accessories

Marie Trendy Marie appears in four sets between 1998 and 2001. This casually dressed version is from Marie in her Studio (3142).

Sparks Unlike his mining colleagues, Sparks' torso is not exclusive to him. In fact, his torso can also be seen on a 2001 minifigure from the Town theme.

Articulated right arm for throwing rocks

Head and body are all one piece

Building knobs on left shoulder and back

Rock Monster Two Rock Raiders sets came with this supersized alien foe, who just wanted to protect his underground home!

New, unique head piece

LEGO ADVENTURERS

Johnny Thunder and the Adventurers team were back for their second year. This time, they were heading to the South American jungle in search of the mysterious sundisc, and many new minifigures and new pieces took part in this quest. The Adventurers were determined to obtain the artifact before their rivals Señor Palomar and Rudo Villano. Of course, Johnny won in the end!

Gabarros A new character this year, the South American sailor uses his local knowledge to help both Señor Palomar and Johnny Thunder find the sundisc.

Villano wears a black version of Johnny Thunder's hat

Backpack

Villano has two pistols tucked into his belt

Rudo Villano Another new arrival for this year, Rudo (also known as Max in the UK) has a new, exclusive scruffy torso and scarred head. He also has a variant without a backpack.

Face print also used in LEGO® Studios and Town themes

Pith helmet was first produced in 1998

Compass detail print on torso is exclusive to Pippin Reed

New head piece also used on a 2003 LEGO® Sports NBA player

Classic white LEGO stetson

Backpack clips around neck

CURSES! I FORGOT MY SUNSCREEN!

Torso with white jacket and brown vest is unique to Señor Palomar

Señor Palomar New for this year, Señor Palomar appears in Spider's Secret (5936). In this set, he has a backpack, but in two others released this year, he does not.

Jungle Surprise This set (1271) features a small Jungle temple inside which lies a sundisc waiting to be found by a minifigure.

Backpack is worn by several minifigures in this theme

Pippin Reed Eager journalist and partner to Johnny Thunder, Pippin (sometimes known as Gail Storm) is ready for anything with her jungle gear.

LEGO® DUPLO®

LEGO DUPLO continued to entertain in 1999. Construction workers drove big, yellow trucks; cave people continued to co-exist with dinosaurs; and Little Forest Friends rode on snails and ladybugs!

Smiling face with stubble detail

Construction Worker This figure was hard at work in 1999, appearing 10 times in five sets. He seems pretty happy, though.

Fur bib printed on torso

Cave Baby This cute prehistoric baby appears with three other figures in Dinosaurs Fun Forest (2821).

All members of the Strawberry family wear red

Melba Strawberry Little Forest Friends figures like this were not posable, but had gripping hands and feet that could be built onto LEGO DUPLO knobs.

The Meadowsweet family all wear white

Sleepyhead Meadowsweet Part of another Little Forest Friends family, Sleepyhead wears a flower for a hat and a pinecone onesie!

2000s

LEGO® *Star Wars*™ was just the start of licensed play themes. Other world-famous characters soon followed, from student wizard Harry Potter to the web-slinging Spider-Man. New design revolutions led to the advent of human skin tones for licensed LEGO themes. The minifigures of the new millennium gained extra faces on the backs of their heads, threw basketballs, shrank down on shorter legs, landed on Mars, and even dabbled in some movie-making!

SAVE! AND A BEAUTY, IF I SAY SO MYSELF!

Different national flag stickers are supplied. This minifigure wears the German flag

Black gloves—the ball won't slip through his fingers

Black Team Goalkeeper This black-capped minifigure is the goalkeeper from the Black Team Bus (3404). Like all team bus goalies, he has a plain green torso.

2000

PICKING THE BIGGEST LEGO® event of 2000 is no easy task. Was it the release of some of the most iconic LEGO® *Star Wars*™ sets ever? How about exciting new subthemes for LEGO® Adventurers and LEGO® Castle? Or the snowy action of the LEGO® Arctic subtheme? Could it be the amazing success of LEGO® Soccer (known as LEGO® Football in other countries), which went on to launch dozens more LEGO® Sports sets? One thing is beyond any doubt, 2000 was a year when excitement and sheer fun ruled—and what's more, it held the promise of an incredible decade to come!

LEGO SOCCER

The LEGO Group scored in the world of sports in 2000 with the launch of the first LEGO Soccer sets. (The LEGO Sports brand would not be used until 2003.) These were a surprise hit, spawning future sets for basketball, hockey, and extreme sports. Soccer player minifigures were designed to be personalized, so they could play for different teams and countries.

Hair piece introduced in 1979 is still in style for many LEGO soccer players!

German flag sticker on front torso

TEAM BUS SETS
To play, teams must first get to the stadium! Five team bus sets were brought out in 2000, including an Americas Team transport and buses for Red, Blue, and Black teams. Each included six minifigures and a soccer ball.

Black Team Player With a change of sticker, this minifigure could play for any one of five teams in the Black Team Bus (3404).

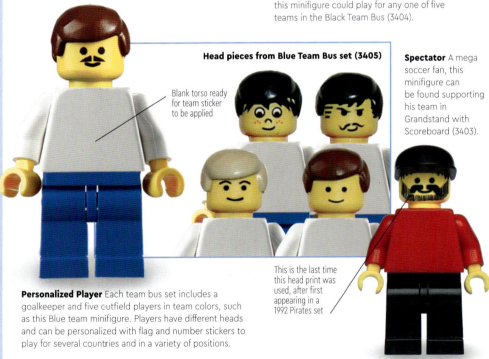

Blank torso ready for team sticker to be applied

Head pieces from Blue Team Bus set (3405)

Spectator A mega soccer fan, this minifigure can be found supporting his team in Grandstand with Scoreboard (3403).

This is the last time this head print was used, after first appearing in a 1992 Pirates set

Personalized Player Each team bus set includes a goalkeeper and five outfield players in team colors, such as this Blue team minifigure. Players have different heads and can be personalized with flag and number stickers to play for several countries and in a variety of positions.

Blue Team Bus This set (3405) contains the bus elements, six minifigures, and sticker sheets with a choice of national flags for their front torsos and numbers for their backs.

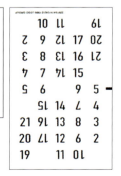

Flag stickers (above)
Number stickers (right)

SOCCER SETS

The most popular Soccer set was the Championship Challenge (3409), which featured 10 outfield players, two goalkeepers, and a field of play. Mounted on flexible stands, minifigures could flick the ball. The set was such a hit that it inspired a sequel, Championship Challenge II (3420), in 2002.

Green and White Team Player In the Field Expander set (3410), players wear the same shirt, but they have different numbers on their backs.

He shoots, he scores— and he looks pretty pleased with himself!

Scraggly hair peeking out from under cap

Stubbled face

Studs protect his body and intimidate the opposition

Angry Goalie This assertive-looking goalie appears only in the Championship Challenge set (3409).

Same head piece as Green and White Team Goalie

Studded top saves him from bruises when he's saving goals

Blue Goalie The Goal Keeper set (3413) comes with a blue variant of the angry goalie. A stick and turntable arrangement allows him to move around the goal to make some agile saves.

SHOOT 'N' SCORE

This small set featured two minifigures—a soccer player and a goalie. It was ideal for young builders who wanted to practice shots on goal before moving on to actual competition.

Soccer Legend French soccer superstar Zinedine Zidane got his own minifigure in the Shoot 'n' Score with Zidane set (3401). Magnifique!

New head with intense, smoldering expression

Sideburns are printed on head and hair piece is separate

Adidas sponsor logo printed on legs

LEGO ADVENTURERS

The Adventurers faced prehistoric peril this year in LEGO Dino Island, the third subtheme in the series. Fourteen sets were released, but most contained fewer than 100 pieces, making this the second-smallest subtheme in Adventurers history—but not in popularity!

DID YOU KNOW? LEGOLAND® California features a land based on the LEGO Adventurers theme.

Aviator helmet and goggles

Shady, wide-brimmed hat

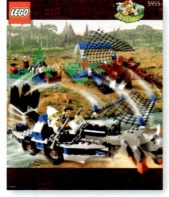

Another variant has brown hips instead of black

Pippin Reed Also known as Gail Storm, this fearless minifigure seeks out flying reptiles in her twin-propeller airplane, the Island Hopper (5935).

Mr. Cunningham This tough henchmen is a master of disguise. He's currently wearing a crop top, which is a new torso design.

All-Terrain Trapper The three minifigures in this set (5955) include the villains' leader, Baron Von Barron.

Hair piece worn by around 100 minifigures in black

Pursed lips—she's concentrating!

Belt has lots of pouches to hide things in

Alexia Sinister The sister of Baron Von Barron, Alexia is always scheming to steal treasure. The Baron himself used the name "Sam Sinister" in some sets this year.

Mike This minifigure likes to partner with other Dino Island heroes. He's a mean shot with his trusty slingshot!

Brown cavalry cap

Exclusive torso design

Slingshot tucked away in belt

Horns clip to helmet via a dragon's mouth crest

Unique head has angry, scowling face

Red gloves make him stand out from his troops

Cheek guards protect his face (and hide his unkempt hair)

Cedric the Bull This villain appears in two sets with his bull horns on and one where they're at the cleaners.

Brown leather scale mail torso pattern

Gilbert the Bad Gilbert has an eye (just the one) for designing foul war machines, like the giant catapult in the Catapult Crusher set (6032).

Broad-brimmed archer's helmet with chin guard

Detachable breastplate over scale mail torso

John of Mayne The king's most trusted advisor wears a chest plate designed for the LEGO® Pirates theme.

NINJA

Only three LEGO® Ninja sets were released this year, none of them building sets. Instead, they were known as Mini Heroes Collections (3344, 3345, and 3346) and contained just minifigures, display bases, and collector cards.

Ninja crest appears on three minifigures' helmets

DID YOU KNOW? The headwraps designed for the Ninja subtheme feature in 12 LEGO® NINJAGO® sets.

Red plume fits into hole on visor

Richard the Strong Richard is the best and bravest among King Leo's knights. He features in the Royal Joust set (6095).

Knights' Kingdom plate armor printed on legs

LEGO® KNIGHTS' KINGDOM

King Leo lived in the first medieval-style LEGO castle made since 1995, which was also the first to come with a complete royal family. Cedric, the villain, had no castle, so he and his Bulls made it their mission to knock down Leo's castle using catapults, battering rams, and more.

WATCH US DISAPPEAR BEFORE YOUR EYES!

Green Ninja The second female ninja in this Castle subtheme is part of a triple pack with the White Ninja Shogun and a male ninja, also in green.

Ninja hides a shuriken and dagger in her robes

Red bandana printed on head under helmet

White Ninja Shogun This fierce ancient warrior minifigure is equipped with metallic leg armor and golden antlerlike helmet crest in set 3346.

LEGO CASTLE

This year saw the end of the LEGO Ninja subtheme. The ninja would slip quietly into the shadows until 2011, when the concept would return with LEGO NINJAGO (although one Ninja would briefly sneak back in 2009 as a Vintage Minifigure). Elsewhere, LEGO Castle continued, returning to medieval Europe with the first Knights' Kingdom subtheme. This line focused on the battle between King Leo's knights and Cedric the Bull's raiders. The two kings were locked in a ferocious feud over the future of the minifigure kingdom.

Crown and helmet are one piece

Aged, lined face; after all, he has reigned for a long time

Torso features King Leo's lion head shield

King Leo This regal minifigure of King Leo is the central character in Knights' Kingdom and appears in all five sets.

Hinged visor can be raised and lowered

No other minifigure wears this gold and silver armor

Princess Storm King Leo's brave daughter is the first female knight minifigure in the LEGO Castle theme.

King Leo's Castle This set (6098) comes with seven minifigures, including King Leo, Queen Leonora, and Princess Storm—and a creepy skeleton figure, too.

Queen Leonora King Leo's wife has a printed sloped piece instead of legs. She thinks King Leo's Castle (6098) has the wrong name!

Headdress based on medieval hennin

Outer red robe printed across torso and skirt

Keys to the castle safely attached to chain belt

LEGO® TOWN

LEGO Town headed due north in 2000, with the Arctic subtheme creating a short, sharp blizzard of activity. But while things were ice cold in some places, they were red hot in others. LEGO® Race burned up the racetrack, Space Port headed for the Red Planet, and there were new Fire Fighters sets. A year of variety indeed!

Crystal Aput Rescue helicopter pilot Crystal makes sure the Red Medic always drops in where he's needed. Like him, she wears a red snow suit.

Transparent blue visor on helmet

Flat beaked blue cap

Polar bear image for Arctic theme

Captain Ross The minifigure Captain wears a plain blue cap when he's chilling out in Mobile Outpost (6520).

Crocodile motif— she's snappy around the track

Safety helmet fitted with breathing hose

THAT'S NOT THE ENGINE ROARING— IT'S ME!

Smirk—Chip is confident he will win!

He loves tigers, so chose one as his race motif

Gloves help her keep a firm grip on the wheel

Lucky Clad in her favorite color, Lucky is all set to try her racing luck in Green Buggy (1284).

RACE

The Race subtheme made its final pit stop this year, with 13 sets that included new driver and pit crew minifigures and vehicles such as buggies, dragsters, and monster trucks. A new line, Racers, would begin revving up in 2001.

Chip Driving through flame obstacles won't send Chip into minifigure meltdown in Turbo Tiger (6519). His protective race suit and helmet will save him.

ARCTIC

Brrrrr! Brave explorers headed to the freezing Arctic in this Town subtheme, which lasted for a year. They were hunting for meteorites that had fallen to Earth with alien life trapped inside. Ten sets came out, featuring realistic snow vehicles and the first ever polar bear figures to appear in a LEGO set.

Scooter Scooter is ready to face chillier challenges in his snug hoodie. The subtheme was the first to feature fur-lined hood pieces.

Hood fits over head piece and torso

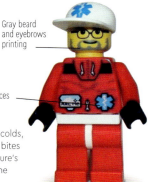

Gray beard and eyebrows printing

Star of Life is symbol of emergency medical services

Red Medic Dealing with colds, frostbite, and polar bear bites are all part of this minifigure's job. He appears only in the Polar Base set (6575).

Rocket Dragster This set (6616) includes a long, aerodynamic yellow racer and a Chip minifigure.

CITY CENTER

The largest City Center set this year was Highway Construction (6600) with five minifigures. Fire Fighters' HQ (6478) was in second place, featuring a hose-bearing helicopter, a motorcycle with trailer, and four minifigures.

Badges on uniform

Walkie-talkie to pass on orders

Patterned red belt

Fire Chief Like all firefighters released in 2000, this City Center minifigure wears a new gray uniform.

LEGO® BELVILLE™ FAIRY TALES

LEGO BELVILLE continued its flight through fairyland in 2000, delighting fans with five sets featuring good fairies, royal coaches, palaces, and other classic fairy tale elements.

Silver moon pattern

Pink floral pattern on white figure

Fairy Tales The LEGO BELVILLE Fairy figures came with optional fabric fairy wing attachments and plastic bow ties.

CLASSIC

In spite of a trend toward detail, the pre-1989 classic minifigure face still made an appearance now and then. This happy fellow remains, to many, the iconic symbol of the LEGO minifigure.

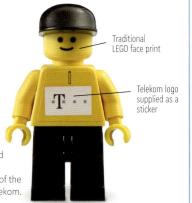

Traditional LEGO face print

Telekom logo supplied as a sticker

Telekom Cyclist This minifigure is included in set 1199—a promotional set for the Tour de France bicycle race. He bears the logo of the German telecommunications company Telekom.

DID YOU KNOW? This Fire Chief uses a megaphone to give orders (and win arguments) at the Fire Fighters' HQ.

LEGO *STAR WARS*

The Force was strong with LEGO *Star Wars* fans this year, as some of the most famous characters in the epic saga—Han Solo, Princess Leia, Emperor Palpatine, Boba Fett, C-3PO, and Chewbacca—became minifigures for the first time. A total of 19 sets were released in 2000, including the first *Millennium Falcon* starship.

I'VE ALWAYS BEEN A BIT OF A REBEL.

Specially created braided buns hair piece

Flowing senatorial gown printed on torso

Silver belt symbolizes Alderaan royalty

Trademark lopsided grin on head piece

"Han style" black vest and light shirt

Legs printed with blaster holster pattern

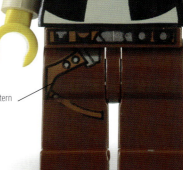

Princess Leia The first minifigure of Princess Leia Organa is dressed in her senatorial robes and features her famous bun hairstyle.

Han Solo This is one of three minifigure variants of lovable pilot Han Solo released in 2000. He wears the casual, open-necked shirt and vest *Star Wars* fans know so well.

Audio sensors on either side of head

Bowcaster ammunition bandolier

Unique head piece has hair that flows down his chest and back

C-3PO A new head piece was made for C-3PO's minifigure, which debuted in the *Millennium Falcon* set (7190).

Plain pearl gold legs unique to C-3PO

Chewbacca This Wookiee hero is taller than humans, so his special head piece is designed to add height. It sits on a torso also used for two Ewok minifigures.

TIME FOR A FACIAL.

Angry, distorted face print unique to this minifigure

Black cloth cape

Sith robes printed on torso

DID YOU KNOW?
Three of this year's LEGO® Technic™ sets were also based on *Star Wars*.

Helmet covers black head piece with no face

Rocket power for quick getaways

All in one Boba's detailed helmet and jetpack are one piece.

Mandalorian body armor printed on gray torso

Boba Fett This is the original minifigure of the Mandalorian bounty hunter.

Uniform printed on torso is unique to the Security Officer

Cap has been worn by many minifigures, such as Stan Shunpike with his purple version in LEGO® Harry Potter™

Naboo Security Officer
This smiling minifigure helps keep the peace on Naboo, at the controls of a green Flash Speeder (7124).

Emperor Palpatine The evil Lord of the Sith has a suitably scary, wrinkled face for his first appearance in the LEGO *Star Wars* theme. His minifigure features the same hood piece as the Darth Maul minifigure from 1999.

LEGO® STUDIOS

Fans got a chance to make their own movies this year with the LEGO Studios Steven Spielberg MovieMaker Set (1349). This innovative item came with a stop-motion camera and editing software, and included a recreation of a scene from *The Lost World: Jurassic Park*.

Stylish white bandana

Pen for jotting down notes

Shades protect his eyes from the glare of studio lights

Grip This guy brings a bit of bare-armed muscle to the set. He'll lift or shift anything the film crew needs him to.

Padded gloves for carrying heavy equipment

Utility belt holds screwdriver for dismantling props

Like all crew members, she wears an ID badge

Assistant Director This minifigure wields a working clapperboard in the MovieMaker Set (1349).

Practical orange vest

Same face design as Docs from the Rock Raiders theme

Beard and glasses like those worn by Steven Spielberg

Director Looks familiar? This minifigure is based on filmmaker Steven Spielberg. He features in nine sets, including Explosion Studio (1352).

Camera operator's emblem

CREW

Along with the director and cameraman, the LEGO Studios theme featured a grip, an assistant director, a stunt performer, and a firefighter in case things got a bit heated on the movie lot.

Camera Operator This cinematographer is always right at the center of the on-set action, tracking, panning, and zooming. That's how he rolls!

CAST

The actors in this set played Adventurers Johnny Thunder and Pippin Reed in an exciting scene where they flee from a rampaging dinosaur. They were the first of a number of actors to grace the LEGO Studios' big screen.

Tumbling tresses

Crop top under open jacket

Compass for checking directions

Red bandana protects against harsh winds

Stunt Performer When there are dangerous stunts to be done, this highly trained (and highly insured) minifigure steps in.

Female Actor This star plays a modern-day action hero in the MovieMaker Set (1349).

Female Actor as Pippin Reed Our versatile star looks just like the real LEGO® Adventurers in Dino Head Attack (1354)!

Protective gloves also provide grip

Same outfit as the Male Actor

Male Actor The male lead of the film being shot in MovieMaker Set (1349) is styled as a rebel with a heart of gold!

LEGO® ROCK RAIDERS

The Rock Raiders' adventures came to an end this year. The four sets produced were all promotional models. Some Rock Raider minifigures were also released as part of a LEGO® Mini Heroes Collection set (3347).

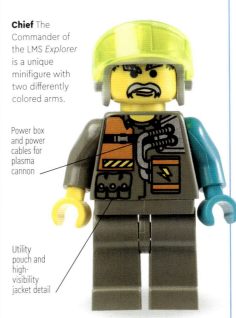

Chief The Commander of the LMS *Explorer* is a unique minifigure with two differently colored arms.

Power box and power cables for plasma cannon

Utility pouch and high-visibility jacket detail

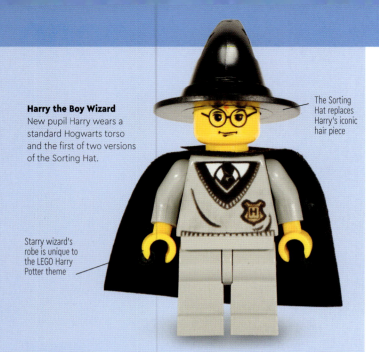

Harry the Boy Wizard
New pupil Harry wears a standard Hogwarts torso and the first of two versions of the Sorting Hat.

The Sorting Hat replaces Harry's iconic hair piece

Starry wizard's robe is unique to the LEGO Harry Potter theme

2001

SUPER-SPIES, SORCERERS, and space aliens helped make 2001 a magical year for LEGO® fans! Two major themes, LEGO® Harry Potter™ and the nonminifigure based BIONICLE®, launched in 2001, but that was only the beginning. Exciting LEGO® System themes such as LEGO® Alpha Team and LEGO® Life on Mars also joined the line-up. Aspiring movie-makers had a lot of LEGO® Studios sets to choose from, while younger builders could enjoy the new LEGO® Jack Stone models. LEGO building was bigger and better than ever in 2001!

LEGO HARRY POTTER

Gryffindor uniform

Trademark lightning-shaped scar

LEGO Harry Potter was the second major licensed theme to be released after LEGO® Star Wars™, premiering with 11 sets and 30 new minifigures based on the *Harry Potter and the Sorcerer's Stone* movie. Also appearing were the first sets of Hogwarts Castle (4709) and Hogwarts Express (4708), which would both prove so popular that several updates would be issued over the next few years.

THE WIZARD AND HIS FRIENDS
Fans just couldn't get enough of Harry and his friends. The theme's first year saw no fewer than four variants of Harry, three of Hermione Granger, and three of Ron Weasley.

Harry Potter™ A new, violet variant of the cloth robe was introduced specially for the theme. Harry wears the colorful robe in three sets.

Gryffindor crest

Hogwarts school crest

Hermione Granger™ All Gryffindor minifigures, including Hermione, wear the scarlet-and-gold uniform in years one and two. Their torsos and legs are identical.

Hogwarts Witch This Hermione minifigure is not yet in Gryffindor, so she wears a school crest on her torso piece instead of a Gryffindor one.

Bowl-shaped hair piece in Earth orange

Face printed with arrogant sneer

Draco Malfoy™ This is the first of more than 20 Draco Malfoy minifigures. As a member of Slytherin, his uniform bears the green-and-silver snake crest of his house.

Ron Weasley™ The first 18 Ron minifigures feature this quirky, grinning face, with eyebrows colored to match his hair piece.

Yellow hands and face were used for all Harry minifigures until 2004

Casual Harry This is one of more than 75 different Harry minifigures. He wears these casual clothes to board Hogwarts Express (4708).

Unique knitted sweater pattern

Casual Hermione Hermione has changed into a casual but stylish blue sweater and jeans for Diagon Alley Shops (4723).

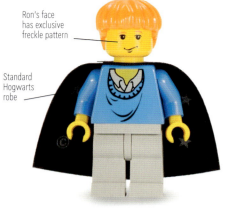

Ron's face has exclusive freckle pattern

Standard Hogwarts robe

Casual Ron Ron's robe keeps him warm when he's relaxing in the common room in Gryffindor House (4722).

Shaggy beard and hair are one piece

Supersized legs are unposable

Extra-long torso piece gives Hagrid his half-giant height

Rubeus Hagrid™ There are seven variants of Hogwarts' half-giant gamekeeper. Each one stands a whole head taller than his minifigure friends.

CASTLE RESIDENTS

Not all LEGO Harry Potter minifigures are human—or even alive! Peeves was the first LEGO ghost to be built from standard minifigure parts; the Silver Knight was a statue in Hogwarts Castle; and the Chess Queen was a minifigure-sized chess piece guarding the Sorcerer's Stone.

Face printed onto a light gray standard LEGO head

Ghostly markings of jacket and shirt

Peeves the Poltergeist This gray-bodied minifigure appears in two LEGO sets (4705 and 4709).

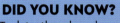

Shiny silver crown

Faceless head is a cylindrical LEGO brick

Chess Queen Harry and Ron come up against this ghastly game piece in The Chamber of the Winged Keys (4704).

A spooky gray face lurks under the two-piece helmet

Silver Knight The warrior statue minifigure holds a large LEGO sword and stands guard at Hogwarts Castle (4709).

HOGWARTS PROFESSORS

It wasn't just about the students! Professors Dumbledore, Snape, and Quirrell joined in the fun this year. Quirrell was the first Defense Against the Dark Arts teacher minifigure, and many more have followed in his footsteps.

DID YOU KNOW?
To date, there have been seven minifigure-scale versions of the iconic Hogwarts Express.

Face printed with sarcastically raised eyebrow

Glowing complexion

Professor Snape™ The Potions Master is the first minifigure to have a glow-in-the-dark head.

Long, purple frock coat

Plain black cloth robe

Albus Dumbledore™ The first minifigure of the Hogwarts headmaster has detailed purple robes and a purple wizarding cloak.

Ornate details on robes can be seen if beard is removed

Hair and beard are two separate removable pieces

Legs printed with wizarding gadgets

Unique purple turban hides a hideous secret

Purple jacket and scarf match color of turban

Evil face Voldemort's features are printed on the reverse of the head

Professor Quirrell The Professor Quirrell minifigure is the first to have a special double-sided head. Turn it around and Lord Voldemort's face is revealed!

LEGO® SPACE

LEGO Space traveled to the Red Planet for the first time with the Life on Mars subtheme, which focused on astronauts exploring Mars and encountering a friendly species of alien. Adventures revolved around the humans helping the good Martians stop a planned rebellion by a bad Martian. Life on Mars lasted for only one year, and its sets would be the last in the Space theme until 2007.

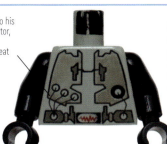

Chrome visor

Wired up to his heart monitor, Mac never misses a beat

Special unit Mac's exclusive torso is printed with the heart-monitoring unit he has to wear in space.

Front **Back**

Knobs

Breathing apparatus

Simple face detail with messy orange hair

BB's helmet BB's headgear has two knobs on the back, which allow him to attach to space vehicles so he can "hover" above the ground.

Doc Ailing astronauts can rely on this dedicated doctor to fix them up. His minifigure appears in two sets (7315 and 7312).

Gray beard and eyebrows show he is a mature medic

Torso printed with new detailed space suit

Black gloves

Large helmet and breathing apparatus cover torso detail

Mac Found only in the Solar Explorer set (7315), Captain Mac isn't headed for the sun. His ship gets its name from its large solar panels.

BB Mac's Solar Explorer co-pilot is very young and very eager. He wears the same helmet as his hero Mac over his unique tousle-haired head.

LEGO JACK STONE

Jack Stone sets focused on hero Jack saving the day in various guises. The figures were "midfigs," midsized figures that could not be taken apart.

Helmet worn when piloting rescue boat

Torso printed with rescue overalls

Res-Q Worker This figure shows Jack Stone in his role as an intrepid rescuer at the Aqua Super Station (4610).

MARTIAN COLONY

All named after stars, the Martians used an air pump and tube transport system to get around. They had more advanced tech than the astronauts, so it's lucky they were friendly!

MY JUMPSUIT IS OUT OF THIS WORLD!

Air tube mask printed on Martian head

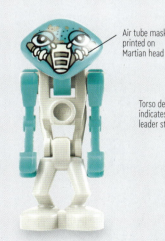

Torso design indicates leader status

Cassiopeia Rigel's daughter Cassiopeia is the only female Martian in the theme.

Angled legs are only used for Martians

Pollux Like all the Martian figures, Pollux is taller than a standard LEGO minifigure.

Rigel This green Martian has years of experience at leading his people. He's also the General of the Aero Tube Hangar (7317), a Biodium mining outpost on Mars.

Hat designed for LEGO Adventurers

LEGO® STUDIOS

Fans had gone wild for the LEGO Studios Steven Spielberg MovieMaker Set in 2000. To follow up on its success, 14 more sets were released this year, all designed to be part of LEGO fans' homemade films. Two of the sets were based on the making of the *Jurassic Park III* movie, with LEGO® Adventurers Johnny Thunder and Pippin Reed taking the place of the real stars.

Aviator's cap with padded ear flaps

Stubble adds to tough-guy image

Screwdriver close at hand

Grip This versatile technician minifigure has three variants and appears in three sets.

ID badge

Padded jacket protects him from scrapes

Tough Guy Actor This performer seems to have based his on-screen style on the Crook from 1998's Ninja sets.

Camera Operator This minifigure has a unique torso with a large LEGO logo printed on their back.

Stunt Artist This fearless minifigure comes in a set with a catapult for launching him over a wall of fire!

LEGO® TOWN

It turned out to be an unusually quiet year for the usually bustling LEGO Town. Only three sets were released: two promotional sets for real-world airlines (1100 and 2718) and a reissue of 1992's Gas N' Wash (6472).

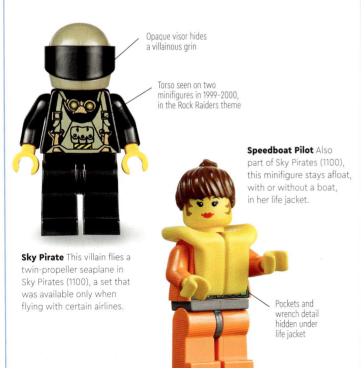

Opaque visor hides a villainous grin

Torso seen on two minifigures in 1999–2000, in the Rock Raiders theme

Speedboat Pilot Also part of Sky Pirates (1100), this minifigure stays afloat, with or without a boat, in her life jacket.

Sky Pirate This villain flies a twin-propeller seaplane in Sky Pirates (1100), a set that was available only when flying with certain airlines.

Pockets and wrench detail hidden under life jacket

Rabbit mask fits over a standard head piece

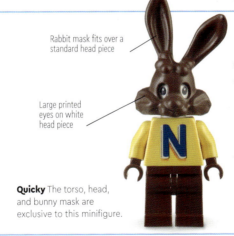

QUICKY

Quicky the bunny is the cute mascot of Nesquik®, Nestlé's popular flavored milk drink. His minifigure, which appeared in three promotional sets under the LEGO Studios banner, was designed to show an actor portraying Quicky for a movie.

Large printed eyes on white head piece

Quicky The torso, head, and bunny mask are exclusive to this minifigure.

LEGO® TIME TEACHING CLOCK

Young fans could now learn to tell the time with LEGO clock (4383). It came with a minifigure whose collection of hats included a chef's hat for meal times, a baseball cap for play times, and a ghost mask for bedtimes!

Wizard's hat shows that it's time for learning

Pocket to hold tools for fixing the clock

Clock Companion This minifigure always has time for LEGO fans and can be built onto a working clock with a top layer of LEGO knobs.

LEGO ALPHA TEAM

Super-spies took on a malevolent mind-manipulator in the first LEGO secret agent theme—Alpha Team. Evil Ogel sought to transform the population into Skeleton Drones using mind control orbs. The seven agents of Alpha Team battled him on land, on sea, and in the air in six new sets featuring nine new minifigures. Alpha Team and Ogel would be back for rematches in 2002 and 2004.

Unique new head piece

Alpha Team logo on necklace

Utility belt holds mechanic's tools

Cam Attaway Alpha Team's mechanic wears her purple glasses for the first and only time in the Alpha Team ATV (6774).

HEY, THAT'S SUPPOSED TO BE A SECRET!

Headset for communicating with the team

Dash Justice At the first sign of trouble, team leader Dash will be there in a flash! Brave Dash pilots the Alpha Team Helicopter (6773).

Utility belt worn over buttoned jacket

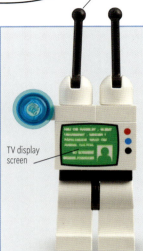

Black levers act as antennae

TV display screen

Tee Vee This first variant of Alpha Team's communications robot is fully programmed and switched on—as you'd expect of a TV set on minifigure legs!

Aviator-style protective helmet

Explosives fixed to clothes

Purple hair is unique to 2001 and 2002 variants

Mouth clenched in concentration

Crunch Working for Alpha Team is a real blast for Crunch. He's the team's dedicated explosives expert.

Three pockets on utility belt

Radia Quick-thinking and super-clever, Radia has a mind as bright as the lasers that she works with.

DID YOU KNOW?
"Ogel" is LEGO spelled backward—he represents the opposite of LEGO fun and play.

Movable chrome gold visor

Pockets on legs for tools

Flex No problem is too tricky for Flex, Alpha Team's ropes expert. He's just happy to be on the team—delighted, in fact!

DIDN'T SEE THAT EVIL ORB COMING!

Epaulettes appear only on first variant

Skeleton head

Menacing red eye

Elaborate shoulder armor

Protective armor clips over torso

Ogel Control Center This set (6776) saw Ogel's first minifigure appearance. He was protected by two Minion Commanders.

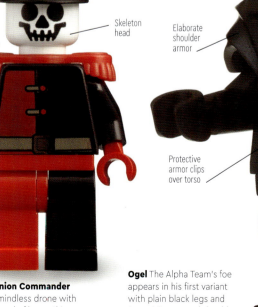

Minion Commander A mindless drone with a head of bone, this minifigure is the first variant of Ogel's minions.

Ogel The Alpha Team's foe appears in his first variant with plain black legs and torso. His armored shoulder protection is so bulky, it almost covers his scowl.

LEGO *STAR WARS*

It was another year of firsts for LEGO *Star Wars*, with the debuts of two classic characters from Episodes IV, V, and VI: the crimson-clad Royal Guard and the iconic Stormtrooper. But they were not the only LEGO *Star Wars* rookies. Watto, from *Star Wars: Episode I The Phantom Menace*, made his first appearance in his very own set—Watto's Junkyard (7186).

Royal Guard This electrostaff-wielding minifigure wears red robes as part of the Emperor's personal guard.

Hood mold specially designed for the Royal Guards

Hood conceals black LEGO head piece with no face details

Imperial emblem on helmet

Ventilated helmet

Special black armor with life-support system

Stormtrooper This year saw the debut of the original Stormtrooper minifigure. There would be many future variants.

Utility belt with blaster power cell reserves

TIE Pilot The original variant of the Imperial Pilot flies the much-feared TIE Fighter (7146).

Simple black uniform with belt

Imperial Pilot This minifigure pilots Emperor Palpatine's Shuttle (7166). Later variants are much less cheerful!

Plain head, wings, and torso fit over standard LEGO torso

Imperial Shuttle This set (7166), featuring Palpatine's infamous spaceship, was introduced in 2001 along with four minifigures, including two Royal Guards.

Watto Appearing only in Watto's Junkyard (7186), this minifigure variant of the winged Toydarian junkyard dealer is both unique and rare.

LEGO® SOCCER

The Women's Team, a brand-new set in the LEGO Soccer theme, was released in conjunction with the Women's European Championships, this year held in Germany. No new pieces were used, but it scored a memorable first nevertheless: a women's team had never before appeared in a LEGO Soccer set.

Ponytail detail on hair piece

Black-haired Player This defender is ready to tackle anything—or anyone—the opposition might throw at her.

Brown-haired Player It takes more than 90 minutes to win a match. This minifigure trains for hours every day in her yellow team bib.

Bib piece fits over neck

Country flag sticker can be stuck here

LET'S GET IT IN THE LEGO NET!

Blonde-haired Player This woman has one aim—putting the ball in the back of the net. She's playing with her teammates for the first time in Women's Team (3416), and they're going for the goal.

Plain blue Women's Team shirt

Dark cap and keeper's gloves

Goalie The Goalie, with smiling LEGO face, looks more carefree than her pals. She's a safe pair of hands and she knows it!

Phase I helmet has a distinctive fin

Black edges depict bodysuit under armor

Gray lines depict body armor

Utility belt carries survival gear

DC-15A blaster

MY UNIT IS ME, MYSELF, AND I.

Clone Trooper This Phase I clone minifigure is the first variant of the clone trooper.

2002

A GLITTERING CAST of famous movie characters entered the minifigure world in 2002. Licensed lines were the hot LEGO® news, with new sets based on *Star Wars: Episode II Attack of the Clones, Harry Potter and the Chamber of Secrets*, and Spider-Man all flying off the shelves. The big Hollywood stars didn't entirely steal the scene, however. The LEGO® Alpha Team was back for Mission Deep Sea, and Pepper Roni from the successful LEGO® Island video game made his debut as a minifigure in the Island Xtreme Stunts line.

LEGO® STAR WARS™

The 25th anniversary of *Star Wars* had arrived. The occasion was celebrated with the release of *Star Wars: Episode II Attack of the Clones*, and with seven LEGO sets tied to the movie. Their memorable minifigures included a grown-up Anakin Skywalker and villains Jango Fett and Count Dooku, who troubled the Jedi for the first time.

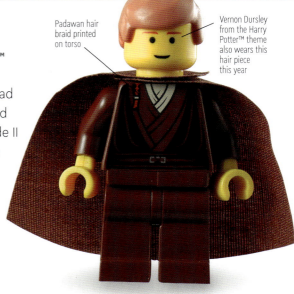

Padawan hair braid printed on torso

Vernon Dursley from the Harry Potter™ theme also wears this hair piece this year

Padawan Anakin Skywalker This minifigure is the first adult version of Anakin. He has lost the freckles of his 1999 younger self.

Original Yoda head has molded but no printed eyes

Shorter, nonposable leg piece debuts this year

Yoda Unique printing on the aged Grand Master's torso includes a blissl—an instrument like a tiny panpipe—worn around his neck.

NEVER TRUST ANYONE NAMED DARTH.

Hair piece recreates the long hair of the movie character

Headset lets him talk to other Jedi while chasing Jango Fett

Torso printed with loose-fitting tan Jedi tunic

Obi-Wan Kenobi Two variants of this Obi-Wan minifigure exist: the other has no headset but is otherwise identical.

Unique head with gray beard and wrinkled skin

Cape clasp and belt on torso unique to Count Dooku

Jedi Starfighter This (7143) set contains a Jedi Starfighter spacecraft and Obi-Wan Kenobi to pilot it. Obi-Wan's droid R4-P17 is also included in the set.

Count Dooku Dooku has fallen to the dark side, and his clothes are a little on the dark side, too—they are all black or brown. His minifigure came with Jedi Duel (7103).

IF ONLY THERE WERE MORE OF ME ...

Boba's face is a childish version of Jango's

Jetpack and helmet are one piece

Custom blasters are actually LEGO revolvers

Short legs are unposable

Young Boba Fett Yoda and this child variant of Jango's clone son are among the first minifigures to feature the short LEGO legs.

Jango Fett A minifigure mercenary and bounty hunter, Jango appears in set 7153. His head is plain black on one side with a stubbled face and balaclava outline on the other.

BATTLE DROIDS

Although the Separatist battle droids had appeared as LEGO figures before, this was the first year for super battle droids and droidekas. The Clone Wars were about to get a lot tougher!

Head is molded as part of torso

Head clips on to torso

Droideka blasters are binocular pieces

Droideka This heavy destroyer droid is made up of 26 pieces, including its weapons.

Super Battle Droid Towering over ordinary battle droids, this imposing figure boasts all-new parts in a unique metal blue color.

Security Battle Droid A red torso identifies this battle droid as one of a few advanced enough to act as prison guards.

Veil worn by Zam when she is posing as a human

Zam Wesell Like Jango, Zam is a bounty hunter. Unlike him, she is also a Clawdite shape-shifter, so her minifigure head has both a human face and a reptilian Clawdite one.

Unique torso and hips with specialized equipment and armor

Mask and goggles offer protection from sun and sand

Humidifier to make dry air easier to breathe

Tusken Raider This mysterious minifigure moves through deserts in his sand-colored shroud and crossed utility belt.

LEGO® SPIDER-MAN™

The web-head swung into the LEGO line-up for the first time, as a subtheme of LEGO® Studios. The Spider-Man Action Studio (1376) featured the first Spider-Man and Peter Parker minifigures, and Green Goblin (1374) included the Green Goblin and Mary Jane. Fans could now drop Spidey into a variety of sticky situations in their own stop-motion movies.

Molded features need no printing

Green Goblin Mask

Green Goblin The true face of Spidey's archenemy, Norman Osborn, is printed on a green head piece and hidden beneath a scary mask.

Armor is printed on his legs and torso

LEGO® STUDIOS

The monsters came out to howl in 2002, as LEGO Studios unleashed four spine-tingling movie sets. The Mummy, the Vampire, the Monster, and the Werewolf were all there—costumed actors, of course—along with directors, camera operators, and other performers. It was also the first time there had been werewolf and vampire minifigures.

Removable neck bracket goes here

THAT PETER PARKER LOOKS LIKE A COOL KID!

Spider-Man's classic hero costume with spider logo

Red gloves ensure that Spidey's body is fully protected

Spider-Man The first ever LEGO version of Spider-Man comes with an exclusive neck bracket, which allows him to be clipped onto a long bar piece and moved around to "climb" walls.

Zipped jacket print on torso

Peter Parker Spider-Man's alter ego has a two-sided head—one side with glasses, one without.

DID YOU KNOW?
There have been more than 30 different Peter Parker Spider-Man minifigures since 2002.

White, lifeless hands

Vampire This scary vampire is thirsty for minifigure blood! Turn his head around to see his mouth open, ready for a bite.

LEGO® HARRY POTTER™

The boy wizard returned for a second magical year in 2002. This time, the sets focused not just on Hogwarts, but on other places in Harry's world, too, such as the house of Harry's Muggle relatives, the Dursleys. Ten sets were released based on the second movie, *Harry Potter and the Chamber of Secrets*, with three more based on the first movie, *Harry Potter and the Sorcerer's Stone*.

SORCERER'S STONE

The new *Harry Potter and the Sorcerer's Stone* sets introduced two new species: goblins and trolls. Goblins would return in 2011.

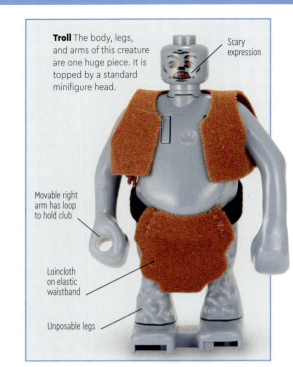

Troll The body, legs, and arms of this creature are one huge piece. It is topped by a standard minifigure head.

Scary expression

Movable right arm has loop to hold club

Loincloth on elastic waistband

Unposable legs

Specially molded head

Bank teller's uniform

Goblin This short-legged minifigure is an employee in Gringotts Bank (4714).

Casual zipped plaid jacket

Ron Weasley This is the last minifigure of Ron to feature a yellow head and the only variant released in 2002.

Cute freckles

Gryffindor crest

Ginny Weasley As a first-year student at Hogwarts, Ginny gets her first minifigure. It is her only variant to feature a yellow head.

CHAMBER OF SECRETS

The 2002 LEGO Harry Potter sets had several new minifigures, including Dobby the house-elf, Professor McGonagall, Professor Lockhart, Tom Riddle, Lucius Malfoy, and Madam Hooch, plus three new variants of Harry.

DID YOU KNOW?
Professor McGonagall is the only LEGO Harry Potter minifigure to wear a green wizard's hat.

Gilderoy Lockhart The ornately printed torso and light pink hips and legs are unique to this minifigure.

Groomed blond hair

Carefully chosen pink outfit

Elaborate gold design on vest

Green Lockhart This stylish variant of the professor is seen in two LEGO Harry Potter sets in this year (4733 and HPG01—a promotional release).

Green wizard's hat

Spell book

Face has wrinkle printing

Professor McGonagall This strict professor's printed sloped piece was seen in two sets released this year (4729 and HPG04—a promotional set).

Pilot's goggles

Madam Hooch The gray striped robe is unique to this variant of the Hogwarts flying instructor.

Light gold stripe as opposed to Malfoy's silver

Quidditch uniform in Slytherin house colors

Draco the Seeker This minifigure comes with a green robe, which can also be seen on Professor McGonagall in this year.

Determined expression

Casual clothes for when Harry is not at school

Harry the Seeker In his bright red Quidditch uniform, Harry is ready for training in Quidditch Practice (4726).

Blue Jacket Harry Harry's minifigure ventures into the Forbidden Forest in this blue zipped jacket.

Comfy cardigan

Vernon Dursley Harry's uncle was the only Dursley to appear as a minifigure until 2020.

Red Shirt Harry This casually dressed variant of Harry is only seen in the Escape From Privet Drive set (4728).

Robes without star pattern

Formal pinstripe jacket

Stern expression

DID YOU KNOW? Dobby's head is made of rubber.

Forlorn expression

Tattered clothes print

Tom Riddle Tom shares his hair piece with Harry, but his face is printed with a much darker expression.

Lucius Malfoy This malicious wizard wears the same hair piece as Ginny Weasley but in a different color.

Dobby the House-elf Dobby's minifigure comes with short legs. His torso is printed with the dirty pillowcase that he wears when in the employ of the Malfoys.

Crew-cut hairstyle

Harry and Goyle This minifigure of Gregory Goyle is actually Harry in disguise. A reversible head piece shows Harry's features reappearing as the Polyjuice Potion starts to wear off.

Hair piece is the same as Draco Malfoy's, but in black

Star pattern on robes

Ron and Crabbe This minifigure is actually Ron disguised as Vincent Crabbe. The double-sided head piece shows Ron's red eyebrows reappearing.

Harry

Ron

LEGO ALPHA TEAM

Ogel took his villainy beneath the waves in the second year of Alpha Team, called Mission Deep Sea. His plan: to use his orbs to mutate sea creatures into monstrous drones. It took all of Alpha Team's skill—and some awesome underwater vehicles—to put a stop to him and his modified Skeleton Army.

Stubble

Communication unit for talking to the team

Crunch Explosives expert Crunch has been underwater for so long, he just hasn't found the time to shave.

Radia The 2002 version of this laser beam expert has purple hair, but by 2004, she favors the same style in black.

Helmet with diving mask

Air tube

Detachable flippers

Dash Justice With a determined, steely look in his eyes, this minifigure is looking forward to taking on the evil Ogel.

Movable diving mask

Cam Attaway This minifigure of Alpha Team's Cam is dressed in full diving gear, ready to accompany Dash on a sea mission.

Scuba tank This scuba attachment fits between the torso and head piece.

Bubble-shaped transparent neon green helmet

Commander The medal print on the torso of this minifigure indicates that he is the appointed commander of the Skeleton Drones.

Red-and-black uniform is the same as 2001 version apart from medal

Huge smile

Flex retains the right orange arm from the 2001 variant

Flex Scuba-diving Flex is happiest working the Sub-Surface Scooter (set 4791), as can be seen from his huge grin.

LEGO Alpha Team logo

Vital diving equipment

Charge This version of the electricity expert, in diving gear, pilots a diving mech in Alpha Team Robot Diver (4790).

Pockets for storing equipment

LEGO® SOCCER

Soccer was riding high for a third year, with sets tied to the 2002 FIFA World Cup™ and a new version of the LEGO Championship Challenge (3420). The Grand Championship Cup (3425) was the largest Soccer set ever released, with 22 minifigures, and would be the last LEGO Soccer stadium set for four years.

V-neck soccer strip

Black Stripe Defender From the Defender 1 set (4443), this player is one of several 2002 FIFA World Cup minifigures to wear Coca-Cola branding.

Cockerel logo on shirt

French Soccer Player This player sports the French team colors of blue, red, and white. His legs display the Adidas logo.

French Football Federation logo

LEGO® CASTLE

This was a relatively quiet year for LEGO Castle— only two sets were released. Black Falcon's Fortress (10039) was a rerelease of a 1986 set, and Blacksmith Shop (3739) was a fan-designed model available only through LEGO.com. These would be the last Castle sets until 2004.

Shiny scale mail

Blacksmith There are two things that this minifigure takes great pride in: the armor he makes and his mustache.

LEGO® ISLAND XTREME STUNTS

Based on the successful LEGO *Island* and LEGO *Island 2* video games, the new theme Xtreme Stunts introduced pizza delivery guy and ace skateboarder Pepper Roni and his enemy, the Brickster, in minifigure form. The sets combined skateboard, boat, and all-terrain vehicle (ATV) stunts with Pepper's efforts to keep LEGO Island safe. After 2002, the theme featured three promotional sets only.

Pizza pattern on torso

WANT YOUR PIZZA WITH A SIDE OF KICKFLIPS?

Green eyes seen through mask

Prison number

Prison uniform worn by several LEGO crooks

23768

Brickster LEGO Island Xtreme Stunts' main villain is always planning a jailbreak or new ways to take bricks that don't belong to him!

Blue glove on left hand

Knee pads protect from falls

Pepper Roni A skateboard expert, Pepper Roni keeps the Island safe from criminals. He is also a pizza delivery boy.

STUNT MANIACS

Pepper was joined by all of his friends from the PC game, including Sky Lane. This theme used a bracket and bar system (see Sky Lane, right) to allow the minifigures to perform their stunts, similar to the LEGO® Gravity Games™ stunt sticks introduced in 2003.

White mustache

Stylish red vest and bow tie

Crop top with string ties

Bar attaches to knob on neck bracket

Neck bracket A bar fits into the knob on the back of the neck bracket so that Sky can do her daring skateboard stunts.

Xtreme Tower The largest set released this year from this theme, Xtreme Tower (6740) includes six minifigures, the Xtreme Tower, a helicopter, and a skateboard.

Sky Lane Pepper Roni's daring friend often helps him fight criminals. She wears a neck bracket while performing stunts.

Infomaniac The creator of LEGO Island has an angled "i" logo on his torso to stand for his name. He appears only in one set this year—Xtreme Tower (6740).

Infomaniac's 1999 variant has black pants

Seven stars pattern on helmet

Left arm different color to right one

Striped green helmet looks like a snake's head

Scorcher Although his torso says "4," this minifigure always comes first in the Hot Scorcher set (4584).

Storming Cobra From the Storming Cobra set (4596), this racer minifigure drives a green racecar over a ramp—just for fun.

LEGO® RACERS

LEGO Racers spun off from Town Race in 2001. This year brought Drome Racers, a subtheme that featured an extensive story and multiple minifigure characters. Centering on a vast indoor racing arena called the Drome, it featured six teams racing for glory. Each instruction booklet included a Drome Racers comic.

Jacket pattern with straps

LEGO® SPACE

This promotional pair hold a special place in LEGO history. After their appearance at the World Space Congress, images of them were launched into space on the NASA Mars Exploration Rovers *Spirit* and *Opportunity* in 2003.

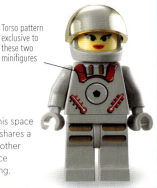

Classic LEGO® helmet with chrome visor

Biff Starling It's not obvious, but this minifigure is nervous—he's hoping he doesn't meet any Blacktron Astronauts on his mission.

Torso pattern exclusive to these two minifigures

Gold ribbing

Sandy Moondust This space robot or "astrobot" shares a torso with only one other minifigure—her space colleague, Biff Starling.

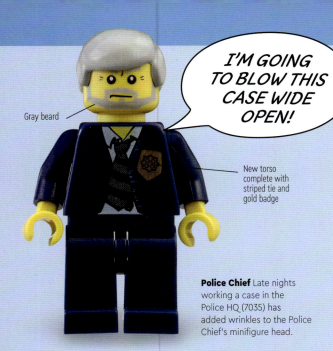

Gray beard

I'M GOING TO BLOW THIS CASE WIDE OPEN!

New torso complete with striped tie and gold badge

Police Chief Late nights working a case in the Police HQ (7035) has added wrinkles to the Police Chief's minifigure head.

2003

THE LEGO® MINIFIGURE celebrated its 25th birthday in grand style. After decades of almost exclusively yellow-skinned minifigures, some of these iconic toys got a major redesign as human skin tones were introduced. A minifigure of Lando Calrissian from the LEGO® *Star Wars*™ theme was among the first to receive this more realistic treatment. 2003 also saw some big changes in LEGO® Town, LEGO® Sports expanded to include a wider range of sports (including LEGO Soccer and Basketball), and the most ambitious LEGO® Adventurers line ever was released.

LEGO® WORLD CITY

LEGO Town became LEGO World City in 2003, and the emphasis was on action. Police sets dominated, with Trains and Coast Guard still featuring, while Construction and Airport took a back seat for a short while. World City would last for two years before being replaced by LEGO® City.

Knitted cap

Wicked smile revealing a gold tooth

Torso with inmate number is new and unique to this minifigure

POLICE

The World City Police featured in six sets in 2003, including a new Police HQ (7035) and a Surveillance Truck (7034). Only two of the sets contained minifigure crooks.

Badge emblem based on a 2×2 LEGO brick

Smiling Officer A smiling Policeman is always reassuring. This one is from the Police HQ (7035).

Crook A bright orange jumpsuit makes this crook easy to spot if he flees from Police HQ (7035).

WORLD CITY IS MY KIND OF TOWN!

Silver sunglasses for flying in sunny skies

Same face as the Smiling Officer

Radio to call for backup

Patrolman torso is new this year

Serious expression is new this year

Police Pilot This helicopter pilot has the word "POLICE" printed on the back of an all-new torso.

The belt has pouches for storing vital equipment

Determined Officer This minifigure comes with a helmet and a cap in Surveillance Truck (7034).

Squad Car Driver This minifigure spans two themes this year, also appearing in the LEGO® Spider-Man™ set, Spider-Man's First Chase (4850).

CITY FOLK

It wasn't all high adventure in World City. Minifigures were still traveling by train, going through Grand Central Station (4513) on their way to their destinations.

Necklace has golden pendant

Tapered jacket print

Passenger This minifigure has a ticket for the High Speed Train (4511) and a hair piece first seen in the LEGO® Harry Potter™ theme.

Heavy luggage to heave onto the train

Square glasses

Open-collared shirt

Orange train ticket

Commuter The commuter minifigure is wearing a new blazer. He'd love to shout about it, but he can't—he's a minifigure.

Flat, gelled hair gives a professional look

Dark glasses keep identity hidden

BE COOL. DON'T BLOW MY COVER.

Tailored suit

Slick suitcase full of secret documents

Undercover Cop Dark hair, dark glasses, and a dark suit ensure that this minifigure cop blends into the background on the High Speed Train (4511).

DID YOU KNOW?
It takes just one second to manufacture 15 LEGO minifigures!

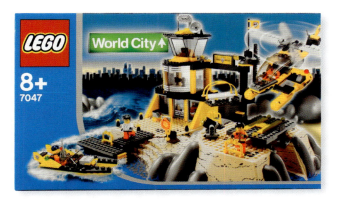

Coast Watch HQ This bright yellow base (7047) includes landing places for a boat and a helicopter, and plenty more to keep its four minifigures busy.

COAST GUARD

The World City coastline is kept safe by new-look coast guard minifigures. Their Rescue Chopper (7044) was the first minifigure-scale helicopter with room for side-by-side pilots.

Same classic hair piece as World City Commuter

I KNITTED THIS BROW MYSELF!

Coast Guard Coast guarding is a serious business—as you can tell from this minifigure's steely expression.

LUCKILY FOR ME, MINIFIGURES FLOAT!

Silver sunglasses shield eyes from sun's reflection on the water

Zipped pockets keep out water

Safety straps for a snug fit

Gray gloves for extra grip on the boat steering wheel

Speedboat Pilot The Speedboat Pilot is very happy indeed—he's the only minifigure to wear this new stickered flotation jacket, exclusive to set 7047.

Coast Guard Pilot Like the World City Police Pilot, this minifigure has a new face print with mirrored sunglasses.

2003

LEGO SPORTS

LEGO Sports was a new theme for 2003, incorporating LEGO Soccer with extreme sports and basketball. But this meant more than just designing new sets; it required the redesign of the minifigure for basketball. The addition of the stunt stick to the Gravity Games sets meant that minifigures could be played with in a whole new way!

The course features jumps and drops

Snowboard features red minifigure outline

Snowboard Boarder Cross Race In this set (3538), two minifigures race to the finish line at the bottom of the snowy and tricky competition course.

Under the goggles, there's a helmet with checkered pattern, which is new this year

Race number is a sticker

Light gray gloves

Big Air Snowboarder This minifigure has the same head piece as Madam Hooch from the LEGO Harry Potter theme, but she prefers snowboards to broomsticks.

GRAVITY GAMES

The LEGO® Gravity Games™ sets featured special stunt sticks that could be attached to the minifigures to allow them to do midair stunts. Vertical ramps made for even more excitement.

Plain black helmet worn by more than 100 minifigures

Gray Snowboarder Being up against the Tough Snowboarder doesn't scare this minifigure—he has years of experience on the slopes.

Even super-cool snowboarders need gloves to keep warm!

Helmet first seen in the 2002 Racers theme

Tough Snowboarder This snowboarder looks tough, but he still likes to protect his minifigure skin from the sun's glare with sunblock.

NBA AND STREET BASKETBALL

Minifigures underwent a radical redesign for the NBA Basketball subtheme and their street basketballer counterparts. Springs were built into their legs, and arms and hands were specially constructed to hold, throw, and slam dunk the ball.

Blue strip of NBA All-Star Game East team

Orange sunglasses take away any glare

Arms modified to hold basketball

Street Player Come rain or shine, this player is always ready to play some b-ball.

East NBA Player Springing off to shoot some hoops is sure to make this minifigure player's team happy.

Springs to "jump" and shoot

Torso design reads "HIGHFLIP"

Stunt Skateboarder Helmet and goggles keep this minifigure safe as she performs stunts at the Skateboard Vert Park Challenge (3537).

Monobrow and goatee printed on head piece

Cool graphics on T-shirt

Park Skateboarder The Skateboarder's bearded head piece appears on six other sporty minifigures.

Sunglasses printed on forehead

Jacket seen on the Stunt Artist in the LEGO® Studios theme in 2001

Duracell Snowboarder This minifigure has a snowboard featuring a LEGO minifigure head design.

LEGO GRAVITY GAMES PROMOTIONAL SETS

Half of the LEGO Gravity Games sets were promotions for companies including battery manufacturer Duracell, something that continued into 2004. Each set featured a minifigure and stunt stick.

LEGO ADVENTURERS

The final year of LEGO Adventurers took our heroes on a mission to India and China. Here, they made many new friends as they tried to stop their old enemy, Sam Sinister, from getting his hands on a series of golden treasures. The detailed story was told over 18 sets, most of which came with comic books. Bonus pieces linked the largest sets to make an exciting board game.

ARE YOU READY FOR AN ADVENTURE?

Four Johnny variants share this face

Torso design introduced in 1998

Johnny Thunder A new version of the adventurer minifigure returns with a new head with sideburns and a chin dimple.

Wide-brim hat

Exploring Johnny The lead adventurer wears a new coat in the mountains but the same old classic hat.

Exclusive torso

Printed map tile

Pockets printed on legs

Hat later used in LEGO Harry Potter sets

New hairstyle print

Red wool scarf

Reporter's notebook in coat pocket

Black gloves

Exploring Pippin This returning hero is protected against the elements and mythical snow monsters in Yeti Hideout (7412)!

Pith helmet

New green torso with red scarf

Pippin Reed Journalist Pippin doesn't just write about her adventures, she photographs them, too! She carries this camera in Elephant Caravan (7414).

ADVENTURERS

Many favorite characters were back for 2003, including Johnny Thunder and Pippin Reed. Their thrilling journey involved steamboats, biplanes, hot air balloons, and elephants!

Dr. Kilroy The brilliant scientist Dr. Kilroy, also known as Dr. Lightning, is certainly a snappy dresser in Scorpion Palace (7418).

White, wispy beard

Paisley pattern on vest

Top hat and monocle add a touch of class

White scarf comes in handy for surrendering

Lord Sam Sinister A hook for his left hand and a battle-scarred face give this minifigure a new look.

UP TO NO GOOD

Sam Sinister (a.k.a. Baron Von Barron) teams up with emperors and yeti hunters on his latest quest for power and riches.

DID YOU KNOW?
LEGO Adventurers was the first minifigure theme to feature elephant figures.

Red turban

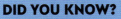

New torso with blue vest and yellow embroidery pattern

Babloo This young man has a talent for communicating with animals, including the supersized star of Elephant Caravan (7414).

Ponytail hair piece

Exclusive torso print

FRIENDS AND ALLIES

Three new faces joined the team in its final year: animal expert Babloo, martial arts whiz Jing Lee, and skilled mountain guide Sangye Dorje.

Jing Lee The Adventurers are stronger than ever with this martial artist on their side.

Identical headgear to Pippin Reed

Ax to cut through slippery ice

Backpack filled with supplies

Sherpa Sangye Dorje The young mountain guide knows that snow shoes are essential wear when traveling to the Temple of Mount Everest (7417).

Red sash tied around waist

Snow shoes attach to legs

LEGO *STAR WARS*

The LEGO *Star Wars* galaxy got bigger this year, with trips to Jabba's Palace (4480) and Cloud City (10123). The first came with a giant Jabba the Hutt figure, while the second included Lando Calrissian with a lifelike skin tone.

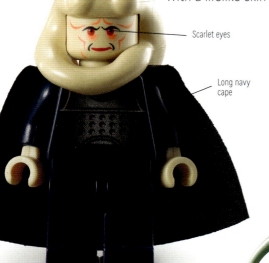

Skull and lekku (head-tails) are all one head piece

Scarlet eyes

Long navy cape

Bib Fortuna Jabba's chief of staff was the first minifigure of the Twi'lek species to be made.

I'M SO RARE, THERE'S A BOUNTY ON MY HEAD!

Boba Fett This unique variant of the bounty hunter—in set 10123—is the first minifigure to have printed arms.

Green Mandalorian armor

Armored knee pads

Blaster

Jabba the Hutt Jabba's head and torso are made from a single mold, but the tail comes in two separate parts.

Plain, unmarked eyes

Fingers molded on hands

Tail pieces fit into torso socket

YOU ARE NOT THE DROID I AM LOOKING FOR.

Breathing filters

Oxygen-filled rebreather pack

Commanders wear orange pauldrons

Black gloves

Printed belt holds blaster ammo

Sandtrooper To aid breathing in the extreme desert climate, this minifigure wears a rebreather pack.

DID YOU KNOW? Boba Fett from Cloud City (10123) is one of the rarest and most collectible minifigures.

Molded antennae

Elongated snout

Arms with painted tan stripes

Brown hips and sand blue legs are unique to Greedo

Greedo A bumpy head mold was designed specially for Greedo. His large eyes are fitted with light reflectors.

Textured hair pieces were not available at this time

Shirt with dark blue collar

Dual-colored cape is blue outside and yellow inside

Lando Calrissian Lando's head piece is the first human skin-colored minifigure head for the *Star Wars* theme.

Blaster made from megaphone piece

Cloud City In part of this set (10123), which features seven minifigures, the villainous Darth Vader has trapped Han Solo in carbonite. The Lando minifigure tries to rescue the Han Solo minifigure.

LEGO® SPIDER-MAN™

The second year of the LEGO Spider-Man theme moved away from LEGO® Studios, with three sets based on the first Spider-Man movie. Major new minifigures introduced were the Green Goblin's alter ego, Norman Osborn, as well as Peter Parker in his wrestling costume.

New balaclava print covers mouth and nose

White gloves

I'M YOUR FRIENDLY NEIGHBORHOOD SPIDER-MAN.

I'M JUST NOT SURE GREEN IS MY COLOR.

Determined expression

Spider-Man's wondrous web

New faded spider and web print on torso

Double-sided head The other side of Osborn's head shows a scared expression.

Norman Osborn This shirtless, yellow-torsoed minifigure represents Norman Osborn before his transformation into the Green Goblin in The Origins (4851).

Wrestling Peter For his fight against Bone Saw McGraw, Parker fashions this costume, which is only found in Spider-Man's First Chase (4850).

LEGO® EXPLORE LITTLE ROBOTS™

The Little Robots from the BBC children's series of the same name was a LEGO Explore theme for two years, starting in 2003. Five sets were released featuring Tiny, Sporty, and the team.

Red shoulder pads

Sporty This beefy robot helps out in the Junk Yard. He has a green, red, and gold body.

Torso has switch pattern

Tiny Specially molded hands help this little robot hold the Day and Night lever in the Junk Yard.

Belt molded around waist

Prominent black nose for sniffing

Messy Tiny's green-and-golden robot-dog pet from the Tiny and Friends set (7441) is always running away.

LEGO® RACERS

This year saw the release of the second Williams F1 Racer set, a 1:27 scale racecar with a driver. The set was based on the well-known British racing team and preceded Ferrari and Lamborghini as Racers licenses. This was the last Williams F1 set and minifigure produced.

New torso with polo shirt and jacket

Same face print as original 2002 Mary Jane

New white-and-pink torso

Peter Parker A studious-looking Parker is off on a school trip to the science lab in The Origins (4851). Watch out for spiders, Peter …

Mary Jane Both of this year's Mary Jane minifigures have the same hair piece. No other minifigure wears it in orange.

Large white eyes

Bright yellow helmet

Sticker can be placed here

F1 Racer The Williams F1 Team Racer (8374) includes an "HP Invent" sticker for this competitive racer's torso.

LEGO® DISCOVERY

LEGO Discovery was a one-year theme focusing on real-life space flight. Only one of the six sets featured minifigures: Lunar Lander (10029). The other sets were replicas of NASA spacecraft.

Helmet disconnect clasp

NASA logo

Apollo Astronaut A NASA space suit is vital for this minifigure's out-of-this-world experiences.

Ogel has one red eye and one black

I CAN'T FAIL THIS TIME ... CAN I?

Black mechanical shoulder pads

Blue hook replaces red one on 2002 version

Ogel The minifigure's only design change since 2002 is the color of his hook. Now, Ogel feels ready for his final battle against Alpha Team.

Transparent blue bubble helmet

New silver outline around scarab logo

Black-and-red torso and legs

Ogel's ice orbs can freeze anything

OGEL AND HIS MINIONS
Ogel's plan is to freeze the world with the help of his Skeleton Drones and ice orbs. Thanks to his powerful mind control orbs, the skeletons follow their leader's orders without hesitation.

Super Ice Drone This drone's black skull head piece with white printing and red eyes is unique.

Skeleton Drone This year, Ogel's underlings wear helmets to protect them from their own ice orbs.

2004

THIS YEAR SAW THE comeback of some old favorites, as LEGO® Alpha Team and LEGO® DUPLO® returned. LEGO® Harry Potter™ and BIONICLE® also remained strong. LEGO® Spider-Man™ swung back into action as *Spider-Man 2* arrived in theaters. Ferrari sets were released for the first time and LEGO® *Star Wars*™ continued to flourish with the launch of iconic classic sets and sets from the Expanded Universe.

LEGO ALPHA TEAM

After a year's absence, Alpha Team returned to stop Ogel in *Mission Deep Freeze*. With a new logo, redesigned minifigures, and two new minifigure heroes—Diamond Tooth and Arrow—it was a new team for a new era.

GOOD THING I WORE MY THERMAL UNDERWEAR!

New head piece features black sunglasses and gritted teeth

New, triangular Alpha Team logo

Magnifying glass

New uniform with blue sleeve and silver zipper details

Dash Alpha Team leader Dash has a completely new look in 2004.

Red robot eyes

Tee Vee Alpha Team's communications expert has appeared in three very different guises—a TV with legs; an underwater vehicle; and now, finally, an android minifigure.

ALPHA TEAM
This year, agents Cam and Crunch were replaced by Arrow and Diamond Tooth. All six of the year's sets featured Alpha Team vehicles in icy colors, including Flex's Chill Speeder (4742) and Charge's Ice Blade (4743).

Special magnifying lens

Bandana printed on head piece

Diamond Tooth New for 2004, Diamond Tooth is the mining expert for Alpha Team and pilots the Tundra Tracker (4744).

Arrow Alpha Team's new mechanic has the same torso as Diamond Tooth, apart from his right arm.

LEGO *STAR WARS*

2004 saw the release of a number of classic LEGO *Star Wars* sets, including a new version of the *Millennium Falcon* (4504). This version of the ship featured both Han Solo and Princess Leia in their Hoth outfits from *Star Wars: Episode V The Empire Strikes Back.*

Hoth Princess Leia This variant features Leia's iconic bun hairstyle. In 2011, the rebel leader has braids instead.

NEXT TIME, I'M DRIVING!

Print details on torso include the rebel leader's insignia

Skin-colored hands—the 2011 variant has white-gloved hands

Printed hood—Han's 2011 variant comes with detachable hood

Furry hood protects Han in a chilly blizzard

Hoth Han Solo The rebel pilot is dressed warmly for the icy conditions on Hoth.

Hoth Han Solo Variant This rare yellow variant featured in a promotional version of set 4504 with all-yellow minifigures.

Han's handy electrobinoculars hang from a strap

Large sensor dish

Chewbacca and Han sit in the cockpit of the promotional set, featuring yellow minifigures

Millennium Falcon The ship's triangular shaped panels can be pulled open on their hinges to reveal all the action inside.

DID YOU KNOW?
Eight minifigure-scale versions of the *Millennium Falcon* have been released so far.

LEGO® RACERS

Ferrari was introduced to LEGO Racers in 2004, with minifigures of pit crew members and real-life Formula 1 drivers Michael Schumacher and Rubens Barrichello. Four System sets were released this year, as well as Ferrari-based LEGO® Technic sets. The LEGO Racers relationship with Ferrari would prove to be a long-lasting one.

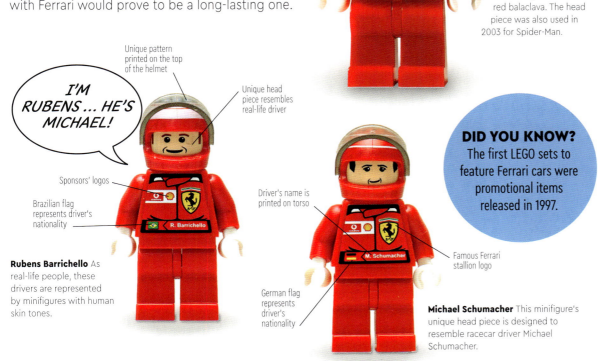

Removable helmet

F1 Ferrari Pit Crew Member Underneath his helmet, the minifigure wears a red balaclava. The head piece was also used in 2003 for Spider-Man.

I'M RUBENS ... HE'S MICHAEL!

Unique pattern printed on the top of the helmet

Unique head piece resembles real-life driver

Sponsors' logos

Brazilian flag represents driver's nationality

Rubens Barrichello As real-life people, these drivers are represented by minifigures with human skin tones.

Driver's name is printed on torso

German flag represents driver's nationality

Famous Ferrari stallion logo

Michael Schumacher This minifigure's unique head piece is designed to resemble racecar driver Michael Schumacher.

DID YOU KNOW?
The first LEGO sets to feature Ferrari cars were promotional items released in 1997.

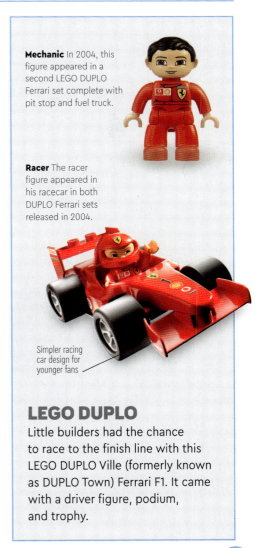

Mechanic In 2004, this figure appeared in a second LEGO DUPLO Ferrari set complete with pit stop and fuel truck.

Racer The racer figure appeared in his racecar in both DUPLO Ferrari sets released in 2004.

Simpler racing car design for younger fans

LEGO DUPLO

Little builders had the chance to race to the finish line with this LEGO DUPLO Ville (formerly known as DUPLO Town) Ferrari F1. It came with a driver figure, podium, and trophy.

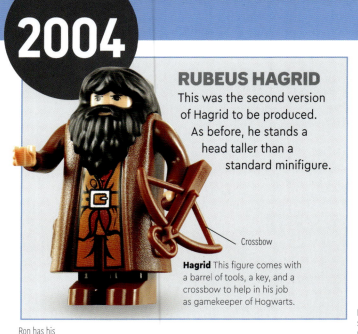

RUBEUS HAGRID

This was the second version of Hagrid to be produced. As before, he stands a head taller than a standard minifigure.

Crossbow

Hagrid This figure comes with a barrel of tools, a key, and a crossbow to help in his job as gamekeeper of Hogwarts.

Ron has his trademark orange hair piece

Neville has the same torso and legs as the 2004 variants of Harry and Ron

Hermione wears the Time-Turner around her neck

Casual Ron Weasley Ron's torso with striped sweater and open shirt is unique to two Hogwarts Express sets released in 2004.

Neville Longbottom Harry's friend Neville is a minifigure for the first time. His unique head piece has a nervous face in Professor Lupin's Classroom (4752).

Time-Turner Hermione Granger Hermione has a unique detail on her Gryffindor uniform—a magical Time-Turner. A robed variant was also released.

For the first time, Harry Potter's head is not yellow

Harry's tie and sweater are printed with the Gryffindor house colors

Third-Year Harry Potter
Three minifigures of Harry in his Gryffindor uniform were released this year. Each has the same head, torso, and legs, but two have robes.

STUDENTS

This year brought new versions of Harry Potter, Hermione Granger, Draco Malfoy, Ron Weasley, and Neville Longbottom. Harry actually appeared in six different incarnations, although many of the variations were very minor.

LEGO HARRY POTTER

Harry Potter and the Prisoner of Azkaban got the LEGO treatment in 2004. Sets included new versions of Hogwarts Castle (4757), Hagrid's Hut (4754), and the Hogwarts Express (4758), along with several models depicting key scenes from the film. There were 10 new sets in total, plus the first mini-set—the Knight Bus (4695). In this year, all the minifigures were remade with representative human skin tones, apart from Snape, who retained his glow-in-the-dark head.

DID YOU KNOW?
2004 saw the release of the first and only motorized version of the Hogwarts Express train (10132).

The head is printed with a gaping mouth but no eyes

The 2011 version has a gray head and arms instead of green

Tattered gray robe and hood

Dementor The first version of the ghoulish Azkaban guard was released in four sets. It comes with a LEGO dish piece that can be attached to the base to keep it upright.

Unique light purple witch's hat

Shimmering blue gown with purple accessories

Unposable sloped piece

Professor Trelawney Harry's Divination teacher stands out from the other minifigure professors, wearing a unique outfit.

Snarling mouth

Werewolf mask This removable piece can be put over Lupin's human head in place of his hair piece.

TEACHERS

New teacher minifigures graced the LEGO Harry Potter line this year. Professor Sybill Trelawney appeared for the first time in minifigure form, as did Remus Lupin (in both human and werewolf forms). Professors Dumbledore and Snape both got updates, with the latter also being imitated by a Boggart.

Gray robes

Professor Lupin The scratches on his face and his tattered suit hint at this minifigure's secret. A full moon would reveal it ...

Glow-in-the-dark head

Unique torso is printed with Neville's grandmother's cardigan and scarf

Boggart This shape-shifter has taken the form of Neville Longbottom's worst fear: Professor Snape!

LEGO® CASTLE

The second LEGO Castle subtheme to be called Knights' Kingdom featured minifigure-scale sets and buildable action-figure sets. The Villainous Vladek and his army of Shadow Knights battled the forces of King Mathias and his four brave knights: Rascus, Danju, Jayko, and Santis. Seven sets were released in this first year of the line.

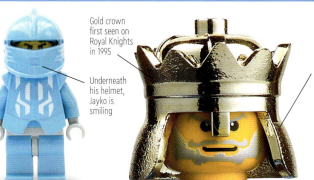

Gold crown first seen on Royal Knights in 1995

Underneath his helmet, Jayko is smiling

Jayko The youngest of the four knights, Jayko is often known as "the Rookie." His main color, medium blue, is new.

Crown covers the sides of the head and the nose

Danju's hair is dark tan underneath his helmet

Danju The oldest of King Mathias' four knights, Danju is also the wisest. His dark purple color is also new this year.

All four heroes have lift-up visors

Printed torso

Removable armor

Rascus This great warrior is famous for his agility and flexibility.

Rascus Without Armor Of the four hero knights, only Rascus gets a nonarmored variant.

Medieval helmet protects face

Angry expression

Red breastplate with scorpion symbol

Mathias' symbols are a crown and a lion

King Mathias Appearing in two sets this year, King Mathias rules his kingdom, Morcia, with wisdom and nobility.

Plain torso under printed armor

Santis wears dark gray gloves

Santis This knight is famous for his great strength. Santis was also released as a larger action figure, along with six other Knights' Kingdom characters.

The Guardian does not have a hat or hair piece—just printed hair

Detachable gray beard

The Guardian This wise old minifigure protects the Heart of the Shield of Ages in the Citadel of Orlan. He will only give it to those who are worthy.

Brown torso and legs with gray details

This striking minifigure wears black armor with red details

Shadow Knight Vladek's loyal Shadow Knight minifigures help him carry out his schemes and stratagems.

Vladek Leader of the Shadow Knights, the wicked Vladek captures King Mathias and tries to take his place as ruler.

Hat and head pieces are unchanged

The tie on the previous version was black

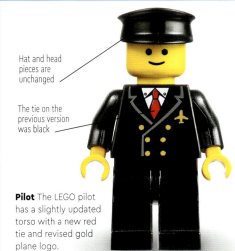

Pilot The LEGO pilot has a slightly updated torso with a new red tie and revised gold plane logo.

LEGO® WORLD CITY

Ten years after its first release, the classic LEGO Town set, Century Skyway (6597) was reissued as a LEGO World City set (10159). The 12 minifigures that came with the new set had minimal changes from their original 1994 versions.

The passenger is casually dressed

Passenger The 2004 version has a new head, featuring eyebrows and a wide smile.

Spider-Man's Street Chase Spider-Man is out to catch two crooks in this 73-piece set (4853).

New minifigure trike design

HEY, COME BACK HERE WITH THAT!

Web line

City rat

Mary Jane Watson As well as a new head piece, this year's Mary Jane minifigure also gets a more realistic hair color.

Unique torso print

DID YOU KNOW? 2004 included the first appearances of J. Jonah Jameson and Harry Osborn as minifigures.

LEGO SPIDER-MAN

LEGO Spider-Man returned in 2004 as *Spider-Man 2* hit movie theaters. This time, Aunt May, Mary Jane, and the other minifigures had faces and hands matching the on-screen characters' skin tones. The line included five new sets and 17 minifigures, including four different versions of Doctor Octopus. LEGO Spidey would next swing into action as part of the LEGO® Marvel Super Heroes theme in 2012.

Aunt May is the only minifigure with this light gray ponytail

Head piece is unchanged since 2003

Aunt May This Aunt May's minifigure is unique to Doc Ock's Bank Robbery (4854).

Unimpressed expression

J. Jonah Jameson In his first LEGO appearance, Peter's boss becomes the 10th minifigure to wear this severe black hair piece.

Loosened collar and tie

Spider-Man The wall-crawler keeps the same head seen on his 2002 and 2003 versions, but has an updated web design on his torso and legs.

New web design in 2004

Spider-Man's costume is a darker blue in 2004

Casual vest over zipped jacket

Casual blue pants

Peter Parker The first Peter minifigure with a realistic skin tone was also the last Peter minifigure until 2019!

Same hair piece as J. Jonah Jameson, but in brown

This blue suit can also be seen on Bruce Wayne in 2006

Hand piece

SPIDER-MAN AND FRIENDS

This was the third time Spider-Man had appeared in minifigure form. Along with the webbed wonder, the 2004 sets showcased all the first film series' major characters, including Aunt May, Peter Parker, Harry Osborn, J. Jonah Jameson, and Mary Jane Watson. The new Peter Parker figure was more casually dressed than previous versions and was not wearing glasses.

Harry Osborn Peter Parker's best friend has two minifigures in 2004: one wearing a blue suit (above) and the other wearing a gray pinstripe suit.

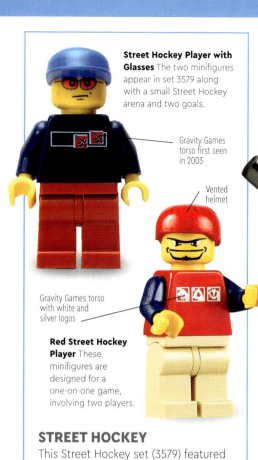

Street Hockey Player with Glasses The two minifigures appear in set 3579 along with a small Street Hockey arena and two goals.

Gravity Games torso first seen in 2003

Vented helmet

Gravity Games torso with white and silver logos

Red Street Hockey Player These minifigures are designed for a one-on-one game, involving two players.

STREET HOCKEY

This Street Hockey set (3579) featured two minifigures on movable bases controlled by levers. One seemed to be much more confident of winning than the other!

Standard helmet visor worn upside down

WHAT DO YOU MEAN I HAVE TO BUILD MY OWN PENALTY BOX?

Black body armor

Stubbled Hockey Player The minifigures are divided into two teams—black and white. Their body armor shows their team colors.

Helmet originally designed for LEGO® Adventurers pilots

White body armor

Determined Hockey Player Ice Hockey can be dangerous, so the minifigures protect themselves with body armor and helmets.

LEGO® SPORTS

The Hockey subtheme of Sports first appeared in 2003, but there were no minifigures—just brick-built players. In 2004, one set featured minifigures: NHL Championship Challenge (3578). There were eight ice hockey players, each with a different face. They were attached to movable bases, controlled by levers and designed for a two-player game.

Doc Ock uses his tentacle arms to ensnare his foes

Doctor Octopus Thanks to his grabber arms, Doctor Octopus is slightly more complex than the other 4+ figures.

Peter Parker Unlike minifigures, 4+ figures have molded noses and ears.

Spider-Man The 4+ figure has similar costume detailing to the minifigure version.

Doc Ock Due to his unique design, Doc Ock is made up of 26 different LEGO pieces.

Bendable tentacles

I GIVE GREAT HUGS!

A special neck clip attaches Doc Ock's robotic arms to his minifigure.

DOCTOR OCTOPUS

The villainous Doc Ock came in four versions in 2004: frowning, smiling, angry, and in his Fusion Lab outfit.

Green suit

LEGO 4855

Spider-Man's Train Rescue In this set (4855), Spider-Man battles Doc Ock on top of a subway train. It also features minifigures of J. Jonah Jameson and a subway train conductor.

SPIDER-MAN™ 4+

LEGO Spider-Man was the only licensed theme in the 4+ line, which was first introduced in 2003. At 4 in (10 cm) tall, the figures were larger than minifigures, with little or no building required—perfect for little hands.

Classic grin • 1978
• Townsperson • LEGOLAND Town

Full beard, bangs, and eyepatch
• 1989 • Captain Redbeard
• LEGO Pirates

Bangs and defined lips • 1989
• Female Pirate • LEGO Pirates

Mustache and stubble
• 1989 • Blue Pirate • LEGO Pirates

Headset and eyebrows
• 1992 • Space Police Chief
• LEGO Space

Purple eyeshadow and glasses
• 2001 • Cam Attaway
• LEGO Alpha Team

Scary skull • 2004
• Super Ice Drone
• LEGO Alpha Team

Scared face • 2007
• Crown Knight • LEGO Castle

Alien head with fangs • 2009
• Kranxx • LEGO Space

Alien head with tongue • 2009
• Squidman • LEGO Space

Toy robot head • 2012 • Clockwork
Robot • LEGO Minifigures

Minotaur head with horns • 2012
• Minotaur • LEGO Minifigures

HEADS UP, EVERYONE!

THE BASIC DESIGN of the standard minifigure head—a rounded piece with a knob on top—has not changed since the early years. The first heads all looked the same, but in 1989, LEGO® Pirates introduced new prints featuring facial hair, bangs, and more. The launch of licensed themes in 1999 saw a massive innovation—specially molded heads created for less humanlike characters— and soon many other themes introduced these, too. The reversible head debuted in 2001, which allowed a minifigure to change his or her expression when they felt like it.

Windswept face • 2013
• Skydiver • LEGO Minifigures

Queasy face • 2014
• Queasy Man • LEGO Creator Expert

Full beard (with gray) and eyepatch
• 2020 • Captain Redbeard
• LEGO Ideas

Two heads • 2021
• PoulErik • LEGO NINJAGO

Cool shades • 1992 • Pool Guy
• LEGO Paradisa

Robot head • 1994 • Spyrius Droid
• LEGO Space

Droid head with large eye shield
• 1997 • Blue Droid • LEGO Space

Ringlets • 2000
• Queen Leonora • LEGO Castle

Huge grin • 2001 • Flex
• LEGO Alpha Team

Cold cheeks • 2009
• Carol Singer • LEGO Creator Expert

Large-jawed alien head • 2011
• Alien Trooper • LEGO Space

Hammerhead shark head • 2011
• Hammerhead Warrior
• LEGO Atlantis

Ancient Egyptian jackal head
• 2011 • Anubis Guard
• LEGO Minifigures

Big-eyed alien head • 2012
• Classic Alien • LEGO Minifigures

Snake head with fangs • 2012
• Lizaru • LEGO NINJAGO

Two-headed snake head • 2012
• Fangdam • LEGO NINJAGO

**Lion head mask over lion head
print** • 2013 • Laval
• LEGO Legends of Chima

Insectoid head • 2013
• Winged Mosquitoid • LEGO Space

Cookie-shaped head • 2013
• Gingerbread Man
• LEGO Minifigures

Alien head with tentacles
• 2015 • Alien Trooper
• LEGO Minifigures

Hairy monster head • 2015
• Square Foot • LEGO Minifigures

Fairground face paints • 2019
• Girl • LEGO City

Possessed face • 2019
• Mr. Branson • LEGO Hidden Side

Anthropomorphic pig head
• 2020 • Pigsy • LEGO Monkie Kid

Happy alien head • 2022
• Space Creature • LEGO Minifigures

Snowperson head • 2022
• Snowman • LEGO Minifigures

Face mask • 2023 • Paramedic
• LEGO City

Glasses and colorful eyepatch
• 2024 • Train Kid • LEGO Minifigures

"Invisible" head • 2024
• Mr. Pale • LEGO NINJAGO

Breathing apparatus

Air tanks

Protective visor

Fire extinguisher

THIS YEAR WAS SMOKING HOT!

Heroic Firefighter This firefighter looks every bit the rugged hero, with a dimpled chin and determined expression.

2005

IT WAS A YEAR full of new play themes and new innovations for the LEGO Group. A new LEGO® City theme (an evolution of LEGO® Town and World City), plus LEGO® Dino Attack, LEGO® Power Racers, and LEGO® Tiny Turbos all made their first appearances. The LEGO® Factory initiative allowed fans to design sets for other fans to order. Sets based on *Star Wars: Episode III Revenge of the Sith* and *Harry Potter and the Goblet of Fire* helped fans bring the movies to life. Minifigure star power was also on display in new LEGO® *Star Wars*™ video games and mini-movies.

LEGO CITY

A new LEGO City theme took over from World City this year and immediately expanded its scope by adding construction to the traditional police and fire sets. LEGO City gave builders the chance to play in the "real world," with minifigures representing both everyday heroes and the ordinary folks who keep a city running.

Cool Firefighter Appearing on Day 1 of the 2005 City Advent Calendar has given this minifigure a confidence boost!

White helmet

Reflective stripes

First time this helmet appeared in a color other than black or white

FIRE
The LEGO City Fire minifigures were on the job in 2005, with a new Fire Station (7240), Fire Truck (7239), Fire Helicopter (7238), and Fire Car (7241). To the rescue!

Flame on badge

Radio

Happy Firefighter With a cheerful smile, this minifigure is always happy to help his fellow citizens.

Signal paddle

Working flashlight

SOUND THE ALARM! SOMEONE DRANK MY COFFEE!

Gray beard and mustache

Flashlight Cop This police officer has a light-up flashlight to shed some light on mysteries.

Traffic Cop His stern expression suggests that this cop is not to be messed with!

POLICE
The LEGO City Police made its first appearance in two years with four new sets, including a Police Station (7237). After this, the theme would virtually disappear until 2008.

Police Chief This officer shares the same head as the chess piece version of Jayko from Knights' Kingdom in 2005.

Knitted cap

New head with dark blue shades

Gold tooth

Leather jacket

Inmate number

DID YOU KNOW?
Police dogs made their debut in LEGO City sets this year.

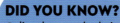

Crook With an arched eyebrow and a sly grin, this new minifigure looks like trouble!

Police Biker This minifigure comes with a new torso, designed to look like a leather jacket.

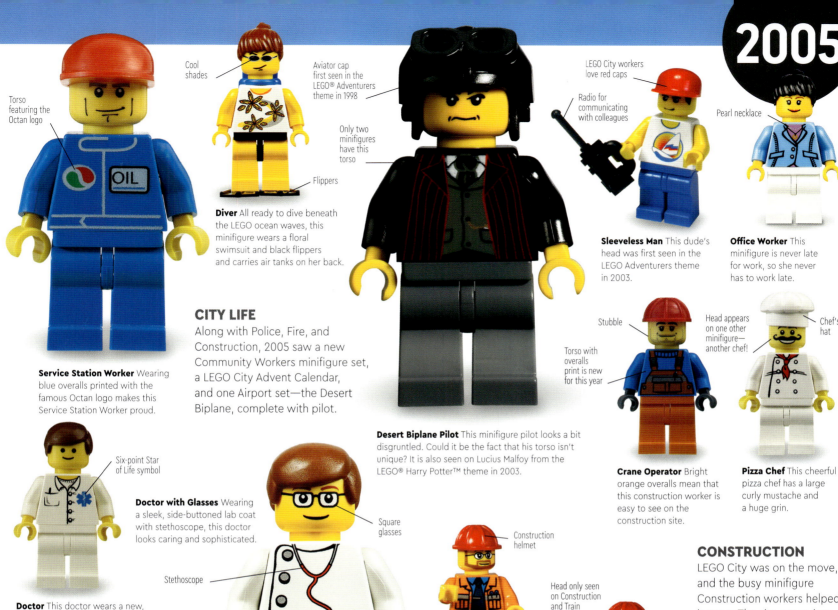

Cool shades

Aviator cap first seen in the LEGO® Adventurers theme in 1998

Only two minifigures have this torso

Flippers

Diver All ready to dive beneath the LEGO ocean waves, this minifigure wears a floral swimsuit and black flippers and carries air tanks on her back.

Torso featuring the Octan logo

OIL

Service Station Worker Wearing blue overalls printed with the famous Octan logo makes this Service Station Worker proud.

LEGO City workers love red caps

Radio for communicating with colleagues

Pearl necklace

Sleeveless Man This dude's head was first seen in the LEGO Adventurers theme in 2003.

Office Worker This minifigure is never late for work, so she never has to work late.

CITY LIFE

Along with Police, Fire, and Construction, 2005 saw a new Community Workers minifigure set, a LEGO City Advent Calendar, and one Airport set—the Desert Biplane, complete with pilot.

Desert Biplane Pilot This minifigure pilot looks a bit disgruntled. Could it be the fact that his torso isn't unique? It is also seen on Lucius Malfoy from the LEGO® Harry Potter™ theme in 2003.

Stubble

Torso with overalls print is new for this year

Crane Operator Bright orange overalls mean that this construction worker is easy to see on the construction site.

Head appears on one other minifigure—another chef!

Chef's hat

Pizza Chef This cheerful pizza chef has a large curly mustache and a huge grin.

Six-point Star of Life symbol

Doctor with Glasses Wearing a sleek, side-buttoned lab coat with stethoscope, this doctor looks caring and sophisticated.

Stethoscope

Square glasses

Doctor This doctor wears a new, buttoned shirt featuring the blue EMT Star of Life emblem.

HOSPITAL

The first hospital-themed model in 17 years appeared in 2005, with a promotional Paramedic set offered in Czechia and at LEGOLAND® Windsor, UK. A new torso design with the Star of Life symbol also made an appearance this year.

Construction helmet

Formal shirt and tie

Site Supervisor As the head of the team, the foreman must look the part—he wears a shirt and tie under his jacket.

Head only seen on Construction and Train minifigures

Tired eyes

Worker with Broom He may look weary, but this worker loves making a clean sweep of things.

CONSTRUCTION

LEGO City was on the move, and the busy minifigure Construction workers helped it grow. The site supervisor minifigure kept an eye on the workers as they operated heavy machinery and started another new building.

DID YOU KNOW?
These were the first construction-themed sets in five years.

LEGO® CLIKITS™

LEGO CLIKITS was an arts and crafts line for creating room decorations, gifts, and accessories. Only three CLIKITS figures were released, and each one came in a separate set.

Flower in hair

Star With the name Star, it's no surprise that this figure came in a set (7535) with lots of star pieces.

Hip hairstyle

Daisy This figure was included in set 7534 with pieces designed to make jewelry.

Aqua skirt

Construction Site This set (7243) includes a large crane, a dump truck, a rock crusher with a conveyor belt, and three minifigures to operate all the machinery.

LEGO® STAR WARS™

Star Wars: Episode III *Revenge of the Sith* dominated the LEGO assortment in 2005, with 13 sets devoted to the new movie. As well as several new minifigures, light-up lightsabers were added to some sets. Anakin Skywalker's transformation into Darth Vader provided the climax to the three prequels and a compelling LEGO set.

Head button turns lightsaber on and off

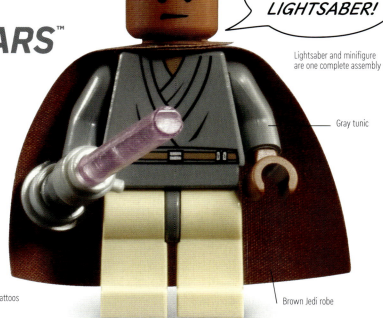

THESE PUT THE "LIGHT" IN LIGHTSABER!

Lightsaber and minifigure are one complete assembly

Gray tunic

Brown Jedi robe

Molded hood

Light-up Lightsaber Obi-Wan Kenobi This new variant of Obi-Wan appears in Ultimate Lightsaber Duel (7257), where he must fight his former apprentice, Anakin Skywalker.

Light-up Lightsaber Mace Windu This Mace Windu minifigure is pretty special—he is the only minifigure to wield a purple light-up lightsaber.

Mirialan headdress is exclusive to Luminara

Facial tattoos

Mirialan symbol

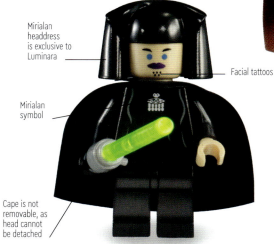

Cape is not removable, as head cannot be detached

Light-up Lightsaber Luminara Unduli This skilled Jedi Master has a unique head piece with facial tattoos that represent her physical accomplishments.

THE LIGHT SIDE

2005 saw the first appearance of Jedi Mace Windu and Luminara Unduli in minifigure form. There was also a new version of Obi-Wan Kenobi.

THE DARK SIDE

The *Star Wars* villains have their share of minifigures, too, with two versions of battle-scarred Anakin, a new Darth Vader, and an exclusive and highly valued Scout Trooper.

Jawa This shady character hides under a large hood element. It's perfect for snooping around and carrying out shady droid deals.

Orange eyes glow with mischief

Ion blaster

Specially fitted cloak for short-legged minifigures

Hilt of the light-up lightsaber is joined to arm piece

Battle scars

Cyborg hand

Light-up Lightsaber Anakin Skywalker This powerful Jedi is the only minifigure to have this hair piece in this color.

Gray, scarred head under helmet

Single-piece helmet used for all Vader minifigures until 2015

Control panel

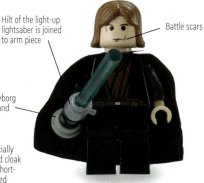

Darth Vader This is the first variant of the Vader minifigure to come without a cape.

Plain black head visible through visor

Ammo pouches

Scout Trooper Camouflaged armor keeps this minifigure well hidden during operations in the jungles and swamps.

FIRST APPEARANCES

Fierce cyborg General Grievous made his debut in LEGO form in 2005, alongside brick-built versions of the Buzz Droid, the FX-6 Surgical Droid, and the Dwarf Spider Droid.

Unique skull-like head piece

General Grievous This fearsome cyborg figure can hold four lightsabers at once.

CLONE TROOPERS

Two new styles of clone trooper, an Aerial Trooper and a new Clone Pilot, were released in 2005. Both featured a new clone helmet based on *Revenge of the Sith*.

Grievous has two blue lightsabers and two green ones

Republic symbol

Air supply hose

Clone Pilot With a life-support pack on his torso, this minifigure is ready for takeoff!

Life-support pack

Missiles made from spear gun pieces

Jetpack attached with a neck bracket and back knob

Blaster

Aerial Trooper This minifigure has a jetpack and specializes in air attacks.

New style of helmet with side holes

Scale mail armor

Barbarian armor new this year

Gritted teeth

Barbarian Armor Viking
Barbarian-style armor really helps this Viking get in the mood for a rampage.

Scale Mail Viking Despite a new torso with scale mail resembling the scales of a fish or a reptile, this Viking still seems peeved!

LEGO® VIKINGS

Courageous Scandinavian warriors battled mythological monsters in five exciting LEGO Vikings sets in this theme. Minifigures featured many new torsos and heads, as well as a new small white barb piece used as the horns for the helmets. Vikings would be replaced by the new Castle line in 2007.

Dragon figurehead

Fearsome Viking warrior

Cage prison

Viking Ship Challenges the Midgard Serpent
This set (7018) features the first galley made by the LEGO Group and is the first set to include a sea serpent (not shown). It features the Viking King minifigure and six Viking warriors.

Golden helmet reflects his status

White beard and sideburns

Black cape

Viking King As leader of the Vikings, it's only right that the caped Viking King is regally dressed in red.

White barb used as horn

Lines add to rugged look

Handsome Viking This Viking has a rugged charm and is one of the few Viking minifigures to have a happy expression.

Armor breastplate

Stern Viking Featuring the new speckled armor breastplate, this Viking is ready to defend his village from fearsome monsters.

Studded collar

Leather belt

Patterned round shield

Serious Viking This minifigure is included in only one set—Viking Fortress (7019), in which the Vikings fight the Fafnir Dragon.

DID YOU KNOW?
Most of the monsters in the Vikings sets came from Norse myths.

LEGO DINO ATTACK

Dangerous dinosaurs go on a rampage and only the Dino team can stop them in this new theme. Each set included a Dino team vehicle and a mutant dinosaur. The minifigures featured new head prints and detailed torso designs showing a range of equipment.

DID YOU KNOW?
LEGO Dino Attack was released in Europe as Dino 2010, with some changes to the sets and story.

Battle scar

Viper This dino tracker never leaves the house without his well-equipped zipped-up vest.

Digger This Digger minifigure features the new torso with red harness and binoculars pattern.

A steady hand, even in the face of danger

Utility belt

Balaclava

Specs The balaclava-clad head on this minifigure is also featured on a LEGO® Mars Mission astronaut from 2007.

Specs with Tools Specs' new torso has tools with lime green handles and a red book.

Rope

Clothes hold various tools

Shadow This minifigure's new head is specially camouflaged for creeping up on the dinosaurs undetected.

Sir Rascus In combat, Rascus is agile and flexible, just like the monkey emblem on his shield and armor.

Blue sword

Monkey emblem

Sir Santis A new shield and breastplate features a bear, reflecting Santis' strength and fortitude.

The bear's ferocious teeth are visible

Danju wields his sword with skill

Sir Danju The wise Danju's emblem is a wolf, printed on his new armor breastplate and his shield.

Wolf emblem

Each of the knights' visors is slightly different in design

Sir Jayko Although he is the youngest of the knights, Jayko is powerful and fast. The new hawk emblem design reflects this.

Hawk emblem

Vladek is an expert sword fighter

Dark Lord The new Vladek minifigure now features a red breastplate with an image of a scorpion.

Beneath the helmet is a scowling face

LEGO® CASTLE

LEGO® Knights' Kingdom returned for its second year in 2005, with seven sets. Both the story—King Mathias and four brave knights versus Vladek and his Shadow Knights—and the majority of the minifigures remained largely the same as in 2004. Many of the new minifigures released for this theme were part of a chess set.

Black ponytail hair piece

Evil skull face

Black Chess Queen This sinister, skeleton-faced minifigure is a chess piece.

Royal staff

Chrome gold crown

Black fabric cape

Black Chess King Chess minifigures were only released as part of the chess set (851499).

Head is also used on the Jing Lee the Wanderer minifigure from the LEGO Adventurers theme in 2003

Same armor as the 2004 Jayko knight minifigure

Sloped piece

White Chess Queen This minifigure is one of the queens from the Knights' Kingdom chess set.

BIONICLE®

2005 brought more ways to play in the BIONICLE universe. Characters previously depicted only as buildable models became smaller single-piece figures, battling new Visorak spider pieces. Despite having no articulation, each one was posed for action.

Distinctive design based on larger buildable version

Toa Hordika Matau All four of this year's playsets included the same six Toa Hordika figures, including the brave Matau.

Hands can grip standard minifigure accessories

Toa Hordika Nuju The Toa of Ice is completely white. He rubs his Hordika Teeth tools together to create an ultrasonic hum.

Toa Hordika Nokama All in blue, this figure is the Toa of Water. She can create anything from water—from a stream to a tidal wave.

Base fits on to standard LEGO knobs

White and black mandibles

Visorak Keelerak Agile and strong, this figure has large mandibles and razor-sharp legs.

LEGO® HARRY POTTER™

The LEGO Harry Potter play theme focused on *Harry Potter and the Goblet of Fire* in 2005, with four new sets. Three of the four sets dealt with the three deadly tasks from the Triwizard Tournament. Three new versions of Harry appeared this year, and new minifigures included Viktor Krum, Professor Karkaroff, and Mad-Eye Moody.

Bowl-cut hair

Torn uniform

Ron Weasley This minifigure's head is reversible—turn it around to see Ron sleeping!

"POTTER" is printed in large letters on the back of the torso

Harry Potter™ This is one of three Harry Potter minifigures released for *Harry Potter and the Goblet of Fire*. Each one wears a different outfit suitable for the trials Harry must face.

False eye

Unique torso printed with a shirt and a buckled jacket

Until 2018, all versions of Dumbledore have the same beard

Whiskery facial markings

Ratlike teeth

Gloved replacement hand

Mad-Eye Moody With his scarred face and false eye, this minifigure has a unique head piece.

Professor Dumbledore In this variant, the headmaster wears blue dress robes.

Same uniform as the 2004 minifigure

Hermione Granger This minifigure has a reversible head. The other side shows her in an enchanted sleep.

Wormtail This minifigure's unique head shows signs of his Animagus form—a rat.

Shark head piece fits over minifigure head

Head glows in the dark

Lord Voldemort This is the first actual minifigure of Lord Voldemort. Prior to this, he featured only as a face on one side of Professor Quirrell's head.

Large furry hat

Jacket with toggle fastenings

Face now has smaller nostrils and eyes changed from red to clear

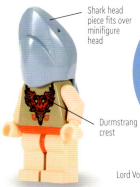

DID YOU KNOW?
In set 4767, LEGO designers created a dragon's egg with a magnetic piece on one side. Harry has a magnetic handle so he can hold it.

Durmstrang crest

Shark Head Viktor This minifigure shows Viktor Krum when he is half-shark, half-human.

Lord Voldemort

Graveyard Duel This is one of the alternative builds that could be made from the pieces in Graveyard Duel (4766).

Viktor Krum This torso piece is identical to Igor Karkaroff's, but Victor's younger-looking face makes it easy to distinguish between the two.

Igor Karkaroff The scowling face with goatee is unique to this minifigure.

Merperson This Merperson's unique head, torso, and tail prints are not found on any other minifigure.

Hair piece also used for Poison Ivy from LEGO® DC Batman™

Black Death Eater mask

Wormtail

Black skeleton is unique to this set

Robe used on the minifigures of Voldemort and the Dementors

Death Eater This Death Eater resembles Lucius Malfoy and has a reversible head.

Death Eater

The first LEGO merperson tail

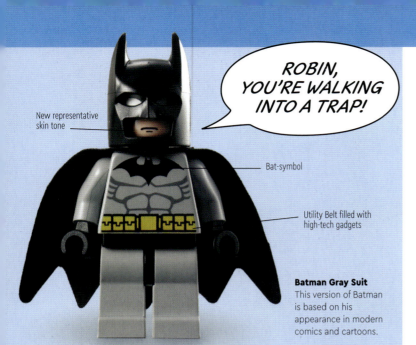

New representative skin tone

Bat-symbol

Utility Belt filled with high-tech gadgets

> **ROBIN, YOU'RE WALKING INTO A TRAP!**

Batman Gray Suit
This version of Batman is based on his appearance in modern comics and cartoons.

2006

A CAPED CRUSADER, a powerful Airbender, a yellow sponge from beneath the sea, brave young warriors in mighty battle mechs—these were just some of the new LEGO® minifigure "faces" to appear in 2006. Building on its success with *Star Wars™*, LEGO play themes embraced pop culture by welcoming some of the hottest licenses around. Lines such as LEGO® EXO-FORCE™ and LEGO® Aqua Raiders would also provide the adventure and role-play LEGO fans craved, while new soccer sets revived LEGO® Sports.

LEGO® BATMAN™

LEGO fans and comic fans both had reason to cheer when the new LEGO Batman theme premiered in 2006. The Dark Knight appeared with some of his best friends and his worst enemies in six sets (a seventh, the Ultimate Batmobile set, featured no minifigures). Many of the minifigures also appeared in three magnet collections.

Wavy hair piece

New torso this year with "R" symbol and yellow Utility Belt

DID YOU KNOW?
Batman's "blank" eyes are created by printing a white band across the minifigure's forehead.

Robin The minifigure of Batman's ally is based on the third Robin from the comics, Tim Drake. He was the first to wear long pants instead of shorts.

New head piece with mustache and laugh lines

Alfred Bruce Wayne's loyal butler, Alfred, wears a new torso this year, with a suit jacket, gray vest, and blue bow tie.

Alfred is always impeccably dressed

New masked head

Nightwing symbol

Unique feline mask

Silver goggles visible underneath mask

Double-sided head

Nightwing After retiring as Robin, Dick Grayson became Nightwing. His hair piece is also seen on Hitomi, from the LEGO EXO-FORCE theme.

Catwoman This jet-black catsuit, new this year, allows Catwoman to remain undetected during her nocturnal criminal activities.

THE BATMAN FAMILY

Two versions of the Batman minifigure, plus Robin, Alfred the butler, Nightwing, and Batman's alter ego Bruce Wayne are featured in the 2006 sets.

> **THIS BRUCE WAYNE GUY LOOKS REALLY COOL. I BET HE'S MODEST, TOO!**

Batman Black Suit
This all-black variant resembles Batman's suits from the comics of the late 1990s. It features gold torso detai s.

Well-groomed hair

Suit is pressed to perfection

Bruce Wayne The Caped Crusader's civilian torso was first seen in 2004 on Harry Osborn from the LEGO® Spider-Man™ theme.

Teeth of a predator

Unique reptilian torso

Killer Croc The scaly-skinned menace has the appearance and the strength of a crocodile.

Top hat is a favorite with minifigure villains

The Penguin This dapper crook wears a tuxedo, with a vest and bow tie, and a monocle over one eye.

Torso pattern resembles the leaves of a plant

Short legs

Poison Ivy This villain has a brand-new, unique head with green lips and red eyebrows.

First time a hair piece is printed

Acid damage

Two-Face's black-and-white suit reflects his split personality

Two-Face This criminal has all new elements that are unique to him. His head is unremarkable on one side, but purple and scarred on the other, with a large exposed eyeball.

THE VILLAINS

Most of Batman's minifigure archenemies surfaced in 2006, either individually in sets or together in Arkham Asylum (7785). The Joker, Penguin, Two-Face, and Killer Croc all had their own vehicles in the assortment.

Question mark emblem

The Riddler Nothing makes The Riddler happier than leaving complex clues to his crimes for Batman to solve. This year, the Riddler has a new head with purple mask detail.

Green jumpsuit

Permanent grin

The Joker calling card

The Joker This Joker minifigure featured in a limited edition box set given away at the 2008 San Diego Comic-Con, as well as in set 7782.

Mr. Freeze This cool character's clear bubble helmet was first seen on minifigures from the LEGO® Insectoids theme in 1998.

Freezer blaster

Cryogenic suit

Pointed black hat made originally for LEGO® Castle witches and wizards

Scythe

The Scarecrow This sinister red-eyed minifigure has a transparent head that glows in the dark. His torso has printed stitching and a rope belt.

LEGO® VIKINGS

In 2006, the LEGO Vikings Chess Set was released, as well as two Vikings sets. These included the Army of Vikings with Heavy Artillery Wagon (7020), which came with seven minifigures—the most included in any Vikings set.

White facial hair makes him appear old and wise

Red Chess King The Viking chess pieces have the same torso pattern as the Fantasy Era dwarf minifigures from the Castle theme in 2008.

Horns are glued to helmet

Red Chess Bishop So that the chess minifigures did not get mixed up, some of the pieces were stuck together with glue.

On the chessboard, he holds a sword in each hand

Red legs

Blue Chess Queen The blue and red queens in the Viking chess set are the only ones that have happy expressions. They must be enjoying the game!

Gray hair piece

Gray sloping piece for skirt

LEGO® EDUCATION

This minifigure is one of two featured in Science and Technology Base Set (9632). The LEGO Education set for schools came with building instructions for 12 LEGO® Technic models.

Black ponytail hair piece

Pretty orange flower pattern

Teamwork Minifigure The Science and Technology Base Set was designed to encourage teamwork.

LEGO® AVATAR THE LAST AIRBENDER™

Based on the popular animated Nickelodeon series, *Avatar: The Last Airbender* was a one-year theme in 2006. Two sets were released, featuring six new minifigures. Aang is the only minifigure to appear in both sets and, like the others in the theme, he features manga-style eyes.

> NO, I DON'T KNOW WHAT I'M SMILING ABOUT EITHER.

Aang As the last Airbender, Aang must try to save the world, but as his smile suggests, he would rather have fun than fight the Fire Nation!

Master Airbender Tattoo

Bright yellow torso

Orange poncho

New brown legs with yellow printing on the thighs

Strap holds a boomerang on his back

Smirk

Blue robes

Sokka Katara's warrior brother, Sokka is brave and loyal. His unique torso has a printed strap detail.

Classic Castle helmet, but in a new color

Armor breastplate

Fire Nation Soldier Serving fiery Prince Zuko is no joke—this soldier is the only minifigure with this new serious head.

Firebender This scary-looking minifigure has the power to control fire. He has a new head piece with a skull-like mask.

New head has ponytail on the back

Prince Zuko The exiled heir to the Fire Nation throne has quarreled with his father. He got the scar on his face in a duel.

Fireproof armor pattern is unique to the Zuko minifigure

Loop of hair

Dark blue robe with white trim

Katara This minifigure has a brand-new, unique head that features loops of hair that drape over her face.

LEGO® CITY

When there was an emergency, the LEGO City Emergency Medical team was on the job in 2006. Doctors and air ambulance pilots made up just some of the minifigures released with four Emergency sets. Also in 2006, LEGO® Train (now a subtheme of City), converted to remote control, with two sets featuring seven minifigures.

Flying Doctor This air ambulance doctor has a new torso with a jacket print that includes a radio, zippers, and the EMT Star of Life logo.

Star of Life logo

Radio

Zipper

Doctor with Stethoscope With a new torso featuring pens and a stethoscope, this doctor is ready to help the ailing citizens of LEGO City.

Open collar

Stethoscope

Silver shades

Tools in pocket

Construction Worker New overalls with a handy pocket for storing essential tools have made this construction worker's day.

Glasses

The conductor wears his uniform with pride

Train logo

Conductor Charlie This friendly conductor really enjoys helping the passengers.

LEGO® CASTLE

LEGO Knights' Kingdom continued the story of the heroic knights of Morcia and their battle against Vladek. The struggle shifted to the mighty Mistlands Tower, and King Jayko was promoted to the throne from his previous rank of knight. Apart from Lord Vladek and King Jayko, all the other characters were new for 2006, including noble hero Sir Adric.

Black cape

Gray beard fades to white at edges

Hawk symbol

King Jayko This royal minifigure has a new pearl gold armor breastplate. It features a silver-and-black hawk pattern.

Bushy eyebrows meet in the middle

Villainous scowl

Dracus The leader of the Rogue Knights, this menacing minifigure stands out in his yellow pants and sleeves.

Fierce facial expression for battle

Bronze studs

Karzon Vladek's wicked weapons master is very proud of his bronze armor and likes to show it off with plenty of bad-tempered shouting.

Little of Vladek's face is visible under the visor

Scorpion emblem

Bright red cape

Lord Vladek This returning foe now wears a black armor breastplate, embellished with a large silver scorpion.

Helmet has also been worn in red by the knight Santis in 2004

Striking red armor

Sir Adric Raring to defend King Jayko in battle, Sir Adric just needs to make sure he can see out of his chunky helmet first!

LEGO® SPONGEBOB SQUAREPANTS™

SpongeBob SquarePants This minifigure has a unique head piece printed with SpongeBob's face, which fits over a plain yellow torso.

Small holes on edges to reflect the texture of a sponge

Goofy expression

Square pants

DID YOU KNOW? Plankton also appears in a tiny, single-cylinder brick form this year.

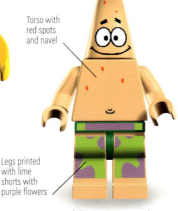

Torso with red spots and navel

Legs printed with lime shorts with purple flowers

Patrick Star SpongeBob's dopey best friend Patrick has a unique cone-shaped head piece.

High-waisted blue pants

Unique features

Shirt collar pattern

Short legs

Mr. Krabs The owner of the Krusty Krab restaurant has a unique molded head piece and eyes on stalks.

Squidward Tentacles SpongeBob's grumpy neighbor has a regular head piece that is printed with a big nose and large yellow-and-red eyes.

Small lever

Sticker with Plankton's features

PLANKTON! This large version of Plankton is made from three round bricks covered by a sticker. This was the only figure in Build-A-Bob (3826). The set references the TV episode in which Plankton takes over SpongeBob's mind.

Who lives in a LEGO set under the sea? SpongeBob SquarePants! Three sets appeared this year, featuring minifigures of all the major characters. The SpongeBob theme earned a reputation for having many interesting elements and variations of minifigures over the years.

LEGO® STAR WARS™

Classic Star Wars characters making their LEGO debuts in 2006 included Grand Moff Tarkin, Wedge Antilles, and the bounty hunters Dengar and IG-88. Luke, Han, and Lando got updated looks in Jabba's Sail Barge (6210), while Ten Numb became the first Sullustan minifigure in B-Wing Fighter (6208).

Green lightsaber

Later variants all have a black right hand

Jedi robe pattern

Jedi Knight Luke The latest variant of Jedi Luke is the first not to have yellow skin.

Ax head first seen in 2005 LEGO® Vikings sets

Lando Calrissian In Jabba's Sail Barge (6210), Lando is disguised as one of the Hutt gangster's guards.

Unique helmet hides smiling face

Deadly vibro-ax

Boarlike head and armor are all one piece

2003 variant has sand green hands

Brown tunic and gold armor

The torso on the 2010 variant has creases on the shirt

Han Solo This Han variant is the first not to have a holster print on his legs.

Gamorrean Guard This variant of a 2003 minifigure is exclusive to Jabba's Sail Barge (6210).

Helmet printing is unique to Wedge

> LUKE ISN'T THE ONLY SUPERSTAR PILOT AROUND HERE!

Orange Rebel Alliance flight suit

Wedge Antilles Luke's pilot pal is exclusive to X-Wing Fighter (6212), which could be customized as Luke or Wedge's ship.

Stern, pinched features

Governor's large rank bar

Imperial officer's kepi

2010 variant has a sterner face

Imperial code cylinder

All variants wear gray tunic

Imperial Officer This minifigure seems surprisingly happy to work for scary Grand Moff Tarkin.

Grand Moff Tarkin The first minifigure depiction of this gruff Imperial governor commands a 1,367-piece Imperial Star Destroyer (6211).

Mug piece

Goblet piece

Tray is a 2×4 plate

R2-D2 A built-in tray turns this droid into a reluctant bar cart in Jabba's Sail Barge (6210)!

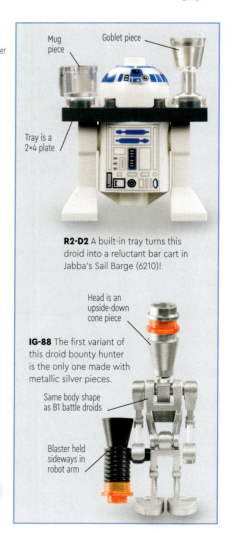

Head is an upside-down cone piece

IG-88 The first variant of this droid bounty hunter is the only one made with metallic silver pieces.

Same body shape as B1 battle droids

Blaster held sideways in robot arm

Same style hat as Imperial Officer

No other minifigure wears the classic LEGO smile on this color head

Unique torso with rank print on arms

Blaster made from megaphone accessory

Bespin Guard Providing security for Cloud City makes this minifigure smile. So does having a unique head!

A 2014 variant wears a red flight suit

Printed air mask and Sullustan features

Ten Numb This rebel pilot was the only LEGO Sullustan until Nien Nunb was made into a minifigure in 2024.

Head wrap first worn by LEGO Castle ninja

Torso pattern unique to this minifigure

Dengar This bounty hunter meets his rivals Boba Fett and IG-88 in one 2006 set.

LEGO EXO-FORCE

LEGO minifigures met Japanese manga in this exciting new line. Daring young fighters in massive mechs challenged the might of an army of robots with equally massive mechs in 16 sets. The human minifigures featured new torsos and new, cartoon-style hair pieces, as well as anime-inspired facial designs.

New angular hair piece

New torso with EXO-FORCE uniform

Ha-Ya-To As the joker of the team, Ha-Ya-To is always smiling—even in the face of danger.

Orange visor

Hikaru The serious Hikaru has a new hair piece and double-sided head with an orange visor printing.

Utility belt

Keiken The leader of the EXO-FORCE team is the eldest and most experienced. Turn his head around to reveal his fighting face.

DID YOU KNOW?
Every LEGO EXO-FORCE set in 2016 features a light-up brick called a "power core."

Scar

Intense expression

Red headband

Uplink equipment

Takeshi This minifigure has a new torso design with a dark gray armor breastplate over a red suit.

Ryo The technical expert of the team, there's nothing Ryo can't fix or invent!

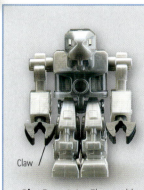

Blaster

Large feet for stability

Meca One This cunning golden figure is the leader of the robots.

Claw

Blue Devastator These cold and calculating robots have fearsome mechanical claws.

Iron Drone The drone figures are the strongest robots, but are less intelligent than the Devastators.

THE ROBOTS

The enemy robots have a clear hierarchy, beginning with the Iron Drone figures, moving up to three different colors of Devastator (red, blue, and green), and finally to the golden leader, Meca One.

LEGO® RACERS

Four more Ferrari sets sped toward the finish line for LEGO Racers this year. Along with a new version of driver Felipe Massa and a number of pit crew members, this year's line-up included announcers, camera operators, and a race official. A Fuel Filler minifigure was also introduced, wearing modern protective gear.

Checkered pattern

DID YOU KNOW?
Five new minifigure characters make their first appearances in the 2006 LEGO Racers sets.

Head piece also used for the 2004 Rubens Barrichello minifigure

Felipe Massa This new minifigure represents the real-life racecar driver Felipe Massa. A torso sticker shows his name and the Brazilian flag.

Camera operator Capturing all the race action with his camera, this minifigure wears a stickered bib to show that he's a member of the press.

Torso printed with name

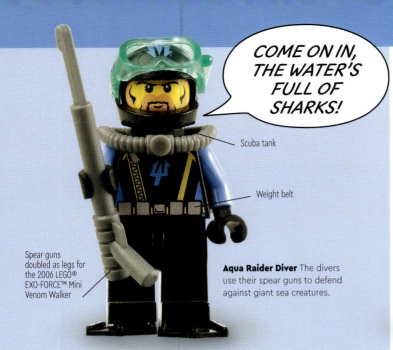

COME ON IN, THE WATER'S FULL OF SHARKS!

Scuba tank

Weight belt

Spear guns doubled as legs for the 2006 LEGO® EXO-FORCE™ Mini Venom Walker

Aqua Raider Diver The divers use their spear guns to defend against giant sea creatures.

2007

THE EXCITEMENT was building in 2007 as the LEGO Group helped celebrate the 30th anniversary of *Star Wars* with a host of new sets and a special 14-carat gold C-3PO minifigure. Harry Potter™ returned in one set, his last until 2010. Meanwhile, new LEGO play themes took center stage, including the undersea LEGO® Aqua Raiders, the out-of-this-world LEGO® Mars Mission, and the fantasy-themed LEGO® Castle. LEGO® Modular Buildings made their first appearance, giving experienced builders the chance to assemble realistic buildings in scale to their minifigure residents.

Mechanical robot arm

Lobster Strike
A fearsome giant lobster, an underwater exploration rover to withstand it, and two minifigures are included in this set (7772).

Dinosaur tail end piece is also used on the Jabba the Hutt minifigure, first released in 2003

Huge claws

Antennae also used as Barraki spines in the BIONICLE® sets

Spinning drill for collecting underwater crystals

Knitted hat has kept more than 160 minifigures warm, including robbers and farmers

Aqua Raiders trident logo

Hatted Diver After a long day seeking treasure deep in the ocean, this minifigure dons a knitted hat to keep warm.

LEGO AQUA RAIDERS

Aqua Raiders plunged beneath the ocean waves in 2007 in seven sets. Unlike previous underwater teams, the Aqua Raiders don't fight other minifigures, but search for treasure along the sea floor. They need to watch out, though—dangerous sea creatures stand between them and their prizes!

LEGO® SPACE

2007 saw the first new LEGO Space theme in six years: LEGO Mars Mission. A sequel of sorts to 2001's LEGO® Life on Mars, it differed by making the alien figures a menacing, rather than peaceful, force. Eight sets were released in 2007, featuring astronauts with new torsos and glow-in-the-dark aliens.

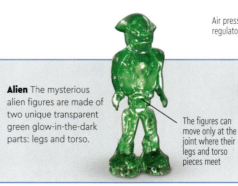

Air pressure regulator

Alien The mysterious alien figures are made of two unique transparent green glow-in-the-dark parts: legs and torso.

The figures can move only at the joint where their legs and torso pieces meet

Mars Mission Astronaut
A version of the classic LEGO Space logo adorns this explorer's environment suit.

Zipped black mask and red eyes

Bane This mighty minifigure only ever appears in one set, The Bat-Tank: The Riddler and Bane's Hideout (7787). He gets a redesign in 2012 and switches to a black suit.

Bulging muscles and scars

Unique torso with yellow Utility Belt

LEGO® BATMAN™

Two sets appeared in 2007, featuring a new dark blue costume for the Caped Crusader. Only one new character was released—the muscle-bound Bane.

Dark Blue Knight Batman receives a makeover with a dark blue mask, cape, hips, and hands.

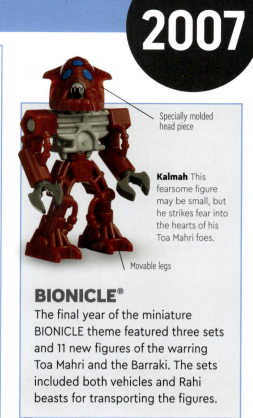

Specially molded head piece

Kalmah This fearsome figure may be small, but he strikes fear into the hearts of his Toa Mahri foes.

Movable legs

BIONICLE®

The final year of the miniature BIONICLE theme featured three sets and 11 new figures of the warring Toa Mahri and the Barraki. The sets included both vehicles and Rahi beasts for transporting the figures.

LEGO MODULAR BUILDINGS

Modular Buildings sets were launched this year, giving minifigures the most realistic and detailed street scenes yet to hang out in. The first was Café Corner (10182), part of the Advanced Models theme, which features more challenging models. This was followed by Market Street (10190), a LEGO® Factory exclusive created by talented fan Eric Brok. Both sets came with three very busy minifigures.

Market Street Vendor This trader can't wait for a lunchtime trip to Café Corner.

Green overalls

Spiky hair, seen on EXO-FORCE minifigures and LEGO® DC's Nightwing minifigure

Super Goalie The Super Goalie's hair piece is usually enough to distract the opposition.

LEGO® SPORTS

This exclusive goalie minifigure was part of a promotional set given out free with the purchase of some types of Adidas sneakers. It also included a golden soccer ball and a stand for the figure. The minifigure came with flat gloves with Adidas goalie glove pattern stickers, which attached to his regular minifigure hands.

Neat ponytail

Market Street Resident Modular living is the only way for this minifigure!

Blue jacket

Market Street Shopper Buying fresh produce is part of this local's daily routine.

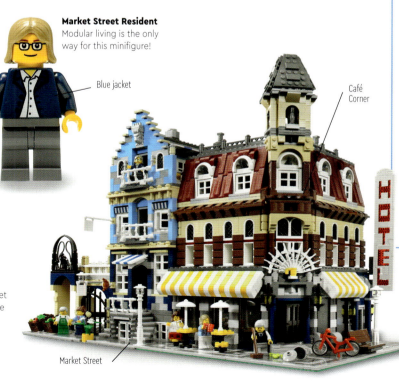

Café Corner

Market Street

Market Street This modular set (10190) contains a market place and a four-story townhouse, plus three minifigures.

Café Corner This modular construction set (10182) can be combined with other LEGO sets, as it is here, to create a whole neighborhood.

LEGO® HARRY POTTER™

2007 saw the release of one set in the LEGO Harry Potter theme, the third version of Hogwarts Castle (5378), from *Harry Potter and the Order of the Phoenix*. Nine minifigures came with the set, including Harry Potter in a new school uniform and new versions of Hermione Granger, Draco Malfoy, Professor Snape, and a Death Eater.

Death Eater This version of the Death Eater is exclusive to set 5378.

Ornate silver mask

Pink blush to match pink suit

Stern mouth

Molded hair

Cat brooch

Smart school tie

Harry Potter Harry's tie is printed with the colors of his house—scarlet and gold for Gryffindor.

Professor Dolores Umbridge The unpleasant Umbridge makes her minifigure debut in Hogwarts Castle (5378). Her hair is also seen on a worker minifigure in the Modular Green Grocer (10185) from 2008.

Double-sided sleeping/smiling head

Gryffindor uniform

Hermione Granger This version of Hermione is unique to set 5378, but the individual parts have been used in other sets.

Frowning expression

Professor Snape Like the Hermione minifigure, this version of Professor Snape is also unique to set 5378.

DID YOU KNOW? The mandrake plants from Hogwarts Castle (5378) included their very own unique minifigure heads.

Hogwarts Castle This version of the famous castle (5378) was the only LEGO model released for *Harry Potter and the Order of the Phoenix* until 2020.

The castle's interior has hidden items for Harry and his friends to find

Owl perched in alcove

LEGO® EXO-FORCE™

LEGO EXO-FORCE returned for a second year in 2007 with 11 new sets. Inspired by Japanese manga and animation, the theme featured a team of human pilots battling against the cunning robot army for control of their mountain home. Most LEGO EXO-FORCE sets were battle machines that both sides created to try to win the war.

DID YOU KNOW? Hitomi becomes leader of EXO-FORCE when the Sensei disappears.

Hair piece is also used for LEGO Sports Goalie minifigure

New double-sided head. Turn it around to see her angry expression

New gold amulet-patterned armor torso

Hitomi The granddaughter of Sensei Keiken, this is courageous Hitomi's first and only appearance in minifigure form, in Fight for the Golden Tower (8107).

Bright red angular hair

New gold-and-violet flight suit torso

Ha-Ya-To Ha-Ya-To's specialty is flying, which explains his windswept hair.

LEGO® RACERS

The Ferrari™ 248 F1 Team roared into action in 2007 in a new set for LEGO Racers. It included eight minifigures: a new variant of Felipe Massa, the minifigure debut of Kimi Raikkonen, two crew members, three engineers, and a record keeper. A second edition of this set contained different racecars and a Michael Schumacher minifigure in place of Raikkonen.

Ferrari red legs and torso

Felipe Massa With a new torso and new standard helmet, Massa is ready to burn some rubber.

Crown Princess The king's daughter features in the Castle Chess Set (852001) and alongside a new dragon figure in Skeleton Castle. (7093).

Gold crown details on costume

New dark blue sloped skirt

CROWN KNIGHTS

Led by the brave Crown King, the Crown Knights are made up of foot soldiers and cavalry. They have new torsos with armor breastplate printing and appeared in every 2007 Castle set.

Broad brim helmet

Chest strap

Crown emblem

Scared Crown Knight
Maybe this scared Crown Knight has just spotted a Skeleton Warrior?

Chrome gold crown

Golden broadsword

Crown King with Cape
Ruler of the Crown Knights, the caped Crown King has new pearl gold armor to protect him in battle.

Dark blue cloth cape

LONG LIVE THE BLING!

LEGO CASTLE

The new LEGO Castle series featured human Crown Knights battling against a scary Skeleton Army led by a power-hungry wizard. This popular theme, referred to as "Fantasy Era" by LEGO fans to distinguish it from Classic Castle sets, lasted for three years. Seven sets were released this year, along with a Castle Chess Set (852001) and Tic Tac Toe (Noughts and Crosses) game (852132).

Hood

Studded breastplate

Crown Bishop From the Fantasy Era Chess Set, the Crown Bishop is hoping his fierce expression will scare the Skeleton Army.

New torso with scale mail and belt detail

Staff with lightning bolts

Double-headed ax

Skeleton Warrior shield

Crown Knight with Visor
The Crown Knight's standard helmet and pointed visor is metallic silver for the first time this year.

Shield with printed crown emblem

Skull head is new this year

Red-robed torso underneath breastplate

Evil Wizard His hat and legs are exclusive, but the Wizard's head is similar to Ogel's in the Alpha Team theme.

One red eye

Wizard's hat with printed skull and lightning bolts

Evil Queen The red-headed Evil Queen wears a new armor breastplate, with a silver-studded ribcage pattern and skeleton head detail.

Charms for sorcery

Skeleton Warrior
This warrior's speckled armor was first seen on the Vikings minifigures in 2005.

THE SKELETON ARMY

The Evil Wizard's army consists of Skeleton Warriors who ride skeleton horses. Other sinister minifigures, such as the Evil Queen and Evil Bishop, appear only in the Fantasy Era Chess Set.

New shoulder joints

Black Skeleton The standard Fantasy Era skeleton is black instead of white. Its body and limbs have also been redesigned to hold poses.

LEGO® STAR WARS™

2007 brought the 30th anniversary of *Star Wars* and new excitement to the LEGO *Star Wars* play theme. There were new sets from across the original and prequel trilogies, new and exclusive minifigures, a special commemorative 30th anniversary C-3PO minifigure, and the release of one of the largest LEGO *Star Wars* sets to date!

GUESS WHAT I'M GOING TO BE WHEN I GROW UP?

Tousled hair

Freckled face

Short legs

Anakin Skywalker This third representation of Anakin as a young child features a new head and torso.

Green lightsaber

Qui-Gon Jinn The wise Jedi Master has a new head with mustache, beard, and chin dimple.

Jedi robe first seen in 2005

Light blue lightsaber

Obi-Wan Kenobi This young version of the Jedi Padawan is exclusive to the Republic Cruiser set (7665).

Hood with cape

THE PHANTOM MENACE

One of the highlights of the new Episode I LEGO sets was the new version of Anakin Skywalker, the first to feature short LEGO legs. Short legs had been introduced to minifigures in 2002, three years after the last young Anakin minifigure.

Red markings

Clone troopers are always ready for battle

Unique torso with Jedi robes and silver belt detail

Back of specially designed head has more sensory tentacles

New torso, with black shadow armor design, is exclusive to this minifigure

White C-3PO head

K-3PO Exclusive to the Hoth Rebel Base set (7666), this minifigure is highly collectible.

New helmet with red Imperial symbols

REVENGE OF THE SITH

Four new sets for this episode were released this year, featuring a new specialist clone trooper minifigure, as well as battle droid and super battle droid figures.

Shock Trooper Every clone trooper is created from the DNA of bounty hunter Jango Fett, but this minifigure has a unique helmet and torso.

Kit Fisto Jedi General Kit Fisto is the first LEGO *Star Wars* minifigure to have a head made from soft rubber instead of ABS plastic.

Tentacles

Shadow Trooper This shady Shadow Trooper is ideal for undercover work, with advanced dark armor.

Pilot helmet

Torso with breathing equipment detail is new this year

AT-AT Driver This clone driver pilots an All Terrain Armored Transport (AT-AT).

General Veers The stern Imperial Officer Veers makes his debut this year.

Officer torso first introduced in 2005

Snow gear for fighting on the ice planet Hoth

Backpack for equipment

Hoth Rebel This is the second version of this character, and it features a new head.

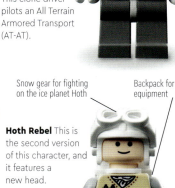

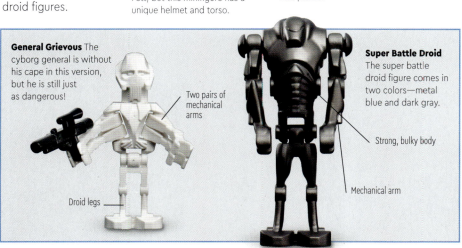

General Grievous The cyborg general is without his cape in this version, but he is still just as dangerous!

Two pairs of mechanical arms

Droid legs

Super Battle Droid The super battle droid figure comes in two colors—metal blue and dark gray.

Strong, bulky body

Mechanical arm

ORIGINAL TRILOGY

A handful of brand-new Original Trilogy minifigures appeared this year, including the Shadow Stormtrooper, K-3PO, and General Veers. The character of K-3PO did not appear again for nine years, until 2016 in Assault on Hoth (75098).

Main sensor

Forward floodlight

Han and Chewie sit in the cockpit

Millennium Falcon This Ultimate Collector Series *Millennium Falcon* (10179) is built from a whopping 5,197 pieces and comes with a 311-page instruction booklet!

EPIC SET

One of the most sought-after LEGO *Star Wars* sets was also the biggest ever made at the time—the Ultimate *Millennium Falcon* (10179). It featured five minifigures of classic characters: Luke, Han, Leia, Obi-Wan, and Chewbacca.

Lines under eyes

Obi-Wan Kenobi Obi-Wan's minifigure has a furrowed brow and gray hair.

Smirking expression

Han Solo There have been 40 different Han Solo minifigures released since the first one in 2000.

Tatooine Luke Skywalker An update of a 1999 variant, Luke now has longer hair, a skin-toned head and hands, and new torso and leg printing.

Side buns

Leia is wearing red lipstick

Princess Leia This skin-toned Princess Leia is dressed in her all-white senator's uniform.

Belt pouch

Tan pants

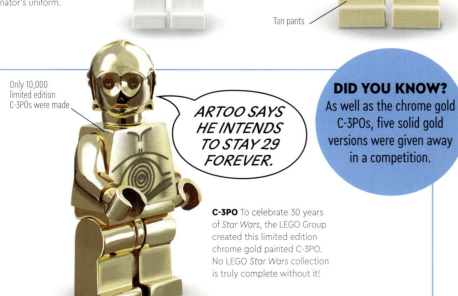

Only 10,000 limited edition C-3POs were made

ARTOO SAYS HE INTENDS TO STAY 29 FOREVER.

DID YOU KNOW?
As well as the chrome gold C-3POs, five solid gold versions were given away in a competition.

C-3PO To celebrate 30 years of *Star Wars*, the LEGO Group created this limited edition chrome gold painted C-3PO. No LEGO *Star Wars* collection is truly complete without it!

Biker This minifigure visits the Service Station (7993) to fill his motorcycle with Octan-brand fuel.

Classic Space logo

Sleeveless top worn by 15 minifigures

Life Guard This Life Guard is dressed for a hot day and is ready to keep all the beach-goers safe.

LEGO® CITY

Adventure had no limit in the 2007 LEGO City sets. From Fire Station (7945) and Harbor (7994) to the busy Train Station (7997), LEGO City was a bustling place to be. The vast majority of minifigures introduced this year used new combinations of existing elements to make nonetheless compelling new characters.

This megaphone has featured in many sets, from Batman to *Star Wars*

Construction Worker With his bright orange jacket and megaphone, this worker is both seen and heard on the building site.

Silver hard hat matches shades

Silver shades to protect eyes from the glare of fires

Firefighter The brave LEGO City firefighters battle fires and rescue any people or animals that need their help.

Helmet with visor

Police badge

Gray beard

Anchor logo

Neat tie

Police Pilot Like the Life Guard, this minifigure was part of a promotional giveaway set.

Boat Captain This minifigure's torso is new, with an anchor logo and blue tie and pocket detail.

"I'M WORKING ON A SPELL TO MAKE LEGO SETS BUILD THEMSELVES ..."

New hat print with gold buckle and stars

Beard piece fits between the wizard's head and torso pieces

Good Wizard Four LEGO Castle minifigures and a Viking have previously used this head, with its stern but kind face.

Potion, pouch, and amulet hang from belt

2008

THIS YEAR WAS a memorable one in the history of LEGO® play. As well as being the 50th anniversary of the patent of the LEGO brick and the 30th anniversary of the LEGO minifigure, it brought fans an amazing array of new themes. LEGO® *Star Wars™: The Clone Wars™* made its debut, along with the action-packed LEGO® *Indiana Jones™*. LEGO® Agents went on their first secret mission and the Vintage Minifigure Collection brought back favorites from the past. All in all, a year to remember!

Green eyeshadow and black lipstick

Magic lightning bolt for zapping unsuspecting minifigures

Spider necklace

Advent Calendar Witch This magical minifigure is one of seven in the LEGO Castle Advent Calendar (7979), which also includes two skeletons.

LEGO® CASTLE

The Crown Knights of LEGO Castle got a new enemy this year—the mighty Troll Warriors. Fortunately, they also acquired a new ally in the equally fierce Dwarf Miners. Six major LEGO Castle sets were released this year, plus three smaller sets. An exciting new Castle Advent Calendar also made its appearance as the holiday season approached.

Broom first seen in LEGO® FABULAND™ sets

DWARVES

The brave dwarves appeared in four sets, including the impressive Dwarves' Mine (7036). The minifigures wore new helmets and intricate beard pieces and carried accessories from the LEGO® Vikings theme.

Intricately braided beard

Apron keeps dust off her skirt

Advent Calendar Woman This minifigure may have borrowed her broom from the Advent Calendar Witch!

Winged helmet exclusive to dwarves

Dwarf Pawn In LEGO Castle Giant Chess (852293), dwarf minifigures like this one serve as pawns.

Tasty drumstick

Advent Calendar Dwarf This minifigure from the Advent Calendar is making the most of the festive fare.

New head with extra-wide smile

Fantasy Era torso with crown buckle

Jester This all-new Jester waits behind the day 24 window of the Castle Advent Calendar (7979). He is clearly having a happy holiday.

TROLLS

Two kinds of Trolls were made: minifigures and Giant Troll figures. Not just enemies of the Dwarves, Trolls battled the Crown Knights, too, using siege engines and a ship.

Copper troll helmet with cheek guards

Belts, chains, and buckles on chest

Copper Troll Pawn This troll pawn is one of 33 minifigures in the LEGO Castle Giant Chess Set.

Silver-black variant of troll helmet

Troll symbol on buckle

Silver Troll Pawn This troll pawn variant wears a breastplate with integral shoulder guards.

Spikes run from his head down his back

Giant Troll At 3 in (7.5 cm) tall, this muscle-bound, club-wielding Giant Troll is twice the height of a standard minifigure.

Hands attach via LEGO® Technic pins

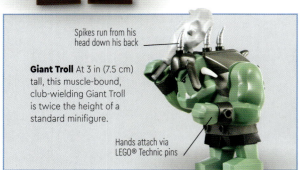

LEGO AGENTS

Agents replaced Alpha Team as the LEGO super-spies theme and leapt into action by sending secret operatives up against the villainous Dr. Inferno. The eight sets were numbered ("Mission 1," "Mission 2," and so on), and each included a comic strip on the box. Unlike Alpha Team, most of the minor villains in Agents had unique names and powers.

Agent Chase As team leader, Chase appears in six of this year's eight sets—more than any other Agents minifigure.

Double-sided head

Same head as standard Chase (this is the reverse face)

Crew-cut hair piece in reddish brown

Agents logo on left of torso

Diver Chase Chase may be ready to go under, but he'll still come out on top in the Deep Sea Quest (8636).

ID card attached to belt

Gun is hose nozzle piece

Powerful glasses for detailed work

Agent Charge Unlike most Agents, Charge has only one face. He says it's the only one he needs!

Helmet with visor—he is an air, land, and sea pilot

Agent Trace Fearless Trace is on the case in three of this year's sets.

Radio keeps him in touch with the team

Rocket Charge In Mission 2 (8632), Charge swaps his hair for a helmet to ride a high-tech rocket cycle.

AGENTS

The Agent minifigures came equipped with jetpacks, speedboats, and an awesome Mobile Command Center (8635). They needed them all to fight not only Dr. Inferno and his minions, but also a glow-in-the-dark octopus!

Agent Fuse An alternative scared face comes in handy when Fuse enters Dr. Inferno's Volcano Base (8637)!

Blaster made from camera and cones

Unique face print

Same torso print as Saw Fist

Accessory first used as a hosepipe nozzle

Unique metallic gold hair

Four robotic eyes printed on face

Knitted cap

Legs are robotic arm pieces

Break Jaw This fierce-looking foe is made extra scary by his jawlike helmet.

Fire Arm This cyborg baddie has a blaster built onto his robotic right arm.

Gold Tooth With gold teeth and hair, this must be one of the shiniest minifigure minions ever.

Spy Clops This multilegged figure is a creation of Dr. Inferno. He is made up of 19 parts, including 6 helmet horns used as feet.

Accomplice This rather overlooked villain can't wait to get a nickname of his own!

Hand grips like a standard minifigure's

Head piece also found in LEGO Castle Advent Calendar

Black is dominant color in outfit

Claw-Dette Dr. Inferno's second-in-command loves her prosthetic arm, which matches Inferno's exactly.

Mechanical arm and robot hand

Badge based on hairstyle—or is it the other way around?

THOSE AGENTS ARE JUST JEALOUS OF MY HAIR!

Unique hair piece is one of the most unusual ever

Slime Face This minifigure's head is colored transparent neon green to make it look like slimy green jelly.

Slime drips printed on torso

Transparent neon bubble-style helmet

Chainsaw piece in use since 1993

Crew-cut hair piece in black

INFERNO AND CREW

Dr. Inferno planned to conquer the world, aided by his team of minions with their futuristic weapons and gigantic laser cannon. They were an eclectic bunch, with names like Break Jaw, Slime Face, and Spy Clops. None of these minifigures would reappear after 2008.

Dr. Inferno There are two variants of this minifigure, but only their claw color varies. This one has pearl light gray; the other has silver.

Saw Fist This cyborg is aptly named! He is the only minifigure to use the LEGO chainsaw piece as a limb.

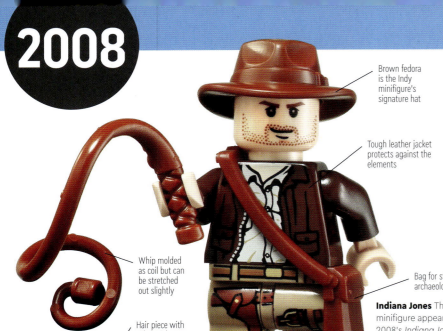

Brown fedora is the Indy minifigure's signature hat

Tough leather jacket protects against the elements

Whip molded as coil but can be stretched out slightly

Bag for stashing archaeological finds

Indiana Jones The same new Indy minifigure appeared across all three of 2008's *Indiana Jones* subthemes: *Raiders of the Lost Ark*, *The Last Crusade*, and *The Kingdom of the Crystal Skull*.

LEGO *INDIANA JONES*

The big name in LEGO adventure in 2008 was without a doubt Indiana Jones. Sets based on three of the hit movies arrived in stores this year. (Another, *Indiana Jones and the Temple of Doom*, would be represented the following year.) The play theme was an immediate hit, both with eager young builders just meeting the whip-cracking adventurer for the first time via *Indiana Jones and the Kingdom of the Crystal Skull*, and with their parents who remembered the original movies first released in the 1980s.

RAIDERS OF THE LOST ARK

Indy sought the Ark of the Covenant in this subtheme's five sets. Movie characters Indiana Jones, Marion, Satipo, and Belloq became minifigures. The only significant absence was Major Toht, who appeared in the LEGO® *Indiana Jones* video games but never as a minifigure.

Hair piece with side braids drawn back

Flower and bow detail on top

SNAKES, INDY! LEGO SNAKES!

Marion Ravenwood Marion must end up escaping the snakes, because the reverse of her head is calm and smiling.

Dark tan pith helmet

Gun not just used for self-defense

INDIANA? HIS NAME IS HENRY JONES JR.

Steel-rimmed specs—nothing escapes his eagle eye

Signature bow tie

Temple Escape In this set (7623), Indy's minifigure faces all the traps from the opening of *Raiders of the Lost Ark*.

Dark tan clothes help him blend in with sand

René Belloq Indy's rival shares his smirking face with another minifigure villain: Draco Malfoy from the LEGO® Harry Potter™ theme.

THE LAST CRUSADE

In the three sets of this subtheme, Indy and his father went on a quest for the Holy Grail and fans got their first Sean Connery minifigure. (He played Indy's father, Henry Jones Senior, in the movie.)

Henry Jones Senior Judging by his sharp suit and the diary in his pocket, Indiana's father values neatness and good record-keeping.

New head, old hair (that maybe needs combing)

Leather biker jacket for this motorcycle hero

Unique torso with name on jacket front

THE KINGDOM OF THE CRYSTAL SKULL

An older, wiser Indy teamed up with a young man named Mutt on his strangest adventure yet—finding a mystical crystal skull. It was the largest subtheme, with seven sets, and featured new versions of Indy and Marion plus new minifigures Irina Spalko, Colonel Dovchenko, and more.

TELL ME ALL YOU KNOW ABOUT MINIFIGURES ... NOW!

Mutt Williams Indy's long-lost son Mutt debuted in this subtheme. His minifigure was included in three sets: Jungle Duel (7624), Temple of the Crystal Skull (7627), and Peril in Peru (7628).

DID YOU KNOW? Every set in the LEGO *Indiana Jones* theme features a minifigure of Indy himself.

Irina Spalko On her relentless quest for power and knowledge, minifigure Irina maintains a cool (and new) head.

Ice-cold expression

No frills on this no-nonsense minifigure's shirt!

LEGO® CITY

LEGO City continued to be a busy place in 2008, and a safe one for its minifigure citizens, too. Not only was there a brand-new Police Station in town, but the Coast Guard was back after four years away. The new Coast Guard minifigures kept watch on the shoreline of LEGO City, rescuing surfers and boaters from sharks, spills, and stormy weather.

Alert, ever watchful expression

Patroller This is one of two Patroller minifigures in the Coast Guard Patrol Boat and Tower (7739).

Fully waterproof jacket

Crash helmet often used for sports minifigures

THE OCEAN IS MY BEAT.

POST OFFICE

The Cargo subtheme entered its second year, with two of its four sets centered on delivering mail. Both the Postal Plane (7732) and Mail Van (7731) sets included a postal worker minifigure.

Determined look— nobody gets lost at sea on his watch!

Helicopter Pilot The pilot flies his chopper over treacherous seas to rescue minifigures from such hazards as snapping sharks!

Radio used to report back to base

COAST GUARD

After a brief absence, Coast Guard returned under the LEGO City banner, with the minifigures sporting new blue-and-yellow uniforms. Eight sets included Coast Guard Platform (4210), Quad Bike (7736), Helicopter and Life Raft (7738), and Patrol Boat and Tower (7739).

Life jacket in use since 1990

Speedboat Pilot Under his life jacket, this minifigure wears the standard 2008 Coast Guard top with zippers, logo, and radio printed on it.

Mail taken from mailbox for delivery

Glasses help him read badly addressed mail

New envelope logo for 2008 Post Office workers

Front of mailbox opens

Mail Van Worker There's no chance of this Mail Van Worker deserting his post! He's never far from his trusty yellow van.

LEGO® VINTAGE MINIFIGURE COLLECTION

Old minifigures were suddenly new again with the launch of the LEGO Vintage Minifigure Collection. Each set in this series would feature five reissued minifigures, usually with little to no change from the original. The first set featured a Red Astronaut, Firefighter, Octan Driver, Scientist, and crook named Jailbreak Joe.

Astronaut wears the updated helmet, first seen in 1987

Classic planet logo on torso

Sunglasses popular with City minifigures since 2003

Both workers have this new torso but old legs and heads

Air Mail Worker The dedicated Air Mail Worker is very proud to be flying the flag (and the plane) for LEGO City Post Office.

Red cap with peak shades their eyes

Octan Driver Fourteen sets (other than this one) have included this gas truck driver minifigure.

Logo of Octan—the LEGO gas brand

Red Astronaut This minifigure from the Classic Space theme was launched into the LEGO universe in 1978.

Helmet ensures a cool head at all times

Five-button jacket

Firefighter This cheerful firefighter got a foot on the first rung of the ladder in 1981's Town theme.

Standard helmet with red "M"

Standard white helmet has no visor

Dragon design printed on torso and legs

SEE HOW FAST I SPEED-READ THIS PAGE!

Silver chest panel printed on torso

LEGO® RACERS

The LEGO Racers theme got a new licensed subtheme this year, based on the movie *Speed Racer*. All four of its sets focused on the heroic Speed Racer and his efforts to win the Casa Cristo 500 against the mysterious Racer X. More than a dozen new minifigures were introduced, including two versions of Speed Racer, his girlfriend Trixie, the villainous Cruncher Block, and Racer X.

Taejo Togokhan Taejo drives in the Casa Cristo Classic race wearing this white race suit with an intricate dragon design.

Speed Racer This motoring minifigure has an intense, driven expression and wears a sleek white jumpsuit.

Visor can be raised or lowered

White "X" on torso and helmet

Even hands are under cover

"R" is logo of Royalton Industries team

Silver chains pattern

Racer X Black overalls conceal this undercover minifigure's identity. Are they hero or villain?

Cannonball Taylor Speed Racer's arch-rival wears chest armor. He's expecting a rough race!

Gray Ghost This stylish minifigure and his car, the Fumeé, appear in Grand Prix Race (8161).

Short, wind-ruffled hair

BE CAREFUL, SPEED!

Silver glitter printed on top and skirt

Lopsided smile with mustache to match

Pops Racer Speed Racer's dad has a unique torso and head piece with dark, bushy brows.

DID YOU KNOW?
The Grand Prix Race set (8161) included a figure of Spritle's pet, Chim-Chim the chimpanzee.

Flashy red silk vest

Spritle Speed Racer's little brother has a unique torso, but a face print found on more than 80 minifigures.

Spritle is a fan of chimps

Short legs

Trixie A racing champion in her own right, Trixie knows Speed Racer has got what it takes!

Race Commentator This minifigure's head was used for Viktor Krum in the Harry Potter™ theme.

Piercing stare

Pinstriped vest and red silk tie

Gold shades can't disguise his mean expression

Belt buckle features two snakes design

Vest and striped tie printed on torso

New female head with steely gaze

Dark blue pants match his shirt

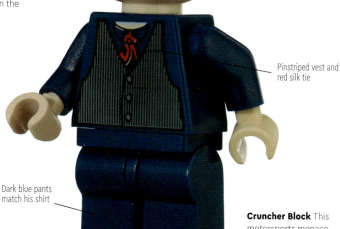

Snake Oiler This cheating racer is less trustworthy than the snakes depicted on his belt!

Cruncher's Driver Like many Speed Racer minifigures, Cruncher's car-driving sidekick has only printed hair.

Cruncher Block This motorsports menace likes to decide each race's winner long before it starts!

BREEZY TODAY, HUH?

"V" logo comes as a sticker to be applied to the torso

Vestas Worker The worker minifigure drives the Vestas maintenance van.

WIND POWER

Sometimes, LEGO sets are made in conjunction with real companies. A limited edition set appeared in 2008 promoting Vestas, a Danish wind power company. Vestas Wind Turbine (4999) featured a maintenance van and a motorized wind turbine on a small house.

SPECIAL EVENT

To mark the 50th anniversary of the LEGO brick patent, a commemorative logo was created and a LEGO® *Collector's Guidebook* published. A souvenir minifigure bearing the logo was packaged with the first edition of the book.

The logo shows a 2×4 LEGO brick from above and below

Anniversary Minifigure This minifigure bears the original and classic yellow head.

LEGO® FACTORY

The LEGO Factory theme started in 2005 and gave us three sets in this year. Two of these were space-themed and the third a Custom Car Garage (10200). Factory was tied to LEGO® Digital Designer, a software program that allowed for virtual LEGO building. The theme was replaced in 2009 by LEGO® DesignByMe.

Helmet with trident design from Aquazone theme

Plaid shirt often used in Town and City themes

Plaid Hot Rod Driver The three driver minifigures, including this plaid-shirted one, were made up of parts from a range of LEGO themes.

Stickered torso shows silver star badge

Star Justice Astronaut Two of these smiling minifigures are provided with Star Justice (10192).

Crew-cut hairstyle

Naboo fighter pilot torso from LEGO *Star Wars* theme

Grinning skull face seen through transparent visor

Custom Car Garage (10200) This set includes a LEGO Digital Designer CD, so fans can build a virtual version, too.

Jacket is sticker on plain black torso

Battle droid arms from LEGO *Star Wars* theme

Hot Rod Driver A neat line in hair—goatee, sideburns, and a crew-cut style—gives this minifigure his cool look.

Space Skull Commander The nemesis of the Star Justice team is a gang of galactic looters called the Space Skulls. They are led by this malevolent minifigure.

Star Justice Droid This little helper robot and his variant buddy are made from small LEGO pieces, including tiles, dishes, plates, and levers.

LEGO® STAR WARS™

LEGO *Star Wars* went from strength to strength in 2008. An exciting development was the launch of the first ever sets based on *The Clone Wars* TV series. Classic *Star Wars* was well represented, too, with sets from Episode IV, Episode V, and the Expanded Universe. With so much to smile about, LEGO *Star Wars* fans may have found their only problem was keeping up with the new releases.

Rebel Trooper The first rebel trooper minifigure has a new helmet, combined with a standard LEGO visor piece.

Helmet chin-strap printed on head

Short blaster is easy to handle when on the move

New torso with blue shirt and black vest

Emperor Palpatine This Emperor Palpatine minifigure from the Death Star (10188) shows him in the black robes of a Sith Lord.

Like all Sith lightsabers, Palpatine's has a red blade

No other droid has this head piece in black

Standard protocol droid design on torso

New bluish-gray head with heavily wrinkled face

Imperial Protocol Droid Unlike most protocol droids, this minifigure has no name or model number. He may forever remain anonymous.

Black gloves for handling dark deeds

Long black cloth cape

Three Luke variants wear this hair piece

Belt holds blaster power cell reserves

Luke Skywalker Old parts are used for this minifigure, but in a new combination. Luke's 2007 head and hair top a standard stormtrooper torso and legs.

LEGO *STAR WARS* ORIGINAL TRILOGY

The highlight of the year in classic LEGO *Star Wars* was the release of a fantastically detailed, multidecked Death Star (10188). It came with 24 characters, six of which were exclusive to the set. These included Luke Skywalker and Han Solo in borrowed stormtrooper armor, an Assassin Droid, and an Interrogation Droid.

New head and side part hair piece

WHEN DO I GET TO SING "SEND IN THE CLONES"?

Clone trooper-style armor

Obi-Wan Kenobi Like other *Clone Wars* minifigures, Obi-Wan has the big, cartoonlike eyes of his animated TV character.

Posable arms

Molded features augmented with printed eyes

Rotta the Huttlet This tiny baby Hutt figure can attach to other elements by a single knob.

Mask is not detachable, as Plo Koon rarely removes it

Head made from rubber

Blue lightsaber shows he fights for the light side

A tense tussle has left his hair tousled

Green lightsaber used by Ahsoka in the Clone Wars

New torso with black tunic over brown shirt

Detachable head-tails piece

Undershirt seen at neck of Jedi robe

Torso print found in five Clone Wars sets

THE CLONE WARS

LEGO *Star Wars* went storming into the Clone Wars era in 2008 with 10 new sets. New minifigure versions of Anakin Skywalker, Yoda, and Obi-Wan Kenobi were joined by a host of debuting characters, including Ahsoka Tano, Plo Koon, and General Grievous' MagnaGuards.

Anakin Skywalker This heroic minifigure's new head is scarred and battle-worn. His hair and torso are new for 2008, too.

Plo Koon This minifigure Jedi Master has a unique head. He wears a special mask that protects him from breathing a harmful excess of oxygen.

Ahsoka Tano A bright orange torso and head mark out Anakin's Padawan as a minifigure member of the Togruta species.

Red helmet markings are unique to this minifigure

Pauldron protects upper body

Helmet has orange stripes and visor

Commander Cody Like Captain Rex and Commander Fox, minifigure Cody wears a kama and carries two small blasters.

Kama fits over standard clone trooper legs

Commander Fox This minifigure wears a new piece—the kama—which is a form of anti-blast leg armor.

I'LL BE BACK, HARLEY—AND THAT'S NO JOKE!

Very serious expression

Body armor printed on new torso

Batman This updated Batman minifigure wears an outfit like that of the character in the newly released *The Dark Knight* movie.

New design for Utility Belt

Domino mask

DID YOU KNOW?
All 2008 *The Clone Wars* minifigures and figures are new and exclusive to the subtheme except the Buzz Droid.

Five o'clock shadow—it's been a long mission

Small blaster is a new piece for 2008

Captain Rex All Clone Wars clone troopers share the same new head except Rex. His has extra features—stubble and a scar on his chin.

Startling white face with blood-red lips

Her twin lightsabers have unusual curved hilts

Asajj Ventress Making her minifigure debut in set 7676, this cold-eyed Sith came with a variety of unusual new pieces.

First minifigure to wear a cloth skirt

Head and head wrap are one piece

Fabric cape sits underneath molded head wrap

MagnaGuard Count Dooku's tall, metal bodyguard cuts a menacing figure in a tattered cape.

Harley Quinn Harley wears a new dual-colored jester cap in The Batcycle: Harley Quinn's Hammer Truck (7886). She and Batman were the only minifigures in the set.

Oversized mallet is not for playing croquet!

Diamond shapes printed on legs

LEGO® BATMAN™

The Caped Crusader was back this year for what were to be his last four sets until 2012. The big news was the release of an all-new minifigure. Harley Quinn—mischievous villain, Poison Ivy's best buddy, and Joker's sometime girlfriend—arrived on the scene to give Batman some ha-ha-hard times.

LEGO® EXO-FORCE™

The anime-inspired EXO-FORCE theme came to an end in 2008, delivering seven sets that included a massive Hybrid Rescue Tank (8118). Minifigures making a final stand against their robotic foes included new versions of the EXO-FORCE battle machine pilots. Sensei Keiken also appeared for a second time.

Other side of head has angry expression

Double-sided head with closed-mouth expression

Blue tubes run between the armor and belt

Camo patterns feature on all 2008 pilot torsos

Ryo The 2008 version of repair expert Ryo is back in his orange suit, this time with a new armored torso.

Ha-Ya-To The third and last Ha-Ya-To minifigure has the same head, hair, and legs as earlier versions, but his torso is new. He now wears body armor printed over a camouflage pattern suit.

HOW LONG DO I HAVE TO HOLD THIS? TAKE THE PICTURE ALREADY!

Pickax

Helmet with breathing gear and headlamps first introduced in 1999 in the LEGO Rock Raiders theme

Star logo

Doc The team's leader and also the medic, Doc has been on many adventures. His head is also double-sided: determined and grinning.

2009

IT WAS AN EVENTFUL year in the world of LEGO® minifigures. A new theme, LEGO® Power Miners, was launched, with the help of an animated mini-movie. LEGO® *Star Wars™* celebrated its 10th anniversary in *Clone Wars* style. Old favorites LEGO® Pirates were reintroduced after more than a decade's absence, and the LEGO® Space Police patrolled the galaxy again. The games figure also made its first appearance this year as LEGO® Games hit the shelves, giving board games an exciting LEGO makeover.

LEGO POWER MINERS

Considered by many to be the follow-up to 1999–2000's LEGO® Rock Raiders, LEGO Power Miners would become one of the most popular LEGO play themes, until the arrival of LEGO® NINJAGO® in 2011. It was the ninth play theme in which all the minifigure characters had names.

Metal plate in forehead

Bomb logo

Rex This minifigure's job is to handle explosives, so he has a bomb logo on his uniform.

Safety goggles

Flashlight

Stubbled Rex Rex's other variant has a head with two stubbled faces. One looks determined, the other scared.

Hair piece seen on more than 240 minifigures

Duke This veteran miner thinks he has seen it all—until he meets the Rock Monsters!

POWER MINERS

Doc, Rex, Duke, and Brains made up the team of minifigure miners in 2009. The brave Power Miners dug beneath the Earth, discovering amazing powerful crystals and fearsome Rock Monsters.

Glasses with power lens

Boom! LEGO dynamite

Brains The Power Miners' scientist, Brains, can also be found in 2010's LEGO® Atlantis theme.

Thunder Driller With this powerful, double-geared drill (8960), the Power Miners Doc and Duke can easily tunnel through solid rock.

Duke

Rotating drill

Doc

Energy Crystals

Stored Energy Crystals

Articulated arms can launch rocks … or smaller rock monsters!

Geolix Even when it's fighting, Geolix won't let its Energy Crystals go—it holds them on its back.

ROCK MONSTERS

The Rock Monster figures used all-new molds and came in five colors. Small versions were included with most sets, and two larger versions were included with the fall 2009 releases.

Hinged mouth can open and close to gobble up crystals

Firox If this Rock Monster is allowed to eat an Energy Crystal, it becomes super fast.

LEGO PIRATES

LEGO Pirates minifigures sailed the seas for the first time in 12 years. Eight new sets appeared in 2009, featuring Captain Brickbeard and new versions of the Imperial Guard. However, after the release of the exclusive Imperial Flagship (10210) in 2010, the pirates mostly went back into hiding until 2015.

Castaway In the 12 years since the last LEGO Pirates release, the castaway has had no hope of rescue. His pants have become ragged and his beard shaggy.

Hopeful wave

Tattered vest

Patched and ragged pants

Cutlass

Bicorn hat with skull and crossbones

Customary pirate's eyepatch

Gold detail on outfit

Gold epaulettes

Gold hook piece is new for 2009

Wooden leg

Eyepatch

Long, brown hair

Green bandana worn at a jaunty angle

Matching green pants

Treasure map

Telescope Pirate This treasure-hungry pirate debuts new head and torso pieces for this year. Her map tile has appeared in 15 sets since 2008.

Green Bandana Pirate This pirate doesn't see why he can't look good while being bad. His bandana and his pants match perfectly!

Captain Brickbeard The pirates' new leader replaces Captain Redbeard. This greedy pirate is only interested in one kind of treasure—gold.

PIRATES

Captain Brickbeard led a crew of minifigure pirates in search of treasure. The pirates had a variety of heads, hats, and leg colors. New elements included a gold hook on Brickbeard, a grizzled head with an eyepatch on another pirate officer, and a new castaway minifigure.

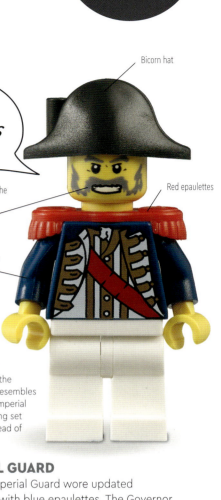

WE WILL HAVE TO SEARCH THE SEVEN SEAS FOR THOSE PIRATES!

Bicorn hat

Red epaulettes

Gray mustache and stern expression

Grand blue uniform

Governor This important minifigure is in charge of the Soldiers' Fort (6242). He resembles the Admiral from 2010's Imperial Flagship advanced building set (10210), but with red instead of gold epaulettes.

IMPERIAL GUARD

The new Imperial Guard wore updated red jackets with blue epaulettes. The Governor wore a blue jacket with red epaulettes. In 2009, for the first time, the Imperials sailed a bigger ship than the pirates.

Tricorn hat

Nervous Officer This minifigure has good reason to worry—he's a lowly pawn in a LEGO Pirates chess set.

Impressive plume of red feathers

Blue epaulettes

This soldier has a knapsack printed on his back

Imperial Officer Attention! This soldier could win the prize for best dressed minifigure, thanks to his plumed hat and fine epaulettes.

Vintage Soldier
This minifigure retains all the original pieces of the 1989 minifigure.

Smart epaulettes

CLASSIC PIRATES

Two Classic LEGO Pirate theme minifigures were reissued in 2009 as part of the Vintage Minifigure Collection. The Soldier was originally produced in 1989 and the Pirate in 1996.

The pirate's original vest was darker

Vintage Pirate The LEGO designers kept all the details from the 1996 version, apart from the pirate's vest color.

There have been two variants—the original had solid black pupils

Celebration Luke Skywalker Originally available only as part of DK's LEGO *Star Wars Visual Dictionary*, this exclusive minifigure celebrates the rebels' victory over the Empire at the end of Episode IV *A New Hope*.

Exclusive torso with gold medal

Blaster belt detail on brown pants

HEY DAD, WANT TO SEE THE MEDAL I GOT FOR DEFEATING YOU?

This Mon Calamari head piece can be seen on two other minifigures from the LEGO *Star Wars* theme

Unique torso with Mon Calamari officer's uniform

LEGO *STAR WARS*

The tenth anniversary of LEGO *Star Wars* meant special minifigures. Among the treasures from this year were Luke Skywalker with a celebration medal, a chrome Darth Vader, a silver Stormtrooper magnet, and the first minifigure appearance of Admiral Ackbar. Of these celebration minifigures, only Ackbar appeared in a standard LEGO set. The brave Ewoks also received a more realistic look.

The 2009 Wicket has detailed printing on his face

Combined head-and-torso piece fits over standard torso

Wicket W. Warrick Wicket was one of the first Ewoks to appear in minifigure form in 2002. This year, he's given a makeover and is seen in his distinctive orange hood.

Underneath his helmet, the stormtrooper's head is blank

Same helmet and torso pattern as a regular white stormtrooper

Silver Trooper This shiny minifigure appears in a magnet set in 2009 and in an exclusive polybag for Toys 'R' Us in 2010.

Underneath his shiny helmet lies Vader's scarred human face

KIDS, HUH? WHAT CAN YOU DO?

Admiral Ackbar This version of the rebel leader appeared in just three sets, so it is especially prized by collectors.

Chrome Vader This 10th anniversary Darth Vader is shinier and more menacing than ever, thanks to his chrome-black finish. Only 10,000 were produced.

This version has a cape but no lightsaber

LEGO® *INDIANA JONES*™

The minifigure archaeologist with the famous hat was back in 2009 with two new sets based on *Indiana Jones and the Temple of Doom*—the only movie not featured in the theme's 2008 debut. The highlight of the 2009 theme was the Temple of Doom set (7199), featuring not only six new minifigures, but also a thrilling temple/mine rollercoaster track build that was more than 3 feet (1 meter) long.

Indiana Jones This version shows Indy dressed in a smart tuxedo, with his 2008 head piece.

Indy is dressed up to visit Club Obi Wan in Shanghai

Mola Ram The villain has many unique details, including his headdress (excluding the horns), his torso, and the red paint on his forehead.

These detachable horns also appear on the Minotaur in LEGO® Minifigures Series 6 from 2012

Red crown piece

Willie Scott Ready for a performance at Club Obi Wan, singer Willie Scott wears a glamorous outfit.

Unique red outfit with gold details

Elusive diamond

Rock bin trap

Guards pursue Willie and Short Round

Glow-in-the-dark spikes

Temple of Doom

Temple of Doom This set (7199) boasts many exciting features, including a trapdoor, several booby traps, and glow-in-the-dark spikes.

LEGO SPACE

The intergalactic law enforcers were back after 11 years with a new play subtheme, chasing down the galaxy's worst thieves in 10 sets. Nicknamed Space Police III by fans, the theme featured numerous new alien heads. Every set included at least one alien minifigure, from the four-armed Frenzy to the eight-eyed outlaw Snake!

Alien head piece also used on Rench in the Space Police III subtheme in 2010

A large skull is also printed on the back of Kranxx's vest

Kranxx The leader of the Black Hole Gang, Kranxx is also a skilled pilot with a taste for high speeds.

Spiked helmet on top of green alien head

Slizer This spiky alien criminal is the chief mechanic of the Black Hole Gang.

Spiked armor printed on torso and legs

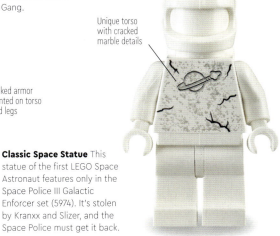

Unique torso with cracked marble details

Classic Space Statue This statue of the first LEGO Space Astronaut features only in the Space Police III Galactic Enforcer set (5974). It's stolen by Kranxx and Slizer, and the Space Police must get it back.

Unique head piece

Red cape—to match his eyes

Scales and muscles printed on torso

Squidman This alien criminal is always thinking up schemes to make himself rich, but they usually fail.

Extra-large eyes

Extra arms

Torso extension piece

Frenzy This four-armed baddie has a unique head piece featuring a huge, gaping mouth.

Double-sided head underneath the helmet. One side has two eyes, the other side has three

Black uniform with "Octan" printed on it

Skull Twin Just one of these criminals would be bad, but unfortunately there are two scary Skull Twins. Double trouble!

Visor can be used to hide his identity

Eighth eye

Protective helmet

Symbol of the Black Hole Gang

Knee pads printed on legs

Snake This prolific criminal appears in five sets—more than any other alien villain in this theme.

Snake Variant In Space Speeder (8400), slimy Snake appears without his visor.

CLASSIC SPACE

Four brave astronaut minifigures returned to outer space in 2009 as part of the Vintage Minifigure Collection. These minifigures were originally produced in the first nine years of the Classic Space line. The reissued versions looked identical, apart from their helmets, and are more robust than the originals.

Excitement hidden behind calm, professional smile

White Spaceman This intergalactic explorer has been on ice since 1987 and can't wait to journey into the 21st century.

Classic Space insignia

Yellow Spaceman It's been 20 years, but piloting a rocket is like riding a bicycle for this minifigure.

Space Police badge

Rookie Officer This officer is on his first mission. He seems confident enough, but his alternative face looks scared.

Flick-fire missile launcher

Special Ops Officer Orange glasses ensure that this minifigure looks good, even in space.

Large visor

Space Police Officer Compared to this year's colorful crooks, the Space Police uniform is positively restrained. Luckily, gray is this officer's favorite color.

GREAT CROP OF BRICKS THIS YEAR!

Farm Hand The hardworking farm hand has some familiar parts: her shirt was worn by Cloud City Luke Skywalker in 2003.

Cheerful red pants

Crouching cat from set 7637

Tan sun hat

Head piece popular in LEGO City theme—it is used for several policemen and construction workers

Printing continues on the back of the torso

Farmer This farmer has a new torso with a red plaid shirt and green overalls.

Green overalls for doing mucky farm work

DID YOU KNOW?
LEGO City Farm (7637) includes a grain silo, barn, cow pen, tractor, and three minifigures.

LEGO® CITY

Farm made its first appearance in a LEGO System theme in 2009 as part of LEGO City. Five sets and eight new minifigures and various animals populated this line, which initially lasted for two years. Three of the minifigures were farmers, each with a different head and torso. Prior to this release, Farm was primarily a LEGO® DUPLO® theme for younger fans.

Casual blue plaid shirt

Spotless pants are free from mud—so far!

Four-wheel Driver This minifigure is taking his four-wheel drive with horse trailer for a spin in the country. He's no farmer!

This hat piece is more commonly seen as a construction helmet

The horse cannot be disassembled

Horse Rider This well-dressed rider and her horse are found in 4WD with Horse Trailer (7635).

LEGO® AGENTS

The second and final year of LEGO Agents was known as Agents 2.0. Its five sets added steadfast Agent Swift to the team and the likes of Dyna-Mite and Dr. D. Zaster to their opponents' forces!

Same uniform as 2008's Agent Trace

Agent Swift The Agents' latest recruit pilots a hulking helicopter in Aerial Defense Unit (8971).

Head piece shared with Slime Face from 2008

Dr. D. Zaster This slimy villain has the same hair as Dr. Inferno, but in gruesome green.

Unique lightning-bolt torso print

Dyna-Mite This crook does her worst when working with her sidekick, Dollar Bill.

Antenna in place of standard head

Magma Drone Three of these headless minifigures patrol Dr. Inferno's latest volcano base.

Troll King This green minifigure is the leader of the wicked Troll Warriors. He plans to capture the Crown King and imprison him in his Mountain Fortress.

Tattered cloak is new this year

Pilot torso

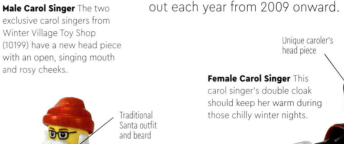

DECK THE HALLS WITH LEGO BRICKS! FA LA LA ...

LEGO® CASTLE

2009 was the last year of the fantasy-based LEGO Castle theme before LEGO® Kingdoms took up the quest in 2010. In 2009, a mighty minifigure king and his knights battled the evil forces of the Troll King in three sets.

LEGO SEASONAL

LEGO minifigures have always been a great holiday gift for LEGO fans. This group from the Winter Village Toy Shop and LEGO City Advent Calendar were the first of many designed to double as holiday decorations. They did not appear in any other sets. One set in this festive line would come out each year from 2009 onward.

Male Carol Singer The two exclusive carol singers from Winter Village Toy Shop (10199) have a new head piece with an open, singing mouth and rosy cheeks.

Unique caroler's head piece

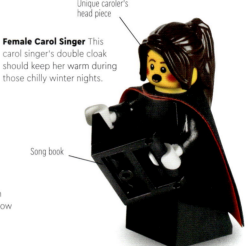

Female Carol Singer This carol singer's double cloak should keep her warm during those chilly winter nights.

Golden sword

First hair piece to feature a hole for accessories

Traditional Santa outfit and beard

Sack for presents

Song book

Medieval-style blue dress

Detachable breastplate armor

Crown King The 2009 version of the King has new printing on his torso and legs and a blue plume in his crown. Unlike the 2007 version, this minifigure does not have a cape.

Crown Queen The Queen has a double-sided head: now she is happy and smiling, but she can easily turn to her annoyed expression if something makes her royally cross.

Santa Perhaps not surprisingly, Santa can be found behind window 24 on the LEGO City Advent Calendar.

Lava Dragon—Knight In this two- to four-player game, the winner is the first knight to reach the top of a fiery mountain.

Red feather

VINTAGE CASTLE

Three Vintage Minifigures were reissued this year: a Forester and Knight from the Classic Castle sets, and a Ninja Warrior from the Ninja sets.

Simple hat

Classic Castle helmet

Knight This noble minifigure debuted in 1978 as part of the Castle Mini Figures set (0016). He reappears, unchanged, as a Vintage Knight for 2009.

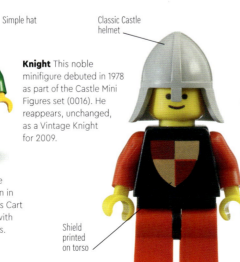

Minotaurus—Red Spartan Playing as red, blue, white, or yellow Spartans, the object is to travel to the center of a maze, avoiding the Minotaur.

Lunar Command—Green Players must build space stations to launch a Lunar Rocket.

Ramses Pyramid—Blue Explorer Blue, red, yellow, and orange explorers try to get to the top of Ramses Pyramid.

LEGO GAMES

Standing two bricks tall with a knob on the head, the games figure burst onto the scene in 2009 in LEGO Games such as Lava Dragon, Minotaurus, Lunar Command, and the award-winning Ramses Pyramid.

Ninja head wrap later used in NINJAGO play theme in 2011

Forester This Vintage Forester was last seen in 1990 in the Crusader's Cart (1877) and Hay Cart with Smugglers (1680) sets.

Shield printed on torso

Red Ninja The Red Ninja minifigure first adventured in 1999 in sets such as Ninja's Fire Fortress (3052).

2010s

Minifigures went massive in the 2010s! First, they received their own dedicated theme, introducing hundreds of new characters across the decade. Then LEGO® NINJAGO®: *Masters of Spinjitzu* took the small screen by storm before THE LEGO® MOVIE™ and its follow-ups turned minifigures into genuine film stars. Meanwhile, pop culture icons from Fred Flintstone and The Beatles to Mickey Mouse and Minecraft "mobs" all got the minifigure treatment—along with dozens of Super Heroes and Super Villains from Marvel and DC!

ME LIKE ROCK MUSIC!

The spiked club is new for this Minifigure

Underneath his removable hair and beard, the Caveman has a heavy brow and a wide smile

Hairy chest and animal-hide clothes

Caveman This Minifigure loves inventing things. If only he would invent a razor, then everyone could see his unique face!

2010

LONG THE HEART of many a play theme, minifigures were the actual theme in 2010! The simply named LEGO® Minifigures range was all about the characters and began a collection that is still going strong today. LEGO® *Prince of Persia*™ and LEGO® *Toy Story*™ launched as the first minifigure-scale themes to be based on Disney movies, with the latter pushing the boundaries of how tall a minifigure could be! Meanwhile, the heroes of LEGO® Atlantis looked for a fabled underwater city, the LEGO® World Racers made everywhere their racetrack, and LEGO® Castle revealed new rival Kingdoms!

Turkey leg

Shovel

Zombie The first-ever Zombie Minifigure would be followed by four more in 2012's LEGO® Monster Fighters theme.

LEGO MINIFIGURES

The collectible LEGO Minifigures theme was a major hit in 2010, with the first two series each providing 16 exclusive Minifigures to excited fans. Each character was packed individually in a series-colored bag, so collectors wouldn't be able to tell which Minifigure they were getting until they opened it.

A black version of this hair piece can be seen on the Disco Dude in Series 2

Clown face is unique to this Minifigure

Horn

Ninja katana, used for slicing sandwiches!

Ninja hood

Torso and legs are also exclusive to this Minifigure

Circus Clown This Minifigure can't talk, but fortunately he can honk his horn.

Ninja This ninja-in-training is one year early for the launch of LEGO® NINJAGO®!

Red cape has been seen on more than 20 other LEGO® minifigures, including a 2002 Quidditch Harry Potter™

Rare blue head piece with unique red mask printing

Wrench

Head, torso, and legs are exclusive to this Minifigure

Super Wrestler Life's just one big wrestling match for this Minifigure, and he's determined to win!

Demolition Dummy This unique Minifigure has a one-track mind: he just wants to dismantle everything.

PA7 70

License plate from a dismantled car

This hair piece is making its debut in blonde

Hands fit inside pom-poms

SERIES 1

The Series 1 line-up featured nine new LEGO parts. The new theme was more popular than anticipated, and supply issues made this first series of collectible Minifigures the rarest in the entire theme.

Cheerleader "2, 4, 6, 8, LEGO bricks are what we rate!" This enthusiastic pom-pom-shaking Minifigure is the first to feature side-printing on her legs.

SERIES 2

LEGO Minifigures Series 2 introduced more new Minifigures and also redesigned some old ones, including the Vampire. The series included 13 new elements and innovations, such as giving the Mime three interchangeable heads.

This head piece was also used on a rocker in a store-exclusive Minifigure three-pack in 2012

1970s outfit includes medallion and white suit

ROCK MUSIC? HOW PREHISTORIC!

Number shows this skier is in a race

Retro record

Skier This minifigure knows it's all downhill from here, but that's the way he likes it!

New spear has a soft tip

Ski poles and skis are new parts

Disco Dude Remember when pop music was played on funky vinyl things called records? No? The Disco Dude does!

New textured version of the witch/wizard's hat

Helmet, head, torso, and legs are unique to this Minifigure

Spartan Warrior He'd love to meet another Spartan Minifigure to spar with, but the Spartan Warrior is just too unique.

New microphone piece

The Witch was the first to have a bright green head

Shield has a handle on the back and a knob on the front

Witch This Minifigure spells trouble. Watch out for her in 2012; she reappears in a Halloween accessory set.

This is the first appearance of the sloped base in the Minifigures theme

Sandals printed on feet

Exclusive pink outfit with silver details

Pop Star She might be one of the LEGO world's most popular singers, but the Pop Star is just an ordinary Minifigure at heart.

This hair piece was first seen on the Cheerleader in Series 1

Beret is also seen on the Artist in Series 4

Rescue float can be gripped by two Minifigures

I DYE MY HAIR TO MATCH MY BELT!

Two alternative heads: frowning and frightened

Trophy piece also used as a microscale figure

Printed black belt

Lifeguard This Minifigure scans the seas looking for swimmers in trouble. The initials of LEGO sculptor Gitte Thorsen can be seen printed on her swimsuit.

Mime The Mime can convey extreme emotions and make other Minifigures fall over laughing without even making a sound.

Karate Master This martial artist is eager to show off his trophy—a brand-new element for 2010.

Double-sided head: smiling and sad

WHY DID THE DRAGON CROSS THE ROAD?

1×1 round plates for juggling

LEGO® CASTLE

In 2010, the new LEGO Kingdoms series took over from the 2007–2009 LEGO Castle theme, focusing on a battle between the rival Lion and Dragon kingdoms. Eight new sets were released this year, featuring wizards, knights, royalty, and other new minifigures. A Kingdoms Advent Calendar was the jewel in the crown of this year's assortment.

Quiver of arrows

Broad-brimmed helmet in shiny dark gray

Dragon Bowman Who knows what this bowman is up to with his cheeky smirk? Perhaps he has a plan up his sleeve to ambush the Lion Kingdom Knights.

If the Queen kisses him, this LEGO frog may turn into a prince!

Jester This medieval clown is only the second jester minifigure ever created. The first wore a similar outfit in blue and red and was in the 2008 Fantasy Era sets.

Same torso as Lion King

Smiling head piece with chin dimple

Lion Prince The heir to the throne has the same torso and legs as the King without the armor. The Lion Prince only appears in the 2010 Kingdoms Advent Calendar.

Green is the color of the Dragon Kingdom

The Queen's dress has lace-up details printed on the back

Queen The Queen has a new outfit in 2010 with gold details and a sloped skirt piece, but her head and crown were used on the Fantasy Era Queen in 2009.

Gold crown with detachable plume of feathers

Hair piece also seen on Hermione in the LEGO® Harry Potter™ theme

Dragon insignia

Dragon Knight One of five knights in the Green Dragon Knights Battle Pack (852922), the Dragon Knight features the new dragon torso printing.

Lion Princess This princess's regal torso and matching sloped skirt piece are new for 2010.

The Dragon Knight wears a cape instead of armor

Standard LEGO cape found in more than 200 sets

New torso can be found underneath this armor

Hat with dragon print is unique to this minifigure

DRAGON KINGDOM

The Dragon Kingdom had no king, so the Dragon Wizard minifigure usually acted as the leader. The Dragon Knights used the same helmet as the Lion Knights, but wore dark and pale green outfits with a golden dragon design.

This wizard is the first minifigure to have this beard piece in black

New printed legs with gold detail

Lion King As befits the noble leader of the Lion Kingdom, the king has many new elements, including a torso with Lion head medallion and fur trim pattern.

LION KINGDOM

The heroic Knights of the Lion Kingdom featured a new helmet with a cross shape on the front and a new breastplate with a golden lion print. They were led by the Lion King, who had a new crowned head, a new torso, and new legs.

Dragon Wizard This powerful minifigure would love to defeat the Lion Kingdom. He really doesn't like the Lion King!

LEGO ATLANTIS

Minifigure divers went in search of the mysterious city of Atlantis in this underwater play theme, but aquatic guardians were determined to stop them. Many exciting new elements and molds were introduced to create the amazing undersea creatures of LEGO Atlantis. The theme was a huge success, leading to more sets and minifigures in 2011. The new Atlantis elements also provided LEGO fans with colorful and unique pieces to use in their own creations.

Eyepatch is unique to Ace minifigures

Propeller blade attached to air tank

Ace Speedman
The leader of the Salvage Crew, Ace Speedman pilots the Neptune Carrier. He wears a distinctive eyepatch— his eye is fine, he just thinks an eyepatch looks cool!

Standard-issue green diving flippers

FIRST THING I DO IN ATLANTIS? VISIT THE SWIMMING POOL!

Shark Warrior Comprising three unique pieces, the Shark Warrior has the head of a shark but the torso and legs of a human.

There is no standard minifigure head underneath, unlike Viktor Krum's 2005 LEGO Harry Potter minifigure

Gold-and-black speckled helmet

Trident

Gold-and-black speckled breastplate

Portal key

ATLANTIS DEEP SEA SALVAGE CREW

The lime-green-and-silver Atlantis minifigures featured a new breathing apparatus mold, new torsos (printed front and back), and new heads. All but two of the Atlantis sets came with specially molded portal keys, which were the object of the divers' quest in the 2010 storyline.

UNDERSEA GUARDIANS

Atlantis featured some of the most innovative minifigure designs to date, particularly its fierce underwater warriors. The Portal Emperor included a new helmet with a never-before-seen gold-and-black speckled paint pattern.

Portal Emperor This minifigure is made of five parts, four of which are unique. Only his breastplate appears on another minifigure—the Atlantis Temple Statue in 2011.

Double-sided head: smiling and annoyed

Detachable headgear

DID YOU KNOW?
Atlantis was the first LEGO play theme to feature 3D content on its website.

Manta Warrior Featuring unique head, headgear, and torso pieces, this Manta Warrior is a fearsome foe for the Salvage Crew. His trident can fire blasts of electricity!

Headgear reflects the shape of a manta ray fish

Squid Warrior Instead of legs, the Squid Warrior has a new tentacle piece. The piece was used in a different color on the 2011 Alien Commander in the LEGO® Alien Conquest theme.

Detachable headgear

Harpoon gun

Detachable headgear

Portal key

Unique torso

New tentacle piece instead of regular legs

Like the other underwater warriors, the Squid Warrior wields a gold trident— new for 2010

Professor Samantha Rhodes Although not technically a member of the Salvage Crew, scientist Sam Rhodes accompanies them because she is determined to prove that Atlantis exists.

151

White wand piece

STUDENTS

Luna Lovegood She's a unique character in many ways, and Luna Lovegood was also the only Ravenclaw minifigure for many years.

Spectrespecs

Exclusive pink jacket

Unique skirt-over-pants design

All of Harry's friends got minifigure redesigns this year. The only new character was Luna Lovegood, complete with reversible head with Spectrespecs on one side and a smile on the other.

Voldemort Look out, Harry Potter! He Who Must Not Be Named looks scarier than ever in 2010. He can be found in Hogwarts Castle (4842).

Unique torso

LEGO® HARRY POTTER™

LEGO Harry Potter reappeared after a two-year absence in 2010 with six fun sets. Rebranded for the new movie *Harry Potter and the Half-Blood Prince*, the characters had mostly been released before. One set, The Burrow (4840), was brand new and taken from that film.

Hair piece is dark brown version of ones used on Draco Malfoy

Fenrir Greyback This snarling werewolf has bared teeth for biting other minifigures, even when there isn't a full moon.

Unique torso and head

Wavy hair piece

Ron Weasley Harry's best friend has a new haircut in 2010 and a double-sided head featuring smiling and scared faces.

Dementor The gray-and-green 2004 Dementor figures were scary enough, but the spooky 2010 ones are terrifying.

Dementors have a skeleton body underneath their tattered robes

Long, curly hair piece is unique

Bellatrix Lestrange The personality and unique style of one of Voldemort's most loyal supporters is brought to life as a minifigure for the first time in 2010.

Torso and skirt piece are decorated with silver and blue details

DARK LORD AND FOLLOWERS

The redesigned Lord Voldemort had new minifigure allies this year. Those joining his wicked crew included the dangerous witch Bellatrix Lestrange and the vicious fiend Fenrir Greyback.

Same torso and legs as Hermione, Ron, and Ginny

Harry Potter In set 4842, this version of Harry Potter comes with his Invisibility Cloak.

2010 Quidditch minifigures have a helmet that can be placed on the head when the hair piece is removed

QUIDDITCH

Game on! 2010 saw new minifigures of Harry Potter and Draco Malfoy in redesigned Quidditch robes and a new character, Marcus Flint.

Marcus Flint The Slytherin captain wants to win the Quidditch Cup. His unique head piece shows his large sneer.

Blond hair piece is unique to both 2010 versions of Draco

Lion badge denotes Gryffindor house

Only nine other minifigures wear this colored robe

Double-sided head: frowning or smiling

Ginny Weasley Ron's sister's minifigure looks much more grown up than the 2002 version.

Gloved hands

Draco Malfoy For 2010, Malfoy's Quidditch minifigure has a new dark green uniform and white pants. His double-sided head can look worried or smug.

Green is color of Slytherin house

Gloved hands

Harry Potter Unique to Quidditch Match (4737), this version of Gryffindor's scarlet Quidditch uniform appears twice—on Harry and on Captain Oliver Wood, also released in 2010.

TEACHERS AND OTHERS

Four new minifigures joined the supporting cast this year: Professor Flitwick, Argus Filch, and Ron's parents Arthur and Molly Weasley. The Molly minifigure went through numerous prototypes before the final look was achieved.

Hair piece also seen on Dumbledore

Crumpled outfit is unique to this minifigure

Argus Filch Making his first appearance in 2010, the Hogwarts caretaker has a hefty collection of keys hanging from his belt.

Unique head and torso

Arthur Weasley It was easy for the LEGO designers to make Mr. Weasley look like his sons—they just used the same red hair piece as Fred and George's minifigures.

Hair piece also used on Mary Jane Watson in the 2004 LEGO® Spider-Man™ theme

Molly Weasley Ron Weasley's caring and hardworking mother is portrayed in a unique minifigure with an orange-patterned apron.

2002 version had unpainted eyes

Large ears

Small silver glasses

Bushy brown mustache

Professor Flitwick The Charms Professor's tiny stature is reflected in his short LEGO legs.

Rumpled vest and bow tie

Ragged outfit made from pillow case

Dobby The heroic house-elf's minifigure had an impressive makeover in 2010. His unique head mold and authentic outfit bring his character to life.

Plain head piece underneath helmet

Gryffindor Knight Statue This statue of a knight appears in the Gryffindor common room in Hogwarts Castle (4842).

Movable hands

Hagrid A head taller than most other minifigures, this version of Hagrid the Hogwarts gamekeeper appears in one set in 2010 and two more in 2011.

LEGO® ADVANCED MODELS

Since 2000, LEGO builders wanting a bigger challenge have looked to the Advanced Models theme. These LEGO sets were larger in size and piece count and generally used more advanced building techniques. Popular subthemes in 2010 included Modular Buildings and Space.

Mannequin Bride and Groom The huge clothing store Grand Emporium (10211) featured wedding mannequins, a cashier, a window cleaner, a child, and two shopper minifigures.

Wedding dress used again in a LEGO® Education set in 2011

Head piece is turned to show blank side—the other side features face printing

Detachable gold visor

Astronaut This minifigure appears in Space Shuttle Adventure (10213), which was the second ever LEGO® Space Shuttle set.

LEGO SEASONAL

The holidays meant more fun minifigures this year. This unusually undressed Santa minifigure is from the LEGO® City Advent Calendar. He's fresh from the bathtub!

Santa keeps his hat on, even in the bathtub!

Nude yellow torso and legs. Black hips represent briefs

Bathtub Santa He makes an unusual appearance on day 18 of the 2010 LEGO City Advent Calendar, but by day 24, Santa is dressed again.

LEGO® WORLD RACERS

World Racers was a new theme in 2010, the first racing-related theme since *Speed Racer* to have minifigures and a story behind it! World Racers pitted two teams—the Backyard Blasters and the Xtreme Daredevils—in a bruising series of races all over the globe.

Another variant has the same helmet but with a red visor

Torso exclusive to Bart Blaster variants

Racing Helmet Bart Blaster
There are four variants of this minifigure released in 2010, each with different helmets.

Aviator Helmet Bubba Blaster
This monobrowed minifigure has three variants.

Detachable goggles

Unique torso with Backyard Blasters logo

Team logo on helmet

Removable goggles

Dirtbike Helmet REX-treme Rex has four variants. Three are distinguished by their helmet, but the fourth, from a promotional set, has plain white legs.

Suit pattern continues on legs

Aviator-style helmet

Helmet with red visor

Double-sided head: evil grin and determined expression

Red Visor Billy Bob Blaster
Underneath his helmet, Billy Bob has red eyes and an unusual glasses pattern.

All the Backyard Blasters have the same legs

Aviator Helmet Bart Blaster
This determined driver has a double-sided head—one face is scowling and the other is half covered by a balaclava.

Torso is unique to all variants of this minifigure

TEAM X-TREME DAREDEVILS

MAX-treme, DEX-treme, and REX-treme made up the heroes of World Racers, driving sleek vehicles armed with an array of missiles. All three featured new, double-sided heads and torsos printed front and back.

BACKYARD BLASTERS

The Backyard Blasters were the "bad guys" of this theme. Bart, Billy Bob, and Bubba would try anything to beat their opponents. The team drove large, chunky vehicles with an array of explosive and destructive weapons, such as giant cannons and saws.

Lime green helmet is exclusive to variants of Dex and Max

Green Helmet DEX-treme
The three Dex variants all feature the same torso with radar detail on the front and belt detail on the back.

Radar detail

CREW AND OFFICIALS

Other minifigures came along for the World Racers ride—three Team X-Treme crew members and three race officials. The latter minifigures had little to do, since no one was paying attention to the rules anyway ...

Each crew member variant has the same torso

Orange legs also used on rebel pilots from the LEGO *Star Wars* theme in 1999

Race Official The three versions of the race officials had the same torso but different heads and headgear.

Crew Member Three crew members were released with different heads.

Black gloves to protect hands

Visor can be worn up or down

Standard Helmet MAX-treme One side of his head is grinning and the other is determined, but thanks to his shades, it can be hard to tell what Max is really thinking.

Cad Bane All the elements of the ruthless Duros bounty hunter, apart from his legs, are new for 2010 and exclusive to this minifigure.

Trademark wide-brimmed hat

Detachable breathing apparatus

Aayla Secura Twi'lek Jedi Knight Aayla Secura makes her first minifigure appearance in 2010 in the *Clone Wars* set Clone Turbo Tank (8098).

Exclusive Twi'lek head-tails

Unique torso and head

Head piece is the same as the 2008 Clone Trooper, although Senate Commandos are not clones

Lightsaber

Printing also continues on the back of the torso

Exclusive white markings denote rank of captain

Luke Skywalker The fifth variant of Luke as an X-wing pilot features more details on his g-suit and helmet. The g-suit is also worn by fellow rebel Zev Senesca, also released this year.

LEGO *STAR WARS*

2010 proved to be a great year for LEGO *Star Wars* collectors, as new characters and new versions of fan favorites entered a galaxy not-so-far-away. Ruthless bounty hunter Boba Fett was back with a more movie-accurate look, and Aayla Secura, Cad Bane, and Bossk became minifigures for the first time.

Detachable range finder

Senate Commando Captain Tasked with guarding Chancellor Palpatine and the Senate, this minifigure's elite status is reflected in his unique helmet and torso.

Unique sand green head

Flight suit has breathing apparatus printed on the back

Blaster rifle

Bossk The Trandoshan bounty hunter's reptilian head piece and flight suit torso were specially created for this minifigure. This version of Bossk is exclusive to two sets.

Battle-damaged helmet with new, battle-scarred head underneath

Blaster with LEGO® Technic piece on barrel

YOU'RE WORTH A LOT OF CREDITS TO ME.

Removable jetpack on back

Boba Fett This new variant of the famous bounty hunter is available in just one set (8097). The minifigure has a new torso and cape.

Underneath his helmet, Boba Fett has a plain black head piece

Minimalist black line printing

Limited Edition Boba Fett Designed to look like the original all-white concept art for Boba, this promotional minifigure was given away as part of the 30th Anniversary of *Star Wars: The Empire Strikes Back*.

LEGO *TOY STORY*

The first LEGO theme to be based on Disney Pixar movies included sets based on *Toy Story*, *Toy Story 2*, and the all-new *Toy Story 3*. They mixed traditional minifigures with new, long-limbed figures for Woody and Jessie, and unique molds for the likes of Rex, Hamm, and Lotso. There were also large-scale buildable figures of Buzz Lightyear and Zurg.

Head fits over space suit

Dome fits over unique head

Wings fit onto back of suit

Standard minifigure legs and torso

Buzz Lightyear This Space Ranger stands two bricks shorter than Woody but flies high with an exclusive four-piece wingsuit.

Alien Five sets, including the large-scale Construct-a-Buzz (7592), feature aliens from the faraway world of Pizza Planet.

Pizza Planet logo

Short legs

This Jessie figure has a worried expression

Scuffs and dirt from a trip in a garbage truck

Woody With his long arms, long legs, and unique head piece, Woody towers over his best friend, Buzz!

Hat is part of head piece

Long arms attached to standard torso

Legs are about one standard brick longer than usual

Jessie In *Toy Story 3* sets, Jessie, Woody, and Buzz all get figures with dirt stains and sad-looking faces.

DON'T TELL ANYONE, BUT SPINJITZU MAKES ME DIZZY!

Detachable beard covers goatee printed on head

Traditional Japanese hat

Spinner

First release minifigure wears black obi sash

Master Wu LEGO ninja practice the art of Spinjitzu—spinning at high speed—to fire up their energy. Spinners such as this one allow Master Wu and his students to practice Spinjitzu.

Katana is a traditional ninja sword

Gold fireball pattern

Hidden identity

Nya One of the few NINJAGO minifigures with a double-sided head, Nya is Kai's sister. Her alternative face has a mask covering her mouth.

Cole As the Ninja of Earth, the Cole minifigure wears black to represent the energy stored below the ground.

Bushy eyebrows

Earth symbol attached to cords

LEGO NINJAGO

LEGO NINJAGO was one of the most ambitious play themes ever launched, and its success proved to be beyond anyone's expectations. Combining colorful and exciting ninja sets with a social game (NINJAGO Spinners), it boasted a successful TV series and a best-selling graphic novel line. Originally planned to be a three-year line, the popularity of NINJAGO later led to it being extended to far beyond.

Scarred eyebrow

Jay Although only their eyes are seen, the ninja minifigures all have distinctive features. Jay, the Ninja of Lightning, has a scarred right eyebrow.

Lightning symbol

2011

THIS WAS A BIG YEAR for the LEGO Group. LEGO® NINJAGO®, one of its most successful play themes, was introduced; aliens invaded Earth in the new Alien Conquest line; LEGO® City launched a successful space program; and bold adventurers went on a Pharaoh's Quest. And with new sets appearing in the LEGO® Atlantis, LEGO® SpongeBob SquarePants™, and LEGO® Stars Wars™ themes, action continued from the depths of the ocean to the farthest reaches of outer space, and everywhere in between!

Red robes indicate that Kai is the Ninja of Fire

Kai DX This variant of the Kai minifigure bears a golden dragon design. It shows that he has tamed a dragon and attained Dragon Extreme (DX) status.

DID YOU KNOW? Although the Kai minifigure has scars around one eye, these were not present in the TV series.

Zane The Ninja of Ice, Zane, wears all-white robes. He is the fourth of the four original ninja minifigures in the LEGO NINJAGO theme.

Dragon breathing fire design

Tail of dragon printed on legs

Ice symbol on robe

Gray sash keeps robes in place

NINJA

The four ninja minifigures each wear different-colored robes tied to their element: red for Fire, blue for Lightning, white for Ice, and black for Earth. The colored robes were featured in play theme sets and spinner packs.

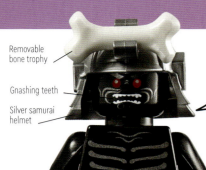

Removable bone trophy

Gnashing teeth

Silver samurai helmet

DOESN'T EVERYONE HAVE A DOG BONE ON THEIR HAT?

VILLAINS
Lord Garmadon's plot to escape the Underworld leads to a conflict that spans all Ninjago. Aided by General Samukai and the Skeleton Army, Garmadon quests for the Four Golden Weapons of Spinjitzu.

Lord Garmadon Nemesis of the ninja, Garmadon cuts a suitably sinister minifigure in black. The bone on his helmet marks him out as the commander of the Skeleton Army.

Sideswept hair with front curl

Superman The promotional Superman minifigure would later reappear in 2012's Superman vs. Power Armor Lex (6862).

Famous S-shield

Muscles printed on torso

Red cape

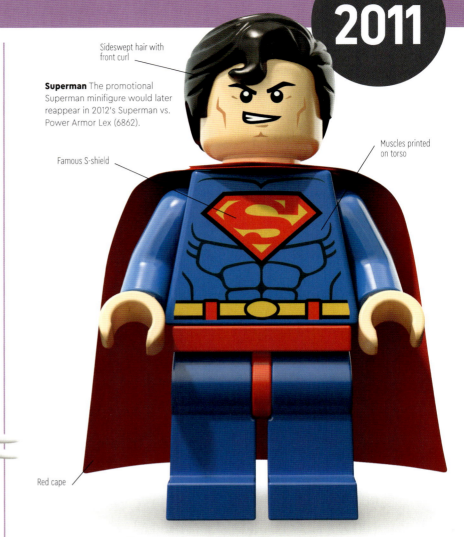

Removable armor

Metal plate replaces lost eye

New booted leg piece

Kruncha The General Kruncha figure wears a military cap that cannot be removed.

Frakjaw This Frakjaw figure hides his metal-plated head firmly under his hat.

Nuckal The skeleton figures have vertical grip arms—their hands are rotated 90 degrees to their arms.

Dual-colored jester hat

Bonezai Like the ninja, each skeleton has his own theme. Bonezai is the Skeleton of Ice.

Krazi Skeleton Krazi's hat was last seen on a jolly court jester in 2009's LEGO® Castle theme.

Chopov The first Chopov figures were hatless, but he later gained this simple black helmet.

SKELETONS
Soldiers of Lord Garmadon, skeleton figures each have a unique weapon. They appear in both play theme sets and spinner packs. Despite their fearsome look, they play a comic role in the story.

Bamboo hat

Protective chest plate of a skeleton general

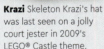

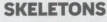

Wyplash His torso may be standard skeleton issue, but the General Wyplash figure's worm-eaten head and bone armor are all his own.

LEGO® DC UNIVERSE SUPER HEROES
Super Hero excitement started to build in July with the announcement at San Diego Comic-Con that the DC Universe would be coming to LEGO sets in 2012. Batman and Green Lantern minifigures were given away at that show as a free promotion, with a Superman minifigure offered at New York Comic-Con that fall.

Bat cowl

Batman Another Comic-Con exclusive, this Batman minifigure bears the logo from *The Dark Knight* movies instead of the classic black-and-yellow one.

Grimly set mouth

Bat logo

White eyes peer through mask

Green Lantern logo

Green Lantern On one side of the Green Lantern minifigure's head is this fierce snarl; on the other is a confident smirk.

Five-pointed cape

LEGO® PHARAOH'S QUEST

A team of minifigure adventurers unleashed an ancient curse in this one-year play theme. Pharaoh's Quest featured six sets and 12 new minifigures. The sets also included six mystical treasures, such as swords and scarabs, all but one of which were colored gold.

Earnest expression

Map

Large pickax

Professor Archibald Hale The pith helmet may be old hat, but the bespectacled head is brand new for the Professor Hale minifigure.

READY FOR ADVENTURE

Professor Hale is aided by a team of brave minifigure heroes. Their names all refer to types of weather—a homage to the names of the original LEGO® Adventurers, including Johnny Thunder and Charles Lightning.

Werewolf Some microfigures recur in several games, but the Werewolf appears only in Waldurk Forest.

Dark Druid Druids may be either Heroes or Monsters. The Dark Druid is among the Monsters.

Missing eye

Goblin General Goblins are Monsters, easily identified by their green faces and red eyes.

Shaggy bangs

LEGO® GAMES HEROICA™

LEGO Games plunged into the fantasy world of HEROICA in 2011, with microfigures of Heroes and Monsters scattered across a total of five games. The HEROICA line would last until 2012.

Ranger The Ranger is a bow-wielding Hero who can defeat a Monster up to five spaces away.

Extravagant sideburns

Jake Raines With a wry grin, bold stare, and facial scar, this dashing minifigure conveys Jake Raines' fearless nature.

Cross-body bag to store finds

Helena Tova Skvalling Two versions of Helena's minifigure exist—one with yellow hands and one wearing brown gloves.

Scorpion Pyramid Set 7327 features seven minifigures, including three explorers on the hunt for treasure.

Simple, smiling face

Speech Bubbles Minifigure Minifigures got to talk—in a way—with the LEGO® Speech Bubbles Minifigure (81087). It came with a minifigure, attachable speech bubbles, and stickers with quotes.

MINIFIGURE MANIA

Some LEGO minifigures do not fit into a theme, but they are no less popular. They have played a part in all sorts of celebrations, from topping cakes at weddings to being a giveaway at LEGO® Fan Weekends in Denmark. The fellow in the red and blue even came with his own speech bubbles—he always had something to say.

Tiara and veil

Top hat

Bride and Groom Fans could now tie the knot in LEGO style with these Bride and Groom cake toppers.

Sloping pieces form skirt

LEGO® MINIFIGURES

The second year of the collectible LEGO Minifigures series featured three assortments, totaling 48 new Minifigures. The bar code—which in the past allowed some people to work out which Minifigure was in a package—was removed, so the selection was truly random. Forty-eight new parts featured this year.

Gold hat with minifigure head detail

Gold teeth

Gold mic

Rapper This minifigure brings the beats and the bling with all his gold accessories.

Pointy elfin ears

Elf The Elf warrior is the first minifigure to have ears attached to his hair piece.

Scale mail armor

Stag head emblem on shield

SERIES 3

Fans were particularly excited to get their hands on the first LEGO Elf Minifigure in Series 3. New parts for this series included the Elf's bow and arrow, the Tennis Player's racquet, and the Hula Dancer's maracas.

Tennis racquet

Upturned alien eyes

Breathing tubes

Tennis outfit printed on torso and legs

Tennis Player This sporty minifigure wears traditional tennis whites.

Space Alien Lime green is the go-to LEGO color for aliens. This one has a contrasting red tongue.

> ### DID YOU KNOW?
> Series 4 Minifigures featured more back printing and decorated accessories than any previous series.

Plumed hat with turned-up brim

Stylish Van Dyck beard

Musketeer The fleur-de-lis on the Musketeer's torso is a classic symbol of French royalty.

Board used in a 2014 LEGO® Friends set

New hair piece with quiff

Sailor hat unique to this minifigure

SERIES 4

Among the new parts created for Series 4 were Kimono Girl's fan and the Sailor's hat. The Ice Skater and a Hockey Player shared the ice—and the limelight—as they both debuted new minifigure ice skates.

Bright orange hazard suit and helmet

Radioactivity warning symbol

Hazmat Guy Judging by his alarmed expression, the Hazmat Guy Minifigure is in the wrong job.

Snowboard bindings printed on feet

Snowboarder This daredevil minifigure is the first to ride a snowboard since 2003.

Fabric skirt fits over legs

Ice Skater Silver skates attach to the Ice Skater Minifigure's feet.

Telescope for spotting land

Sailor This skilled seafarer is the first collectible Minifigure to have a winking facial expression.

SERIES 5

Series 5 Minifigures showcased 20 new parts, including the Boxer's gloves, the Evil Dwarf's round shield, and the Egyptian Queen's sharp bob.

Minifigure hands replaced with a new glove element

Boxer The Boxer packs a real punch in his flashy all-red gear. Instead of ordinary minifigure hands, he has two boxing gloves.

Winged scarab printed on hair

Venomous green snake

Egyptian Queen The ancient Queen's snake has appeared in various colors in more than 100 sets.

Winged metal helmet

Two blades attach to ax individually

Rock club

Evil Dwarf This beard piece debuted in 2008 in the LEGO® Castle theme. It is only ever used for dwarf minifigures.

Cave Woman One of the locks on the Cave Woman's hair piece acts as a clip to attach her bone ornament.

Mature features

ADU logo

Helmet protects their powerful brain

Detachable jetpack

ADU-issue azure blue suit

ADU Sergeant Gray facial hair and wrinkles mark this minifigure out as the senior ADU member.

Computer Specialist Orange glasses protect this minifigure tech-expert's eyes from screen glare.

ADU Rookie The slightly overconfident Rookie isn't laughing on the other side of their face!

LEGO® SPACE

Aliens invaded Earth for the first time in a LEGO line in this one-year Alien Conquest theme. The strange aliens and their UFOs were opposed by the Alien Defense Unit, who drove the invaders off Earth at the end of 2011. The Alien Conquest story crossed over into numerous other play themes, including LEGO® City Space.

ALIEN DEFENSE UNIT

The brave minifigures of the ADU have new torsos, printed legs, a belt pattern on the hips, and reversible heads. The team includes old and young, male and female, and brave- and scared-looking minifigures!

THOSE ALIENS HAVE MADE THEIR LAST CROP CIRCLE!

Breathing apparatus

High-grip gloves

Double-barreled blaster

ADU Soldier This soldier scans the horizon for UFOs, ready to launch into action.

Specs for spotting toxic spills

Radio to transmit warnings

Scientist Cleaning up alien toxins is this green-spattered scientist's job.

Shocked expression

Farmer Except for his standard hair piece, this agricultural abductee is made of all new parts.

Sharp, sleek hairdo

Microphone

Clipboard

Lotta Brix A new head and torso grace this pushy news reporter minifigure who is about to get the full scary story!

CIVILIANS

The aliens need brainpower to make their ships go, and they have realized that Earth people are a good supply. These civilian minifigures all have reversible heads so they can look scared when the aliens appear.

Staring, single eye

Alien Clinger The Alien Clinger can fit onto any civilian minifigure's head. Once in place, it sucks out their brainpower to fuel the alien ships.

I RULE AN EMPIRE, BUT I CAN'T FIND PANTS THAT FIT!

Gold epaulettes show rank

Alien blaster

Six tentacles are one piece

Alien Commander Separate brain and face elements make up the head of the self-styled "Supreme Overlord" alien.

ALIENS

Four new alien minifigures were introduced in this line, with new head pieces and new torsos. Their blasters had previously only appeared in the collectible Minifigures theme. The Alien Commander has tentacles instead of standard LEGO legs.

Alien Android The easily fazed android sports the standard Alien Conquest alien colors—black, magenta, silver, and lime green.

Semitransparent brain

Mechanical eye

Mechanical arm with barb

Metal leg

Very small brain

Huge, powerful jaw

Alien Trooper This ferocious minifigure is the land soldier of the alien invaders.

LEGO® HARRY POTTER™

The LEGO Harry Potter theme featured two sets related to *Harry Potter and the Deathly Hallows*™ in 2011, as well as the largest LEGO Harry Potter set at the time, Diagon Alley (10217). This year saw the release of 28 minifigures, with some—including Narcissa Malfoy, Mr. Ollivander, and the Weasley twins—appearing in minifigure form for the first time.

Ron Weasley The 11th Ron minifigure wears a tartan tank top with brown pants. A 2010 variant had the same top with black pants.

Two-colored hair piece

Narcissa Malfoy Narcissa's sleek minifigure has fancy blue-gray embroidery on both sides of her torso.

Red-and-brown color scheme

DID YOU KNOW? The strip of paint on some minifigures' torso pegs (underneath the head piece) helps the printing machine recognize which side of the torso is the front or back.

Lightning-bolt scar

White bow tie and dress shirt

Familiar Harry Potter hairstyle

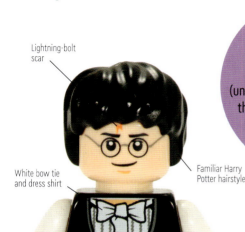

Witch's hat with buckle

Professor Sprout A sprig of leaves adorns the torso of the Hogwarts' Herbology teacher.

Stan Shunpike This Knight Bus conductor minifigure doesn't have printed sideburns, unlike his 2004 predecessor.

Hollow, lined cheeks

Ticket machine print on torso

Magic wand

Teeth gritted in concentration

Zipped cardigan

Knitted cardigan with hood

Side braids drawn back

Hermione Granger The new 2011 Hermione minifigure has swapped her school uniform for casual clothes.

Yule Ball Harry Potter DK's book LEGO® Harry Potter™ Building the Magical World came with this minifigure, looking suave in his Yule Ball dress robes.

Neville Longbottom Unlike the 2004 version, Neville's new minifigure has a reversible head.

Casual pants

LEGO ATLANTIS

The adventure beneath the sea continued in 2011, as the minifigure heroes of LEGO Atlantis found the lost city itself, complete with a Poseidon statue that turned out to be its Golden King. The King would be the only Atlantis minifigure to appear as a microfigure in the LEGO® Game Atlantis Treasure. Ten minifigures and five sets rose from the depths this year.

Classical architecture

Gold fish ornament

City of Atlantis A ruined city, a deep sea sub, five minifigures, and a giant crab come with the City of Atlantis set (7985).

Barracuda Guardian

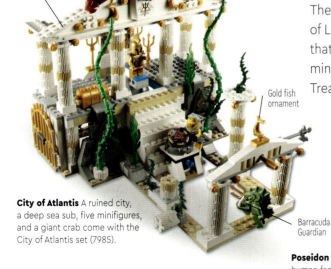

Spartan warrior's helmet

Poseidon Statue A yellow human face is printed on the reverse of this golden minifigure's head.

Lobster Guardian This demonic decapod guards the temple with a golden trident gripped in one of its big claws.

Long, spiky spines

Strong pincers

I USED TO STYLE WOOKIEE HAIR IN MY OLD JOB.

Curved top to helmet

Filter

Lightweight armor

Black gloves

Shadow ARF Trooper A new black Advanced Recon Force Trooper came free with some online purchases as part of a *Star Wars* Day promotion.

T-shaped visor

Unique ponytail plugs into knob on head

Twin blasters

Mandalorian Trooper Four of these warriors from *The Clone Wars* feature in the Mandalorian Battle Pack (7914).

Eight-horned head top piece

Orange jumpsuit

Aurra Sing Like other *Clone Wars* characters, Aurra has large, stylized eyes.

Savage Opress A yellow pattern on Opress' head represents clan tattoos.

Bowcaster

Embo The printed radar dish helmet is unique to the Embo minifigure.

Head piece and hair piece have both been seen before

Padmé Naberrie This is the first update of the Padmé minifigure since the *Star Wars* theme's debut in 1999.

Rare double-ended lightsaber

Yellow eyes of dark side devotee

LEGO *STAR WARS*

The LEGO *Star Wars* theme went from strength to strength this year, with both fan-requested minifigures and minifigures based upon *The Clone Wars* appearing. Some characters, such as the crimson R-3PO, had never before been seen in LEGO form. Others became exclusive minifigures unlikely to reappear in future sets. All of this helped make 2011 a great year for LEGO *Star Wars* collectors.

DID YOU KNOW?
The R-3PO minifigure uses the same mold and printing as C-3PO. Only its color is different.

New torso details for fourth Darth Maul minifigure

Darth Maul The spiked piece on top of Maul's head is the same as that of Opress, his minifigure brother, but with different printing.

Removable head wrap

Patched-together armor

Dengar Bounty-hunting has left its mark on Dengar's battle-scarred minifigure.

Photoreceptor eyes

Printing continues on reverse

R-3PO This protocol droid minifigure is only available with the Hoth Echo Base set (7879).

New, tousled hair piece

Breathing mask on reverse face joins air tube

Bacta Tank Luke The latest Luke Skywalker minifigure shows the hero ready for immersion in a healing bacta tank.

Straight ears

HALLS TO BE DECKING I HAVE!

Backpack attaches at neck

Short legs

Santa Yoda The head of this festive minifigure is based on Yoda's appearance in *The Clone Wars*. His outfit, not so much!

Hair parts on different side to adult Han

Short legs

Young Han Solo In animated adventure *The Padawan Menace*, young Han has his first adventure with R2-D2 and C-3PO.

Medal given to Han in *Star Wars: A New Hope* movie

Han Solo with Medal This minifigure makes a pair with the medal-wearing Luke in 2009's LEGO *Star Wars: The Visual Dictionary*.

THREE OF A KIND!

These three minifigures are limited edition exclusives. Santa Yoda was part of the 2011 LEGO *Star Wars* Advent Calendar (7958). Young Han came with the Blu-ray edition of animated adventure LEGO *Star Wars: The Padawan Menace*. Medal Han was packaged with the first ever LEGO *Star Wars Character Encyclopedia*, published by DK.

LEGO® ADVANCED MODELS

The Pet Shop (10218) was the first Modular Buildings set to include two structures—a three-story pet shop and a townhouse. This was the sixth set released for this line. LEGO fans blasted off into outer space again with Shuttle Expedition (10231), which was a slightly revised version of the Space Shuttle Adventure set (10213) from 2010.

Hair falls forward over shoulder

Classic smiling face print

Logo shows shuttle flying above a planet

Pet Store Customer This shopper's torso print was first worn by a LEGO Castle queen.

Female Shuttle Astronaut The 2011 female Astronaut has acquired a new hair piece, as well as a new head.

Red-and-white jester hat

Quiver attaches at neck

Jester For the first time, a female minifigure gets to play the fool!

Dragon Knight Of the six Dragon Knight variants released this year, only this one is missing a tooth.

LEGO® CASTLE

Four LEGO sets joined the Kingdoms subtheme in 2011, including the large Mill Village Raid (7189). Elsewhere, the first female LEGO jester appeared in the LEGO® Education Fairytale and Historic Minifigure Set (9349).

Detailed medieval outfit

Reverse face has cross expression

Villager Mill Village Raid includes three exclusive villager minifigures and two rare goat figures.

LEGO® PIRATES OF THE CARIBBEAN

As the fourth *Pirates of the Caribbean* film sailed into theaters, a fresh LEGO theme dived into its treasures. Sets inspired by the all-new *On Stranger Tides* were accompanied by one based on first film *The Curse of the Black Pearl*; two focused on its follow-up, *Dead Man's Chest*; and one depicting saga-spanning ship the *Black Pearl* itself.

Barnacles printed on new style of pirate hat piece

Captain Jack Sparrow No *Pirates* set is complete without this swaggering swashbuckler, in one of his eight minifigure variants.

Double-sided head found in just one set

Hairstyle created for this theme

Bandana and jewelry printed on hair piece

Beardlike tentacles attach between head and torso

Alternative face shows Jack as a cursed skeleton

New claw hand piece

Davy Jones The scourge of the Seven Seas is found aboard The Black Pearl (4184) and no other set—thank goodness!

Elizabeth Swann Marooned on Isla De Muerta (4181), Elizabeth and Jack battle minifigure and skeleton versions of villainous Hector Barbossa.

LEGO® BRAND STORE

2011 saw the tradition of exclusive LEGO sets offered at LEGO® Store openings continue. These sets featured one or more minifigures, some specially made for the sets and others reissues of classic minifigures. Several new stores opened this year in Denmark, the US, Canada, and the UK.

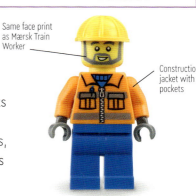

Same face print as Mærsk Train Worker

Construction jacket with pockets

Mission Viejo Worker This minifigure was available at the opening of a LEGO Store in Mission Viejo, California.

I'M ON A KNIGHT SHIFT.

Helmet with nose guard

Long side bangs

Pretty yellow flowers

Sunrise Lion Knight Early visitors to the LEGO Store in Sunrise, Florida, could add this knight to their LEGO collection.

San Diego Stylist This minifigure came with a hairbrush accessory at a LEGO Store opening in San Diego, California.

Standard wizard's hat

Gandalf the Gray As you might expect, all parts of Gandalf's minifigure but the face and hands are gray.

New torso with rope and belt pattern

Gray beard encircles smiling face

2012

EXCITEMENT GREW in 2012, with adventure stepping up to the next level. New licensed themes LEGO® *The Lord of the Rings*™, LEGO® DC Universe Super Heroes, and LEGO® Marvel Super Heroes spawned some of the most sought-after building sets yet. Brand-new play themes such as Monster Fighters delighted fans, while continuing favorites LEGO® NINJAGO®, LEGO® Minifigures, LEGO® *Star Wars*™, and LEGO® City found new ways to spark their imaginations. Of the huge number of new and refreshed minifigures released this year, many represented some of the greatest characters in fiction. Little surprise, then, that 2012 became a banner year for collectors of every age.

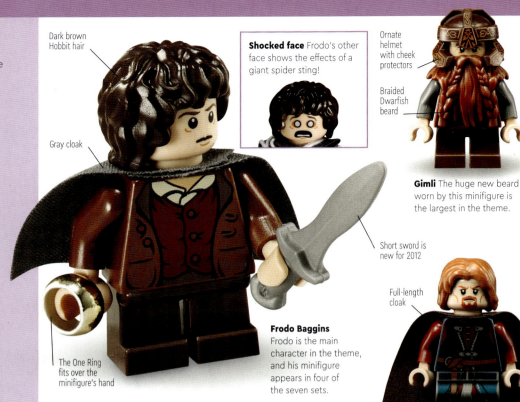

Dark brown Hobbit hair

Gray cloak

The One Ring fits over the minifigure's hand

Shocked face Frodo's other face shows the effects of a giant spider sting!

Frodo Baggins Frodo is the main character in the theme, and his minifigure appears in four of the seven sets.

Ornate helmet with cheek protectors

Braided Dwarfish beard

Gimli The huge new beard worn by this minifigure is the largest in the theme.

Short sword is new for 2012

Full-length cloak

Boromir A grimacing face appears on the reverse of this brave warrior's head.

Gold crest on helmet

Breastplate covers entire torso

King Théoden The heroic Rohan king minifigure has new ornate legs, helmet, torso, and breastplate.

Scale mail pattern on legs

LEGO *THE LORD OF THE RINGS*

It was one of the most hotly anticipated LEGO play themes launched in 2012, with seven sets based on the three hit *The Lord of the Rings* movies. All the major characters appeared as minifigures, with new heads, torsos, and printed legs. The many new elements included swords, shields, and helmets, and an entirely new element was created to represent the One Ring.

Elven ears attached to hair piece

Slightly bigger bow and arrow version introduced in 2011

Legolas This minifigure's new hair piece is worn by all 2012 Elves in this theme and for 2013's LEGO® *The Hobbit*.

Elven tailcoat

EXCLUSIVE ELF

This exclusive version of Second Age Elrond was available only with preorders of LEGO® *The Lord of the Rings*™: *The Video Game*.

Open-mouthed angry expression

Pearl gold spear

Same hair piece as Elves Legolas, Haldir, and Tauriel, but in brown

Elrond Young Elrond carries a long spear and has a reversible face: open- and closed-mouthed.

GOLLUM

This small LEGO figure requires a minimum 2×2 brick to stand on because of his hunched shape. He appears in two variants and in two sets, one from 2013's *The Hobbit* theme and one from *The Lord of the Rings*.

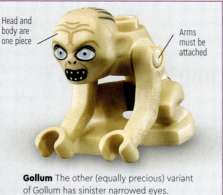

Head and body are one piece

Arms must be attached

Gollum The other (equally precious) variant of Gollum has sinister narrowed eyes.

All-black outfit includes tattered cloak and hood

Ringwraith The shadowy Ringwraiths, also known as Nazgûl, have only appeared in one set to date (9472).

Handprint In set 9476, an Uruk-hai can be found with a handprint on his helmet.

Terrifying warpaint printed on face beneath helmet

White hand of Saruman

Standard gray breastplate piece

Uruk-hai Four variants of these fierce warrior creatures have been released with and without helmets and armor.

Pointed greatsword

Evenstar pendant printed on torso

Flame and telescope form torch

Shirt tails on torso extend to legs

Aragorn Brave Aragorn has a new torso, legs, and reversible head, but his hair piece has been worn by more than 20 other minifigures in this color since 2010.

I PUT THE HISSSSSS IN MINIFIGURE HISTORY!

Boa crest on hood

Gray scale markings

Ready to grip Constrictai Fang Blade

Snike Short, unposable legs set the tunneling Constrictai apart from the other Serpentine tribes.

LEGO NINJAGO

In its second year, LEGO NINJAGO upped the action as the five ninja and Nya took on the Serpentine tribes. The villains had new snake heads and snake prints, and some even had snake tails instead of legs!

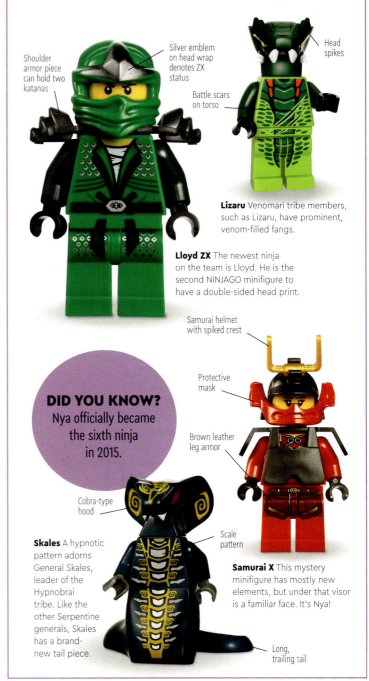

Shoulder armor piece can hold two katanas

Silver emblem on head wrap denotes ZX status

Head spikes

Battle scars on torso

Lizaru Venomari tribe members, such as Lizaru, have prominent, venom-filled fangs.

Lloyd ZX The newest ninja on the team is Lloyd. He is the second NINJAGO minifigure to have a double-sided head print.

Samurai helmet with spiked crest

Protective mask

Brown leather leg armor

DID YOU KNOW? Nya officially became the sixth ninja in 2015.

Cobra-type hood

Skales A hypnotic pattern adorns General Skales, leader of the Hypnobrai tribe. Like the other Serpentine generals, Skales has a brand-new tail piece.

Scale pattern

Samurai X This mystery minifigure has mostly new elements, but under that visor is a familiar face. It's Nya!

Long, trailing tail

Bizarro This rare minifigure of Superman's troubled clone was a prize in a raffle at the 2012 San Diego Comic-Con.

Unique head has sad expression on other side

One-off torso

Purple cape

LEGO DC UNIVERSE SUPER HEROES

After releasing a few exclusive minifigures at Comic-Cons in 2011, the DC Universe burst into life with an explosion of LEGO minifigures in 2012. It was the first year that non-Batman DC sets joined the assortment, a trend that would long continue. New minifigures, including Wonder Woman and Lex Luthor, made their debuts, and old favorites got an exciting new look.

Tiara is part of hair piece

Alternative face has a smile

Star-spangled shorts

Wonder Woman The minifigure Amazon warrior comes complete with a golden lasso accessory.

Angry expression

Stylish black suit

Lex Luthor Lex is one of three minifigures in Superman vs. Power Armor Lex (6862).

SUPERMAN

The giveaway Man of Steel from 2011's San Diego Comic-Con made a welcome return in 2012. This time, he was packaged with Wonder Woman and Lex Luthor, who, unlike Superman, were new and exclusive to the set.

Cowl piece in use since 2006

Eye holes in cowl show white head printing

Utility Belt is larger than on other Batman minifigures

Subtly updated cowl shape for 2012

Bat-symbol in blue

I TAKE CRIME APART, BRICK BY BRICK.

Five-pointed cloth cape

Electrical wires and plates printed on legs and torso

Electrosuit Batman This minifigure was exclusive to LEGO® Batman™ *The Visual Dictionary*, published by DK.

Batman Two variants of this minifigure exist: this one and another with a new-style cowl.

DID YOU KNOW?
To date, there have been more than 90 variant Batman minifigures!

Chiseled features

Expensive gray business suit

BATMAN II

The Dark Knight returned in five sets this year, with a new minifigure head and torso. Many of Batman's foes were similarly refreshed for 2012, including Poison Ivy, The Joker, The Riddler, Two-Face, and Catwoman.

Bruce Wayne Bruce's head print is the same as his alter ego's, but without the headband that makes minifigure Batman's eyes.

WHICH ROBIN AM I? I GET CONFUSED.

Robin The first new Boy Wonder minifigure since 2008 wears all red instead of the classic red and green.

Bat-wing tail fins

Cord printed on torso represents cape attachment

Reverse of head has expression of open-mouthed alarm

"R" logo appears on all Robin minifigures

Lightning-bolt symbol

Shazam! Another San Diego Comic-Con raffle prize, this was the only Shazam! minifigure until 2019.

Black cape is the same as Batman's

Batman in cockpit

Batmobile and the Two-Face Chase This set (6864) comes with two vehicles, five minifigures, and a bank with a safe.

Hubcaps same color as bat-symbol

Black on yellow bat-symbol

Whip to whisk stolen goods into her grasp

Classic jester hat

Wrestler mask printed on head

Zipped catsuit printed on torso

Diamond pattern on legs

Catwoman Batman's feline foe has a new mask, torso print, and head print with purple lips.

Harley Quinn Aside from her classic hat, the Joker's mischievous minifigure sidekick has all new parts.

Bane Tubes that carry a strength serum to Bane's brain are printed on the back of his torso and head.

Vest laced up with string

Fedora shields eyes from sun

SEEN A T.REX? CALL REX T!

Compass attached to belt

Rex Tyrone This dashing dino tracker has the same taste in hats as LEGO® *Indiana Jones*™—and the same disregard for his own safety!

LEGO® DINO

Deep in the jungle, LEGO explorers discovered dinosaurs that had somehow survived into the modern era. The intrepid minifigure heroes tried to capture the dinos in the seven-set theme. Each set came with a dinosaur, at least one hero minifigure, and a vehicle.

NEW HEAD, NEW TORSO ... SAME SENSE OF HUMOR! HA HA HA!

Old hair piece appears in green for first time

Torso printed with lime vest, bow tie, and squirty flower

Same hair piece as 2006 Two-Face

Purple on front and back of torso is printed

White hands match face

Left arm and leg are molded in purple

Two-Face Bold new colors give this updated good guy/bad guy minifigure an eye-catching look.

The Joker It's smiles all around for the Joker. His new head has a different kind of grin on the reverse.

Utility vest holds screwdriver and radio

Nervous expression

Tousled hair

GPS device to locate T-rex

Binoculars for spying dinosaurs

"Tracer" Tops A chin dimple and mirrored shades give this tracer a rugged look.

Belt holds pocket for pen and paper

Chuck "Stego" Jenkins A new head is introduced for this wildlife photographer. He clearly has bigger things to worry about than shaving.

ID tag necklace

Leaves printed on hair piece

Bowler hat in light gray

Crowbar resembles a question mark

DID YOU KNOW?
The Riddler's hat is a gray version of the one debuted by the 2011 collectible LEGO® Minifigures Small Clown.

Loosely tied scarf

Sue Montana Ponytailed Sue is ready to face the action dressed in hardy safari gear.

Poison Ivy A printed vine trails its leaves all over this minifigure's torso and legs.

The Riddler Three question marks on this minifigure's new torso and hat leave no doubt as to the trickster's identity!

Riddler's question-mark motif

Josh Thunder This minifigure hero is a descendant of Johnny Thunder from the LEGO® Adventurers theme.

Belt pocket

LEGO MARVEL SUPER HEROES

Spider-Man had first spun his webs in a LEGO set in 2002. Ten years later, he was back—this time as Ultimate Spider-Man—along with a whole wave of Marvel characters making their minifigure debuts. They included the X-Men, the Avengers, and some of their most formidable foes!

Scabbard on back holds two katanas

Muscled torso

Extra utility belt on leg

Deadpool A black-and-red mask is printed directly onto the minifigure mercenary's head.

Sideburns printed on head

Wolverine The X-Men's wild mutant minifigure has a hair piece previously seen only on vampires.

Claws attach to minifigure hands

Flaming red hair

Symbol of phoenix rising

Phoenix This minifigure shows fiery X-Men telepath Jean Gray in her classic costume as Super Hero Phoenix. Her reversible head has two faces—one friendly and one fierce.

Gray eyebrows show his age

First minifigure to wear cape in medium lilac color

Gray platform

Magneto The platform supplied with this X-Men foe minifigure represents the metal disc on which he flies.

X-MEN

Wolverine was the first X-Men mutant to achieve minifigure status, in Wolverine's Chopper Showdown (6866). Phoenix would show up next, as a promotional giveaway at San Diego Comic-Con in July of this year.

Wolverine's Chopper Showdown In this set (6866), Wolverine needs his chopper motorcycle to escape the Magneto and Deadpool minifigures and their helicopter.

HEY DOC OCK, CAN YOU SCRATCH MY BACK?

On reverse face, red eyeglass shades are lowered

Mask printing covers half of minifigure's head

Dragon symbol

Life-preserving technology on chest panel

Arms attach to neck bracket

Small spider logo

Mask has rounded eye shapes and black webs

Large white eyes

Black suit is really a living alien being!

Symbiote Suit Spider-Man Raffle winners at the 2012 San Diego Comic-Con got this special minifigure as a prize.

Iron Fist The symbol on this minifigure's torso shows that he fought the magic dragon Shao Lao.

Doc Ock The Doc Ock minifigure has four extra arms that are all detachable and posable.

SPIDER-MAN

Spidey and martial arts master Iron Fist teamed up to take on Doctor Octopus in Spider-Man's Doc Ock Ambush (6873). It was one of three 2012 sets to include minifigures based on characters from the *Ultimate Spider-Man* TV series.

Spider-Man The new Spidey minifigure is modeled on the cartoon version from the *Ultimate Spider-Man* animated TV series.

The usual red Spidey gloves

DID YOU KNOW? The 2012 Doc Ock minifigure is made up of an amazing 26 parts.

MARVEL'S THE AVENGERS

Smash hit movie *Marvel's The Avengers* became an exciting LEGO subtheme in 2012, with four action-packed sets. Black Widow, who appeared only in Quinjet Aerial Battle (6869), was the most sought-after minifigure.

Only Thor has this hair piece in light yellow

Unique torso with circular armor plates

Thor The Asgardian minifigure shows off gritted teeth on the other side of his head.

Gold mask fits over helmet

Repulsor beam

Iron Man Transparent elements attach to Iron Man's hands to represent repulsor beams.

Toy Fair Iron Man Just 125 minifigures like this one were given away at the International Toy Fair in New York.

Mask printed on head

Arc Reactor on chest

No metal plates on knees

Striped panel is straighter than on Toy Fair variant

Captain America There have been more than 20 Captain America variants since this one.

"A" for America (but it could also be for Avengers)

Printed mask has white eye covers

Toy Fair Cap A special promotional Captain America minifigure came packaged as a set with Iron Man at the International Toy Fair in New York.

V-shaped red-and-white panel

Unique horned helmet

Armor based on *Marvel's The Avengers* movie costume

Loki Six other variants of the god of mischief have worn the same helmet.

Strap for archer's quiver

Hawkeye A black bow was designed specially for this minifigure.

Gloved hand for holding bow

Black, tousled hair

Well-muscled torso

Smile can be swapped for a determined look

Weapon holsters strapped to both legs

Black Widow This black-clad Avenger makes her minifigure debut flying the first ever LEGO quinjet.

Head, torso, and legs are one piece

Pants molded on figure as well as printed

Detachable hands turn at wrist

HULK GROW!

The Hulk figure in Hulk's Helicarrier Breakout (6868) is far from mini. He's been scaled up to match Hulk's relative size in the movie. Ten more "big figure" Hulks would follow in the years to come.

Large Hulk Huge hands enable this supersized Hulk to grip standard minifigures by their legs.

HULK SMASH BIGGER HULK!

Incredible Hulk This Hulk minifigure was an exclusive gift-with-purchase at LEGO® Stores and the online LEGO® Shop.

LEGO CITY

LEGO City left town for a while in 2012, with the introduction of the City Forest Police subtheme. New Forest Police minifigures and their adversaries appeared in seven sets, including a new Forest Police Station (4440). Forest firefighters also got four sets. Ranger, pilot, and crook minifigures featured new heads and torsos, and firefighter minifigures had new torsos.

New torso with life jacket worn over it

Forest Police campaign hat

Aviator-style sunglasses

Police Boat Pilot This officer shades his new face print with a new wide-brimmed hat.

Standard crash helmet

Police badge

Torso common to Forest Police

Police ATV Rider An All Terrain Vehicle gives this officer the edge in Police Pursuit (4437).

Respirator attaches to neck

Firefighter This hose-wielding hero is one of four in a LEGO City Accessory Pack (853378).

Water cannon with water jet

Fireproof suit

LEGO MINIFIGURES

The LEGO collectible Minifigures line returned for its third year in 2012, with 48 new Minifigures spread over three series. As in previous years, many new elements were introduced in each of the series.

Clockwork Robot A bracket that fits over the Clockwork Robot's neck holds a turnable key.

Block-shaped head with knob on top

Panel of gauges, knobs, and screen

Skater Girl The third skateboarding collectible Minifigure might just be the coolest so far!

Printed hair streak matches outfit

Smiling skull with pink bow

Winged heart design

Pants with pockets and studded belt

Bright colors as seen on vintage toys

Throwing spear

Metal rivets on feet

Removable surgical cap

Surgical mask printed on head

Surgeon This smooth operator comes with syringe and X-ray minifigure accessories.

Patient's X-ray shows a broken rib!

Helmet has cheek pieces and neck guard

Roman Soldier From helmet to sandals, this soldier Minifigure's costume is fully authentic.

SERIES 6

Series 6 introduced 18 new pieces and contained the largest number of new head molds in any assortment at that point—three. The Roman Soldier, Clockwork Robot, and Surgeon were among the most sought-after Minifigures from this set.

Lightning wings and arrows pattern

Sandal printing continues on sides of feet

Seven-pointed crown

Torch made from plume and telescope pieces

DID YOU KNOW?
The LEGO Friends range has introduced more than 160 named mini doll characters since its launch in 2012.

All parts except flame are sand green

Tile printed with America's date of independence

Lady Liberty The green color of Lady Liberty mimics the copper patina on the Statue of Liberty monument.

LEGO® FRIENDS

Meet the mini dolls! These more realistic figures changed LEGO play forever when the LEGO Friends range launched this year.

Dark red tie

Ice cream sundae

Shoe straps printed on legs

Andrea Mini dolls have the same swappable elements as minifigures, but Andrea's in no rush to change her look!

Emma Artist Emma is one of the five original core Friends, alongside Andrea, Mia, Olivia, and Stephanie.

Peter Male mini dolls like Olivia's dad are a slightly different shape to female mini dolls.

Head cover has rabbit ears

Bunny Suit Guy A veggie diet has put a spring (or a hop) in this Minifigure's step.

Gold shell crown

Fish tail with silver scales

So far, only this little Minifigure has worn this hood in red

Rocker Girl There's a touch of stardust about this musician's zig-zaggy makeup.

Rubbery basket used in LEGO Friends theme

Guitar decal matches stage makeup

Giant carrot accessory

Swim cap so tight, it has wrinkles

Ocean King The stormy sea king's gold trident is right out of the LEGO® Atlantis theme.

Grandma Visitor This is the first female in the LEGO Minifigures theme to have short legs.

Winner's medal

SERIES 7

When Series 7 hit the stores, it brought 16 new parts and more printing than any LEGO Minifigures collection to date. Its rarest Minifigures included Bunny Suit Guy and the Ocean King.

Swimming Champion The swimmer's medal would resurface in the Team GB series.

Brawny Boxer Team GB's lion head logo appears on the Brawny Boxer's head guard.

Horse Rider The Rider's helmet will later be worn by two minifigures in the LEGO Friends theme.

Blue mouth guard protects smile

Helmet and hair molded as one piece

Large boxing gloves

Team GB sash

TEAM GB

Nine Minifigure athletes were produced to commemorate the 2012 London Olympic Games. Each came with a white stand and gold medal and were available only in the United Kingdom and Ireland.

New Santa hat

Santa Santa's sack accessory can be gripped by minifigure hands or attached to a brick.

Short, detachable beard

Helmet has antennae

Sack bulging with gifts

RESISTANCE IS ... JUST GOING TO BE FRUSTRATING FOR YOU.

Magenta skis coordinate with jacket

Conquistador This seeker of gold wears a metallic gold breastplate over his dark red torso.

Detachable plume

Helmet is metallic gold

Standard skull

Glaring red eyes

Goggles shield eyes from glare

Laser weapon made from ray gun and red bar

Actor Alas, poor Actor! He wears a scratchy ruff that feels a bit uncomfortable during long plays.

Ruff is separate

Claw arm

Evil Robot Robot armor covers this Minifigure's torso and legs. Under his helmet, his face is silver metal with rivets.

Ski poles

Downhill Skier Colors taken from the LEGO Friends theme adorn this Minifigure's gear.

SERIES 8

Series 8 had a more even distribution of Minifigures than past releases, making it easier for fans to collect a complete set. The Downhill Skier was perhaps slightly more difficult to find.

LEGO® MONSTER FIGHTERS

The LEGO Monster Fighters theme focused on villainous Lord Vampyre's plan to use the powerful moonstones to help monsters rule the world. Only the valiant Monster Fighters could stop him! Heroes and monsters clashed in nine sets in this one-year line. Although some of the monsters had appeared in previous LEGO sets, they all got new heads and torsos for this play theme.

I KNOW THE MONSTERS ARE DOWN THERE ... THAT'S WHY I'M UP HERE!

New color for bowler hat this year

Unique steam-powered artificial leg

Dr. Rodney Rathbone The dapper minifigure team leader appears in three Monster Fighters sets.

Harpoon clips to topknot

Crossbow

Vampire-repelling garlic attached to belt

Ann Lee Ann's two faces—one smirking and one scowling—both bear a scar left by a witch's nail.

Telescopic eye

Map tucked into cross-body belt

Major Quinton Steele This old-school adventurer carries a unique monster-fighting weapon.

Hammer held by steam-powered artificial arm

Bushy beard and eyebrows

Slicked-back hair

Oil stains on undershirt

Pink moonstone coveted by zombies

Jack McHammer Jack's hammer was first wielded this year by the Thor minifigure in the LEGO Marvel Super Heroes theme.

Frank Rock Biker Frank rarely takes his shades off, but his alternative face shows him with uncovered eyes.

FIGHTERS

All five Monster Fighter minifigures in the theme featured new heads, new torsos, and new printed legs (except Rathbone), and all appeared in at least two sets.

MONSTERS

One of the monsters—the Swamp Creature—had never appeared in any LEGO set prior to this. Like the Werewolf, Mummy, and the Zombie Bride and Groom, he appeared in just one set in the theme.

Unique head with bared teeth

Glow-in-the-dark claws attach to minifigure hands

Werewolf Both the torso and legs of the minifigure Werewolf are printed with ripped clothing.

Seaweed and scales pattern on legs

Detachable head cover with fins

Swamp Creature Big, froglike eyes peer through eyeholes in this minifigure's head cover.

Head bandages coming undone

Mummy This is the first mummy minifigure with glow-in-the-dark details.

Tightly wrapped torso and legs

Manbat Two toothy Manbat minifigures defend Lord Vampyre's abode in the Vampyre Castle (9468).

Hair piece has huge bat ears attached

New arm pieces have bat wings attached

Shaggy fur pattern printed on torso

Hair piece has widow's peak

Special bat moonstone accessory

Cloth cape with huge, pointed collar

Lord Vampyre A red moonstone gives Lord Vampyre power over all other monster minifigures.

Double-ended
saberstaff

Zabrak tattoos
on face

Yellow eyes
on chrome
silver head

Pattern on both
sides of torso

TC-14 She may look
like a silver C-3PO,
but this protocol
droid is one of
a kind!

Darth Maul This
same Maul also
came in an equally
rare Mini Sith
Infiltrator set,
available only at
the 2012 San Diego
Comic-Con.

Exposed
wires on
torso

"REVENGE OF THE FIFTH"

The unofficial *Star Wars* Day on May the Fourth
was followed by a cleverly titled "Revenge of
the Fifth" day. To celebrate, the LEGO Group
offered two exclusive minifigures free with
LEGO.com and LEGO store purchases.

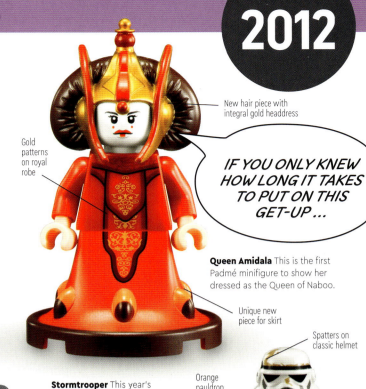

New hair piece with
integral gold headdress

Gold
patterns
on royal
robe

*IF YOU ONLY KNEW
HOW LONG IT TAKES
TO PUT ON THIS
GET-UP …*

Queen Amidala This is the first
Padmé minifigure to show her
dressed as the Queen of Naboo.

Unique new
piece for skirt

Helmet with breathing mask
and vision enhancer

LEGO *STAR WARS*

The big news for LEGO *Star Wars* in 2012 was the
arrival of Queen Amidala. Padmé Amidala (or Padmé
Naberrie) minifigures had been around since 1999, but
this was her first appearance in royal robes. It featured
in only one set, Gungan Sub (9499). Other highlights of
the year were a more
detailed Gamorrean
Guard and the debut of
bounty hunter Boushh.

Stormtrooper This year's
stormtroopers are the first
to have faces printed on the
heads beneath their helmets.

Spatters on
classic helmet

Orange
pauldron
over one
shoulder

Tatooine Stormtrooper
Dirt stains cover 2012's
second new stormtrooper.

Helmet dented
by past battles

Standard
blaster found
in more than
250 sets

Helmet style
introduced
in 2009

Thermal
detonator

New, more
detailed
torso print

Face facts This year's
stormtroopers, sandtroopers,
and TIE fighter pilots all share
this head print.

Boushh Removing this minifigure's helmet
reveals its true identity. It isn't Boushh the
bounty hunter at all—it's actually Princess
Leia in disguise!

Boba Fett A new Boba
minifigure has orange knee
pads and silver boots.

Blaster is pistol set
in a lightsaber hilt

LEGO® CUUSOO

LEGO CUUSOO was the original name for
the LEGO® Ideas platform, which sees
the best fan creations turned into real
LEGO sets. The second CUUSOO set,
Hayabusa Unmanned Asteroid
Explorer (21101), was the first to
include a minifigure and the first
to be made available worldwide.

Junichiro Kawaguchi This
real-life professor led the
Hayabusa space
exploration project.

JABBA THE HUTT

This second version of Jabba is more
detailed than the one that appeared in
2003, and features a head that can
swivel 360 degrees. His hands are
capable of holding minifigure
accessories.

Jabba the Hutt The
head and torso of
this Hutt figure
are made as
one piece.

Tattoo on right arm

Faint stripes
indicate skin
wrinkles

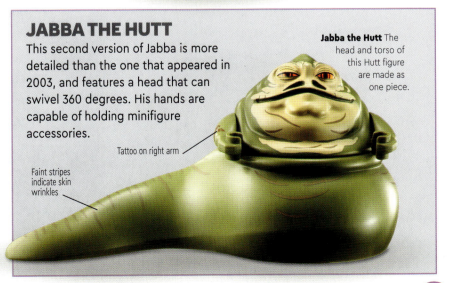

Seagull The Sea Captain's faithful friend perches on his hand when it wants a rest.

Camera The hockey puck on the opposite page becomes a zoom lens with this accessory!

Shovel Minifigure shovels have been around since 1978, but 2019 saw the first green one—for scooping up after dogs!

Balloon This party essential is guaranteed never to pop, deflate, or float away!

Keytar There are lots of minifigure musical instruments, but few are as funky as this one!

Briefcase and ticket This Passenger minifigure looks businesslike with his briefcase accessory. Clip his ticket to his hand and off he goes to board the train.

MINI GEAR

MINIFIGURES WERE given C-shaped hands so they could carry things—and they have certainly carried a lot of things! LEGO® minifigure gear can be practical, such as a shovel for digging a hole (or scooping a poop), or just for fun, such as sports equipment or a cool keytar. The kind of gear they carry helps distinguish one minifigure from another and is great for role-play. For example, the crook might have the stolen money in his hand, but the police officer is ready for him with the handcuffs! Watch for new gear every year.

Money There's a sinister squid on the loose! The Squidman minifigure flees the scene of the crime, carrying his stolen loot in his hand.

Magnifying glass First seen in 1998, the minifigure magnifying glass really magnifies!

Handcart The Railway Employee minifigure transports the passengers' luggage. He doesn't look very thrilled about it!

Book This style of LEGO book really opens and is also used as a minifigure laptop.

Cup Minifigures have been using cups of all colors since 1979, but they are most common in red.

Hockey stick Over the years, sports minifigures have made use of tennis racquets, baseball bats, and pool cues, too!

Baby's bottle This Nurse Android Minifigure can hold a baby's bottle just as easily as she holds a baby!

Paintbrush and palette The Artist's paint-splattered palette and brush accessories were brand new for 2011.

Tools The Harbor Worker is a busy man, but luckily tools like his handy wrench and mallet make life a little easier.

Umbrella How do minifigures keep their hair so immaculate? Umbrellas are part of the secret!

Steak and cleaver The Butcher's brand-new T-bone steak has a bone to make it easier to hold.

Ax Minifigure firefighters have always carried axes, but 2019's City sets introduced the most realistic choppers on the block!

Police badge and handcuffs The Policeman's badge is printed on a 1×2 tile. His handcuffs can really be worn by minifigure crooks.

Pearl gold CHI harness gives Longtooth awesome power

Battle scar on unique head mask

LET ME AT THOSE CROCS!

Longtooth This older foot soldier has spent many years on the Lion Tribe's front line, where all the action is—and his minifigure has the battle scars to prove it!

2013

LEGO® FANS WERE introduced to a whole new world of play in 2013 with the launch of LEGO® Legends of Chima™, a fantasy theme set in a world where animals rule and the power of CHI is the key to peace ... or power. But there were plenty of other high-stakes conflicts going on this year, as the ninja of NINJAGO battled a Stone Army, LEGO® Galaxy Squad fought off a bug invasion, and two new licensed themes— LEGO® Teenage Mutant Ninja Turtles™ and LEGO® *The Lone Ranger*™—took the battle between good and bad to new heights.

LEGO LEGENDS OF CHIMA

Tribes of sentient animals clash over a mysterious source of power called CHI in this exciting new theme. Its story centers on the battle for control of the CHI between the powerful Lion and Crocodile Tribes, which then draws other tribes of Chima into battle. In 2013, LEGO Legends of Chima featured more than 30 new minifigures, all with completely new designs and accessories.

Eagles have the same wings as Ravens, but in white

Unique head mask features flowers and happy grin

G'lonna This lovable little girl Gorilla likes to adorn her fur with braided vines and pink flowers.

Eris The gleaming gold tiara on Eris' head shows that she is the daughter of one of the Eagle Tribe's Ruling Council members.

G'lonna stores her CHI in a decorative harness

Legs feature feathers, talons, and Eagle Tribe armor

HEROIC TRIBES

The brave Lions, quirky Eagles, and laid-back Gorillas are allied in an effort to preserve peace and harmony in Chima. They want to ensure fair distribution of CHI for all tribes—even their hostile enemies!

Only Laval is important enough to wear this unique head mask

Powerful CHI staff is a symbol of his high status in the tribe

Lagravis Laval's father commands great respect as king of the Lion Tribe. The aging leader is the only Lion minifigure with a gray mane.

CHI-orb-encrusted crown

Royal armor features Lion Tribe symbols

Laval Dressed in a gleaming gold crown, a regal cape, and dark blue battle armor, Laval looks every inch the royal prince of the Lion Tribe.

Only Lagravis wears this elaborate CHI armor in pearl gold

LEGO® DC Universe Super Heroes Riddler has same purple hands in 2012

Head mask with beak and feather texture fits over regular minifigure head piece

Artificial leg is also worn by Alien Android in 2011 in LEGO® Alien Conquest theme

Razcal This minifigure is in charge of valuing the Ravens' stolen treasures. The gold markings on his head mask suggest that he keeps some for himself!

Rizzo This ragtag Raven has a silver artificial leg and eyepatch made from scavenged metal.

Jagged scales poke through his gold head mask

King Crominus The gruff, tough king of the Croc Tribe has gold teeth to match his royal head mask.

I'M THE KING—DO WHAT I SAY AND MAKE IT SNAPPY!

Only Croc royalty wear capes

Battle scars over both eyes from numerous dogfights

TIME TO CHI UP!

Worriz is first minifigure to wear this jagged cape

Wakz wears scary-looking fangs on his leg straps

Red robe features animal bones

Sharp claws

Wakz Bushy eyebrows and white whiskers mark this minifigure out as the oldest warrior of the Wolf Tribe.

Crawley This formidable foot soldier's tough scales provide natural body armor, so all he wears in battle is a red bandana and a loincloth.

Vine necklace has a place for storing CHI

Worriz His minifigure's gray cape shows that Worriz is the lead negotiator of the Wolf Tribe, but that doesn't mean he is the boss— all members of the pack are equal.

VILLAIN TRIBES

Motivated by greed, the Crocodiles want to seize control of all the CHI in Chima. They persuade the ferocious Wolves and sharp-tongued Ravens to side with them and do battle against the Lions and their allied tribes for power.

LEGO® MARVEL SUPER HEROES

The armored Avenger Iron Man flew into battle in sets based on the movie Marvel Studios' *Iron Man 3*. From his Malibu mansion to a high-speed chase over water, Tony Stark challenged the forces of the Mandarin with the help of War Machine. Other minifigures this year included Doctor Doom, Nova, and Venom.

Freckled face

Pepper Potts The CEO of Stark Industries is exclusive to Iron Man: Malibu Mansion Attack (76007). Turn her head around to see her scared expression.

Arc Reactor

Iron Man This minifigure has an updated torso, with Arc Reactor and gold Heartbreaker armor.

Transparent blue jets

Shoulder cannon

Determined face can be swapped for neutral look

Double-sided head: confident or scared

War Machine Wearing the same helmet as Iron Man, but in gray, this minifigure comes with a shoulder cannon and transparent red repulsors and jets.

"Danger" printed on torso

Tony Stark This first version of Tony without armor appears in Iron Man: Malibu Mansion Attack (76007).

LEGO® MINIFIGURES

The collectible LEGO Minifigures theme reached its landmark tenth series in 2013, celebrating with the rare and remarkable Mr. Gold. But the year's shiny star would have been the first to admit: none of it could have been possible without the hardworking Minifigures of Series 9, and the characters in Series 11 were some of the very best yet.

I'D LIKE TO THANK MY DESIGNER.

Mr. Good and Evil This character has a split personality after an experiment went wrong. Even his clothes and face are divided—one side torn and messy, the other side neat and tidy.

Tattered top hat

Potions bottle containing suspicious purple liquid

Movie award for best actress

Diamond pendant

Hollywood Starlet This icon of the LEGO screen wears a stylish dress with 372 stars printed on it.

SERIES 9

The year's first series could hardly have been more varied, boasting monsters, movie stars, and more! A new roller skate piece also made its debut—in the first of almost 250 set appearances to date.

WHY DID I CROSS THE ROAD?

Large wings

Traditional British court dress

Brand-new gavel

Judge The ceremonial wig worn by this formidable character is new this year.

Helmet with unique star printing

Roller Derby Girl Don't try to stop this roller-skater—her super-fast wheels mean she's not going to slow down for anything!

New roller skate design can attach to LEGO knobs

Chicken Suit Guy This is the first minifigure to have a torso with arms that are the same from the front and back.

Claws for pretending to scratch the soil

EXCLUSIVE MINIFIGURE

This 19th-century Toy Soldier minifigure is exclusive to DK's LEGO® Minifigures Character Encyclopedia. Although he carries a rifle, this is just for dress purposes and his real mission is to find a fun adventure and make new friends.

A black version of this helmet first appeared in the LEGO® Pirates sets in 1989

Toy Soldier This smiling, bright-eyed and rosy-cheeked minifigure wears the uniform of a Napoleonic era British soldier.

SERIES 10

Not everyone could own a Mr. Gold, but there were no disappointments to be found in the Series 10 mystery bags. The Roman Commander had legions of fans, and there was a real buzz around Bumblebee Girl ...

Librarian The *Oranges and Peaches* title on the Librarian's book comes from a joke about a mishearing of *On the Origin of Species* by Charles Darwin.

"Shhh!" is written on the mug—a message for those who make noise!

Reading glasses

Helmet first appeared on the Roman Soldier

Wolf symbol represents Rome

Roman Commander Fans requested this character to command the Roman Soldier from Series 6.

Classy gold monocle

Stylish gold tie

Mr. Gold Just 5,000 editions of this dazzling character were created to celebrate the 10th series of LEGO Minifigures. Mr. Gold is also the only character that can't be found in every box of Minifigure bags.

Fancy gold suit

Grandpa Although he dislikes anything new, Grandpa's bald cap is a brand-new hair piece.

Balding head with comb-over

First time this pot has featured printing

Hiked-up pants

Old news is good news

Bumblebee Girl This is the first female costumed LEGO Minifigures character.

Same wings as the Series 8 Fairy, but clear instead of transparent blue

> *I LOVE WORKING ON SUNDAES!*

Diner Waitress LEGO designer Tara Wike inspired the look of this retro roller-skater, hence her "Tara" name badge.

Hair like whipped cream

Ice cream piece has come in 11 colors since 1995

Notepad in apron pocket

Hair is braided into braids at the back

Pretzel piece found in more than 20 sets

Pretzel Girl This traditionally dressed Bavarian minifigure shares her passion for pretzels with the Lederhosen Guy from Series 8.

Printed fabric skirt piece

SERIES 11
Minifigures conquered the world in Series 11! Diner Waitress, Constable, and Pretzel Girl were icons of American, British, and Bavarian culture respectively, while the Yeti hailed from the dizzy heights of the Himalayas!

Buttons for eyes and stitched-on smile

Ear of corn in top pocket

Scarecrow The crows might not think he's scary, but this straw man is always outstanding in his field!

Unique helmet

Truncheon later used by dentist in Assembly Square (10255)

Chinstrap printed on head piece

Constable There have been lots of LEGO police officers over the years, but none as smartly dressed as this classic British bobby!

Welding mask hides oil-spattered face

Exclusive raggedy overalls print

Gloved hands protect against the heat

Welder This masked Minifigure wields a new welding torch piece. It has since been used as a fancy light fitting!

Ice pop piece introduced in 1998

Same head mold used for 2015's Square Foot Minifigure

Yellowed fangs

Frosty fur printed on legs

Yeti Some call him abominable, but the only scary thing about this snowman is the state of his teeth!

LEGO TEENAGE MUTANT NINJA TURTLES

Turtle power was back with this new theme based on the Nickelodeon TV series. Leonardo, Raphael, Donatello, and Michelangelo minifigures teamed up to fight the villainous Shredder and the Krang, aliens from Dimension X who resemble brains and inhabit robot minifigure bodies. Sets included the Turtle Lair Attack (79103) and the Stealth Shell in Pursuit (79102).

Sculpted red bandana

The four Turtles have different torso designs

Raphael Hot-headed Raph has a chip knocked out of the shell on his torso.

Knee pads are essential when crawling through sewers

Raph carries a sai—a traditional martial arts weapon—in each hand.

Grimace

Leo always wears blue

Katana sword

Leonardo Like his three brothers, Leo has a specially molded head with a unique facial expression and colored bandana.

Long rat ears

Furry chest peeks through

Sloped piece with kimono flower pattern

Fierce, gap-toothed grin

Splinter The Turtles' sensei debuts a new sculpted rat head piece.

New turtle shell piece; the shell is also printed on the back of the Turtles' torsos

Michelangelo Mikey's tongue is stuck out in concentration. Another 2013 variant has an excited smile.

Shell attaches to back with neck bracket

Burn scars to face and eye

Claws are also worn by Setam, a warrior minifigure in the 2010 LEGO® *Prince of Persia™* theme

Shredder The Turtles' archenemy looks fearsome in spiky armor and wielding trademark shredder claws.

Bō staff with extra blade

Donatello This brainy minifigure prefers talking to fighting—but he can use his Bō staff when he needs to.

Unique orange Elf hair piece

Elven ears attached to hair piece

Camouflaged warrior clothing printed on torso and legs

Tauriel The Elvish Guard of Mirkwood wields gold-and-silver daggers that originated with the 2010 LEGO *Prince of Persia* theme.

Same hair piece as 2012 Legolas, with braid running down back

Legolas Greenleaf This version of the Elf appears in just one set, dressed in forest attire for Escape from Mirkwood Spiders (79001).

Golden scale mail

Mean orange eyes

Spiked bone collar

Yazneg Scars and wrinkles mark the torso and bare head of the Orc commander minifigure.

High-rise pants printed on torso and legs

Bald patch printed on hair piece

Unique beard piece includes extra padding to bulk out stomach

Bombur The many Dwarves in this theme all have beard and hair pieces unique to their individual figure.

Tasty sausage

Arms uniquely printed in pearl gold

Goblet raised for a toast

Balin Like his fellow Dwarf minifigures, Balin stands on short legs. His alternative face bears a frown.

Unique new one-piece hair and beard

New hair piece worn by all Hobbits

Mouth opened wide in worried expression

Bilbo Baggins The first of two Bilbo minifigures wears a full Hobbit suit. The other wears just pants, a shirt, and suspenders.

Torso printed with traditional Hobbit clothing

The One Ring

Chain mail seen through shirt opening

Thorin Oakenshield Dwarf leader Thorin shares his new hair piece mold with minifigures Kili and Fili, also from *The Hobbit* theme.

LEGO® THE HOBBIT™

Based on the prequel films to *The Lord of the Rings* trilogy, the launch of LEGO *The Hobbit: An Unexpected Journey* featured eight sets depicting movie scenes. All the major characters were represented, with Gandalf, Gollum, and Legolas also appearing in *The Lord of the Rings* sets. It was a fantastic year for Hobbits and Dwarves, who also turned up as microfigures in a new LEGO game.

Large compound eyes

Solomon Blaze The leader of the Blue Squadron wears a scope over his right eye to help him spot enemy bugs.

Double-sided head features breathing equipment when turned

Chuck was first to wear this helmet in bright green

Exclusive face print with blue lips

Ashlee Starstrider The linchpin of Orange Squadron is on a mission to bag some bugs.

Menacing mandibles

Pointy proboscis

Exoskeleton

Winged Alien Mosquitoid This minifigure has a winged element, introduced in 2013, which attaches with a neck bracket.

LEGO® SPACE

There was a real buzz about 2013's Space subtheme: the insectoid-filled LEGO Galaxy Squad. Summoned to Earth by Lord Vampyre from the LEGO® Monster Fighters theme, the alien bugs swarm through space—and only Galaxy Squad can stop them! The subtheme features Red, Blue, Green, and Orange teams versus a powerful (if not too smart!) menace.

Chuck Stonebreaker Green team leader Chuck wishes he didn't wear the same color as the aliens!

Standard-issue bug blaster

Unique robot head

Alien Mantizoid If his face isn't enough to scare the Galaxy Squad, then this bug's strange alien weapons certainly will!

Red Robot Each team has a unique robot member to help battle the bugs.

Worried expression

Brown jacket with red vest, as in 2012

Frodo Baggins The adventuring Hobbit comes with a new double-sided head in 2013, and no longer wears a cape.

Not happy Frodo's other face is far from happy!

LEGO® THE LORD OF THE RINGS™

The most famous fantasy series of all continued its epic journey in 2013. Five more sets depicted some of the best-known scenes from all three movies. New versions of minifigures were revealed, and even more joined the action, with many featuring new headgear and hair pieces. The adventure continued with new releases later in the year.

Sunken eyes

Patterned neckline

Gríma Wormtongue The evil adviser to King Théoden looks sinister in his dark, subdued robes.

Ornate chain necklace

New hair piece, similar to Elrond's but without the braided detailing

Double-sided head can be either smiling or frowning

Elven dress printed on torso and sloped piece

Arwen This powerful Elf makes her minifigure debut in set 79006.

Aragorn This version of the heir of Gondor has a new torso and legs, ready for battle in set 79007.

Red Elven cloak

Bears same expression as in 2012 sets

White tree of Gondor printed on armor

Braided hair with silver detailing

Orange fabric cloak

Long red coat continues onto legs

Elrond The Third Age version of Elrond shows him to be older, with silver lining his hair, and dressed for life in Rivendell instead of battle.

Wrinkled face partly concealed by bushy beard

Black-and-white wizard's staff

Saruman Saruman the White battles Gandalf the Gray in The Wizard Battle (79005).

Standard cloth cape, in white

Unique helmet

Mouth is only facial feature

Silver chains printed on torso

Crown in an eerie green color

Ghostly skeleton features printed on face and torso

Simple belt detailing on torso

White wizard's staff

Mouth of Sauron Mercifully, this menacing messenger did not appear in another set until 2024!

King of the Dead This creepy king commands similarly scary troops in Pirate Ship Ambush (79008).

Gandalf the White His cloak and clothes might be all-new, but Gandalf's distinctive bushy eyebrows and kindly eyes are clearly visible beneath his new white hair and beard piece.

LEGO® FRIENDS

Following on from its massive success in 2012, LEGO Friends returned in 2013. Twenty-three new sets continued to expand the world of Heartlake City and the adventures of the original five girls.

Glasses printed on unique face

Surfer-style ruffled hair piece

Legs also used on Peter's mini doll figure in 2012

Ms. Stevens The teacher at Heartlake High is one of several brand-new mini dolls for 2013.

Matthew The third male mini doll to feature in the theme, artistic Matthew attends Heartlake High.

LEGO DC UNIVERSE SUPER HEROES

Batman returned to the world of LEGO building this year, accompanied by Superman. The Caped Crusader battled his foes in a new version of Arkham Asylum (10937) and teamed up with Aquaman against Mr. Freeze. Superman was kept busy challenging General Zod in sets based on the *Man of Steel* movie.

Aquaman Usually seen wielding his powerful trident, Aquaman wears a belt with the symbol of Atlantis on it.

Muscular torso with scales

Arctic Batman Wearing an Arctic camouflage Batsuit for taking on Mr. Freeze, this variant is exclusive to Arctic Batman vs. Mr. Freeze: Aquaman on Ice (76000).

Double-sided head: frowning or determined

White headband worn underneath cowl

Dark Knight Batman Exclusive to set The Bat vs. Bane: Tumbler Chase (76001), this minifigure features a copper-colored belt and black Batman logo.

Cape is shorter than previous variants

Staff

Robin A black hood and a short black cape give this variant of Robin a unique look.

New suit with silver-and-gold detail

Superman Turning the Man of Steel's head around shows his eyes in heat-vision mode.

Hair piece is the same as the Black Widow from the LEGO Marvel Super Heroes theme, seen in 2012

Lois Lane Making her debut in minifigure form this year, Lois appears in Superman: Black Zero Escape (76009).

Gray buttoned vest and shirt

DID YOU KNOW? This is the first minifigure appearance of Dr. Harleen Quinzel, although she was seen as Harley Quinn in 2012.

TIME FOR ANOTHER "FOWL" DEED!

2013 head piece features more wrinkles than the 2006 variant

Freeze gun

Silver fish accessory

Eye can be seen through monocle

Harley Quinn costume poking through

ID badge

Mr. Freeze Minus his trademark goggles, Mr. Freeze's icy blue eyes are revealed. His helmet was first seen in 2011 in the Atlantis theme.

2006 variant is wearing a black wizard's hat

Sunken red eyes

Penguin Back to rain on Batman's parade, this version of the Penguin features all-new printing.

The other side of head features red eyes

General Zod's emblem: a sideways omega symbol

Dr. Harleen Quinzel Psychiatrist Dr. Quinzel's hair piece can be swapped for a red-and-black jester's hat.

Scarecrow The nightmarish Scarecrow has a new, more detailed head and a dark brown wizard hat.

General Zod There are two 2013 variants of General Zod: in the other, he is wearing his combat armor.

Each of the ninja received a new elemental sword this year

Silver three-point crown shows he has reached ZX status

WOW, WHO'S YOUR TAILOR, KOZU?

THIS GUY IN THE UNDERWORLD.

Blue-and-silver color scheme for the Ninja of Lightning

Kimono Jay This new variant of ninja Jay wields a powerful new Lightning blade!

He wears a red version of his boss's horned samurai helmet

Elaborate red-and-white armor covers his torso extension piece

General Kozu Look out, ninja! Lord Garmadon's scariest soldier is even taller than his boss, thanks to his torso extender and armor.

Lower body is a standard minifigure torso

This jagged sword element is only carried by the NINJAGO warriors

Protective shoulder pauldrons

Golden Ninja Lloyd When Lloyd Garmadon turns into the Ultimate Spinjitzu Master, he becomes gold from minifigure head to foot!

Green-and-gold elemental robes

Sword hilt is a telescope piece

LEGO® NINJAGO®

Entering its third year, NINJAGO ramped up the action as the ninja faced off against Lord Garmadon and an army of ancient stone warriors. The ninja now wore elemental robes and carried powerful new weapons, but it took the appearance of a gold ninja and an awesome new dragon to finally end the latest threat.

Ice-white ninja head wrap

Gold warrior symbol

Arms are in Kai's elemental color

Ninja leg wraps

New helmet with crest and mask

Horned staff matches his intimidating helmet

Red eyes

This torso extender piece was first introduced on his 2012 variant

Lord Garmadon Master Wu's four-armed, villainous brother has a special torso extender piece to fit his extra limbs!

Purple belt extends from lower torso to leg piece

Kimono Zane Ninja of Ice Zane wears a black-and-white kimono with gold details for the first time in Garmatron (70504).

Kimono Kai Kai and his fellow ninja minifigures wear their elemental robes when they battle Lord Garmadon and his Stone Army.

Kimono Cole This variant of Cole has ZX (Zen Extreme) ninja status, but he wears a formal kimono instead of his regular ZX robes.

LEGO® BRAND STORES

These three minifigures were offered to 300 lucky customers in a promotion at the grand opening of the LEGO Store in Watford, United Kingdom. Packaging for the range featured Watford Junction railway station.

Signaling paddle

LEGO Friends Mia also rode this skateboard in 2012

Passenger Dressed warmly for a long wait, the passenger looks happy that his train isn't delayed.

Station Master This busy worker lets the train driver minifigures know when the train is ready to depart.

Skateboarder The skateboarder isn't allowed to ride his board on the station platform or concourse.

Poggle the Lesser With his specially sculpted head, the Archduke of Geonosis makes his debut in Duel on Geonosis (75017).

Beardlike tendrils

Gold armor printing

Transparent wings

LEGO® STAR WARS™

A big drumroll in the LEGO *Star Wars* universe this year was for the debuts of a whole host of new characters in minifigure form and new versions of familiar minifigures, including Yoda and Darth Maul. 2013 also heralded the release of *The Yoda Chronicles*, an animated miniseries created by the LEGO Group, featuring the wise Jedi Master and other favorite characters.

Jango Fett The redesigned variant of the renowned bounty hunter features silver armor and knee pad printing on the legs.

Blaster accessory

Prominent head crest

Coleman Trebor Making his minifigure debut in AT-TE (75019), the Vurk Jedi Master has a specially molded gray head piece.

General Rieekan This brave rebel general appears for the first time in 2013, sporting a new thermal jacket to keep him warm on icy Hoth.

Same head piece as Professor Snape from the LEGO® Harry Potter™ theme

Count Dooku With distinctive eyebrows and slicked-back hair, the third incarnation of Dooku bears a close resemblance to actor Christopher Lee, who played him in the movies.

Same hair piece as Draco Malfoy from the Harry Potter theme, but in white

Double-sided head has a snarling expression on the other side

The Gran species has three eyes

Ree-Yees With a three-eyed head created just for him, this lawless creature works on Jabba's Sail Barge (75020).

THE MOVIE SAGA

Among the many sets released this year were the all-new Rancor Pit (75005) and a new version of Jabba's Sail Barge (75020). The Rancor Pit set was designed as an add-on to Jabba's Palace (9516), released in 2012.

Wrench for fixing starfighter equipment

Loose white straps

A-wing Rebel Pilot This redesigned pilot, who first appeared in 2000, has a completely new helmet and a new dark green flight suit.

Printed eyes seen on classic Yoda for the first time

Small, curved ears

Yoda It's all about Yoda in 2013! He has a new molded head piece, featuring a focused expression.

Alternative face print has no visor

Rebel insignia

Snowspeeder Luke Wearing a pressurized g-suit, Luke is ready for action against the Imperial forces in the Battle of Hoth (75014).

Life-support chest pack printing is more detailed than on Luke's 2010 flight suit

Pockets and straps printed on legs

Bulbous eyes

Long, droopy ears of the Ortolan species

Max Rebo Jabba the Hutt's musician is entirely blue. Set 75020 is Max Rebo's first appearance in more than 20 years of LEGO *Star Wars*.

Printed braid is longer than on 2002 variant

Episode II Anakin Skywalker This variant of Anakin features him wearing Hawkeye's hair piece from the LEGO Marvel Super Heroes theme.

Padmé was the first minifigure to wear this hair piece

Double-sided head piece also shows determined face

Padmé Amidala Padmé may look happy, but her clothes have been torn by the nexu beast in the Geonosian arena.

THE CLONE WARS

The Clone Wars raged throughout LEGO *Star Wars* in 2013, with new sets including Z-95 Headhunter (75004) and the Mandalorian Speeder (75022), which featured a new Maul minifigure.

Huge bounty hunter blaster

Rako's trademark facial tattoo

Rako Hardeen This minifigure is really Obi-Wan Kenobi in disguise. Luckily for him, the face tattoo isn't permanent!

Double-sided head shows eyes crackling with power

Jek-14 The Force-enhanced clone is the first minifigure to have a transparent arm.

Modified clone trooper helmet

THE YODA CHRONICLES

The Jek-14's Starfighter set (75018) was based on three-part animated miniseries *The Yoda Chronicles*. It featured the first *Star Wars* character to be created jointly by the LEGO Group and Lucasfilm—the mighty Jek-14.

Togruta have hornlike montrals and head-tails called lekku

HEADS OR TAILS ... OR BOTH?

Turn Ahsoka's face and her expression changes to a huge grin

Ahsoka wields two lightsabers to defeat the Umbarans

Four arms means Krell can wield two double-bladed lightsabers and still have a free pair of hands!

Krell has an extended torso with an additional pair of arms

Ahsoka Tano The 2013 minifigure features the same hair piece as her younger 2010 self, but she has a more grown-up look with new head, torso, and leg printing.

Pong Krell The head, torso extension, and extra arms are all one piece, designed especially to capture this Jedi's unique look.

Rare Darksaber

Cyborg Maul Maul now walks on powerful cybernetic legs. Nothing can stop this fierce Sith warrior!

New torso for 2013

Different head mold to classic Yoda in a brighter green, with longer ears and cartoonlike eyes

White tufts of hair can be seen on the back of his head

Yoda This variant of Yoda features new torso printing with a hood on the reverse.

Double-sided head piece also shows Obi-Wan with a stern expression

Jedi robes extend to legs

Obi-Wan Kenobi This calm Jedi minifigure prefers to use his lightsaber to defend instead of attack.

Clawlike robotic legs

LEGO® CITY

Police and Fire took center stage this year, with a new Elite Police Force providing a lot of the action. Chase McCain and the Elite Police team take on cunning crooks in LEGO City and a 2013 video game. Meanwhile, the Fire team got a new Fire Station (60004).

New striped torso features a rope for scaling buildings

Climbing Crook Could you pick this minifigure out in a police line-up? His unique head with stubble and a scowl might help!

Conspicuous red crowbar

Police radio

Chase McCain This Chase first appeared in 2013, but an exclusive variant was also given away with preorders of the LEGO City *Undercover* video game in 2012.

Fire helmets have been worn by minifigures since 1978

New torso features a utility belt and air pressure gauge for breathing equipment

Firefighter This minifigure is wearing the regulation LEGO City firefighter uniform from 2013.

2014

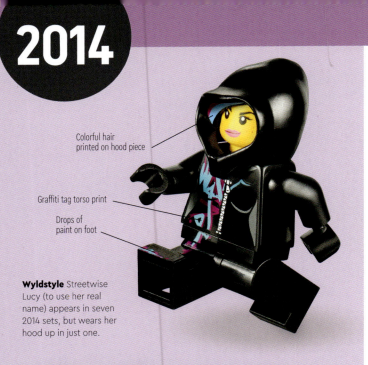

Colorful hair printed on hood piece

Graffiti tag torso print

Drops of paint on foot

Wyldstyle Streetwise Lucy (to use her real name) appears in seven 2014 sets, but wears her hood up in just one.

2014

MINIFIGURES WERE BIGGER than ever when they hit movie screens in 2014! THE LEGO® MOVIE™ was a worldwide box office smash and, of course, there were plenty of themed LEGO sets to go with it. The year also saw minifigures and other LEGO creatures starting to populate the LEGO® Minecraft® world, plus the debut of the LEGO® Ultra Agents and their fiendish foes. Things got a bit chilly in LEGO® City as brave explorers set off for the Arctic, and over in Chima, a whole new range of tribes made their mark, from Bats to Mammoths!

THE LEGO MOVIE

The first ever big-screen LEGO adventure introduced the world to happy-go-lucky minifigure Emmet and his many friends in Bricksburg and its surrounding brick-built worlds. More than 20 sets depicted epic scenes from the movie, from Bad Cop Pursuit (70802) to Lord Business' Evil Lair (70809). Meanwhile, 16 collectible Minifigures included some of the movie's best cameo characters.

Unique metallic beard piece

Treasure chest tummy

LEGO® Technic leg

MetalBeard The captain of the Sea Cow ship has a minifigure head and hat, but no other minifigure parts!

Hair piece designed especially for Emmet

Emmet "The Special" wears the mysterious bright red Piece of Resistance on his back in eight THE LEGO MOVIE sets.

Neck bracket holds Piece of Resistance in place

DID YOU KNOW? In THE LEGO MOVIE, the Piece of Resistance is really just the top from a tube of glue!

THE GOODIES

As "the Special," Emmet meets a host of heroes, from brave Wyldstyle and mystical Vitruvius to swashbuckling MetalBeard and star-trekking Benny. But it is the ordinary citizens of Bricksburg who finally save the day.

Deliberate broken look to helmet

SPACESHIP SPACESHIP SPACESHIP!

Classic Space logo shows decades of wear

Flexible rubber horn piece

Unikitty Seven versions of the Cloud Cuckoo Land princess appeared in 2014, including Angry Kitty and Astro Kitty.

Brand-new tail element

Benny Based on LEGO® Space minifigures from the 1970s and '80s, Benny is designed to look very well played with!

Braces on teeth

Logo used on sets from 1979 to 1989

Fabu-Fan This smiling inhabitant of Bricksburg wears her love for the 1980s' LEGO® FABULAND™ theme with pride!

Mike Monkey appeared in several FABULAND sets

New hat mold with printed sheriff's star

Good Cop

IS THERE SOMETHING STUCK IN MY TEETH?

Helmet and cape shaped like a giant necktie

Unique shoulder armor

Mustache cleverly disguises robot features

Super Secret Police emblem

Bad Cop A turn of the head transforms this tough guy into his alter ego, the far less intimidating Good Cop!

Same uniform worn by Officer Toque in THE LEGO® NINJAGO® MOVIE™

Boot tops are part of special leg piece

THE BADDIES
No minifigure in THE LEGO MOVIE is really, really bad, but some of them give it a decent try! President Business is the big bad guy on the block, aided by his Super Secret Police force.

Each giant heel built from 28 pieces

Posable horse figure introduced in 2010

First of many minifigures to wear this piece

EMMET? NEVER HEARD OF HIM!

Lord Business President Business is ready to give Bricksburg the boot (or both very big boots) in his towering super-villain guise!

Sheriff Not-A-Robot The shiny sheriff of the Super Secret Police in the Old Wild West is (whisper it) a robot!

Tools attached to low-slung belt

Top hat and beard are all one piece

COLLECTIBLE MINIFIGURES
Variants of Emmet, Wyldstyle, President Business, and Bad Cop all feature in the first THE LEGO MOVIE collectible Minifigure range. Mostly, however, the selection is a chance for their lesser-known co-stars to shine!

Gail the Construction Worker Emmet isn't the only notable construction worker in Bricksburg. This one has a new helmet-and-hair piece!

They're literally right here!

Mrs. Scratchen-Post
This animal lover comes with one of her many feline friends and a unique cat-hair-covered costume!

Exclusive concerned face print

Opening lines of Gettysburg Address on printed tile

Abraham Lincoln The first minifigure of a US President is revealed to be a Master Builder in THE LEGO MOVIE!

Unique hat slots into hair piece

Exclusive Hawaiian shirt print

White hip piece serves as underpants

Ginger cat piece found in eight sets

Pouch for carrying cat treats

Antique musket appears in more than 90 sets

Calamity Drone This Wild West dancer is secretly a robot agent for the villainous President Business. Can you tell?

Detailed dress print on sloped brick

"Where Are My Pants?" Guy The first minifigure to come with two sets of legs carries his spare pair as pants!

Steve The theme's hero appears in all of 2014's minifigure-scale sets, armed with different tools, weapons, and armor.

Standard minifigure torso and legs

Pixelated pickax

LEGO MINECRAFT

The first LEGO set based on building and exploring video game Minecraft was part of the LEGO® Ideas theme in 2012. A dedicated LEGO Minecraft theme launched the following year, and in 2014, this spawned the first Minecraft minifigures. Cube-shaped head pieces set these characters apart from traditional minifigures, while other new pieces were introduced to build the world's other blocky inhabitants.

New cube-shaped head

ZOMBIES? WE'RE JUST A MINER THREAT!

DID YOU KNOW?
LEGO Minecraft features the first ever cube-shaped LEGO elements!

Blocky open collar print

Zombie These mean, green mobs menace Steve in two 2014 sets: The Cave (21113) and The Mine (21118).

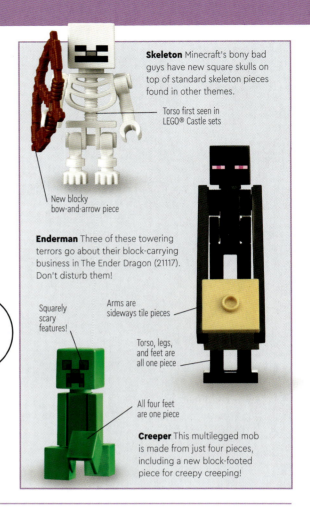

Skeleton Minecraft's bony bad guys have new square skulls on top of standard skeleton pieces found in other themes.

Torso first seen in LEGO® Castle sets

New blocky bow-and-arrow piece

Enderman Three of these towering terrors go about their block-carrying business in The Ender Dragon (21117). Don't disturb them!

Arms are sideways tile pieces

Squarely scary features!

Torso, legs, and feet are all one piece

All four feet are one piece

Creeper This multilegged mob is made from just four pieces, including a new block-footed piece for creepy creeping!

Red minifigure head visible through eye slits

Breez This galactic hero was one of 15 robot figures released in 2014. She is made up of nine pieces.

LEGO® HERO FACTORY

A theme based around large figure builds (much like BIONICLE®), LEGO Hero Factory ran from 2010 to 2015. It was not until 2014, however, that the sets started to include minifigure-scale characters.

LEGO® ULTRA AGENTS

Minifigure play met app-based missions with the launch of LEGO Ultra Agents. Each 2014 set related to a free-to-download story for smartphones and tablets, and playing through six interactive adventures unlocked exclusive building instructions. The action took place in Astor City and saw Solomon Blaze and his trainee Ultra Agents taking on a rogues' gallery of catastrophe-causing villains!

Scar beside right eyebrow

Cybernetic right leg

Solomon Blaze Last seen in 2008's LEGO® Space Galaxy Squad sets, the chief Ultra Agent is now an older and wiser minifigure!

Unprinted areas of helmet reveal green details

Space Invader shirt print

Cyber hacking blaster weapon

Terabyte This techno-terror wears a unique transparent bright green hacking helmet, printed to mostly look like metal.

Transparent bright green head

Slime bombs strapped across chest

Retox A bowler hat can't disguise this radioactive wrongdoer! He is the slimy sidekick of chemical crime queen Toxikita.

Max Burns Just like his fellow Ultra Agents, this firebrand stunt driver has a name with flaming connotations!

Keychain hangs from belt

ID badge with Ultra Agents symbol

Targeting visor is hidden when head piece is turned

Knob shooter new for 2014

Caila Phoenix This heroic martial artist and demolitions expert flies a jetpack in Ultra Agents Mission HQ (70165).

Helmet, shoulder armor, and chest plate are all one piece

Fists first seen in LEGO® Legends of Chima™ theme

Tremor Giant fighting fists and exclusive silver metallic armor make this bad guy look quite unlike any other minifigure!

Spider kept in her pocket

Striped tights print under fabric skirt

Spooky Girl The first Minifigure to be entirely black, white, and gray carries the second all-monochrome bear!

LEGO® MINIFIGURES

In its fifth year, this collectibles theme went digital with the LEGO Minifigures Online game. Each Minifigure in Series 12 came with a code to access its counterpart in the massively multiplayer online world, with characters from older series unlocked via in-game achievements. The game was discontinued in fall 2016, but the physical Minifigures from 2014 are still going strong! This year saw the release of LEGO® The Simpsons™ as collectible Minifigures, with 16 familiar faces from Springfield.

Long spear also wielded by Series 10 Warrior Woman in darker brown

Plume plugs into helmet

Pickax piece introduced in 1978

Battle Goddess With an exclusive shield print, a new helmet piece, and a unique skirt, this warrior wins every time!

Mythical winged horse design

Suspenders curve over plump belly

Prospector This gold-digger's brand-new beard piece is also worn by Wiley Fusebot in THE LEGO MOVIE, albeit in reddish brown.

Headgear also used in a 2019 Chinese New Year set

I PUT THE "STY" IN STYLE ICON!

Juicy apple for pigging out

Piggy Guy Over the years, many collectible Minifigures have dressed like animals, but only Piggy Guy goes the whole hog!

Tail piece can be placed on this knob to make it seem like she is emerging from lamp

Genie Girl What do you wish for? Rub the magic lamp and the Genie Girl will appear to grant you three wishes. Be sure to choose wisely!

Beads dangle from top

Wispy tail piece looks like shimmering smoke

Powerful binoculars for watching the waves

Bright red rescue float

Lifeguard It takes more than stormy waves to ruffle this calm Minifigure. He was trained well by the Lifeguard from Series 2.

Choice of iced and chocolate-chip cookies

Same cape worn by Superman minifigure!

Mrs. Claus Santa's sweetheart carries cookies on a tray and candy canes in her apron in her LEGO set debut.

Hat first worn by Holiday Elf in 2013

Mechanic's tools in overall pockets

Cheeky Elf All four elves in Santa's Workshop wear the same hat piece with pointed ears molded onto it.

LEGO® CREATOR EXPERT

Advanced builders met many new minifigures in 2014. Parisian Restaurant (10243) and Fairground Mixer (10244) were populated by characterful townspeople, while Santa's Workshop (10245) featured four friendly elves, a minifigure Mrs Claus, and the jolly red-suited fellow himself. This new addition to the Winter Village subtheme boasted 883 parts, including bricks to build four adult reindeer and a smaller calf without full antlers.

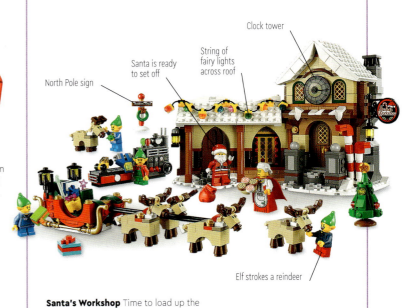

Clock tower

String of fairy lights across roof

Santa is ready to set off

North Pole sign

Elf strokes a reindeer

Santa's Workshop Time to load up the sleigh! This set (10245) features four wrapped presents and four toys, including a yellow car and a blue spaceship.

Stinger tail made from click-hinge pieces

Scutter The largest member of the Scorpion Tribe has six creepy-crawly legs and a spiky, posable stinger!

Unique firebird head mask

Exclusive head mask

Wings can move back and forth

Braptor The leader of the Bat Tribe boasts brand-new wing pieces that clip onto his armor.

Six eyes on head mask

Each leg is a LEGO Hero Factory talon

Two eyes visible through mask

Fire CHI in exclusive harness

Sir Fangar Like other members of the Ice Tribes, the leader of the Saber-Tooth Tigers has transparent icy body parts.

Ragged, battle-worn cape

Sparacon Two fangs, eight limbs, and eight beady eyes make this Spider Tribe soldier a scary sight!

Flame pattern on ceremonial robe

Transparent limbs new for 2014

Fluminox This fiery Phoenix leads the only Legends of Chima tribe to be based on a mythical creature.

LEGO® LEGENDS OF CHIMA™

At the start of its second year, Legends of Chima ventured into the Outlands, where tribes of Spiders, Scorpions, and Bats plotted to steal all the CHI in Chima for themselves! Then, in summer 2014, a wave of "Fire vs. Ice" sets introduced the ancient Phoenix Tribe and their Ice Clan enemies—made up of Saber-Tooth Tigers, Mammoths, and Vultures.

The Flash Who knows why it took the Fastest Man Alive so long to make his debut as a minifigure!

Red hair and cowl are one piece

Batgirl For her first LEGO look, Barbara Gordon wears the costume seen in 2011's "New 52" comic books.

Bat ears are part of hair piece

One of two facial expressions

Lightning-bolt logo

Exclusive lavender cape

Man-Bat This baddie uses parts designed for the similarly named Manbat from the LEGO® Monster Fighters theme.

Wings move as part of special arms

Piercing alien eyes

Torso print based on 2011 comic books

LEGO® DC SUPER HEROES

This year's DC sets drew on the publisher's 80-year history to bring fans the first-ever minifigures of various heroes and villains. Nine sets were released in total, including two San Diego Comic-Con exclusives and two promotional minifigures. Batman's Tumbler (76023) became the largest set of the theme to date, boasting 1,869 pieces, including two special minifigures.

Martian Manhunter The first minifigure of this Justice League member was exclusive to LEGO® Stores and LEGO.com.

Research Scientist This lab-coated chemist works alongside an astronomer and a paleontologist in the 165-piece Research Institute set.

Focused expression

More robust helmet than those of other classic astronauts

All-access pass

Space logo unchanged since 1978

Yve Classic LEGO Space minifigures had never been seen in green before Yve and her fellow astronaut, Pete.

LEGO IDEAS

In 2014, LEGO® CUUSOO changed its name to LEGO Ideas, but stayed focused on releasing sets suggested by fan designers. This year's sets included Exo Suit (21109)—featuring minifigures based on fan builder Peter Reid and his girlfriend Yve—and Research Institute (21110), based around three female scientist minifigures, intended to inspire girls with an interest in science.

Cowl hides second, more intense face

Batman of Zur-En-Arrh This colorful San Diego Comic-Con exclusive is the Batman-inspired protector of an alien world.

Costume first seen in a 1940 comic book

LEGO CITY

City minifigures had to wrap up warm this year as they headed to the Arctic for the first time. A bright orange color scheme made the adventurers and vehicles stand out against the snow, and new polar bear and husky dog figures added animal magic to their missions. Ten Arctic sets were released in all, including ships, planes, plows, and snowmobiles.

Arctic Research Assistant A hat, a gilet, a sweater, and gloves all contribute to the warmth of this minifigure's smile!

Tinted glasses protect against Arctic glare

Clip-on ID badge

Arctic Captain This smiling sailor delivers vital supplies to the exploration team in his intrepid icebreaker ship.

Open version of Arctic Explorer's jacket

Chunky fisherman's sweater

Goggles are part of face print

Pole Star emblem on jacket

NOBODY WARNED ME IT WOULD BE SO COLD!

Arctic Explorer Four sets feature this polar pioneer, who tries to keep nice and cozy inside her new hood piece.

Climbing gear hangs from belt

Head turns to reveal calmer face

Tiara, hair, and Elven ears are all one piece

Witch-King If you dare take this minifigure into a darkened room, you'll see Sauron's second-in-command glow in the dark!

Unique crown piece

Glow-in-the-dark head

Galadriel The mightiest and fairest of all the Elves is made from all-exclusive parts, including a sparkling cape.

LEGO® *THE HOBBIT*™

The final year for the Middle-earth theme focused on the third film in the Hobbit trilogy, *The Battle of the Five Armies*. Four sets depicted scenes from the film, with the largest—The Lonely Mountain (79018)—featuring an enormous figure of Smaug the fire-breathing dragon! Others included the fearsome Witch-King and Orc leader Azog, plus the first Galadriel minifigure.

Exclusive hook-hand

Azog A special head-and-shoulders piece allows this mighty Orc to tower over most other minifigures.

Spider legs can clutch a minifigure

Spider Bytez This moody mutant comes with his human alter ego Victor in TV-inspired Mutation Chamber Unleashed (79119).

Totally unique body piece

Exclusive body mold

Leatherhead The Turtles' alligator ally is a massive presence in the TV series set Turtle Sub Undersea Chase (79121).

Building knob on both arms

Bandana covers top of head

Dark green body parts

Raphael Like the other movie Turtles, Raph wears his new half-shell piece higher on his back than his 2013 minifigure did.

Neck bracket holds half-shell in place

Sunglasses hang from bead necklace

Michelangelo Muted green body parts and printed nostrils set Mike's movie minifigures apart from earlier versions.

LEGO® TEENAGE MUTANT NINJA TURTLES™

The Turtles really came out of their shells in 2014, with starring roles in a brand-new movie, as well as in their ongoing Nickelodeon TV series. Both were the subject of new LEGO releases, with five TV-themed sets appearing in April and three movie tie-ins showcasing new-look Ninja Turtle minifigures in July.

Unique Mandalorian mask print on head

Robes imbued with dark power

Darth Revan This Sith Lord from the Old Republic era was released to mark *Star Wars* Day on May the Fourth.

Festive Astromech Half droid, half Christmas tree, this unique figure lit up Day 22 in the 2014 Advent Calendar.

Printed baubles

Leg parts are exclusive in this color

Detailed new head piece

Tunic print continues on back

Bith Musician Three identical minifigures depict lead singer Figrin D'an and the Modal Nodes band in 2014's Cantina set.

C-3PO The famous droid gets his first printed legs with this Sandcrawler variant, which also shows a restraining bolt on his torso.

Jawa restraining bolt

Leg repaired with silver spare parts

THE ORIGINAL TRILOGY

Episode IV inspired several sets in 2014, from an updated Mos Eisley Cantina (75052) to the Ultimate Collector Series Sandcrawler (75059). The latter boasted 3,296 pieces, including seven new or redesigned droids.

STAR WARS LEGENDS

This year's characters from outside established *Star Wars* lore included names from the *Knights of the Old Republic* video game and *The Yoda Chronicles* TV series. A new LEGO *Star Wars* Advent Calendar (75056) also brought festive fun.

Ithorian Jedi Master The first Ithorian minifigure goes by the nickname Rusty in *The Yoda Chronicles* show.

New "hammerhead" piece

Bare legs and feet under short robes

DID YOU KNOW?

C-3PO's head piece can be found on fellow protocol droids R-3PO and K-3PO, and RA-7, the Death Star droid.

Santa Vader This seasonal Sith could feel your presents when he escaped from Advent Calendars on Christmas Eve!

Gifts attached to belt

Coat print continues on legs

Binoculars piece for eyes

Treadwell Droid This brick-built droid from the 2014 Sandcrawler set has four skeleton arms on a rotating body.

Base made from LEGO Technic parts

LEGO® STAR WARS™

Animated TV series *Star Wars® Rebels*™ took the galaxy by storm in 2014, charting the rise of resistance at the height of the Empire's power. The accompanying LEGO subtheme featured five key rebels in its first year, as well as their two connecting vessels. Not too far, far away, sets based on the movies and more also continued to thrive.

The Ghost Jedi Kanan Jarrus joins Hera and Zeb at the controls of the rebels' stealth ship (75053).

The Phantom (set 75048) can dock between these two engines

Other side Hera shows a more serious expression.

Flying goggles printed on helmet

Hera Syndulla The Twi'lek captain of *The Ghost* has a unique helmet piece that includes her long head-tails (lekku).

Lasat head piece found in just one set

Shark-tail design on shoulder

Zeb Orrelios To date, this Lasat rebel is the only member of his species to be made into a minifigure.

STAR WARS REBELS

Of the six main rebels—Hera Syndulla, Ezra Bridger, Kanan Jarrus, Zeb Orrelios, Sabine Wren, and Chopper the droid—five appeared in 2014 sets. Sabine did not make her debut until the following year.

Gleaming robot eyes

P.I.X.A.L. Circuit-style markings and silver metallic hair make it clear that Cyrus Borg's sidekick is a highly advanced android.

LEGO® NINJAGO®

In its fourth year, Ninjago City was rebooted as a techno wonderland where there was nothing at all to worry about. Well ... only the fact that Master Wu and genius inventor Cyrus Borg had fallen under the control of the Digital Overlord! Luckily, Borg's android assistant P.I.X.A.L. was on hand to help the ninja put things right once again.

Possessed red eyes

Techno Wu Even Wu's hat gets a metallic makeover when he allows himself to be captured by the Digital Overlord!

Only time Wu wears a black beard

Metallic print under unique tech-head

Cyrus Borg When technology gets the better of him, this friendly inventor becomes the terrifying OverBorg!

Stern look can be swapped for smiling face

Wings attach at neck

Falcon The huge wings worn by this hero are one wide piece, made from jewel-like transparent red plastic.

AVENGERS

Two sets in 2014 were based on the animated TV series *Avengers Assemble*. As well as featuring fresh looks for Captain America, Thor, and the Hulk, they also introduced the first minifigures of some unusual characters.

Mind-beam weapon on forehead

MODOK This big-brained villain has the biggest head of any minifigure! Amazingly, it slots onto a standard torso.

Golden chest plate is part of head piece

LEGO® MARVEL SUPER HEROES

This year's big Marvel moment was the Earth premiere of Marvel Studios' *Guardians of the Galaxy* movie. Three LEGO playsets captured most of its heroes in minifigure form. Away from the theater, the comic-book exploits of the X-Men and the animated TV adventures of the Avengers also found new form in LEGO sets.

Shoulder straps are part of head piece

GUARDIANS OF THE GALAXY

Intergalactic outlaws Rocket, Groot, Star-Lord, Drax, and Gamora all feature in 2014's *Guardians of the Galaxy* sets, with antagonists the Sakaaran, Nebula, and the Collector (a San Diego Comic-Con exclusive minifigure) also putting in appearances.

Tail piece fits between torso and leg

Rocket The smallest Guardian might just be the fiercest! He wears this orange outfit in just one set.

Skin tone printed on blue head piece

Cyclops This hero's figure-hugging costume is recreated using printing alone, with no need for a helmet or other extras.

Belt buckle is an "X" symbol

X-MEN Until 2014, Wolverine and Phoenix were the only X-Men with their own minifigures. That changed with X-Men vs. the Sentinel (76022), which added Storm and Cyclops to the mix, along with a new-look Wolverine.

Long hair hides alternative calmer face print

Storm A unique cape loops around this minifigure's wrists, making it ideal for striking Super Hero poses!

Classic 1970s comic-book costume

LEGO® DISNEY PRINCESS™

The second theme to feature mini dolls (after LEGO® Friends) introduced new figure parts, such as a tail for Ariel from *The Little Mermaid* and floor-length dress pieces for the likes of Rapunzel and Cinderella.

Ariel The Little Mermaid is joined by her best friend, Flounder the fish, in Ariel's Amazing Treasures (41050).

First mini doll to wear this hairstyle

No other character has this piece in green

New hair piece with band

Cinderella Thanks to the horse-drawn coach in Cinderella's Dream Carriage (41053), Cinderella will go to the ball.

Magical sparkle print on dress

TRAVEL TO A NEW DIMENSION? THAT MUST BE MAGIC!

Kai Both the Fire Ninja and Cole the Earth Ninja feature in the first wave of LEGO DIMENSIONS sets.

Tournament of Elements robe

"Toy Tag" stand interacts with brick-built portal

Classic "Gandalf the Gray" look

Minifigures can be detached from Toy Tags

Gandalf This wizard from *The Lord of the Rings* is one of three minifigures included with the DIMENSIONS Starter Pack.

LEGO DIMENSIONS

The Lord of the Rings, LEGO® NINJAGO®, *The Simpsons*, *Doctor Who*, *The Wizard of Oz*, and more all came together in the LEGO DIMENSIONS video game! To begin, players built a portal from LEGO bricks and connected it to their games console. They then placed minifigures with special stands on the portal to bring them to life within the game.

LEGO DIMENSIONS Starter Pack Four versions of the Starter Pack (71200) made the game available to PS3, PS4, Xbox One, and Xbox 360 owners.

Wyldstyle from THE LEGO® MOVIE™

Brick-built portal

2015

PLAY WORLDS COLLIDED with the launch of LEGO® DIMENSIONS in 2015. A blend of LEGO® building and console gaming, the theme mixed minifigures from different pop culture realities to create a unique and expandable play experience. The year also marked the minifigure debuts for Rey, Finn, and friends in the first LEGO® *Star Wars*™: *The Force Awakens* sets. Elsewhere, sea shanties were sung for the return of LEGO® Pirates and engines revved in anticipation of the new LEGO® Speed Champions theme.

Alternative calm face print on reverse of head

Fire CHI weapon can be used in the game

Ornate leg armor printing

Eris Chima's Eagle princess has exclusive leg and torso printing for her LEGO DIMENSIONS debut.

Same hat mold as Gandalf

New bright green head piece

Wicked Witch of the West This *The Wizard of Oz* minifigure can really fly once she gets inside the game's reality!

Same Batsuit seen in six DC Super Heroes sets

Taller cowl than other 2015 Batman minifigures

Batman The Caped Crusader comes with a 3-in-1 Batmobile, Batblaster, and Batray build in the DIMENSIONS Starter Pack.

Longbow really works in gameplay

Swirling Middle-earth design on Toy Tag

Legolas Like all DIMENSIONS minifigures, this *The Lord of the Rings* Elf has his own Toy Tag stand with unique Elven-inspired printing.

Gold shades printed on transparent head piece

T-shirt printed with dollar bills

Invizable This show-off likes to be seen, so he dresses to impress to make up for being completely see-through!

LEGO® ULTRA AGENTS

The second year of Ultra Agents sets introduced AppBricks to the LEGO world as the heroes took on eight Antimatter Missions. Each set included at least one carbon-infused AppBrick, which activated interactive comic strips when placed alongside an app-enabled tablet or smartphone screen. New minifigure agents included Trey Swift and Steve Zeal, who faced a fresh array of fantastical foes.

Scary cyborg face

Mechanical spider legs

Spyclops This cyber spider is always on the web! He uses his bug spray on any agent that bugs him.

Rare printed brain piece

Lower body made from 13 pieces

Professor Brainstein This scientist comes in two sets—once as a good guy, and once as a mega-brained monster!

New bandana and flowing hair piece

You can't swashbuckle without buckles!

Pirate Queen Ask this royal rogue about her noble heritage and she'll show you all the priceless antiques she's stolen!

PIRATES

As ever, the LEGO Pirates crew is led by a classic captain with an eyepatch, wooden leg, and hook-hand. But there is also a sea change with the first ever Pirate Cook, Pirate Boy, and Pirate Queen!

Only one bottom tooth

Bare chest under apron

Pirate Cook This scruffy chef keeps a wide selection of exotic cooking sauces. Unfortunately, he keeps them on his apron ...

New-look bandana piece

Rope holds up oversized pants

Pirate Boy The *Brick Bounty*'s freshest face may have based his look on Bo'sun Will from 1989's LEGO Pirates sets.

Adventurous grin

Elegant 18th-century outfit

Governor's Daughter This young civilian is just as handy with a sword as her father's most accomplished soldiers.

Plume is a status symbol

Gaudy gold epaulettes

Governor The graybeard boss of the Bluecoats cuts quite a figure in his unique bicorn hat with decorative cockade printing.

LEGO PIRATES

Six years after the LEGO Pirates were presumed lost at sea, they sailed into view once more with new recruits, new-look enemies, and even their very own chess set! This time around, the marauders made their daring raids aboard the 745-piece ship *Brick Bounty* (70413) and hid their loot behind a giant skull on Treasure Island (70411).

Wig first worn by Revolutionary Soldier in 2013

Admiral This seasoned sailor wears the same uniform as the Governor, but pairs it with a stylish powdered wig piece.

BLUECOATS

These stuffy soldiers have tried to sink the pirates' spirits since the earliest days of the theme. For 2015, they return with their smartest-ever outfits.

PIRATES CHESS SET

With 857 pieces, including 20 minifigures, this is 2015's biggest LEGO Pirates set. Bluecoats and pirate minifigures play the kings, queens, and pawns, while brick-built pieces are used for the rooks, knights, and bishops.

Variant Pirate Queen

Pirates have parrots for rooks

Bluecoat bishops are lookout posts

Gold tooth

Studded leather eyepatch

Pirate Chess King No other LEGO pirate captain combines a plain black bicorn hat with two standard legs.

Pirates Chess Set This serious strategy game (40158) is full of fun details, like the pawn with a banana instead of a sword!

Torso print first seen in LEGO® Castle sets

Bluecoat Chess Queen This VIM (Very Important Minifigure) in Bluecoat society has her own throne on the LEGO Pirates chessboard.

LEGO® JURASSIC WORLD™

In 2001, the LEGO® Studios theme included two sets based around the filming of *Jurassic Park III*. But it was not until 2015's *Jurassic World* that the modern-day dinosaur film franchise got its own LEGO theme. Six sets followed the story of the spectacular new movie, all boasting brand-new minifigures and at least one large dinosaur figure each.

Choice of stern and worried face prints

I SAID SEND ME A TEXT, NOT A T.REX!

Printed mobile phone tile introduced in 2014

Smile can be swapped for angry look

Knife sheath on belt

Owen Grady If anyone can calm Jurassic World's runaway raptors, it's this animal behaviorist, who raised them!

Wings move up and down on hinges

Pteranodon This mold was first seen in 2001's LEGO® DINO theme, but got a new color scheme for 2014.

Tooth-lined jaw can be snapped shut

Dilophosaurus A whole new species in the LEGO ecosystem, this colorful creature has a brand-new frill-necked head piece.

Claire Dearing It's just another day at work for Jurassic World's operations manager when she faces two Velociraptors in Raptor Rampage (75917)!

Overworked expression

Shoulder holster

Vic Hoskins Security chief Vic tackles a T.rex that is four times his height in his only 2015 set appearance.

LEGO® ELVES

The third mini doll theme followed the adventures of Emily Jones in the magical world of Elvendale. It introduced many new parts, including mini doll hair pieces with sculpted elf ears.

Elemental symbol on forehead

Unique die-cut cape

Skyra This Wind Elf guards the portal between Elvendale and the human world. She is found in just one set.

LEGO SPEED CHAMPIONS

Speeding into stores in 2015, this new theme got the green light from car fans everywhere. All seven of the first year's sets featured realistic recreations of famous racecars in minifigure scale and came with minifigure drivers decked out in authentic team colors. The largest set also included a pit stop, a finish line, and a huge Ferrari team truck.

Helmet piece introduced in 1987

Exclusive "Porsche Motorsport" branding

Porsche Driver Eye-catching bright green arms and legs make this minifigure hard to miss—even at 93 mph (150 kph)!

Silver metallic helmet

McLaren speedmark logo

McLaren Driver This smiling sportsman knows he'll soon be back behind the wheel of his McLaren P1™ hybrid supercar.

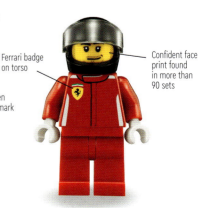

Ferrari badge on torso

Confident face print found in more than 90 sets

Ferrari Driver Clad in Italian racing red, this driver is every bit as stylish as his LaFerrari hypercar (75899).

SERIES 13

Kings, goblins, aliens, and wizards rubbed shoulders in the 13th series of collectible Minifigures. But some of the most lovable characters turned out to be the everyday folk doing the thing that they loved.

ANYONE WANT A SNACK?

Beauty spot

Ripped green crop top

Bone clasp pins skirt together

Lady Cyclops She may wield a heavy club, but Lady Cyclops mostly uses it for playing baseball and scratching her back.

Groovy print on torso and arms

Disco Diva From the top of her perm to the wheels on her roller skates, this singing sensation is pure 1970s!

Roller skate piece introduced in 2013

Hot dog piece goes over standard head and torso

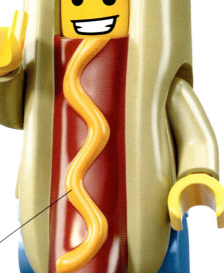

Squirt of mustard

Hot Dog Man With his big buns, this meaty mascot just wants to feed the world—with frankfurters!

Snaking tendrils extend from arms

Plant Monster The face in the mouth of this walking plant belongs to its most recent meal!

Vines cover legs and torso

SERIES 14

Released in time for Halloween 2015, the Monsters series of Minifigures included witches, werewolves, gargoyles, and ghosts. For the easily frightened, it also featured one or two characters who were simply playing at being paranormal!

Peep through the grille to find a grinning face

DID YOU KNOW?
Series 13 was the very first to feature a Minifigure dressed as food.

Foil is also used by the Series 12 Swashbuckler Minifigure, but in gold

Fencer En garde! The eager Fencer wears a pristine white outfit. His torso, legs, and protective masked helmet are all unique.

Mask-string loops around the whole head

Skeleton Guy This harmless trick-or-treater isn't just dressed like a skeleton—he's dressed like a classic LEGO skeleton!

Unique hair piece

Pumpkin basket for Halloween treats

LEGO skeleton limb designs printed on sides

Pom-poms have hand grips inside

LEGO® MINIFIGURES

With its 16 unrelated characters, 2015's first wave of Minifigures followed a familiar and much-loved formula. The second wave followed on from the previous year's *The Simpsons* series, depicting more of Springfield's finest. The third wave was more of a departure as, for the first time, each character was linked by a theme. This time around, every Minifigure was a monster!

Zombie Cheerleader Zombies are well represented in the Monsters series, with Zombie Pirate and Zombie Businessman also on the team.

Patched hat and scraggy hair are all one piece

I AM NAILING THIS PROJECT!

Low-slung tool belt packed with essentials

Carpenter This blue-collar craftsman carries a standard 1×4 LEGO tile printed to look just like a plank of wood.

Unique saw piece

Broomstick has appeared in nearly 80 sets in different colors

Wacky Witch This poor witch is permanently green because she gets airsick attempting to ride her broomstick.

Black cat is not impressed

Striped leggings underneath cloth skirt

Daphne Like the rest of the gang, danger-prone Daphne has a scared face print, as well as a happy one.

Magnifying glass really works!

Shaggy Found in all five sets, Scooby Doo's best friend is more interested in sandwiches than mystery-solving!

Shaggy always needs a shave!

Unique hair piece

Turtleneck collar

Scooby snack found in Haunted Lighthouse (75903)

Velma The smartest member of the gang can never lose her glasses—they are printed on her face!

Fred's alternative expression is not quite so confident!

Ascot tie over white sweater

Fred This dashing detective drives the Mystery Machine through a scary forest in his only set appearance.

Single LEGO knob on back

Head is a separate, posable piece

SCOOBY-DOOBY-S-S-S-SWAMP MONSTER!

Scooby-Doo The greatest of Great Danes appears in all five sets—as happy, scared, standing, and sitting variants.

LEGO® SCOOBY-DOO™

"Jeepers, Scoob, we've got our own theme!" Shaggy and his cartoon chums starred in five fright-filled sets in 2015. Each one was packed with monsters and g-g-g-ghosts, but on closer inspection, they all turned out to be crooks in elaborate costumes! The theme also included a brick-built version of the adventure-loving gang's iconic camper van, The Mystery Machine (75902).

Golden trident from LEGO® Atlantis theme

Swamp Monster Turning the head piece under this monster mask reveals the face of villainous Mr. Brown!

Pumpkin piece also appears in Halloween sets

Mask mold first used in LEGO® Monster Fighters theme

Stalk can be held by minifigure hands

Headless Horseman The face of cunning Elwood Crane is exposed when this new pumpkin head piece is removed.

LEGO® DC SUPER HEROES

The Justice League and their enemies boosted their numbers in this year's DC sets. Goodies Supergirl, Cyborg, and Hawkman all made their minifigure debuts, while the forces of darkness were joined by Black Manta, Captain Cold, Gorilla Grodd, and Darkseid. The last two were the first big figures to be seen in the theme and towered over their adversaries!

Pipes made from flexible plastic

Top of helmet slots on over neck section

Black Manta This fishy foe wears a diving helmet with built-in tubes connected to a breathing tank on his back.

Scuba suit printing continues on back

Bulky body

Hands and arms are posable

Darkseid It takes four members of the Justice League to fight this big blue brute in Darkseid Invasion (set 76028).

Upside-down bat-symbol

Vampire-like teeth

Unfastened pouch on upside-down Utility Belt

Batzarro This corrupted clone of Batman came as part of a limited edition LEGO DC Super Heroes DVD set.

DID YOU KNOW? Raffle winners at 2015's San Diego Comic-Con took home an exclusive minifigure of DC hero Arsenal.

Calm expression can be substituted for gritted teeth

Symbol of the House of El

Supergirl Teenage Kara Zor-El fights beside her Kryptonian cousin Superman in Brainiac Attack (set 76040).

Amy Farrah Fowler Sheldon's soulmate in *The Big Bang Theory* has a unique cardigan print (not that Sheldon will notice).

The LEGO News printed tile

Symbol of Super Hero The Flash

Replica Green Lantern accessory

Sheldon Cooper *The Big Bang Theory*'s central character shows off his love for DC in his minifigure form.

LEGO® IDEAS

Two out of four fan-designed sets came with minifigures in 2015. First up was *The Big Bang Theory* (21302), which recreated the set of the TV sitcom complete with lead characters Sheldon, Leonard, Howard, Raj, Amy, Bernadette, and Penny. Then it was the turn of the world's longest-running science-fiction show, *Doctor Who* (21304), with a bigger-on-the-inside TARDIS build!

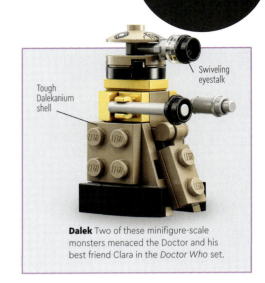

Swiveling eyestalk

Tough Dalekanium shell

Dalek Two of these minifigure-scale monsters menaced the Doctor and his best friend Clara in the *Doctor Who* set.

SWAMP POLICE

Helicopters and hovercraft keep the Swamp Police one step ahead of the crooks and crocodiles in the City's murkiest waters! Thirteen new minifigures in the subtheme include eight new-look cops and five fugitives from justice.

Protective vest

Large, practical pockets

Female Swamp Police Officer Wearing one of two standard Swamp Police uniforms, this ranger rides out in two different sets.

Same hat style as 2012's Forest Police

Radio clips onto shirt placket

Male Swamp Police Officer The second standard outfit of the Swamp Police is more lightweight than the version with vest protection.

Bearded Crook A distinctive look sees this bad guy catch the eyes of the cops in three separate sets!

Missing tooth

Dark orange beard

Ragged suspenders

LEGO® CITY

It was another big year in LEGO City, with a new fleet of demolition vehicles needed to keep up with the ever-changing face of LEGO urban life! The long arm of the law reached into the City swamps—and even the sea proved no boundary for City explorers. City minifigures even went out of this world via the cutting-edge Space Port!

Space Scientist Away from work, this smiling minifigure enjoys reminding all of her friends that what they do isn't rocket science.

Reflective visor protects against solar glare

Stylish half-rim glasses

Red pen in lab coat pocket

Astronaut Two seemingly identical spacewalkers in Utility Shuttle (set 60078) have different faces (male and female) under their golden visors.

CONSTRUCTION

This year's Construction sets were just as much about knocking things down as building them up! Demolition sites and vehicles featured in four sets, assisted by a Service Truck (60073) carrying an all-important portable toilet!

Brown shirt under high-vis vest

Pneumatic hammer drill

Construction Worker A brand-new hard-hat-and-headphones piece protects this worker's invisible ears from the blare of his drill.

Depth and pressure gauges

Scuba Diver Standard City divers' gear gets an update when paired with this explorer's detailed wetsuit print.

DEEP SEA EXPLORERS

Six sets left LEGO City for the seabed in 2015, discovering shipwrecks, sawfish, treasure chests, and whale bones! Each set included at least one exploratory vehicle, closely based on the latest real-world submersibles.

Crowbar for prying open treasure chest

Deep Sea Diver This explorer's heavy-duty helmet with built-in air tanks was first seen in 2010's LEGO Atlantis theme.

Metal toecaps

SPACE PORT

Realistic shuttles and satellites set this returning City subtheme apart from the science fiction of LEGO® Space. Scientists, technicians, and trainee astronauts worked together on the ground, while space-suited minifigures ventured out into orbit.

Finn This friendly ex-stormtrooper and reluctant hero appears in just one 2015 set, the new *Millennium Falcon* (75105).

New hair piece

Jacket "borrowed" from Poe Dameron

THE RESISTANCE

Led by General Leia (who would become a minifigure in 2016), this brave band of freedom fighters combines newcomers including Rey, Finn, and BB-8 with seasoned rebels such as Han Solo and Chewbacca.

Untidy shirt collar

Older Han Solo The 24th Han minifigure is the first to have gray hair (though he retains a boyish grin).

Staff for self-defense

LEGO *STAR WARS*

Ten years after the last live-action *Star Wars* movie, the Skywalker saga returned to theaters in December 2015 with *The Force Awakens*. Three months earlier, on "Force Friday," LEGO *Star Wars* sets based around the new film made their debut in stores. They introduced the world to minifigure versions of a new generation of Resistance heroes and their First Order enemies.

Photoreceptor "eye"

BB-8 It's true that this droid is made from just two pieces, but both are new and boast exclusive printing!

Base connects to a single knob

Hair piece worn instead of mask

Rey The future Jedi comes with a scavenger's bag and a protective desert mask piece in Rey's Speeder (5099).

Helmet hides snarling face

Flametrooper First Order stormtroopers come in several guises, but few are as fearsome as these fire-throwing thugs.

Brick-built fuel pack

Kylo Ren Ren's helmet comes in just one 2015 set. Four years passed before it appeared again (with a different printing).

Exclusive cruciform lightsaber

THE FIRST ORDER

Inspired by the old, defeated Empire, the First Order wants to see the galaxy ruled by fear once again! Its figurehead is the dark side master Kylo Ren, who answers to the mysterious Snoke.

Battle-ravaged cape

Unique silver metallic armor

Black fabric cape with red trim

Captain Phasma The commander of the stormtroopers has a plain head piece under her helmet to keep her identity a mystery.

THE SHIELD HELICARRIER

The biggest ever LEGO Marvel Super Heroes set by far, The SHIELD Helicarrier (76042) is built from 2,996 pieces at microfigure scale. Twelve microfigures are included, along with five hero minifigures.

Transparent red visor built into helmet

LEGO® MARVEL SUPER HEROES

Big-screen adventure Marvel Studios' *Avengers: Age of Ultron* dominated at the box office and in the LEGO Marvel Super Heroes theme of 2015. Six sets included all the familiar heroes, including newcomer The Scarlet Witch. An *Ant-Man* set represented the year's other entry to the Marvel Cinematic Universe, while two sets explored the web-slinging world of animated TV series *Ultimate Spider-Man*.

SHIELD Agent Eight identical microfigures patrol the deck of the Helicarrier, emblazoned with SHIELD emblems.

Microfigure stands 0.6 in (15 mm) tall, including base

Printing even includes pockets!

Nick Fury The director of SHIELD's eyepatch and goatee beard are both less than a millimeter tall on this microfigure.

Ant-Man Shrinking Super Hero Scott Lang rides a giant brick-built bug in Ant-Man Final Battle (76039).

Powered-up red eyes on reverse

Energy bolts in both hands

The Scarlet Witch This Ultron ally eventually teams up with the Avengers, and her two face prints show her different sides!

Skin-tight mask printed on head piece

Darker suit than Peter Parker wears as Spidey

Scary alien smile

Tendrils built on the back of neck bracket

Miles Morales Spider-Man One of many Spider-Heroes in the Multiverse, Miles makes his minifigure debut in an *Ultimate Spider-Man* set.

Carnage This red menace from *Ultimate Spider-Man* turns his tendrils on Miles Morales in Carnage's SHIELD Sky Attack (76036).

Kanji symbol for number six

Only ninja to wear this color

LEGO NINJAGO

The ninja had gone their separate ways at the start of 2015, but were brought back together at the Tournament of Elements. Here, they met villainous Master Chen and his daughter Skylor, a.k.a. the Yellow Ninja. Later in the year, they battled ghosts in the City of Stiix, and Lloyd the Green Ninja was possessed by Morro the Master of Wind!

Skylor The Elemental Master of Amber is the sixth ninja to appear in NINJAGO and wears a symbol denoting this.

Red eyes

Master Chen This sneaky snake-worshipper wears a unique serpent skull helmet with trailing spiky tails.

Serpent-tooth necklace

Sickly skin tone under cowl

Mask and armor are two separate pieces

Evil Green Ninja Lloyd gets a ghostly new look for 2015. He's soon back to his healthy green self, though.

Scythe Master Ghoultar One of 18 Ghost Warrior minifigures, Ghoultar has a brand-new multicolor part in place of legs.

Face print on transparent green head piece

Ghostly lower body connects to LEGO knobs like standard legs

Ponytail print on torso

Alex The minifigure version of what was at the time the default female skin has appeared in more than 20 sets since 2015.

LEGO® MINECRAFT®

Armored skeletons, zombie pigmen, and new brick-built nasties roamed the LEGO Minecraft world in 2015. But most importantly, player minifigure Steve no longer had to face these dangers alone, as he was joined by fellow adventurer Alex! She appeared in The Desert Outpost (21121) and The Nether Fortress (21122), once with a helmet and once without.

Wings clip onto back of armor

Tribe-specific printing on armor piece

Bladvic A member of the Bear Tribe, Bladvic wears distinctive new flame wings and Fire CHI armor.

Same head mold as LEGO Minifigures Yeti from 2013

Breezor This Beaver is the only Chima minifigure not to have a standard head piece beneath an animal mask.

Only second use of short legs in Chima theme

Rinona The Rhino Tribe debuted in 2014, but Rinona and her brother Rogon returned for the Fire vs. Ice showdown!

Printed Fire CHI harness

Hardy rhino-hide leg print

LEGO® LEGENDS OF CHIMA™

Bears and Beavers joined the tribes of Chima for the final year of this theme, and there were reinforcements for the Rhinos, Tigers, and more. Nine sets concluded the "Fire vs. Ice" storyline introduced in 2014, tying in with the third season of the animated *Legends of Chima* TV show, which ended with peace returning to the land of CHI.

Nozzle piece first seen in 2007

Blaze Yellow nozzle pieces and black bricks with side knobs create this monster made from fire and smoke.

1×1 brick with four side knobs

Pixelated pumpkin head piece

Shooter pieces fire snowball knobs

Snow Golem The Snow Golem defends Steve's base by firing snowballs at hostile mobs. It is made from snow blocks and a pumpkin in The Snow Hideout (21120).

Ultimate Macy

Knighton's royal princess is more interested in being a knight than a noblewoman—especially in her Ultimate armor!

Six-knob shooter built onto armor

Power mace weapon

Scannable shield makes maces rain down in the NEXO KNIGHTS app

2016

THERE WERE KNIGHTS to remember in 2016, as LEGO® NEXO KNIGHTS™ powered into toy stores, a TV show, and a dedicated app. Mixing medieval adventure with ultramodern tech, the sets came with special minifigure shields that could be scanned by a smartphone to unlock powers in the app. And as if that wasn't enough excitement, the year also saw some all-time icons becoming minifigures, in the shape of rock band The Beatles, E.T. the Extra-Terrestrial, and a host of Disney favorites.

Jestro He was never a good jester, but Jestro's run-in with Monstrox turns him into a really bad one.

Skulls were bells before Jestro turned bad

Cape torn in battle with Merlok

LEGO NEXO KNIGHTS

Peace reigns in the Kingdom of Knighton—until Jestro the jester messes with the Book of Monsters! As fiery fiends burst forth from its pages, it falls to five brave NEXO KNIGHTS to save the day ... More than 50 new minifigures plus other new figures featured in the first year of this fantasy theme, including knights, robots, and lava monsters!

THE KNIGHTS

All five NEXO KNIGHTS came in standard and Ultimate versions in 2016. Each Ultimate minifigure came with three scannable shields, which unlocked NEXO Powers inside the LEGO NEXO KNIGHTS: MERLOK 2.0 app.

Only Lance wears this pointed visor

Cutout in armor reveals fox print on torso

Lance The most laid-back (some would say laziest) knight likes fame, fashion, and fighting monsters!

Aaron This thrill-seeking knight wears a slightly more serious expression on the reverse of his head piece.

Ultimate Clay In his Ultimate outfit, the leader of the NEXO KNIGHTS wears exclusive transparent blue armor and visor parts.

New helmet mold shared with Aaron and Axl

Arms move like a standard minifigure's

Axl By far the biggest of the NEXO KNIGHTS, Axl has an all-new extended torso part and unique armor-clad arms.

THE VILLAINS

Long ago, the evil wizard Monstrox was transformed into a book and locked away in a dusty library. But when Jestro gets his hands on the book, Monstrox's power compels him to free its monstrous contents!

Book of Monsters Two hinged parts make up Monstrox's book-bound form, which can be held by a minifigure.

Printed face found in two sets

Detachable horn pieces

One of four different Scurrier faces

Scurrier All the monsters in NEXO KNIGHTS' first year are based around fire and lava, including this pear-shaped pest.

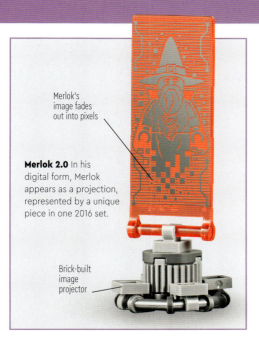

Merlok 2.0 In his digital form, Merlok appears as a projection, represented by a unique piece in one 2016 set.

Merlok's image fades out into pixels

Brick-built image projector

THE OTHERS

One of Knighton's most important citizens is the wise wizard Merlok, who becomes a computer program after an explosive encounter with Jestro. The Kingdom is also kept running smoothly by teams of tiny robots!

Beard hides memory stick pendant print

Merlok The only minifigure version of Merlok came with the DK book, LEGO NEXO KNIGHTS: *The Book of Knights*.

All-exclusive printing

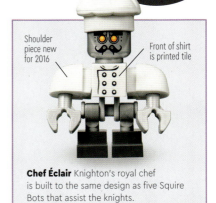

Shoulder piece new for 2016

Front of shirt is printed tile

Chef Éclair Knighton's royal chef is built to the same design as five Squire Bots that assist the knights.

LEGO® CITY

New-look firefighters blazed a trail through the City in 2016, while an aerial display team lit up the sky. Beyond the urban sprawl, police officers dealt with daring escapees on isolated Prison Island and scientists discovered secrets waiting to be found in active volcanoes! Meanwhile, ordinary citizens from every age group enjoyed a relaxing day out at the park.

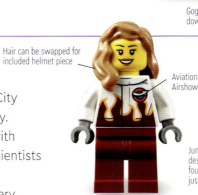

Hair can be swapped for included helmet piece

Aviation Airshow logo

Jumpsuit design found in just one set

Female Stunt Pilot This daredevil performs wing-walking stunts in one of five airport-themed sets from 2016.

Goggles can fold down over eyes

Male Stunt Pilot The wing-walker's identically dressed partner flies their vintage biplane in Airport Air Show (60103).

Zip-up top under life jacket

Police Officer Island life clearly agrees with this perky patrolman, who appears in two of the year's Prison Island sets.

New kindly face print

Both knitwear designs new for 2016

Grandparents These two older city-dwellers enjoy the outdoors in People Pack—Fun in the Park (60134).

Sweat beads on serious face print

Body is all one piece

New rear wheel piece

Volcano Explorers compass logo

Vulcanologist This scientist wears a silver heat suit to explore a lava flow in Volcano Heavy-Lift Helicopter (60125).

Young Family A new baby figure was born in 2016, proudly parented by two minifigures from the Fun in the Park set.

Dog Owner This minifigure is the first to use a wheelchair piece. He loves to take his faithful pooch to the park.

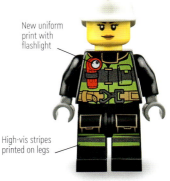

New uniform print with flashlight

High-vis stripes printed on legs

Firefighter This first responder keeps her cool when she attends an oil barrel blaze in Fire Ladder Truck (60107).

Same front wheels as LEGO skateboards

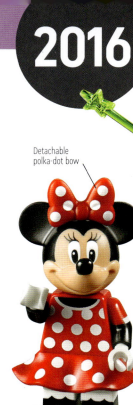

Detachable polka-dot bow

Wings first worn by LEGO® Minifigures Fairy in 2008

Fabric "leaf" skirt

Tinker Bell The Peter Pan pixie is forever associated with Disney magic and appears exclusively in the Disney Castle set.

Skirt piece fits over standard legs

Minnie Mouse Both Minnie and Mickey wear exclusive outfits in the Disney Castle set. Minnie's includes a new skirt piece.

Same head piece as Minnie but with different printing

Legs have printed dress-suit piping on sides

Mickey Mouse A fabric coat-tails piece fits between Mickey's torso and legs, completing his formalwear look.

I THINK YOU'LL FIND I'M A MICKEY-FIGURE!

Firework launcher

Disney Castle This 4,080-piece set (71040) recreates the famous Cinderella Castle at Walt Disney World Resort in Orlando, Florida.

Daisy Duck

Unique horned headdress

Magical staff

Two-tone fabric collar

Bottle labeled "Drink Me"

Same skirt mold as Minnie Mouse

LEGO® DISNEY

This year saw the LEGO Group and Disney celebrate their long-standing relationship with one of the biggest sets ever. Standing 29 in (74 cm) tall and 19 in (48 cm) wide, Disney Castle (71040) played host to seven minifigures, including Mickey Mouse and Donald Duck. The year also saw a host of classic Disney characters making magical appearances in the LEGO® Minifigures line.

Clamshell bikini print

Ariel The star of *The Little Mermaid* comes with a unique hairstyle and an opening oyster shell accessory.

Brand-new lower body piece

Alien A native of the Pizza Planet restaurant, this little green guy first appeared in the LEGO® *Toy Story*™ theme in 2010.

Same head mold as original

All printing updated from LEGO *Toy Story* variant

Maleficent This Minifigure depicts the animated antagonist of *Sleeping Beauty* (1959) instead of the live-action version of more recent movies.

Alice The title character of *Alice in Wonderland* comes with a potion that might just restore her to human size!

DISNEY MINIFIGURES SERIES 1

Favorites from across the Magic Kingdom came together in the first Disney Series of collectible LEGO Minifigures. Eighteen grab-bag characters included Aladdin and the Genie, Mr. Incredible and Syndrome, and Alice and the Cheshire Cat.

Iconic round glasses

John Lennon Purple flowers sail on a sea of green on John's psychedelic shirt—the perfect match for his two-tone pants!

Printed LOVE tile

Paul McCartney Paul's shirt is almost invisible beneath the waves of his enormous kipper tie, worn with a fab frock coat.

LEGO® IDEAS

Fifty years after Beatlemania made them the world's most famous faces, the Fab Four reformed—as minifigures! The Beatles Yellow Submarine (21306) was based on the band's 1968 animated film of the same name and began life as a design by fan builder Kevin Szeto. It also included an exclusive figure of The Beatles' cartoon friend, Jeremy Hillary Boob.

Sideburns printed on head piece

Ringo Starr When the band begins to play, it's Ringo's drums, not his style, that sets the pace!

Submarine motor accessory

George Harrison Though his friends are all aboard, George just isn't up for wearing such groovy-colored gear!

Detachable tiara

Huge skirt piece covers eight LEGO knobs!

SERIES 15

There were lots of unusual parts to play with in Series 15! Three Minifigures had new leg or skirt pieces, while Clumsy Guy came with unique crutches and Tribal Woman cared for a swaddled baby.

Queen As if plucked from a playing card, this royal wears hearts and diamonds on the hem of her unique gown.

Bar piece printed with flute design

Goaty goatee beard

New goat legs piece

Faun This mythical musician is all man in the middle but mostly goat around the head and the hooves!

Reflective gold visor

Classic logo of LEGO Space

Astronaut This off-world explorer travels the galaxy, flying the flag for his love of classic LEGO® Space sets!

Brand-new shark-head helmet

Fins rotate like standard arms

Shark Suit Guy This is the first Minifigure to have fins instead of arms. Luckily he has no fingernails to bite with those sharp teeth.

LEGO MINIFIGURES

Four sets of collectible Minifigures hit the shelves in 2016: the first Disney Series (see opposite), two regular series, and a special DFB Series marking the Euro 2016 soccer tournament. The latter was named after the Deutsche Fussball-Bund (German Football Association) and featured nothing but soccer players! The regular series, meanwhile, covered every career choice from monarch to banana-man ...

German National Football Team logo

DFB SERIES

Unusually, all but one of the DFB Series of 16 German national team players came with the same accessory: a soccer ball! The only one who didn't was coach Joachim Löw, who held a tactics board.

Manuel Neuer This goalkeeper is set apart from his fellow players by his black, long-sleeved shirt and white gloves.

Skin-colored printing separates shorts and boots

Sticker design is printed on

Banana Suit Guy This a-peelingly fruity fellow thinks he's the pick of the bunch among costumed LEGO characters.

Boxing gloves instead of standard hands

Red helmet first seen on Series 5 Boxer

Kickboxer This martial artist can swap her head guard for a flowing hair piece. But the gloves always stay on!

Wings attach with neck bracket

Tail piece fits between torso and legs

Cute Little Devil This mini trick-or-treater's costume features brand-new devilish tail and headgear.

SERIES 16

Things looked to have taken a darker turn when Series 16 included an Ice Queen, a Cyborg, and a Spooky Boy. But there were also friendly faces, including a Babysitter and even a Cute Little Devil!

Hood mold first worn by Ice Fisherman Minifigure in 2011

Wildlife Photographer Behind her hood, this naturalist has a second face print without any goggles—it's ideal for spotting the perfect picture.

Penguin piece later seen in THE LEGO® BATMAN MOVIE sets

LEGO® BRAND STORES

In November 2016, the world's biggest LEGO Store opened in London's Leicester Square. To mark the occasion, 275 individually numbered packs were given away to some of the first customers, each including the store's mascot minifigure, Lester. The ever-so-British character was later reissued in greater numbers and different packaging, but remained available exclusively in the London flagship store.

ACTUALLY, I COME FROM THE BRICKISH ISLES!

Rare bowler hat piece

Umbrella found only in reissue set (40308)

Union Flag vest print

Lester With his red, white, and blue vest and black bowler hat, this dashing dandy could only be a Brit!

2016

Goggles clip onto combined helmet/hair piece

Jyn Erso This rogue rebel has a unique helmet and a detailed bodywarmer print underneath her thick fabric poncho.

Shoulder bag helps hold poncho flat

Rank insignia plaque

Identity disc on belt

Orson Krennic The original director of the Death Star is the first *Star Wars* minifigure to wear a white cape.

LEGO® STAR WARS™

After 17 years of sets starring existing characters, 2016 saw the LEGO Group launch its own family of heroes into the *Star Wars* galaxy! The lovable Freemakers appeared in sets and in their own TV show, which ran until 2017. New names from the big screen and from video games also made the jump to minifigure scale during the year.

ROGUE ONE: A STAR WARS STORY

The first *Star Wars* film beyond the Skywalker saga introduced a host of new characters, from rebels Jyn, Bodhi, Baze, and Bistan to Imperial villain Orson Krennic. All were made into minifigures across five fan-pleasing sets.

Choice of helmet or spiky hair piece

Rowan Freemaker The youngest Freemaker uses the Force to build working LEGO starships in his brick-based version of the galaxy.

Kordi Freemaker Rowan's sister pilots the family's salvage ship in StarScavenger (75147), which also includes their older brother, Zander.

Macrobinoculars worn around neck

Same leg print as Zander Freemaker

K-2SO This reluctant rebel droid is one of five characters found exclusively in Krennic's Imperial Shuttle (75156).

Unique head-and-torso piece

Imperial emblem on shoulders

Same leg piece as super battle droid figures

Blue breastplate denotes a captain

Brown pants under lightweight armor

Shoretrooper What do stormtroopers wear to the beach? In *Rogue One*, they favor this sand-and-sea-colored armor!

THE FREEMAKER ADVENTURES

Animated TV series LEGO® *Star Wars™: The Freemaker Adventures* follows the Freemaker family as they try—and fail—to live a quiet life in the era of the Galactic Empire. Two Freemaker sets were released in 2016.

Same hair as 2009's Endor Leia, but in a lighter color

Frown can be swapped for a smile

General Leia The 15th Leia minifigure was the first to depict her in her role as leader of the Resistance.

THE FORCE AWAKENS

Sets based on the seventh installment of the Skywalker saga proved just as popular this year as they had in 2015. Key scenes from the planets Jakku and Takodana were recreated, complete with favorite characters.

Unkar Plutt A "sandwich board" piece over a standard torso creates the Jakku junk dealer's broad head and bulging belly.

Head, shoulders, and belly are all one piece

Bottom of tabard is printed on legs

Eyes magnified by goggles

Wrinkles continue on torso print

Maz Kanata This pocket-sized pirate has a unique head piece combining a cap, goggles, and Kanata's wrinkled features.

STAR WARS® BATTLEFRONT™

Since 2007, LEGO *Star Wars* battle packs have featured multiple unnamed troopers for building up minifigure armies. Both battle packs released in 2016 were based on the recently revamped *Star Wars Battlefront* video game.

Blaster burns on armor

Handheld knob shooter

Jet Pack Trooper Two of these battle-scarred bullies were among the all-exclusive minifigures in Galactic Empire Battle Pack (75134).

DID YOU KNOW? Minifigure battle packs also feature in the LEGO® Castle, Pharaoh's Quest, and Alien Conquest themes.

New Panther ears head topper

Iconic claw necklace

Black Panther For his first minifigure outing, the King of Wakanda teams up with Captain America in one Civil War set.

Printed gray streaks in hair

Doctor Strange The Sorcerer Supreme and his cloak can both be made to levitate in 2016's only Doctor Strange set!

Powerful Eye of Agamotto amulet

CINEMATIC UNIVERSE

Following his minifigure debut in 2015, Marvel's Ant-Man returned in two alternative forms in Super Hero Airport Battle (76051). Black Panther Pursuit (76047) and Doctor Strange's Sanctum Sanctorum (76060) were other highlights from an action-packed year.

Same figure mold used as a trophy piece in some sets

Face printed on large semicircular piece

Giant Man This brick-built version of Ant-Man maintains the proportions of a minifigure, but stands 5 in (14 cm) tall!

Ant-Man This one-piece microscale version of Ant-Man has detailed printing to match his Giant Man form (right).

LEGO® Technic parts make up hands

Legs move like a minifigure's

LEGO® MARVEL SUPER HEROES

In 2016, Marvel Studios released *Captain America: Civil War* and *Doctor Strange*. Both inspired new Marvel minifigures, with Black Panther and Stephen Strange both joining the fray for the first time. There were also sets based on animated series *Avengers Assemble* and the world of Spider-Man, plus a new range of compact and comical "Mighty Micros."

Printed web-shooters on wrists

Same hood mold as Wyldstyle from THE LEGO® MOVIE™

Ghost Rider This hot-headed hero shares his new head mold with a flaming pumpkin from another 2016 Spidey set!

Head piece combines white and transparent parts

Fiery glow shows through holes in jacket

MIGHTY MICROS

Set apart from other Super Heroes sets, this new subtheme starred short-legged minifigures only. Each hero or villain had a comically exaggerated expression and drove a fun car based on their super abilities.

Huge, lopsided grin

Larger facial features than most minifigures

Exaggerated belt size in relation to tiny legs

Thick black outlines on torso print

Captain America This compact Cap has simpler graphics than most minifigures for a bold and almost cartoonish look.

Red Skull The Cap's crimson foe looks furious at being brought down to size for the Mighty Micros subtheme!

Scarlet Spider This Spidey clone is one of three Super Heroes to wield a new web piece during 2016.

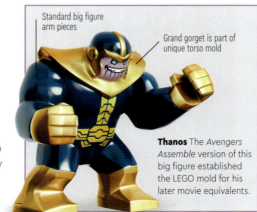

Standard big figure arm pieces

Grand gorget is part of unique torso mold

Thanos The *Avengers Assemble* version of this big figure established the LEGO mold for his later movie equivalents.

SPIDER-MAN

The largest of three Spidey sets this year was Web Warriors Ultimate Bridge Battle (76057), which saw three Spider-Heroes allied against the Green Goblin. Another fiery friendship also featured in Spider-Man: Ghost Rider Team-Up (76058).

AVENGERS ASSEMBLE

In 2016, the Avengers went deep underwater and into orbit with Iron Skull Sub Attack (76048) and Avenjet Space Mission (76049). Both introduced new minifigure characters and took their design cues from TV's *Avengers Assemble*.

Classic Captain Marvel emblem

Captain Marvel Carol Danvers comes with two heads in Avenjet Space Mission: one masked and one with her identity revealed.

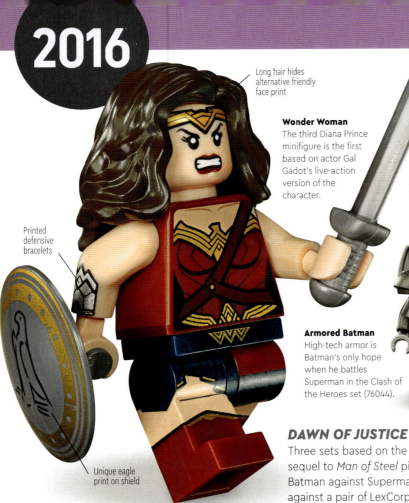

Wonder Woman
The third Diana Prince minifigure is the first based on actor Gal Gadot's live-action version of the character.

Long hair hides alternative friendly face print

Printed defensive bracelets

Unique eagle print on shield

Glow-in-the-dark eyes

Armored Batman
High-tech armor is Batman's only hope when he battles Superman in the Clash of the Heroes set (76044).

Armor mold first used in Ultra Agents theme

LEGO® DC SUPER HEROES

Classic heroes and villains got very different looks this year thanks to three new Super Heroes subthemes. Sets based on *Batman v Superman: Dawn of Justice* matched their minifigures to the latest movie, while a single huge set stepped back in time to celebrate the style of the 1960s. Finally, the new Mighty Micros line ramped up the comic-book charm.

Robin The Boy Wonder swaps the Batmobile for his own red-and-yellow Robin racer for his Mighty Micros outing.

Cartoonish face print

Highly stylized mask

Simple torso design

Over-the-top emblem

MIGHTY MICROS

Big on character but short in stature, these minifigures are no ordinary Super Heroes! Instead, the Mighty Micros come in small, self-contained sets, each featuring one hero, one villain, and two outlandish concept cars.

Bane This miniaturized muscleman drives a dragster with a spinning silver drill in Mighty Micros: Robin vs. Bane (76062).

DAWN OF JUSTICE

Three sets based on the big-screen sequel to *Man of Steel* pitted Batman against Superman; Batman against a pair of LexCorp henchmen; and Batman, Superman, and Wonder Woman against a new-look, long-haired Lex Luthor.

Building knob on head

Standard minifigure arms

Piggy Ten piggies appear in *The Angry Birds Movie* sets, all with different faces on the same new body mold.

LEGO® THE ANGRY BIRDS MOVIE™

Video game stars the Angry Birds got their own movie in 2016, along with a new LEGO theme. Six sets captured the fun of the film, complete with working catapults!

Face print found in Bird Island Egg Heist (75823)

Red The angriest bird appears in five sets out of six, each time with a different—but always unimpressed—expression.

Wings move like minifigure arms

Smile can be swapped for scowling face on other side

Riddler An enigma wrapped in a bright green bodysuit, this puzzle-loving pest is out to dynamite the classic Batcave.

1960s villains lack the muscle definition of modern foes

Lighter hair than most of the Joker minifigures

Choice of grin or surprised face

The Joker Based on the actor Cesar Romero, this Joker's bristly mustache shows through his white clown makeup!

BATMAN CLASSIC TV SERIES

On its release, the 2,526-piece *Batman* Classic TV Series Batcave (76052) was the biggest ever LEGO DC Super Heroes set. It included nine colorful minifigures based on the larger-than-life characters from the 1960s TV show.

Unique bear ears hat piece

Flower brought back to life by E.T. in film

Toy Tag unlocks exclusive battle arena

Finn The *Adventure Time* star is joined by pals Jake the Dog and Lumpy Space Princess in 2016's DIMENSIONS sets.

E.T. The adorable alien film star comes with a pot plant and a buildable telephone for calling his home planet.

LEGO® DIMENSIONS

Even more movie, TV show, and video game characters went through the LEGO DIMENSIONS portal in 2016! Newcomers adding to the play possibilities included the stars of animated series *Adventure Time*, SEGA gaming icon Sonic the Hedgehog, and movie stars from *E.T. the Extra-Terrestrial* to the *Gremlins*. Those that came with gold-colored Toy Tags also unlocked new gameplay arenas.

LEGO® MINECRAFT®

Two brick-built Iron Golems and a three-headed Wither were among the foes faced by Steve and Alex in 2016's LEGO Minecraft sets. New molded figures included wither skeletons and peaceful villagers, while a pair of "skin packs" featured a total of eight new minifigures. These packs reflected the wide range of character customization options available to Minecraft players online.

Barbute helmet print

Pixelated lava armor print

Knight Skin The minifigure parts found in skin packs are ideal for mixing and matching to create new playable characters.

Linked arms do not move

Long torso suggests a knee-length robe

Villager Combined with standard short legs, a new long torso piece makes this figure as tall as a minifigure.

Printed "no ghosts" shoulder patch

Brick-built proton pack on back

Peter Venkman Ectoplasm oozes over this original Ghostbuster's suit—the result of an encounter with Slimer in the 1984 film.

New sideswept hair piece

Ghost grenades on bandolier

Jillian Holtzmann Part of a new generation of Ghostbusters in the 2016 film, Holtzy takes the wheel in the updated Ectomobile.

Posable arms for grabbing food

Slimer One of five ghosts found in Firehouse Headquarters, this goopy ghoul also appears in a LEGO DIMENSIONS set.

LEGO® GHOSTBUSTERS™

The original 1980s Ghostbusters were first made into minifigures for a 2014 LEGO Ideas set. Two years later, they were back in the 4,634-piece Firehouse Headquarters (75827), at the time the third-largest LEGO set ever! Also in 2016, new movie *Ghostbusters: Answer the Call* introduced a fresh team of female ghoul-getters, as seen in the set Ecto-1 & 2 (75828).

Clever torso design covers none of the letters in the Ford logo

Ford Model A Hot Rod Driver The most casually dressed driver in 2016 wears the Ford logo under his shirt.

LEGO® SPEED CHAMPIONS

Three more makes of car joined the starting grid for the second year of this realistic motorsports theme. Audi, Chevrolet, and Ford lined up with two sets each, while Porsche returned with the largest set of the 2016 wave. A vintage car also joined the collection for the first time, in the shape of a flame-decorated Model A Ford Hot Rod.

New ponytail piece

Armor built into upper torso piece

Classic LEGO® Pirates hook-hand

Nadakhan With two torso pieces and a proud plume of hair, the creepy Sky Pirates chief towers over other minifigures.

Same hairstyle as Zane, but in gold

Old-fashioned mechanical design

Echo Zane The ninja meet this rusty replica of Zane in the largest Sky Pirates set, The Lighthouse Siege (70594).

Headwrap masks a wide and eager grin

Homemade "purple ninja" costume

Lil' Nelson This adoring young fan of the ninja dons purple robes to ride with Cole in Rock Roader (70589).

Nya The Master of Water goes without a mask in 2016, after years of wearing her Samurai X disguise.

New shoulder armor piece

Water Ninja symbol

Earth Ninja symbol

Traditional ninja leg wraps

Ghost Cole The Master of Earth has the same ghostly green head piece with dual expressions in two 2016 sets.

LEGO® NINJAGO®

By 2016, Nya was a fully fledged member of the ninja team, bringing their number to six. Together, they fought scallywag Sky Pirates led by the giant genie Nadakhan, and the spirits of their old enemies as summoned by the malevolent Master Yang. Cole was briefly turned into a ghost, while Zane met his "brother"—a clockwork copy of himself.

Bunny Suit Guy
• 2012 • Series 7

Chicken Suit Guy
• 2013 • Series 9

Bumblebee Girl
• 2013 • Series 10

Piggy Guy
• 2014 • Series 12

Unicorn Girl
• 2C15 • Series 13

Shark Suit Guy
• 2016 • Series 15

Penguin Boy
• 2016 • Series 16

Spider Suit Guy
• 2018 • Series 18

GO WILD!

COLLECTIBLE LEGO® MINIFIGURES are the most diverse LEGO characters of all. Since 2010, they have dressed as artists, sports stars, musicians, and monsters. But if there's one look they like more than any other, it's a cool (or possibly quite hot) animal outfit! Special helmet-style pieces are key to these costumes, but some also come with wings, fins, tails, or (in the case of Spider Suit Guy) eight extra legs!

Elephant Girl
• 2018 • Series 18

Fox Costume Girl
• 2019 • Series 19

Llama Costume Girl
• 2020 • Series 20

Ladybug Girl
• 2021 • Series 21

Pug Costume Guy
• 2021 • Series 21

Turkey Costume
• 2022 • Series 23

Raccoon Costume Fan
• 2022 • Series 22

Reindeer Costume
• 2022 • Series 23

T-rex Costume Fan
• 2023 • Series 24

Hamster Costume Fan
• 2025 • Series 27

Robin Dick Grayson's eye-popping glasses are part of a new Boy Wonder hair piece made specially for his minifigure.

Worried look can be swapped for a wide grin

Suit based on Batman's "Reggae Man" outfit

Sash continues onto back

THE LEGO BATMAN MOVIE

LEGO® Batman got his first theme in 2006 before Batarang-ing onto the big screen in 2015's THE LEGO® MOVIE™. Few minifigures were so deserving of their own film, so it was no surprise that he struggled to share the limelight when the moment arrived! Nevertheless, THE LEGO BATMAN MOVIE sets found room for Bruce Wayne's ego alongside his best friends and foes.

2017

TWO BRICKBUSTER LEGO® films thrilled moviegoers in 2017, and themes based on THE LEGO® BATMAN MOVIE and THE LEGO® NINJAGO® MOVIE™ kept the excitement building long after the credits had rolled. Also bringing big-screen heroes down to minifigure size were sets inspired by *Star Wars: The Last Jedi*, DC's *Justice League*, Disney's *Pirates of the Caribbean: Dead Men Tell No Tales*, and the latest installments in Marvel's Infinity Saga. Meanwhile, in Denmark, the new LEGO® House experience opened its doors to visitors ...

Jim Gordon Gotham's top cop wears this ceremonial uniform at his retirement party and in The Scuttler vehicle set (70908).

New not-much-hair piece

Legs and cape first seen in 2016's Batman Classic TV Series Batcave (76052)

Alternative face shows gritted teeth

Chunky new body armor accessory

Barbara Gordon Jim Gordon's daughter follows in her father's footsteps to become Gotham's police commissioner in THE LEGO BATMAN MOVIE.

Alfred Pennyworth Batman's faithful butler appears in three movie sets, but wears this 1960s-style Batsuit in just one of them.

THE HEROES

Spoiler alert! At the end of THE LEGO BATMAN MOVIE, even the villains join forces with Batman to help him save the day. But for most of the film, his allies are more familiar faces ...

Updated head piece has two expressions

Batman The Caped Crusader's classic look is updated for the movie with a new bright yellow Utility Belt piece.

Rocking "The Joker" sign

Rollercoaster encircles whole building

Joker Manor The theme's biggest set (70922) includes exclusive disco versions of Batman and Robin among its 3,444 pieces.

THE VILLAINS

All of Batman's most famous adversaries appear in the movie, along with some rarely remembered villains from the hero's storied history. That's right: the likes of Polka-Dot Man and Calendar Man are real *Batman* comics characters.

Unique hair piece

Skull print on belt

Harley Quinn Harley's Smylex-branded top is a reference to the Joker's trademark weapon in the 1989 *Batman* movie.

Mismatched roller skate accessories

Chinless helmet mold first used for collectible Minifigure Hockey Player in 2011

Mask print makes eyes looks like polka dots, too!

Polka-Dot Man This colorful crook is based on a villain who first faced Batman in *Detective Comics* in 1962.

Fabric coat-tails fit between torso and legs

Calendar grid printed on swimming cap piece

The Joker Batman's best frenemy appears in seven movie sets and wears these extra-long coat-tails in three of them.

Even Joker's trick guns can be dangerous!

Exclusive flame-print helmet

Cape and collar are two separate pieces

Calendar Man This everyday evildoer is dated in more ways than one: he made his comic-book debut in 1958!

Stray tufts of straw ruin Scarecrow's disguise!

Disguised Scarecrow If you like your pizza with extra fear gas, place an order with Scarecrow Special Delivery (70910).

COLLECTIBLE MINIFIGURES

Twenty LEGO® Minifigures from the movie could only be found in collectible mystery bags. They included six very different versions of Batman, some ultra-obscure and oddball villains, and Dick Grayson wielding a can of Shark Repellent.

Helmet is a hollow 2×2×2 dome brick

Unique molded cape part covers shoulders

Red Hood Who is the Red Hood? Lift off this villain's unique red dome helmet and you'll find ... another mask!

One-of-a-kind head piece

Notepad accessory

Eraser 2B or not 2B? That is the question posed by this pencil-thin pest with a talent for making things disappear.

Shoes styled like pencil points

Pink sweatband under cowl

YOU CAN'T SPELL BALLET WITHOUT EL BAT!

Fairy Batman Is this Batman's most unusual minifigure? Fairy Batman comes with a tutu, a wand, and an exclusive pink Bat-cowl.

Tutu piece first worn by Ballerina Minifigure in 2016

Wand and wing molds first used for 2012's Fairy collectible LEGO Minifigure

Printed salad leaves on oversized plate piece

Silk robe print

Lobster element new for 2017

Lobster-Lovin' Batman After a long night's crime-fighting, LEGO Batman just loves a microwaved lobster—alone or with new friends.

213

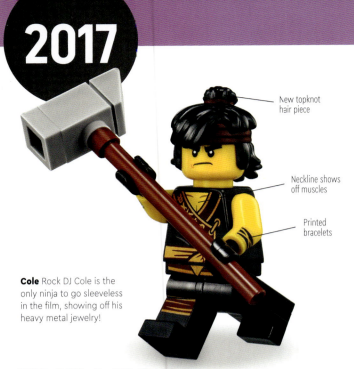

New topknot hair piece

Neckline shows off muscles

Printed bracelets

Cole Rock DJ Cole is the only ninja to go sleeveless in the film, showing off his heavy metal jewelry!

THE LEGO NINJAGO MOVIE

After six years of animated TV adventures, the WJ Crew made the big leap to the big screen in September 2017. THE LEGO NINJAGO MOVIE took the team in a new direction, with a comedy adventure that stood apart from the ongoing TV show. And so the movie sets were released as a standalone theme, alongside a range of collectible LEGO® Minifigures.

Printed dental braces

Nancy Hot dogs and the classic LEGO® Space theme M:Tron keep this young city-dweller smiling, even when Lord Garmadon attacks.

M:Tron logo on undershirt

Hair piece has ponytail at back

Logo of 2002 LEGO theme Galidor

Mother Doomsday This cheery comic book seller is one of 10 ordinary citizens in the 4,867-piece Ninjago City set (70620).

CITIZENS

The everyday inhabitants of Ninjago City appear throughout THE LEGO NINJAGO MOVIE theme. Some of these supporting characters had already been seen in the TV show, but none had been made into real minifigures before.

Unique flamelike hair piece

Bandage above left eye

THIS HAIR IS GIVING ME SIDEBURNS!

Kai On film—and on his minifigure—the Master of Fire has a scar across his right eye. On TV, it is located on the left.

New diamond-print legs

THE NINJA

All six ninja got makeovers for their movie debut, including new clothes, new hairstyles, and even new faces! But each new look stayed true to the characters' much-loved TV personalities and established Elemental Powers.

Exclusive ponytail piece

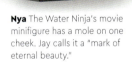

Fabric kusazuri armor piece

Nya The Water Ninja's movie minifigure has a mole on one cheek. Jay calls it a "mark of eternal beauty."

Helmet made from two dome-shaped pieces

Stud-shooting "fish-zooka"

Printed jellyfish tendrils on torso

Jelly When it comes to fighting, this aquatic fanatic floats like a jellyfish and stings like … a jellyfish!

Combined shark mask and breathing gear piece

Fish and blade make a scale weapon

Hammer Head Variants of this big-mouthed bully get up to something fishy in three THE LEGO NINJAGO MOVIE sets.

Scowling face hidden by octopus mask

Breathing gear separate from mask piece

Four Eyes Octopus officers like this one are the most extensively armed soldiers in Garmadon's Shark Army.

THE SHARK ARMY

Four-armed is not forewarned, as the evil Lord Garmadon is repeatedly foiled by the ninja in THE LEGO NINJAGO MOVIE! He uses insect, bird, and fruit forces against them before finally unleashing his Shark Army.

COLLECTIBLE MINIFIGURES

THE LEGO NINJAGO MOVIE series of collectible characters featured a total of 20 minifigures. These included several of the ninja in casual clothes, a new Master Wu, and three very different versions of Lord Garmadon.

Hair is part of exclusive hood piece

Lloyd Garmadon All the Green Ninja's movie minifigures have emerald-colored eyes. In previous sets, they had always been black.

Lopsided hoodie hem printed on leg piece

Tousled hair piece worn only by Jay

Scarf piece new for 2017

Jay Walker A zigzag design on his jacket hints that this might just be the famous Master of Lightning.

Severe new haircut with shaved sides printed on head

Unique backpack piece

Zane A straight smile, parallel eyebrows, and perfectly symmetrical creases in his pants give away this ninja's robotic origins.

Garmadon's movie minifigures are the first to smile

Torso extender mold first used for Garmadon minifigures in 2012

Flashback Garmadon In his imagination, this is the groovy 1970s dad that Lord Garmadon could have been to Lloyd.

DID YOU KNOW?
Temple of the Ultimate Ultimate Weapon (70617) is the only movie set to feature all six ninja.

LEGO® DIMENSIONS

The third and final year for this building-and-gaming theme included new Level Packs based on THE LEGO BATMAN MOVIE and '80s adventure film *The Goonies*. Smaller sets added TV stars from *Teen Titans* and *The Powerpuff Girls* to the gameplay, as well as movie minifigures from *Beetlejuice* and Harry Potter. Even LEGO® City's Chase McCain joined in with the fun.

Badge worn on opposite side to earlier Chases

Chase McCain The top cop of LEGO City has appeared in several sets and video games, but his DIMENSIONS variant is unique.

Lighter shirt than 2017 LEGO City variant

First use for this new hair mold

Choice of smiling and grumpy face prints

Beetlejuice The star of a 1988 movie and its 2024 sequel comes with a brick-built Sandworm monster in matching black and white stripes.

Blue and gold replaces Nya's red and black look

Samurai X A printed mask beneath her helmet kept P.I.X.A.L.'s new persona under wraps until the TV show revealed it.

LEGO® NINJAGO®

As the comedy focus of THE LEGO NINJAGO MOVIE was massively successful in theaters, the more character-based original series continued along its own path on TV. Nine sets tied in with the seventh season's "Hands of Time" storyline, introducing the Vermillion Warriors and a new-look Samurai X—a secret identity now passed on from ninja Nya to P.I.X.A.L.

Every Vermillion Warrior is made from hundreds of smaller snakes

Snake hair first used for Medusa collectible Minifigure in 2013

General Machia This Vermillion Warrior comes with standard legs that can be swapped for a long, brick-built snake tail.

"Hand-drawn" LEGO Space flag

Chain mail armor print

Dungeon keys on belt

Smilin This ironically named imp guards the Goblin Village with a spear twice as tall as he is!

LEGO® ELVES

Goblins came to Elvendale in 2017, adding a new figure style to the mini doll theme. Ten characters all shared the same mold, with different colors and characterful face prints to tell them apart.

Short legs

Exclusive spaceship piece slots over head and torso

Rocket Boy The LEGO® Space logo appears on a gray torso for the first time under this youngster's rocket coverall costume.

DID YOU KNOW?

"Yuppie" is a slang term from the 1980s, meaning "Young, upwardly mobile professional."

LEGO MINIFIGURES

Eager to be seen among the stars of Series 17 were a Rocket Boy, a Roman Gladiator, an Elf Maiden, a Professional Surfer, and a Yuppie. Less thrilled by the limelight was the Highwayman— a black-clad crook from another era who appeared as a silhouette on the series' packaging. Finding him in your mystery bag added to the element of surprise!

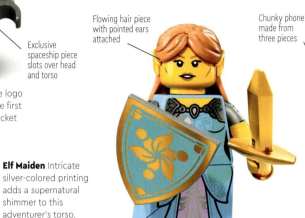

Flowing hair piece with pointed ears attached

Chunky phone made from three pieces

Upper arms molded as separate parts

Elf Maiden Intricate silver-colored printing adds a supernatural shimmer to this adventurer's torso, skirt, and shield.

Leaf-shaped dress layers

Yuppie This high-tech exec is straight out of the 1980s, with rolled-up suit sleeves and a giant mobile phone.

Lightning-tattered clothes

Transparent light blue head piece

Electrified Jestro After being struck by lightning, this jester-turned-TV-weatherman is forecasting all hail—as in "All hail Monstrox!"

Monster face printed on round brick

Round Brickster This column came to life as a foot soldier in the Stone Monster Army—despite not actually having feet!

New arm pieces plug into bricks with holes

LEGO® NEXO KNIGHTS™

A cloud hovered over Knighton in 2017—the villainous Cloud of Monstrox! The sky-high bad guy used lightning bolts to activate a scary Stone Monster Army and to turn the recently redeemed court jester Jestro into a villain all over again. The NEXO KNIGHTS needed all of their app-enabled powers to weather the storm and chip away at their rock-hard foes.

"Helmet" adds furrowed brow and pointy ears

Brand-new lower body part with lightning-effect printing

General Garg Four Stone Army minifigures wear new gargoyle wings, but only Garg gets to rock them in black.

Rogul Two of these rocky wraiths appear in 2017 sets, their bodies floating on a vortex of spinning stones.

Black head piece makes hood look spookily empty

Stone armor piece features unique printing

Lightning-tattered clothes

Printed round tile fits onto unique helmet

Shredded cape

Giant fists fit over standard minifigure hands

Roog This slab-handed stone warrior has a younger brother called Reex and an older, four-wheeled monster-truck brother called Rumble.

Lord Krakenskull As if his helmet wasn't scary enough, this ancient warrior really does have a cracked stone skull underneath.

LEGO® DC SUPER HEROES

Super Hero team-up movie *Justice League* dominated the DC theme in 2017. Batman, Superman, Cyborg, Aquaman, The Flash, and Wonder Woman all battled Parademons across three exciting sets, with Wonder Woman Diana Prince also starring in a set based on her own blockbuster movie. Prince's minifigure got a cool new cloak, while The Flash and Aquaman enjoyed completely new looks.

Alternative face shows eyes white with power

Unique hair piece with printed highlights

Aquaman The second Arthur Curry minifigure is the first to be based on the look of movie actor Jason Momoa.

Hood can be swapped for hair piece

Wonder Woman Everyone's favorite Amazonian dons a cloak and hood to fight villainous Ares in *Wonder Woman Warrior Battle* (76075).

Brighter armor than 2016 variant

MIGHTY MICROS

This year's trio of Mighty Micros sets continued the Justice League theme, starring Superman, Batman, and Wonder Woman respectively. As usual, each set featured a villain and a pair of pocket-sized super-cars.

Back-to-front Superman symbol

Extra-large smile and eyes

Simplified Superman torso print

Bizarro This muddled-up mimic of the Man of Steel drives a similar car to Superman, only built completely backward!

Superman The classic kiss-curl hair piece is the only part this compact Son of Krypton shares with other Superman minifigures.

LEGO® DC SUPER HERO GIRLS

Mini dolls got in on the Super Hero action in 2017, with 10 sets based on animated TV series *DC Super Hero Girls*. Wonder Woman, Batgirl, and Harley Quinn all made appearances in the limited-series theme.

Supergirl The hero also known as Kara Danvers attends Super Hero High School (41232) with Lena Luthor and Poison Ivy.

Detachable fabric cape

Challenger mission patch

Hair can be swapped for helmet piece

Detailed launch entry suit print

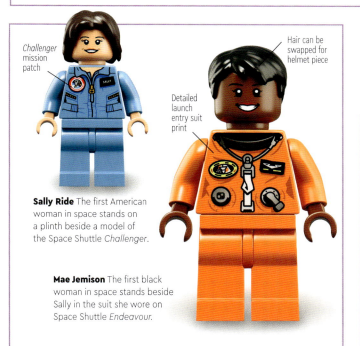

Sally Ride The first American woman in space stands on a plinth beside a model of the Space Shuttle *Challenger*.

Mae Jemison The first black woman in space stands beside Sally in the suit she wore on Space Shuttle *Endeavour*.

LEGO® IDEAS

Four fan-inspired sets were released under the LEGO Ideas banner in 2017, but only two included minifigures. The first was the Old Fishing Store (21310), then the largest set in the theme, with 2,049 pieces and four fishing fan minifigures. The second was Women of NASA (21312), in which four real-life space pioneers were honored in minifigure form.

The Petronas green car graphic features on the leg of the race suit

Mercedes-AMG Petronas Formula One Team Driver This racer is one of six minifigures to wear the iconic Mercedes-Benz three-pointed star symbol in 2017.

Ferrari Engineer Two automotive experts wear this bold branded top in Ferrari FXX K & Development Center (75882).

Same face as LEGO City Rescue Raft Pilot

Face print found in more than 70 sets

Bugatti Chiron Driver The theme's first Bugatti racer wears the famous French company's oval logo on his front and back.

LEGO® SPEED CHAMPIONS

Coming around for a third lap in 2017, the Speed Champions theme added vehicles from Mercedes-Benz and Bugatti to its ever-growing garage of superstar cars. Ferrari was represented by two sets, including a Development Center with a wind tunnel (75882), while McLaren returned with a bright orange 720S car. A single Ford set, meanwhile, included two GT cars, a podium, and a trophy.

Valkyrie This hero is exclusive to The Ultimate Battle for Asgard (76084), in which she battles Hela and her Berserkers.

Warrior face paint

Exclusive asymmetrical cape

Helmet can be swapped for a flowing hair piece

Pointy helmet made from special, flexible material

Baby Groot Made from a single piece, this tiny Guardian of the Galaxy stands waist-high beside his minifigure pals.

Hands can be held in a minifigure's grasp

Feet stand on a single LEGO knob

Hela Thor's power-hungry older sister comes with a brick-built stand so that she can tower over other minifigures.

Ms. Marvel Kamala Khan's shape-shifting arms are represented by a single tube piece that can extend in either direction.

Standard minifigure hands can grip giant fists

Arms can bend in any direction

DID YOU KNOW?
Ms. Marvel's arms are also used by Elastigirl in a 2018 Disney Pixar *Incredibles 2* set.

Smile can be switched for angry face

Same hair piece mold as Ms. Marvel

She-Hulk For her debut LEGO appearance, the Hulk's heroic cousin dons an outfit she first wore in comics during 2004.

Arms can bend in any direction

AVENGERS

Comic books *Iron Man*, *She-Hulk*, and *Ms. Marvel* all provided subject matter for must-have sets in 2017. They included the first minifigures of Agent Coulson, She-Hulk herself, and the Kamala Khan incarnation of Ms. Marvel.

Magneto As a Mighty Micros character, the X-Men's eternal enemy drives a car shaped like a giant cartoon magnet!

Helmet appears in two other X-Men sets

Evil eyes printed on otherwise plain black head piece

MIGHTY MICROS

Made with fewer than 100 pieces each, this year's Marvel Mighty Micros sets pitted Spider-Man against Scorpion, Iron Man against Thanos, and Wolverine against Magneto. All three pairings had short legs but very long histories.

Askew sideburns printed on face

X-Men symbol on belt buckle

Wolverine This mini mutant comes with claspable claw pieces—maybe for styling his square hair and eyebrows.

LEGO® MARVEL SUPER HEROES

The smash-hit Marvel Studios films *Spider-Man: Homecoming*, *Guardians of the Galaxy Vol. 2*, and *Thor: Ragnarok* all inspired LEGO sets in 2017, with the latter two producing the most new minifigures. The comic-book exploits of the Avengers were also depicted in three sets that introduced new "Power Blast" pieces for even more role-play fun. Finally, the Mighty Micros hit the road again in six small super-power-themed cars.

CINEMATIC UNIVERSE

A total of 25 new minifigures debuted in Marvel Studios movie sets during 2017. And as if that wasn't enough for any fan, there were also special figures of giant Gladiator Hulk and tiny Baby Groot.

Captain Salazar This spooky sailor has a hair mold that was later repurposed as a torch flame piece.

Unique black hair piece

Ghostly face printed on transparent head piece

Carina The daughter of Jack Sparrow's former first mate is a talented astronomer and not, as others claim, a witch.

Long hair piece introduced in 2017

Bodice print continues with laces on back

LEGO® *PIRATES OF THE CARIBBEAN*™

Six years after LEGO sets celebrated the first four *Pirates of the Caribbean* movies, a further, huge set was released alongside the fifth film in the series. Measuring 26 in (68 cm) long and featuring 2,294 pieces, *Silent Mary* (71042) captured all the detail of the haunted shipwreck seen in *Dead Men Tell No Tales*. It also came with eight exclusive minifigures.

Vice Admiral Holdo This wise Resistance leader is the first minifigure ever to have lavender-colored hair.

Traditional Gatalentan robe print

Same helmet mold as flametrooper

Blaster found in more than 200 sets

AT-M6 Pilot The pilots controlling the First Order's walkers are never seen in the film, making this minifigure extra-special.

Distinctive gray details on armor and helmet

THE LAST JEDI

Spoiler-free sets for Episode VIII included First Order and Resistance ships as well as a 1,106-piece model BB-8. Nineteen new minifigures appeared in these releases, along with a figure of ball-shaped First Order droid BB-9E.

LEGO® STAR WARS™

Another busy year in the galaxy far, far away saw sets based on the original trilogy, the prequels, *The Force Awakens*, *Rebels*, *Rogue One*, and *The Freemaker Adventures*. But the biggest draw was the new Skywalker saga movie, *The Last Jedi*. Anticipation for this was fueled by seven new sets released in September—three months ahead of the film's premiere.

ROGUE ONE: A STAR WARS STORY

A second wave of sets based on this 2016 film came out in early 2017. It included Battle on Scarif (75171), featuring Jyn in Imperial disguise, and Y-wing Starfighter (75172), boasting two new rebel minifigures.

Moroff The first Gigorian minifigure is a hairy rebel-for-hire with a unique "sandwich board" head and chest piece.

Strapped-on gear is part of sandwich board piece

Exclusive blue hair piece

Fur print on legs and hidden torso

Admiral's rank plaque

Grand Admiral Thrawn
One of the Empire's top tacticians, Thrawn is the first minifigure representative of the blue-skinned Chiss species.

STAR WARS REBELS

Fan-favorite character Thrawn joined the cast of *Rebels* in its third season, having previously starred in best-selling books. A minifigure followed hot on the heels of his animated incarnation, found exclusively in The *Phantom* (75170).

LEGO CITY

A previously unknown side of the City was revealed in 2017, with seven sets exploring its jungles. Ancient ruins awaited discovery in the undergrowth, along with big cats, crocodiles, and minifigure-eating mega-plants! Meanwhile, at the seaside, a new wave of Coast Guard sets sailed into view, complete with several boats that could really float.

Scar over right eyebrow

Drawstrings for hood, printed on back

JUNGLE EXPLORERS

More than 20 different scientists, archaeologists, engineers, and pilots played a part in the Jungle Explorers' various missions. Together, they explored booby-trapped temples; mysterious plane wrecks; and clearings crawling with spiders, snakes, and crocodiles!

Adjustable back legs

Posable head

Tiger This new cat figure was also used for black panthers and distinctively dotted leopards in Jungle Explorers sets.

Male Jungle Explorer A rope, a radio, packed pockets, and a confident grin are all this outdoor adventurer needs.

COAST GUARD

Six sets updated the Coast Guard subtheme after four years lost at sea. They included life rafts, rescue planes, surfers, and sharks, as well as the first new Coast Guard HQ building since 2008.

Rescue Raft Pilot A red life jacket print means this minifigure doesn't always need a separate yellow life jacket piece.

Life jacket print continues on back

Printed spring hook for rope rescues

LEGO® HOUSE

In September 2017, a new 3-acre (12,000-square-meter) attraction opened its doors in the birthplace of the minifigure. Built to resemble a stack of giant LEGO bricks, LEGO House in Billund, Denmark, combines the LEGO Group story with endless opportunities for play. It is also home to some souvenir minifigures found nowhere else in the world!

Later variant has hair instead of a hat

Slogan reads "Home of the Brick™"

Tour Guide This minifigure shows five others around the awesome LEGO House Tree of Creativity (4000024).

I'D LOSE MY HEAD IF IT WASN'T ... OH!

Can carry own head in hand

Nearly Headless Nick The first ever minifigure of Gryffindor Tower's resident ghost is made entirely from white and gray parts.

15th-century costume

2018

THE LEGO GROUP celebrated two big anniversaries in this year. Not only was it 60 years since the LEGO® brick got its patent, it was also the 40th birthday of the minifigure! To mark these milestones, the collectible range of LEGO® Minifigures threw a costume party dressed, among other things, as LEGO bricks and classic characters. Later in the year, the new Wizarding World theme marked the return of Harry Potter sets—and the debut of medium-height minifigures.

Chemical flask piece introduced in 2011

Horace Slughorn Like the 2018 Severus Snape Boggart, Professor Slughorn is found in just one limited edition "Bricktober" minifigure pack, available as a promotion in select stores.

LEGO® WIZARDING WORLD™

Seven years after the previous LEGO® Harry Potter™ sets were released, this new theme brought back the boy wizard and his many friends and foes. But that wasn't all—it also added minifigure versions of Newt Scamander and a host of magical characters from prequel films *Fantastic Beasts and Where to Find Them* and *Fantastic Beasts: The Crimes of Grindelwald*.

Unique torso print

Exclusive face print

Same Gryffindor torso print as Hermione

Shocked face on reverse

The Trolley Witch The fifth version of Hogwarts Express (75955) was the first to feature the train's onboard caterer.

Lucian Bole This little-known member of the Slytherin Quidditch team appears in just one set, with teammate Marcus Flint.

Hermione Granger Hermione got a fresh look in 2018, including short legs and a brand-new hair piece.

Harry Potter The Boy Who Lived also had short minifigure legs for the first time in Wizarding World releases.

HARRY POTTER

Iconic builds such as Arthur Weasley's Flying Ford Anglia, the Whomping Willow, and Aragog the Acromantula were all revisited in this year's Harry Potter sets, which included a total of 33 brand-new minifigures.

Fur stole continues as part of torso print

Severus Snape Boggart This Boggart is what Snape would look like if he was dressed as Neville Longbottom's grandmother!

Neville's grandma's handbag

Jacob Kowalski This minifigure's alternative face print has a chinstrap, for when he wears a helmet instead of hair.

Protective padding over suit

First Newt not to wear an overcoat

Hair mold first seen in LEGO® Friends

Newt Scamander *Fantastic Beasts'* lead character has ditched his overcoat since he first appeared in a 2016 LEGO DIMENSIONS set.

Queenie Goldstein Tina Goldstein's younger sister comes with a choice of smiling and startled facial expressions.

Rubeus Hagrid Far more detailed than the first Hagrid figures, the 2018 version towers over Harry and his pals.

Unique torso and arms with standard hands

FANTASTIC BEASTS

Two sets brought *Fantastic Beasts* to the LEGO Wizarding World in 2018. As well as six all-new minifigures, they included brick-built Erumpent, Occamy, and Thunderbird creatures, plus molded Niffler, Bowtruckle, and Thestral figures.

COLLECTIBLE MINIFIGURES

The Wizarding World launched with a range of 22 collectible LEGO Minifigures from both *Harry Potter* and *Fantastic Beasts*. Seven came with a new medium-length leg piece, used to depict older versions of the Hogwarts gang.

AND HEY PRESTO, MY RIGHT ARM IS AN OWL!

Wand found in more than 70 sets

Exclusive light brown owl piece

Tina is the only one to wear this hat

Only Tina comes with a hot dog bun in this precise shade

Ravenclaw colors on uniform

Tina Goldstein This all-American, hot-dog-wielding witch is a more colorful counterpart to her LEGO® DIMENSIONS set variant from 2016.

Cho Chang The first minifigure of Harry's one-time girlfriend wears a fabric skirt piece over her medium-length legs.

HOGWARTS CASTLE

The biggest set in the Wizarding World theme was the second-largest LEGO set ever released! The 6,020-piece Hogwarts Castle (71043) comes with four standard minifigures plus 24 microfigures in scale with the sprawling building.

Microfigure is all one piece

Ron Weasley Despite standing just four LEGO plates high, this microfigure still captures Ronald's cheeky charm.

Base attaches to a single knob

Combined hat-and-hair element

Brand-new tied-up beard piece

Same hair as 2017 Roman Gladiator collectible Minifigure

Unique printed flag piece

Dean Thomas This Quidditch Chaser made his minifigure debut flying the flag for Gryffindor and wearing a unique scarf print.

Bow is part of head piece

Blossom Like each of the minifigures in the theme, the self-proclaimed leader of the Powerpuff Girls has a unique oversized head mold.

Short minifigure legs

Printed pattern at the bottom of the bowl

Albus Dumbledore Hogwarts' headmaster carries the magical Pensieve bowl, printed on the inside with a swirling blue pattern.

Hedwig figure first seen in 2010

New legs move like those of a full-height minifigure

Harry Potter Fourth-year Harry's medium-length legs make him one LEGO plate taller than his first-year minifigure on the facing page.

LEGO® POWERPUFF GIRLS™

Minifigures based on Cartoon Network series *The Powerpuff Girls* first appeared in a LEGO DIMENSIONS Team Pack (71346) in 2017. They proved so popular that, in 2018, the Girls soared into their own special theme. Just two sets were released, featuring minifigures of heroes Blossom, Bubbles, and Buttercup, alongside the villainous Mojo Jojo and Princess Morbucks.

LEGO® CITY

The brave inhabitants of LEGO City really pushed the boundaries in 2018. While police officers kept order in the mountains, scientists explored an icy Arctic realm and miners dug deep underground. Meanwhile, minifigures in the ever-expanding City Center had fresh opportunities to work and play in brand-new hospitals, hotels, museums, and more!

Branches make carry handles for minifigure hands

Fierce face can be swapped for worried expression

Disguised Crook Known as Stumpy to his pals, this villain is branching out in a unique tree costume, found in just one set.

HE JOINED A SPLINTER GROUP!

Wide-brimmed hat first seen in Swamp Police sets in 2015

Friendly face with laugh lines

Police radio clipped onto vest

WHERE'S STUMPY?

Printed pockets on legs

Police Motocross Biker This off-road officer might look a little stern, but she has a friendly smile underneath her biker's helmet.

Police Chief The head of the Mountain Police leads his team from a high-tech HQ perched on top of a mountain lion's den!

Bear claw scratches on belly

Surprised Crook This bare-chested bad guy is only just out of bed when the Mountain Police come calling at his hideout.

Paw-print design on underpants

MOUNTAIN POLICE

The cops had more than just crooks to contend with in Mountain Police sets. Bears, big cats, and beehives all featured in the subtheme, and officers relied on a new net-shooter gadget to bag the bad guys.

LEGO® Trains emblem on high-vis vest

Crane Operator Two railway workers wear this olive-green outfit in 2018: the cargo crane operator and her train driver colleague.

ARCTIC EXPLORERS

LEGO City scientists first reached the Arctic in 2014. Four years later, they returned to track down prehistoric animals frozen in the ice. These included a saber-toothed tiger and an enormous woolly mammoth.

Temperature monitor on belt

Climbing gear strapped to legs and torso

Arctic Climber This minifigure hasn't turned blue in the cold—he's wearing a full face mask to protect himself from the elements!

Fake-fur hat piece new for 2018

Gloves to keep out the cold

Arctic Photographer Seen in two sets, this brave biologist carries a still camera in one set and a video camera in the other.

New hood piece found in just three sets

Goggles printed onto head piece

Arctic Explorer A cozy hood keeps this Arctic scientist warm, even as she gets chills from digging up ancient polar animals.

Baby figure introduced in 2016

Baby carrier attaches by a neck bracket

Father and Baby A brand-new baby carrier piece lets this dad go hands-free when he goes on a family camping trip.

Reassuring smile

Star of Life symbol on jacket

Doctor The first LEGO City hospital since 2012 includes four medics wearing white coats over bright blue scrubs.

CITY DWELLERS

Large sets such as City Hospital (60204) and Cargo Train (60198) introduced new city workers in 2018. Meanwhile, the Outdoor Adventures People Pack (60202) included 15 unique characters all having fun on Mount Clutchmore!

LEGO® SPEED CHAMPIONS

Ford, Ferrari, and Porsche were the three big names tearing up the racetrack in this year's Speed Champions releases. Across seven sets, all 14 minifigures were new, with drivers, technicians, race officials, and spectators among their number. As ever, the drivers boasted the highest level of printed detail, with real-world sponsor names and logos recreated in tiny type.

White helmet worn by more than 200 minifigures

Ford Fiesta M-Sport WRC Driver Authentic sponsor logos make this racer's torso and leg prints totally unique.

More than 70 minifigures share this face

Classic Ferrari 250 GTO Driver This speed champion wears 1960s-style racing gear to match her classic car.

Classic Ferrari emblem

Same torso print as Porsche 911 RSR driver

Porsche 911 RSR Technician This crucial member of the Porsche pit crew couldn't be happier to be on the team.

Plain white legs found in more than 600 sets

LEGO® JURASSIC WORLD™

Hit movie *Jurassic World: Fallen Kingdom* opened in June 2018, exactly 25 years after the original *Jurassic Park* film was released into the wild. Both were celebrated in LEGO form during the year, with seven sets capturing the new movie and one marking an iconic moment from 1993. An exclusive minifigure pack, meanwhile, combined both in one place.

Choice of scared or serious face prints

Franklin Webb This computer whiz kid is found in just one Jurassic World set: Carnotaurus Gyrosphere Escape (75929).

JURASSIC WORLD: FALLEN KINGDOM

Picking up where 2015's Jurassic World sets left off, the *Jurassic World: Fallen Kingdom* range presented Owen and his pals with a fresh crop of dinosaur danger! These included a spiky Stygimoloch figure and a colossal Carnotaurus.

Ideal camouflage colors

Claire Dearing The Dinosaur Protection Group leader wears green in three 2018 sets and gray in one promotional set.

Dr. Ian Malcolm This chaos theorist mathematician made his minifigure debut in a "Bricktober" promotional set, the Jurassic World Minifigure Collection (5005255), found only in Toys 'R' Us.

Emergency flare to distract dinosaurs

Same quiff as NINJAGO "brown ninja," Dareth

Electric guitar piece introduced in 2014

Rock Star Styled like a 1950s heartthrob, this rock 'n' roller records his hits in a studio above the Downtown Diner.

A single bead of sweat adds to this troubled face

Queasy Rider Builders can choose to give this rollercoaster rider an excited-looking face or one showing the onset of motion sickness!

LEGO® CREATOR EXPERT

After a decade of Modular Buildings in which every minifigure wore the same classic smile, Downtown Diner (10260) introduced a range of expressive faces. Elsewhere, Winter Village Fire Station (10263) added to the seasonal subtheme, and the 4,124-piece Roller Coaster (10261) sent minifigures into a spin!

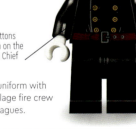

Shiny buttons also seen on the set's Fire Chief

Firefighter A double-breasted uniform with white gloves sets the Winter Village fire crew apart from their LEGO City colleagues.

JURASSIC PARK

Four classic characters were given minifigure makeovers to recreate the iconic kitchen scene in the 25th anniversary set Jurassic Park Velociraptor Chase (75932).

Dr. Alan Grant This gruff paleontologist can swap his hat for a tousled hair piece in the Velociraptor Chase set.

Fedora found in more than 50 sets

Face print based on actor Sam Neill

DID YOU KNOW?
LEGO® Adventurers hero Johnny Thunder starred in a *Jurassic Park III* set in 2001.

Wonder Dog A four-legged friend of the Justice League, this marvelous mutt is based on a dog figure first introduced in 2010.

Unique cape shape

Cowl in dark red for first time

Same hat shape as fellow villain the Penguin

Flaming bat-symbol

Old-fashioned outfit printed in spectral silver

Gentleman Ghost A transparent head piece with a printed monocle makes this minifigure look like a headless specter with a floating hat!

THE LEGO® BATMAN MOVIE

The second year of sets based on THE LEGO BATMAN MOVIE featured more of Gotham City's strangest Super Villains— alongside more of the Caped Crusader's most curious costumes! The largest new set was The Bat-Space Shuttle (70923), which included a section of the Batcave in which the world's best-dressed detective could choose from three stylish Batsuits arranged on a sliding rail.

Reggae Man Batsuit In THE LEGO BATMAN MOVIE, Dick Grayson borrows parts of this outfit to create his colorful Robin costume.

Dreadlocks and hat are all part of mask

"R"stands for "Reggae," or "Robin"!

Specially created dome piece extends bald head

Egg-colored clothing

Egghead Everyone scrambles when this hard-boiled bad guy comes out of his shell. Among other crimes, he is wanted for poaching.

Firestarter Batsuit Batman's face isn't missing here—this blazing Batsuit is in storage in the Batcave until the Caped Crusader needs it.

Unique Bat-hoodie piece

COLLECTIBLE MINIFIGURES

For the second year in a row, THE LEGO BATMAN MOVIE merited its own range of collectible Minifigures. Twenty heroes and villains came complete with unique accessories and display stands emblazoned with the bat-symbol.

Jor-El Superman's dad wears Kryptonian robes and armor and the same hairstyle as Superman—albeit in an exclusive white variant.

Symbol of the House of El

Printed robe piece

Same head mold as Gingerbread Man collectible Minifigure

Clock King This alarming villain is exclusive to the collectible Minifigures theme. He comes with a pair of clock-hand spears.

Bat-Merch Batgirl Barbara Gordon, a.k.a. Batgirl, carries Bat-money for buying more Bat-merchandise in this heavily branded outfit.

Leg print reads "#1 BATFAN"

Unique Bat-hoodie piece

Goggles are part of cowl piece

Belt clock shows same time as head piece

Swimsuit Batman The skimpiest of all Batsuits sees Bruce Wayne's true identity disguised by just goggles, a cowl, and Bat-emblazoned swimming trunks!

Dolphin-shaped pool toy

DID YOU KNOW? The first Jor-El minifigure came as a free gift from LEGO® Stores and LEGO.com in 2013.

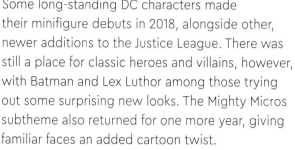

LEGO® DC SUPER HEROES

Some long-standing DC characters made their minifigure debuts in 2018, alongside other, newer additions to the Justice League. There was still a place for classic heroes and villains, however, with Batman and Lex Luthor among those trying out some surprising new looks. The Mighty Micros subtheme also returned for one more year, giving familiar faces an added cartoon twist.

Transparent flames built into head piece

Hands can grip flick-fire Power Blasts

Firestorm This Justice League hero comes with a selection of Power Burst pieces for recreating his flame-throwing abilities.

Red hair and cowl are all one piece

Unique bat-symbol

Green Lantern Jessica Cruz This minifigure was exclusive to the LEGO DC Super Heroes DVD *Aquaman: Rage Of Atlantis.*

Green Lantern Corps symbol over eye

Tail piece visible between legs

The Cheetah This feline felon does battle with Wonder Woman, Batman, and Firestorm in Lex Luthor Mech Takedown (set 76097).

Batwoman Bruce Wayne's Super Hero cousin makes her first appearance in a LEGO set in Batman: Brother Eye Takedown (set 76111).

MIGHTY MICROS

The third and final year of the Mighty Micros line introduced compact cars for Super Heroes Batman, Nightwing, and Supergirl and for Super Villains Harley Quinn, the Joker, and Brainiac.

Exaggerated features

Nightwing's bird symbol

Nightwing Like all Mighty Micros minifigures, Nightwing has short legs, even though he is actually the adult Dick Grayson (Robin).

LEGO® NEXO KNIGHTS™

In its third and final year, the NEXO KNIGHTS storyline revolved around the malevolent Monstrox finding new form as a computer virus. As this digital villain attacked the Kingdom using his Tech Monsters, the knights themselves welcomed former apprentice Robin into their ranks as a fully fledged member of the team.

Tinted visor is part of face print

Armor piece new for 2018

Robin Underwood Previous versions of Robin all had short legs, but in 2018, he stood tall alongside his fellow knights.

LEGO MINIFIGURES

To celebrate 40 years of LEGO minifigures, the collectible Minifigures theme threw a costume party in 2018. Every set in Series 18 contained a costumed character and came with an exclusive orange baseplate for display. Several Minifigures brought gifts along to the party, with three even carrying tile pieces printed to look like tiny LEGO sets.

Brick Suit Girl A special torso piece turns this reveler into a LEGO brick! A red version is worn by her pal, Brick Suit Guy.

Arms attach directly to brick torso

Standard brick knobs on front

Party hat slots into hair piece

Printed torso is a sticker on 1978 version

Minifigure design on bow tie

Police Officer Dressed as one of the very first minifigures from 1978, this partygoer is also carrying the set he appeared in.

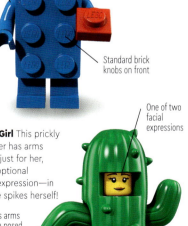

One of two facial expressions

Cactus Girl This prickly partygoer has arms created just for her, and an optional pained expression—in case she spikes herself!

Cactus arms can be posed at any angle

Cake Guy Pink, icing-splattered legs slot inside the cake accessory that this half-baked hero wears as part of his costume.

Six Tech Monsters share this face print

Belt looks like a one-eyed monster

Cezar This spiderlike cyber-fiend stands on four legs made out of blaster weapons and robot arm pieces.

LEGO® STAR WARS™

The penultimate movie in the Skywalker Saga was still in theaters at the start of 2018, and *Solo: A Star Wars Story* followed close behind. There were plenty of LEGO sets to represent both, with younger versions of Han Solo and an older Luke Skywalker minifigure in the mix. As ever, sets based on the original trilogy were featured, too.

Unique helmet design

Cape has hood print on reverse

Han Solo Mudtrooper Young Han's smirking face is the only part of this minifigure not exclusive to just one set.

Double-sided face print on head

Qi'ra Han's childhood friend appears in three Solo sets, each time with a different unique torso print.

SOLO: A STAR WARS STORY

Eight sets depicted the young Han Solo's journey from lowly Corellian scrumrat to lovable hyperspace hero. Minifigures in the subtheme included new versions of familiar characters and a host of new friends and enemies.

Printed sideburns

Metallic scarf print flows from torso to legs

Lando Calrissian This young version of Lando boasts an exclusive blue cape with a collar and printed black trim.

Unusual head armor to protect from sunlight

Blaster

Moloch This villain's robes are made from a new skirt piece introduced in 2018, and his wormlike head is exclusive.

Staff used as a club

Corellian Hound These vicious beasts from Han's homeworld menace minifigures in Moloch's Landspeeder (75210) and Han's Landspeeder (75209).

Ceremonial staff

Unique shoulder armor

Elite Praetorian Guard Leader Snoke's personal protectors come in three varieties—with skirt, with legs, and with variant helmets.

DID YOU KNOW?
Luke Skywalker minifigures have appeared in more than 75 different sets since 1999.

THE ORIGINAL TRILOGY

Key moments from the start of the Skywalker Saga were revisited in 2018 sets, from Luke's Jedi training with Yoda on Dagobah to Leia and the other rebels' fateful trip to the skies over Bespin.

2003 variant has legs instead of skirt

Princess Leia A new variant of Bespin Leia uses the same skirt mold as Moloch for a very different look.

THE LAST JEDI

Important characters held back from the first wave of *The Last Jedi* sets made their debut in 2018. Among them was the older Luke Skywalker, seen in self-imposed exile in Ahch-To Island Training (75200).

New hair piece created for old Luke

Luke Skywalker This Jedi Master minifigure is the first version of Luke to wear a cape and long hair.

Alternative face has closed eyes

Luke Skywalker Luke's Dagobah look had not featured in a set since 2004. This update has a double-sided head with determined and restful faces.

Hairy chest

Unique face print

Wuher The third set to depict Tatooine's Mos Eisley Cantina (75205) is the first to feature its owner, Wuher.

Cat ears attach to standard head mold

Black Panther Wakanda's champion appeared in two 2018 sets based on his own movie and one Marvel Studios' *Avengers: Infinity War* set.

Posable robot arms

Flick-fire Power Blast weapon

Iron Spider-Man Found in just one Marvel Studios' *Avengers: Infinity War* set, this special web-slinger actually has eight limbs!

LEGO® MARVEL SUPER HEROES

Blockbuster movies *Avengers: Infinity War*, *Black Panther*, and *Ant-Man and The Wasp* all inspired LEGO Marvel Super Heroes sets in 2018. Bringing together members of the Avengers, the Guardians of the Galaxy, and more, this ever-expanding theme also set the pace with one last trio of Mighty Micros sets. This concluded the superbeings in supercars subtheme that had launched in 2016.

Unique tree trunk head piece

I AM LEGO GROOT!

Same face as Bespin Leia under helmet

Wing piece connects to torso at neck

The Wasp There was a definite buzz around this minifigure when she made her debut in Quantum Realm Explorers (76109).

Bark print on both sides of torso

Groot The first Groot minifigure followed tiny Baby Groot figures in 2017 and a giant brick-built figure in 2014.

One of four collectible Dragon Armor pieces

Dragon Master A rejuvenated Master Wu is well-protected in this golden armor, which featured in several 2018 sets.

Artificial leg first appeared in this color in 2011

Iron Baron Four Dragon Hunters share this shoulder armor, but only their top-hatted boss wears it on his right-hand side.

LEGO® NINJAGO®

The ninja took on two new sets of enemies in 2018. First up were the Sons of Garmadon biker gang, who used powerful Oni Masks to cause chaos in Ninjago City. Then it was the turn of the Dragon Hunters, who made life a misery for the magnificent beasts in the Realm of Oni and Dragons.

Hair and crown are one piece

Flower print on both sides of cape

Princess Harumi This version of the Sons of Garmadon's secret leader is made up entirely of exclusive parts.

MIGHTY MICROS

The last lap for the Mighty Micros included characterful cars for Scarlet Spider and Sandman, Star-Lord and Nebula, and Thor and Loki. All six minifigures came with short legs and broad expressions for a cute, cartoonish look.

Silver cybernetic arm

Nebula This blue baddie wields an exclusive tile piece printed to look like Star-Lord's famous mix tape!

Star-Lord's signature blaster

Star-Lord Rotate this minifigure's head 180 degrees to reveal the grinning face of Peter Quill underneath his helmet!

Shoulder armor piece first used in NEXO KNIGHTS sets

Ultra Violet This biker wears the Oni Mask of Hatred, one of three special masks found in Sons of Garmadon sets.

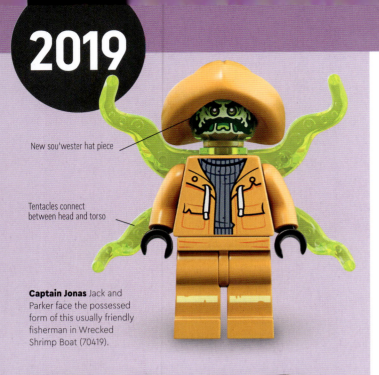

Captain Jonas Jack and Parker face the possessed form of this usually friendly fisherman in Wrecked Shrimp Boat (70419).

New sou'wester hat piece

Tentacles connect between head and torso

2019

CAN A LEGO® SET be haunted? In 2019, the answer was yes, as the Hidden Side theme launched alongside an Augmented Reality app. Viewing the sets through an app-enabled screen let builders see the ghosts that were menacing their minifigures and trap them for virtual rewards. Turning to bigger screens, the year also saw sets based on Netflix smash hit *Stranger Things*; classic sitcom *Friends*; Marvel's *Avengers: Endgame*; *Star Wars: The Rise of Skywalker*; and, of course, THE LEGO® MOVIE 2™!

Newbury Haunted High School
At the flip of a switch, a huge monster's face appears from the walls of this set (70425).

Foldaway eyes

Pop-out giant claws

LEGO® HIDDEN SIDE

Minifigures are turning into monsters in the haunted town of Newbury! As even more people are possessed by ghostly forces, it falls to 13-year-old Jack Davids and his best friend, Parker, to save the town with technology! And with their ghost-catching tech existing as a free real-life app, too, LEGO builders can help the heroes on their Augmented Reality mission ...

New hat-and-hood piece

Jack Davids Hidden Side's hero appears in most sets—sometimes in a jacket, sometimes in gloves, but always in his hood.

Bone-shaped keychain on belt

Exclusive hat-and-hair design

Smartphone accessory shows an approaching ghost!

Parker L. Jackson Newbury newcomer Jack wouldn't last long as a ghost hunter without this street-smart local at his side.

Ripped jeans

Goggles are part of unique hair piece

Monster print on T-shirt

J.B. When not in her lab, this inventor of ghost-catching gear loves to drive the Paranormal Intercept Bus 3000 (70423).

Spencer Jack's faithful ghost dog is a single piece, made from an ethereal mix of white and transparent plastic.

Two-color molding creates wispy effect

Mr. Clarke Nonpossessed appearance.

Wild, haunted hair!

Mr. Clarke This teacher has puzzled and petrified looks on his standard head and a gruesome glare on his ghost one.

Detachable wings

Same swappable ghost head as Captain Jonas

Extra torso and arms first used in LEGO® NINJAGO® sets

DID YOU KNOW?
The Hidden Side app has a multiplayer mode that lets three extra people play as ghosts.

Chef Enzo Swap this chef's extra arms and haunted head for his standard face to free him from ghostly control.

Only Rex wears this new hair piece

I AWAYS LOOK GOOD IN PHOTOGRAPHS!

Reflective high-vis vest print

Blaster as big as his ego

Rex Dangervest This tough minifigure likes danger, traveling through space, and ... wearing vests.

THE LEGO MOVIE 2

Chaos came to Bricksburg in THE LEGO MOVIE 2, turning the home of awesome into Apocalypseburg! Survivalist style was the in look for returning stars from the first film, while new characters from the Systar System went for something far more pink and friendly! Whether they actually were friendly, only time would tell. More than 30 sets featured these clashing sides, mixing minifigures with mini dolls, brick figures, and more!

Goggles are part of printed hair piece

Scarf fits over quiver piece

Lucy The artist formerly known as Wyldstyle comes equipped with scarf, goggles, and a quiver of arrows in six 2019 sets.

Helmet more durable than original 1970s design

Classic minifigure face print

THIS IS WHY WE SEPARATE REDS AND WHITES IN THE SPACE WASH!

Lenny The first minifigure helmet was reintroduced for the first pink LEGO® Space astronaut, who appeared alongside his pals Benny, Jenny, and Kenny.

New funnel hat piece

A heart is all the Tin Man ever wanted!

Tin Man This clockwork collectible Minifigure completes a trio of Oz inhabitants, alongside the Scarecrow and the Cowardly Lion.

Hair piece can be swapped for space helmet

Sweet Mayhem THE LEGO MOVIE 2 theme is the first to mix minifigures and mini dolls, such as this Systar Army general.

Eyes can rotate in any direction

Wings can be raised for flight

Banarnar Anything goes in the Systar System, where brick-built figures like this one can become the best of the bunch!

LEGO® STRANGER THINGS

In the hit Netflix Original Series *Stranger Things*, a brave band of kids explore the boundaries between their own world and its dark underworld reflection. Epic 2,287-piece LEGO set The Upside Down (75810) recreates both of those realities, with a near-mirror-image set that can be displayed either way up! It comes with seven minifigures of the show's main stars, plus one terrifying monster!

New bowl-cut hair piece

Posable medium-length legs

Will Byers A worried face shows that unlucky Will is trapped on the scary side of the Upside Down set!

COLLECTIBLE MINIFIGURES

A bumper crop of 20 collectible characters made up the series of LEGO Minifigures for THE LEGO MOVIE 2. Apocalypseburg inhabitants rubbed shoulders with the strangest Systar System residents, including guest stars from *The Wizard of Oz*!

Eleven Escapee "El" wears a blonde wig and an old dress when she needs to look like an everyday girl.

Printed waffle piece

Fabric skirt piece flexes with legs

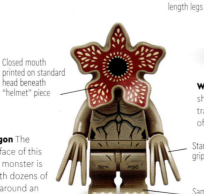

Closed mouth printed on standard head beneath "helmet" piece

Demogorgon The flowerlike face of this nightmare monster is printed with dozens of tiny teeth around an enormous open mouth.

Standard hands grip claw pieces

Same leg mold as Faun collectible Minifigure from 2016

THERE'S NO PLACE LIKE THE SYSTAR SYSTEM.

Exclusive hair piece

Toto the terrier

Dorothy If not in Oz, look to the Systar System for this windswept film star—and her little dog, too!

I ONLY ASKED FOR EYELINER!

Sky Police Officer This deputy drives a truck with working lights and sound effects in Sky Police Diamond Heist (60209).

Combined hat-and-hair piece

New Sky Police uniform print

Sky Police Pilot A new oxygen mask piece helps police pilots to breathe at high altitude in four 2019 sets.

SKY POLICE

LEGO City crime-fighters scaled new heights in six Sky Police sets, using helicopters, planes, drones, and even jetpacks! The subtheme also introduced working minifigure parachutes, used in two sets by cops and crooks alike.

Yellow "skin" visible around painted face

Tiger Girl A paint-splattered artist accompanies this youngster with painted feline features in the Fun Fair People Pack.

Golden rank pins on collar

Fire chief's badge

Freya McCloud Introduced in LEGO City *Adventures*, this friendly fire chief was originally exclusive to just one 2019 set.

Ink from leaky pen on top pocket

Utility belt piece first seen in THE LEGO® BATMAN MOVIE sets

Harl Hubbs LEGO City *Adventures'* star mechanic appears in the Garage Center set (60232), aimed at younger builders.

LEGO® CITY

The fun of the fair came to LEGO City this year, with face-painting, stilt-walking, and more in the People Pack—Fun Fair set (60234). The Sky Police kept an eye on the City from high above, while the latest minifigure astronauts went higher still. Characters from the new animated TV series LEGO® City *Adventures* also appeared in some sets.

Stilt Walker This elevated entertainer follows in the footsteps of an even taller stilt walker from 2014's Fairground Mixer (10244).

Balloon dog accessory introduced in 2018

Each stilt is three times the height of a standard brick

ONE SMALL STEP IS A GIANT LEAP FOR A MINIFIGURE!

SPACE

Last seen in 2015, the LEGO City space program set its sights on the moon and beyond in 2019. Nine sets combined realistic science with near-future innovations, such as the Mars-bound Deep Space Rocket (60228).

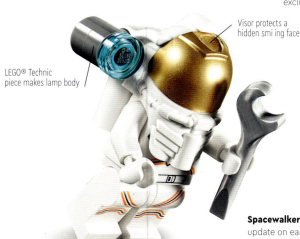

Visor protects a hidden smiling face

LEGO® Technic piece makes lamp body

Spacewalker with Lamp This update on earlier space suits adds orange details—as favored by all of 2019's off-world explorers.

New helmet design fits space-suit-style visor piece

New-look LEGO City space logo

Mars Explorer This astronaut comes with a camera piece, so she could be either winking or focusing on the perfect snapshot!

LEGO® MINECRAFT®

LEGO Minecraft was bigger than ever in 2019, with the launch of large, buildable figures of Alex, Steve, and a Skeleton. Minifigure-scale sets were still in demand, however—new characters introduced this year included a Dragon Slayer in The End Battle (21151), a Pirate in Pirate Ship (21152), and a Blacksmith and a Husk in The Creeper Mine (21155).

Pixelated eyepatch

Shovels make handy oars

Dragon Slayer This brand-new character skin minifigure comes with a Minecraft code that unlocks the same new character look in the game.

Enchanted bow

Pirate This blocky buccaneer encounters brick-built dolphin, parrot, and turtle pals in his only set appearance to date.

Exclusive new hair piece

Double-sided face print on head

Chronal accelerator print

Tracer The original star of Overwatch featured in the very first set of the theme, where she battled her longtime rival Widowmaker.

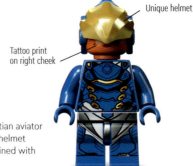

Genji A unique helmet piece on a plain silver head captures the cyborg spirit of this former crime clan member.

Printed visor

Cyborg armor printing continues on back

Unique helmet

Tattoo print on right cheek

Pharah This Egyptian aviator wears a hawklike helmet that can be combined with winged armor.

Ribbon connects to new hair piece

Rice wine bottle hanging from belt

Hanzo This expert archer faces off against his cyborg brother at the Hanamura dojo in Hanzo vs. Genji (75971).

LEGO® OVERWATCH®

Based on the hugely successful video game by Blizzard Entertainment, the LEGO Overwatch theme launched with six sets in January 2019. The futuristic storyline sees a super-intelligent Gorilla named Winston trying to reform the outlawed planetary peace-keeping force called Overwatch. He needs heroes like Tracer, Hanzo, and Pharah on his side to protect the Earth from a dozen different threats!

Face includes printed spectacles

Winston A new big figure mold was made for this imposing ape in 2019's largest Overwatch set, Watchpoint: Gibraltar (75975).

Huge hands grip just like a minifigure's

Rachel Green The *Friends'* fashionista played by Jennifer Aniston is depicted during her time waiting tables in Central Perk.

Iconic "Rachel" hairstyle was actually first seen on 2017's Veterinarian Minifigure

Minifigure shield used as tray

Unique apron print on legs

LEGO® IDEAS

Famous faces populated three LEGO Ideas sets released this year. First up was modern Stone Age family the Flintstones in set 21316, who rocked up with their neighbors the Rubbles. Then Mickey and Minnie Mouse went back to their roots in the black-and-white Steamboat Willie set (21317). Finally, the stars of classic comedy series *Friends* shared coffee in Central Perk (21319).

Ross Geller The *Friends'* persistent paleontologist has loosened his tie while on a break from thinking about dinosaurs.

Tan suit jacket is height of '90s fashion

Newspaper shows a minifigure firefighter with a rescued cat

Exclusive face print

The LEGO *News* accessory found in more than 20 sets

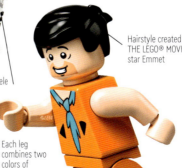

Printed eyelashes distinguish Minnie's head from Mickey's

Minnie Mouse This monochrome mouse carries the sheet music for "Turkey in the Straw," as heard in the 1928 Disney movie *Steamboat Willie*.

Rare white guitar represents Minnie's ukulele

Hairstyle created for THE LEGO® MOVIE™ star Emmet

Each leg combines two colors of plastic

Fred Flintstone Like most minifigures, Fred has no visible nose, but his printed stubble suggests its distinctive shape.

Gingerbread Woman The fourth cookie-based minifigure since 2013 is the first to be depicted as female.

One-off printed skirt piece

LEGO SEASONAL

Three large sets celebrated Chinese New Year in 2019. One featured a family of six sharing a New Year's Eve dinner, another featured a mechanical dancing dragon, and the third was a traditional dragon boat race. Later in the year, a 1,477-piece Gingerbread House (10267) joined the Winter Village theme in time for Christmas.

Exclusive dragon design

Dragon Dancer Four different minifigures wear this traditional Chinese outfit to welcome the new year in Dragon Dance (41896).

Exclusive helmet print

Mismatched, battle-damaged armor

Temperature control unit

Printed harness for ice abseiling

Boolio The first Ovissian minifigure has a head piece molded from two different colors of plastic, with printed facial features.

Din Djarin Boba Fett? Where? The star of *The Mandalorian* may share some similarities, but his minifigure is all new!

THE MANDALORIAN

In fall 2019, the first ever live-action *Star Wars* show was accompanied by a LEGO set featuring four of its characters. AT-ST Raider (75254) included Cara Dune, two Klatoonian Raiders, and the mysterious Mandalorian himself.

LEGO® STAR WARS™

Lucasfilm and the LEGO Group celebrated 20 years of partnership in 2019. Five LEGO *Star Wars* sets included special anniversary minifigures, while the wider theme focused on the future. New shows *Star Wars Resistance* and *The Mandalorian* got their own sets, and of course, there were plenty of fresh-faced minifigures from the ninth saga movie, *The Rise of Skywalker*.

Face print first used in *The Force Awakens* sets

Rey The fourth Rey minifigure swaps her usual gray-and-tan attire for white, but still wears it in a criss-cross style.

Belt buckle replaces cord tie seen on other Rey torso prints

Holster straps crossed over hips

Zorii Bliss This spice-runner-turned-Resistance-fighter has a plain black head piece beneath her unique gold helmet.

THE MOVIES

Five *The Rise of Skywalker* sets came out in October, but the year was also notable for new releases from across the film series. Amazingly, some of these even included characters who had never been minifigures before!

War club

Thermal detonator found in 14 sets

Ushar As one of the fearsome Knights of Ren, Ushar wears unique armor and carries his own choice of weapons.

STAR WARS RESISTANCE

Two 2019 sets are based around this animated series, set between *Return of the Jedi* and *The Force Awakens*. Show and sets alike feature brand-new characters and film favorites such as Leia and Poe.

Unique two-tone hair piece

Kaz Xiono This New Republic racer, stunt pilot, and spy is exclusive to Major Vonreg's TIE Fighter (75240).

New helmet mold

Civilian flight jacket

Major Vonreg First among First Order pilots, this villain's vermillion armor perfectly matches his menacing red-and-black TIE fighter.

Outfit seen in *Rogue One: A Star Wars Story*

Crest of Alderaan on belt buckle

Bail Organa Leia's adoptive father makes his minifigure debut in the Ultimate Collector version of his ship, *Tantive IV* (75244).

Building knob on back of head

D-O A single, specially created droid piece represents BB-8's buddy in two 2019 sets based on *The Rise of Skywalker*.

STAR WARS BATTLEFRONT II

In 2017, Iden Versio first appeared in the *Star Wars* video game as a complex female lead. Two years later, she made her minifigure debut leading three Inferno Squad Agents in a LEGO *Star Wars* battle pack.

Inferno Squad stripes on shoulder

Iden Versio This Imperial commander eventually joins the Rebellion, but here she is equipped solely to serve the Emperor!

Weapon predates blaster pieces

Weapon predates blaster pieces

Princess Leia This retro rebel is one of five reissued minifigures from 1999–2003 found exclusively in 20th anniversary sets.

Classic yellow hands and head

Anniversary logo, which features on Leia's back, too

LEGO® MARVEL SUPER HEROES

In the year that Marvel Studios' *Avengers: Endgame* became the most successful movie of all time, seven tie-in sets included more returning Avengers than you could point the Infinity Gauntlet at. Meanwhile, the Marvel Studios' *Captain Marvel* movie and Spider-Man subthemes also contributed some of the year's most unusual and exciting new Marvel Super Heroes minifigures.

More high-tech look than 2016 Captain Marvel minifigure

Serious face hidden behind new hair piece

Captain Marvel Carol Danvers' movie minifigure first appeared in a *Captain Marvel* set before joining *Endgame*'s all-star line-up.

Hair piece can be swapped for helmet

Canadian maple leaf on belt buckle

Duke Caboom This dashing daredevil jumps through a ring of brick-built fire in Duke Caboom's Stunt Show (10767).

Forky This homemade hero can be held by a minifigure or fitted onto a single LEGO knob.

"Drawn on" details are deliberately childlike

Rust spots printed on helmet

Iron Man Mark 1 Armor This rusty relic appears in a single *Endgame* set, 11 years after its on-screen debut.

Armor plates assembled from scrap parts

MOVIES

More than 20 new minifigures, microfigures, and "big figs" made their debuts in Marvel Studios' *Avengers: Endgame* sets, while Captain Marvel also starred in her own movie build. Another four sets focused on *Spider-Man: Far From Home*.

Swimming cap mold introduced in 2012

Peter Parker The first Peter Parker minifigure since 2004 has a pulled-back mask piece that can be swapped for hair.

Spidey suit visible under clothes

New spherical helmet piece

Intricate armor printing continues on back

Mysterio Alien ally or enigmatic enemy? With a plain silver head underneath his helmet, this *Spider-Man: Far From Home* character is giving nothing away!

LEGO® TOY STORY™ 4

The first LEGO *Toy Story* sets since 2010 introduced updates of Woody, Buzz, and Jessie that used more standard minifigure parts than earlier versions (not counting Buzz's collectible Minifigure from 2016). They also featured fresh faces from the gang's latest adventure, including minifigures of Gabby Gabby and Bunny, and special single-piece figures of Ducky and Forky.

Unique long-hair-and-cowboy-hat piece

Jessie Four exclusive printed parts make this minifigure, including a rodeo shirt torso and cowhide chaps on her legs.

White hood piece first worn by Marvel villain Taskmaster

Costume first seen in comics in 2014

Unique downward-facing spider design

Spider-Man-2099 This futuristic wall-crawler travels through time to join forces with the original in just one 2019 set.

Dots on suit represent advanced "Unstable Molecule Fabric"

COMICS

This year's new minifigures from the Multiverse include a Spider-Man from 80 years in the future and the ghostly Spider-Woman of Earth-65. The scariest version of Sandman so far was also among the updates.

Ghost-Spider This alternative version of Peter's pal Gwen Stacy teams up with Spidey in Spider Mech vs. Venom (76115).

Printed snowflake pieces fit inside gift box

Jack Skellington The star of Disney *Tim Burton's The Nightmare Before Christmas* wears a new bat-shaped bow tie piece.

Pinstripes printed on front, back, and sides

Exclusive new hair piece

Sparking snowflake cape

Giant snowflake accessory

Elsa *Frozen* featured in mini doll sets from 2015 onward, but it was 2019 before Elsa was made into a minifigure.

LEGO® MINIFIGURES DISNEY SERIES 2

Stars from across the history of Disney animation lined up together in the second series of Disney collectible Minifigures. Mickey and Minnie Mouse appeared in their earliest black-and-white outfits alongside cheeky chipmunks Chip and Dale, who first hit screens in the 1940s. Characters from the likes of *Frozen* and *The Incredibles 2* added 21st-century sparkle to the 18-Minifigure mix.

Gift box pieces first used by Series 18 Minifigures

Detachable top hat

Scrooge McDuck Series 2 includes Donald Duck's mega-rich uncle, plus grandnephews Huey, Dewey, and Louie.

Printed spats

1989 Batman A combined cowl-and-cape piece makes this minifigure the most realistic Batman ever seen in a LEGO set.

Choice of smiling or stern face prints

Bat-symbol is built into cowl

Cape is molded with a sideways sweep

LEGO® DC SUPER HEROES

The largest ever DC Super Heroes set was released in 2019, celebrating the 30th anniversary of the 1989 movie *Batman*. Boasting 3,306 pieces, 1989 Batmobile (76139) came with three exclusive minifigures, including a new-look Caped Crusader inspired by actor Michael Keaton's costume in the film. Meanwhile, across the theme, other fan-favorite heroes and villains made big impressions in smaller sets.

One-of-a-kind silver helmet

Ocean Master Exclusive Batman and Aquaman minifigures take on this villain in Batman Batsub and the Underwater Clash (76116).

Lightning-bolt pattern on belt

Shazam! Two new variants of this hero were released in 2019, coinciding with his debut in the DC movie universe.

Dress print continues all down back

Skirt piece is the height of three standard bricks

Madame Maxime This half-giant headmistress appears in two 2019 sets, wearing a different extra-long dress in each.

Face print distinguishes Fleur from Gabrielle

Leg piece is longer than her sister's

Fleur Delacour This young witch and her sister, Gabrielle, wear matching school uniforms in Beauxbatons' Carriage: Arrival at Hogwarts (75958).

LEGO® HARRY POTTER™

The LEGO® Wizarding World™ focused on the Harry Potter series in 2019. Seven sets included characters making their minifigure debuts alongside favorite old friends with updated looks. Four new teenage Harry variants used the medium-length legs introduced for 2018's collectible Minifigures line, while the younger Harry, Ron, and Hermione all featured in the first LEGO Harry Potter Advent Calendar (75964).

Black bowler first worn in 2012 by Businessman LEGO Minifigure

Cornelius Fudge The smartest things about the misguided Minister for Magic are his stylish black suit and bowler hat.

Choice of gritted teeth or smiling face prints

Brick and plate are the same height as medium legs

Hermione Granger The first minifigure of Hermione in her Yule Ball gown uses an exclusive printed brick as a skirt.

Character design inspired by villain Dennis Nedry from the first *Jurassic Park* film

Danny Nedermeyer Crimes against fashion are just the start for this gaudy, grinning bad guy in *Legend of Isla Nublar*!

Hoodie hood printed on back of torso

Smile can be changed to scared face

Souvenir Jurassic World T-shirt

Allison Miles This scientist knows how to stay calm, even when facing a Triceratops Rampage (set 75937)!

Badge identifies Allison as a doctor

Hudson Harper Owen saves this young park visitor from mild peril in Dilophosaurus on the Loose (75934).

LEGO® JURASSIC WORLD™

Animated series LEGO *Jurassic World: Legend of Isla Nublar* brought dinosaurs to TV in 2019, featuring minifigure versions of Owen, Claire, and co., plus a handful of new characters. Four sets pitted the show's most ferocious dinosaurs against these small-screen stars.

LEGO® MINIFIGURES

With Series 19 including the 300th entry in the original LEGO Minifigures line, could there possibly be any more identities to explore? The answer, coming from the 16 characters in this collection, was a resounding "Yes!" Fright Knight, Monkey King, Mummy Queen, Pizza Costume Guy, and Fox Costume Girl were just some of the new names waiting to be found.

Combined helmet-and-hair piece

Wraparound shades to keep bugs out of eyes!

Tire-track design on torso

Mountain bike piece introduced in 2018

Mountain Biker No other collectible Minifigure comes with such a large accessory as this energetic off-roader.

Optional blushing face hidden behind shower cap

Towel attaches between torso and legs like a fabric skirt piece

Shower Guy Take the fabric towel piece away from this Minifigure to find a printed patch of soapy bath bubbles!

Hair piece new for 2019

Printed sweater tied around waist

Programmer The four lines of digits on this techie's T-shirt spell out the LEGO name in binary code.

Laptop accessory can be folded shut

Helmet hides printed alien face

Accessory reads "WANTED: BUILT or BROKEN"

Galactic Bounty Hunter An update of the classic LEGO® Space Blacktron logo suggests the allegiance of this scary-looking seeker.

LEGO NINJAGO

Fire and ice set the temperature of NINJAGO sets in 2019. First, the Serpentine sorcerer Aspheera lit up the city with her flaming Pyro Viper soldiers. Then the ninja faced the Ice Emperor and his army of Blizzard Samurai in the frozen Never-Realm! New friends helped the team along the way, as did the freshly rediscovered powers of Forbidden Spinjitzu.

Samurai helmet with icicle crest

Jagged ice built into armor

Ice Emperor The Never-Realm's ruler wasn't always bad. If only he could remember who he used to be!

Wolf hood hints at dual identity

Akita This shape-shifter appears in two 2019 sets—once as a minifigure and once as a red-and-white wolf piece.

Printed lightning and smiley badges

Transparent flames molded into mask piece

Jay FS All six of the ninja blaze with fearsome Forbidden Spinjitzu powers across a range of Never-Realm sets.

LEGO® SPEED CHAMPIONS

Rally and drag racing were added to Speed Champions' growing list of motorsports in 2019, with sets featuring new entrants Mini and Dodge. The 1967 Mini Cooper S Rally and 2018 MINI John Cooper Works Buggy set (75894) included four new minifigures, while 2018 Dodge Challenger SRT Demon and 1970 Dodge Charger R/T (75893) added another three to the theme.

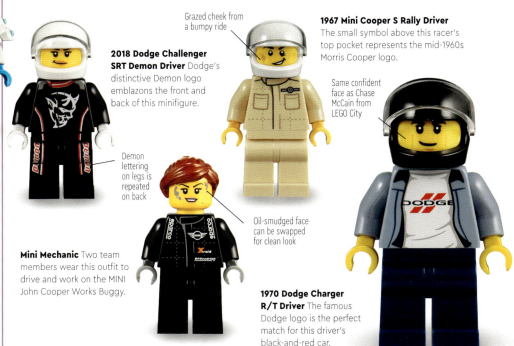

2018 Dodge Challenger SRT Demon Driver Dodge's distinctive Demon logo emblazons the front and back of this minifigure.

Demon lettering on legs is repeated on back

Mini Mechanic Two team members wear this outfit to drive and work on the MINI John Cooper Works Buggy.

Grazed cheek from a bumpy ride

1967 Mini Cooper S Rally Driver The small symbol above this racer's top pocket represents the mid-1960s Morris Cooper logo.

Same confident face as Chase McCain from LEGO City

Oil-smudged face can be swapped for clean look

1970 Dodge Charger R/T Driver The famous Dodge logo is the perfect match for this driver's black-and-red car.

2020s

There was no midlife crisis for minifigures as they soared into their mid-forties! New themes LEGO® Monkie Kid™ and LEGO® DREAMZzz™ introduced all-original characters, while sets based on *Fortnite* and *Animal Crossing* gave gaming icons a minifigure twist. The LEGO® Ideas theme turned Vincent van Gogh and pop band BTS into minifigures, while the LEGO® Icons range transformed minifigures into works of art! Across the board, minifigures were more diverse and representative than ever before.

Detachable plume

THIS IS THE CHINESE YEAR OF THE MONKIE!

Combined hair and ears first worn by a 2019 collectible Minifigure

Shoulder armor designed for LEGO NINJAGO

Monkey King This mythical hero appears in just one 2020 set, but his spirit can be felt throughout the theme.

2020

AT THE START OF a new decade, LEGO® minifigures looked forward and back. The Monkie Kid theme branched out with new characters and elements while also finding its roots in the past. The LEGO® NINJAGO® team had their most high-tech adventure yet, while LEGO® DC Super Heroes revived some super-retro looks in a series of collectibles. Classic Troll Dolls and 1960s soccer stars got the minifigure treatment, while thoroughly modern LEGO® Minions figures introduced all-new pieces.

Double-sided head also features a calmer expression

Princess Iron Fan The giant, brick-built Demon Bull King set (80010) comes with this minifigure version of his equally formidable wife.

LEGO® MONKIE KID™

Roughly 500 years in the making, LEGO Monkie Kid is inspired by the 16th-century Chinese novel *Journey to the West*. In the book, a Monkey King fights demons with his magical staff. In the LEGO theme, the demons are back to cause trouble in modern-day Megapolis, and it falls to a brave delivery boy to wield the staff once more!

Unique new hairstyle

Choice of determined and excited faces

New headphones piece worn around neck

THE HEROES

Noodle delivery driver MK may have a magical staff, but he still needs friends to save the day! Happily, he can always rely on dragon-powered Mei, gentle giant Sandy, and his noodle house boss, Pigsy.

Monkie Kid (MK) The Monkey King chooses this motorcycle courier to be his successor in the battle against demonic forces.

Same chef's hat worn by standard minifigures

New head piece

Dirty dishrag around neck

Mei When MK's best friend battles demons, she uses her ancestral dragon aura for protection and wields a dragon sword.

New hair piece with jade highlights

Outfit hints at White Horse Dragon ancestry

Pigsy MK's guardian and boss runs his own noodle shop. He is famed for his short temper and long noodles!

Head, torso, and legs are one giant part

Meditation beads

Bull-shaped crown on horn-shaped hair

Sandy MK's biggest, bluest buddy has a heart as big as his muscles. He loves cats, calm, and cups of tea.

THE VILLAINS

In the first wave of 2020 sets, Monkie Kid's foes are the Demon Bull Family and their bull clone robots. In the second wave, he takes on the Spider Queen in her robotic spider chariot.

Flame designs on dress

Demon Bull Family medallion

Red Son The half-demon son of Princess Iron Fan and the Demon Bull King is a hot-headed scientist and flamethrower!

Unique spider crown has eight legs and fangs

Thoughtful face can be swapped for a grin

Spider Queen The leader of the Spider Demons rides an eight-legged chariot and uses her venom to control people's minds.

Spider-silk dress

Horn piece first used for cow figures in 2009

Transparent head piece under helmet

Cape marks Ironclad out from other clones

General Ironclad Red Son built General Ironclad and the other bull clone robots to do the Demon Bull Family's bidding.

New breathing mask with headlamps

Classic LEGO® Space style air tanks

Detachable flippers introduced in 2011

Diver This scientist and her diving buddy get close to sharks and shipwrecks in the huge Ocean Exploration Ship (60266).

LEGO® CITY

The popularity of animated TV series LEGO® City *Adventures* saw more of its minifigure stars make the leap from screen to set during this year. Most were cops or crooks, but there was also Harl Hubbs' car mechanic mate, Tread Octane. Later in the year, a whole new wave of heroes took the plunge in the new Ocean Explorers subtheme.

Dark red cap most often worn by LEGO City train crew

Printed letter tile in use since 1982!

Brand-new LEGO Postal Service logo

Air Mail Pilot Aviator sunglasses protect this pilot's eyes when he flies above the clouds in his Mail Plane (60250).

Hair can be swapped for welding mask

Steering wheel chain worn around neck

Seatbelt-style buckle

Tread Octane Tuning Workshop (60258) is where this motorhead checks the oil in his hot rod—and on his hair!

Hearing aid printed on side of head

Same hairstyle as Ice Cream Vendor

Commuter The first minifigure with a printed hearing aid features in this year's largest City set, Main Square (60271).

Hair tied back for working with food

Smart bow tie

Ice Cream Vendor The owner of LEGO City's first Ice Cream Truck (60253) takes pride in having the coolest customers.

POLICE

In 2020, more City sets than ever before featured named characters. In Police sets, they included LEGO City *Adventures* officers Duke DeTain, Sam Grizzled, and Rooky Partnur and crooks Snake Rattler, Vito, and Daisy Kaboom.

Wheeler City Police chief Percival "Wheelie" Wheeler is the first LEGO lawman to speed into action on a skateboard.

First City minifigure to have this hair piece

Ribbon shows awards for service

Skateboard found in more than 50 sets

Rooky Partnur This fresh-faced law enforcer pilots a police chopper that really flies in Police Helicopter Transport (60244).

Hair can be swapped for flying helmet

Gloves help keep firm grip on helicopter controls

Ragged prison gear under jacket

Studded belt

Daisy Kaboom With her dyed, orange-tipped hair and personalized license plate (K4B00M), this crook doesn't care about laying low!

Identifying mole stands out in police line-ups

Intense expression can be swapped for masked face

Vito Police officer Duke DeTain puts the brakes on this crook when he steals a safe using his sports car.

LEGO® HARRY POTTER™

This year's Wizarding World sets went far beyond Hogwarts—venturing from Privet Drive to Diagon Alley via the Forbidden Forest! School was still on the schedule, however, with sets depicting the Room of Requirement and Professor Slughorn's Christmas Party. Things got even more magical with a second series of collectible LEGO® Minifigures, featuring Harry's parents and little baby Harry himself!

Monogram of Slug Club founder Horace Slughorn

Spotless white gloves

Neville Longbottom Of all the minifigures at Professor Slughorn's party, only nonguest Neville has to wear a waiter's uniform.

Petunia Dursley Harry's mean aunt makes her minifigure debut alongside an updated version of her equally unpleasant husband, Vernon.

Stern expression

Dreary fall leaves on blouse

Nymphadora Tonks This Hufflepuff hero makes her minifigure debut battling Bellatrix Lestrange and Fenrir Greyback in Attack on the Burrow (75980).

Tonks has this hair color in *The Half-Blood Prince*

Stylish silk scarf print

Crossbow poised to fire

Centaur A pair of these forest-dwelling beasts share a set with a brick-built version of Hagrid's giant half-brother, Grawp.

New centaur body piece

Target painted on torso

Lower body built from five pieces

Mechanical Death Eater Harry, Hermione, and Luna practice spell-casting on this magical machine in one 2020 set.

COLLECTIBLE MINIFIGURES

The 16 minifigures in this year's LEGO Minifigures Harry Potter Series were a mix of updated old favorites and all-new additions. Several, such as James and Lily Potter, had been on fan wish lists for years!

Lion piece can be swapped for standard hair

Luna Lovegood When she watches Gryffindor play Quidditch, Luna shows her support for the team with this lifelike lion hat!

Blue vest worn over gray sweater

Lily Potter Harry's mom comes with a swaddled baby piece with exclusive printing, representing the newborn Boy Who Lived.

Outfit seen in *The Deathly Hallows—Part 2*

Baby mold introduced in 2016

Printed tile shows Lily and James dancing

Very similar look to Harry

No other minifigure wears this scarf in dark red

James Potter The look of Harry's father is based on a photo glimpsed in the *Prisoner of Azkaban* movie.

Exclusive hair piece

Ginny Weasley A brand-new hair piece and a formal outfit suggest Ginny is off to the Slug Club Christmas Party.

Outfit worn in *The Half-Blood Prince*

The Professor's pet phoenix, Fawkes

Previous Dumbledores all have gray beards

Professor Dumbledore A new hat-and-hair piece crowns the Hogwarts head, while a new phoenix figure sits on his arm!

Hat, hair, and ear protectors are all one piece

Berry brooch befitting a herbology professor

Mud-spattered hem from constant gardening

Professor Sprout The first Pomona Sprout minifigure since 2011 wears ear protectors to protect against the cry of mandrake plants.

Kingsley's 2022 variant wears a plain version of this hat

Robe attached between head and torso

Kingsley Shacklebolt The United Kingdom Minister of Magic is resplendent in a brand-new robe and exclusive kufi hat piece.

LEGO® MINIFIGURES

Collectible Minifigures celebrated two landmarks this year—the tenth anniversary of the theme, and Series 20 of the main range. Peapod Costume Girl led the fresh crop of characters, alongside Space Fan, Super Warrior, Drone Boy, and Llama Costume Girl. The collection included eight female and eight male Minifigures, plus new turtle, piñata, toy rabbit, and keytar (keyboard guitar) accessories.

Elemental blade originally designed for LEGO® NINJAGO® sets

Super Warrior Inspired by Japanese super hero culture, this martial arts master hides his identity under a unique helmet.

Lime green lipstick completes her look

Apple accessory first seen in LEGO® SCALA™ sets

Peapod Costume Girl This fruit-and-veggie-loving Minifigure would like to grow her own food, but she doesn't have green fingers!

Torso print based on a LEGO Space set from 1979

Blueprint for included rocket accessory

Space Fan Goggles disguise the stars in her eyes, but this future astronaut wears her space fandom with pride.

LEGO DC SUPER HEROES

Stars from the DC Universe spanned the decades in 2020! First, a series of 16 collectible Minifigures showed off some classic Super Hero looks ranging from the 1930s to today. Then all eyes were on the 1980s with new movie *Wonder Woman 1984* and its tie-in set. Finally, a special-edition *Supergirl* TV show minifigure brought things up to date.

New hair

Bared teeth can be swapped for a half smile

Cheetah Mild-mannered Barbara Minerva goes wild in *Wonder Woman 1984*. Her Cheetah alter ego is found in just one set.

Claws printed on feet

Hairstyle first seen in LEGO Harry Potter sets

Super sight Alternative face has blue heat-vision eyes.

Costume based on *Supergirl* TV series

Supergirl Fewer than 1,500 fans own this Supergirl minifigure, offered exclusively as a raffle prize at online convention DC FanHome.

New helmet piece has flowing hair at back

Wings first seen in 2016 Super Heroes range

Wonder Woman Everyone's favorite Amazon spreads her wings in *Wonder Woman 1984*, flying into action in gleaming Golden Eagle Armor.

COLLECTIBLE MINIFIGURES

All-time icons and lesser known fan favorites made up the LEGO® Minifigures DC Super Heroes Series. Each one came with a new transparent stand element, for dynamic displays showing them in leaping or flying poses.

Hair worn in bunches

Transparent wing piece

Printed goggles

Energy blast accessories

Bumblebee Teen Titans fans are sure to get a buzz from the first minifigure to depict high-flying scientist Karen Beecher.

Distinctive dog-eared cowl

Exclusive comic book piece

IF THE FLASH IS SO FAST, WHY IS HE STILL ON THIS PAGE?

Transparent "flying" piece

Bat-Mite This bat-fan from the fifth dimension first caused trouble for the Caped Crusader in comics from the 1950s.

Speed Force accessories fit onto neck bracket

Golden wings printed on ankles

The Flash The original speedster, Jay Garrick, can keep up with anything but fashion, so he looks very different from his modern-day counterpart.

American Eagle symbol

Lasso of Truth

Skirt design echoes US flag

Wonder Woman In her classic 1940s outfit, this all-star Amazon flies the flag for the United States—as a skirt!

LEGO® HIDDEN SIDE™

Back for a second year of split-personality sets and Augmented Reality action, Hidden Side was scarier than ever in 2020! With new haunts including a creepy castle, a subway station, and a fairground where the clowns were literally bursting with energy, Jack and Parker needed all their smarts (and their smartphones) to stay one step ahead of the specters.

Combined hair-and-headphones piece

Black-and-turquoise diving suit

Parker L. Jackson Jack's best buddy wears headphones in all her 2020 sets, but dons diving gear in just one.

Scott's everyday welding mask

New ghostly part connects both heads to torso

Ordinary mechanic's overalls

> I'M NOT POSSESSED! I'VE JUST GOT A ROTTEN COLD!

Unhaunted version of head

Unshaven, everyday face

Retro Octan Gas logo

Scott Francis The first minifigure to wear two heads at once also comes with a third, showing his normal appearance!

Hat and hair are one new piece

New double-sided face print on head

Jack Davids The hood is off in 2020, with Jack wearing his baseball cap backward and showing off his hair!

No alternative head—this guy is always ghostly!

Nehmaar Reem Newbury's biggest baddie and his scary Shadow-Walkers menace Jack, Parker, and Vaughn in Mystery Castle (70437).

Smiling retro screen piece

Standard minifigure legs

TeeVee This small-screen sidekick is a close robo-relation of the LEGO® Alpha Team communications robot released in 2001.

Ghost head can be swapped for standard clown head

New haunted body part fits between legs and torso

Ruff first worn by 2012's Actor collectible Minifigure

Standard legs slot into swirling smoke piece

Terry Top This clown looks spooky even when he isn't possessed. He's literally bursting with badness when he *is* possessed!

LEGO® FRIENDS

Chef Lillie made her mini doll debut in 2019, but in 2020, she became a star, hosting a TV show in Baking Competition (41393). In the same set, contestants Stephanie and David wear exclusive aprons.

Stylishly angled toque hat

Monogrammed chef's whites

Lillie This brilliant baker's hat-and-hair piece was first made for the LEGO Minifigures theme and worn by 2017's Gourmet Chef.

Villainous smirk

LEGO® MINIONS

While the LEGO Minions themselves were not technically minifigures, they were led by one—their super-villain leader, Young Gru. The first two sets released to tie in with the upcoming movie, Illumination's *Minions: The Rise of Gru*. One set came with giant brick-built Minion models, and the other with a thrilling motorcycle chase!

Young Gru With a standard head, torso, and legs, Gru is the only true minifigure in this year's Minions range.

Double-height head piece

Kevin Wearing a hard hat and sly expression, Kevin is ready to build with his trusty tools.

Stuart As an alternative to his classic overalls, Stuart wears comfy, striped pajamas. Time for a nap!

Arms rotate just like a minifigure's

LEGO NINJAGO

The six ninja faced their greatest ever challenges in 2020! When video game *Prime Empire* took Ninjago City by storm, they were drawn into its digital realm to face Emperor Unagami and his Rat Pack. Then, back in the real world, they visited the seemingly peaceful kingdom of Shintaro—only to uncover the dark influence of the Skull Sorcerer!

Printed stats bar shows Jay's in-game health levels

Weapon handle shaped like video game controller

Stats bar connects to shoulder armor

Digi Jay All six ninja have "Digi" versions in the Prime Empire, complete with stats bars hanging over their heads!

New ponytail piece also available in black

Unique perfectly pointed beard

Circuit-style pathways printed on torso and skirt piece

Unagami This virtual villain menaces the ninja in three sets—twice on foot and once on his Empire Dragon (71713)!

Pixelated potion in belt

Richie Like the rest of Unagami's Rat Pack, rodent-faced Richie rides a hoverboard and carries in-game bonuses in his belt.

Mask covers plain black minifigure head

Wings first worn by the Bat Tribe in LEGO® Legends of Chima™

Skull Sorcerer This masked menace guards the powerful Blades of Deliverance in two of the year's biggest NINJAGO sets.

Princess Vania Vania teams up with the ninja when she learns that her father, King Vangelis, is the Skull Sorcerer!

Hairstyle first worn by LEGO Friends mini dolls

New visor piece

Swirling clouds design on robes

One armor-clad arm for defense

One bare arm for ease of movement in battle

Armored Cole The Master of Earth and his fellow ninja don gladiator-style gear when they go underground in Shintaro.

LEGO® TROLLS WORLD TOUR

Just like the DreamWorks movie on which the theme is based, LEGO Trolls World Tour was all about dancing to your own tune! Its colorful characters all belonged to musical tribes, and each one rocked their own style. Eight sets captured the film's diverse settings and sounds, from a Techno Reef Dance Party (41250) to the climactic Volcano Rock City Concert (41254).

Poppy The Queen of the Pop Trolls appears in all but one LEGO Trolls World Tour set, wearing four different costumes.

Hair and headband are all one piece

This costume is found in four sets

New skirt piece fits over short legs

Hickory This unique Troll loves to tap his feet to country music—so it's lucky he has four of them!

Huge hat fits onto four knobs on head

Standard minifigure torso

Unique four-legged lower body

Lasso accessory clips onto hat

One-of-a-kind head-and-body piece

Detachable heart-shaped sunglasses

Biggie This huge-hearted Troll takes to the skies in Poppy's Air Balloon Adventure (41252).

Standard short minifigure legs

LEGO® STAR WARS™

LEGO *Star Wars* spanned the entire Skywalker Saga in 2020, with sets based on the prequel, sequel, and original trilogies. The largest of these was Mos Eisley Cantina (75290), which featured 20 minifigures among its 3,187 pieces—many never seen in a LEGO set before! Elsewhere, there were sets based on streaming series *The Mandalorian* and epic Disney Parks attraction Galaxy's Edge.

Brand-new head piece

The Child By far the cutest character in *The Mandalorian*, this Yoda lookalike is doubly adorable in LEGO form.

Unique Aqualish head piece

Spiderlike mouthparts

Ponda Baba This Aqualish smuggler reluctantly lends a hand to Obi-Wan Kenobi when the Jedi Master visits Mos Eisley Cantina.

Unique hair-and-visor piece

Energy bow weapon

Grappling gear attached to belt

Jannah This warrior chief from *The Rise of Skywalker* makes her minifigure debut in Poe Dameron's X-wing Fighter (75273).

WE'RE THE MOS EISLEY CANTEENERS!

Hood piece also worn by Emperor Palpatine

Mask obscures plain, standard head piece

Helmet design also available in white

Exclusive red jetpack piece

Sith Jet Trooper Two of these *Rise of Skywalker* villains are found exclusively in the Sith Troopers Battle Pack (75266).

Jet trooper symbol

Garindan Don't let his thick goggles fool you—this Kubazian spy sees everything that happens at Mos Eisley Cantina.

Flexible head topper with horns and pointed ears

Choice of sly grin or stern face

Labria The regulars at Mos Eisley Cantina know him as Labria, but wanted posters across the galaxy call him Kardue'sai'Malloc!

Face print used for Luke since 2015

One of four hairstyles that have been used for Luke

Luke Skywalker A fabric poncho gives Tatooine's most famous farm boy a unique new look in Luke Skywalker's Landspeeder (75271).

Comlink communications device

Dual-molded hair piece combines two colors without printing

Vi Moradi You can meet this Resistance spy in the interactive world of Galaxy's Edge—or in Resistance I-TS Transport (75293)!

LEGO® DISNEY™

A new chapter of the LEGO *Disney* story began in 2020. A range of storybook-shaped cases opened to reveal fairytale worlds, along with new micro doll figures to inhabit them. Closing the "books" made them easy to store and carry.

Mulan The star of Mulan's Storybook Adventures (43174) has a mini doll head piece on a new single-piece body.

Figure stands around three bricks high

Arms do not move

Eyes are larger than 2016's Beast mini doll

The Beast This cursed prince can be transformed using a human mini doll head also included in Belle's Storybook Adventures (43177).

Hands cannot hold minifigure accessories

I'M MAKING THIS INTO MY WEB PAGE!

LEGO® MARVEL SUPER HEROES

Black Widow went solo with her own film and an updated minifigure in 2020. Meanwhile, Spider-Man teamed up with fellow web warriors Spider-Man Noir, a new Spider-Girl, and the supremely silly Spider-Ham. Elsewhere, other members of the Avengers team faced off against heavily armed A.I.M. (Advanced Idea Mechanics) agents, in sets based on the year's new *Marvel's Avengers* video game.

Half-mask shows off confident smile

Spider-Girl High school student Anya Corazon shows off her web-spinning powers in the Spider-Man vs. Doc Ock set (76148).

A.I.M. Agent These high-tech henchmen use Super Hero-stopping gear against Thor, Black Panther, Captain America, and Hawkeye in 2020 sets.

Molded breather covers a printed one

A.I.M.-branded body armor

Unique cartoon pig head piece

Spider-Ham Also known as Peter Porker, the unlikely hero of Earth-8311 hogs all the attention in Venomosaurus Ambush (76151).

Fedora hat first seen in LEGO® *Indiana Jones*™ sets

Goggles over spider-web mask

Spider-Man Noir This Peter Parker from an alternative Earth dresses all in black to blend into his world's darkest shadows.

Long black trenchcoat

Hourglass belt buckle

Holsters strapped across each leg

Black Widow The fifth Natasha Romanoff minifigure since 2012 takes on the terrible Taskmaster villain in Black Widow's Helicopter Chase (76162).

LEGO Train logo replaces real-world logos used in 1980

40 Years of LEGO Train This set (40370) recreates a 1980 release and was included with certain purchases in LEGO® Stores and online.

Front torso print found in eight 1980 Train sets

Engine Driver This minifigure is identical to one first seen in 1980, but with even sharper, 21st-century printing on his torso.

Plain blue legs found in more than 750 sets

LEGO® EXCLUSIVE

2020 marked the 40th anniversary of the original LEGO® Train theme. For a limited time, fans could get their hands on a special celebratory build. Later in the year, the spectrum of Classic LEGO Space minifigures came closer to completion when a cheery orange astronaut was exclusively designed for DK's LEGO® *Minifigure: A Visual History*.

First bright orange helmet in this style

First bright orange classic oxygen pack

Orange Spaceman This DK exclusive follows in the footsteps of red, white, yellow, blue, black, green, and pink LEGO Space explorers.

LEGO® SUPER MARIO™

Much larger than a minifigure, LEGO Super Mario is an interactive marvel! He responds to his environment and the brick-built characters in it, making faces and sounds as he plays through video-game-style courses.

Hat built onto standard LEGO knobs

Eyes and mouth are digital screens

Arms move like a minifigure's

Overalls can be swapped for other outfits

Mario Unique in 2020, the battery-powered Mario figure has since been joined by similarly interactive Luigi and Peach figures.

Goomba Place Mario on this brick-built baddie to scan the tile on its head and earn a digital reward.

Scannable printed tile

Feet are one new element

New mushroom cap element

Toadette Mario's mushroom pal combines new elements with parts originally designed for LEGO® NEXO KNIGHTS™.

Same torso mold as NEXO KNIGHTS stone monsters

Yoshi Mario's House and Yoshi (71367) is one of many expansion course sets designed to enhance a starter course.

Arms plug into bricks with holes

Same feet as Goomba, but in orange

Headband above eyes

Pixelated version of Kai's 2018 robes

Kai The Master of Fire's Minecraft makeover is inspired by custom character skins made by NINJAGO fans online.

Raid Captain This minifigure is distinguished from other illagers by the Ominous Banner flying above his head.

Unique printed banner piece

Minecraft crossbow new for 2020

Neck bracket used to connect banner

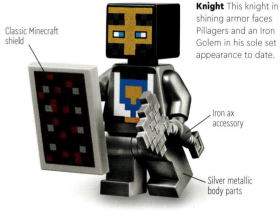

Classic Minecraft shield

Knight This knight in shining armor faces Pillagers and an Iron Golem in his sole set appearance to date.

Iron ax accessory

Silver metallic body parts

Distinctive headband

Long hair flows over shoulders

Valorie New game *Minecraft Dungeons* inspired The Redstone Battle (21163), featuring Valorie and three other playable characters in minifigure form.

LEGO® MINECRAFT®

This enduring video game theme reached its 50th minifigure-scale set in 2020. Brick-built additions to the ever-expanding world included a cuddly pair of pandas and an enormous ravager beast, while a Knight and three rampaging illagers were among the new minifigures. And to top it all off, there was even a special guest appearance from the realm of NINJAGO!

DID YOU KNOW?
Minecraft illagers and pillagers are hostile—and not to be confused with harmless villagers!

Broader neck than similar Elmo head piece

Cookie Monster The street's hungriest resident comes with three printed cookie pieces. At least, there were three a moment ago ...

Medium-length minifigure legs

LEGO® IDEAS

Two fan-inspired LEGO Ideas sets featured minifigures in 2020. The first was Pirates of Barracuda Bay (21322), which revisited Classic LEGO® Pirates on their new desert island home. The second was 123 Sesame Street (21324), based on the much-loved children's television series. Both had all-exclusive minifigures, with the latter boasting brand-new head molds for Cookie Monster and co.

Torso extender adds all-over feather texture

Wings move like standard minifigure arms

Big Bird This yellow fellow lives up to his name with a combined head-and-torso extender for extra height.

Head mold also used as BB-8's body in LEGO *Star Wars* sets

Trash can found in more than 100 sets

Oscar the Grouch Only Oscar is made without new molds—but he's not bitter! His head attaches to his trash can home.

123 SESAME STREET

This is the first LEGO Ideas set to introduce new head molds instead of reusing existing designs. These were essential to recreate the beloved *Sesame Street* characters that have long enchanted children around the world.

Elmo This much-loved monster is something of a *Sesame Street* newcomer. He only joined the 56-year-old show 40 years ago!

Distinctive orange nose

Short minifigure legs

More than 50 minifigures share this confident smile

Torso printed on front and back

Lady Anchor Island life doesn't faze this stylish swashbuckler. She's as smartly dressed today as when she was first shipwrecked!

PIRATES OF BARRACUDA BAY

This modular shipwreck set can be quickly reassembled to make a version of Classic LEGO® Pirates galleon the Black Seas Barracuda. All but one of its eight exclusive minifigures feature brand-new torso prints.

30 years at sea can age any pirate

More detailed torso print than 1989 original

Captain Redbeard This LEGO Pirates icon is instantly recognizable, despite having more gray hair than red on his scallywag chin!

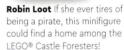

Combined hat-and-hair piece

Grubby face first seen on a LEGO City mountain biker

Robin Loot If she ever tires of being a pirate, this minifigure could find a home among the LEGO® Castle Foresters!

Choice of smiling or stern expressions

Tattooed torso with mermaid, parrot, and anchor designs

Tattooga This bare-chested buccaneer looks just as impressive from behind, thanks to the Black Seas Barracuda tattoo on his back!

LEGO SEASONAL

This year's line-up of minifigure-scale seasonal sets included Chinese New Year Temple Fair (80105), Easter Bunny House (853990), and Charles Dickens Tribute (40410). The latter celebrated the Victorian writer's festive favorite, *A Christmas Carol*. There was nothing Scrooge-like about the set, which was given away free with qualifying purchases from LEGO.com.

New head print with huge Victorian side whiskers

Suit print first seen in a LEGO Harry Potter set

Ebeneezer Scrooge In Dickens' novella, Scrooge goes from nasty to nice overnight. This stern-looking fellow is the nice version!

Alternative face has grubby patches

Tiny Tim Young Tim has sad and hopeful face prints. His hard life gets better when Scrooge changes his ways.

Tim uses a stick to walk

Face print first used in 2019

White-and-pale-blue race suit

Jaguar I-PACE eTROPHY Driver The "e" on this racer's unique outfit shows that she races an all-electric, zero-emissions car.

Lamborghini badge shown in more detail on back

Lamborghini Huracán Super Trofeo EVO Driver Both of 2020's Lamborghini drivers wear the same black-and-white race suit.

LEGO® SPEED CHAMPIONS

The LEGO supercar theme was finely retuned in 2020, with its line of vehicles coming out of the workshop wider and more detailed than ever before. The change in scale was notable, but not enough to stop minifigures from taking the wheel. This year's crop included drivers for Jaguar and Lamborghini, both making their debut in the theme.

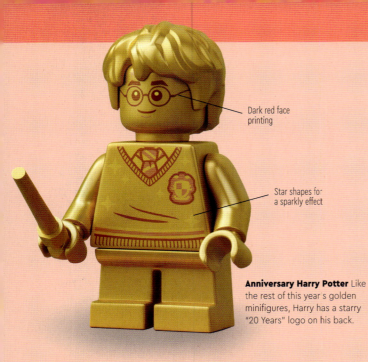

Anniversary Harry Potter Like the rest of this year's golden minifigures, Harry has a starry "20 Years" logo on his back.

- Dark red face printing
- Star shapes for a sparkly effect

2021

IT WAS A GOLDEN YEAR for both LEGO® NINJAGO® and LEGO® Harry Potter™, as gleaming minifigures marked milestone anniversaries. In LEGO® City, new minifigure motorcycles sent the Stuntz team into action, while a guide dog trained to assist people with a visual impairment brought new opportunities for realistic minifigure role-play. Collectible LEGO® Minifigures added stars from Looney Tunes animations and Marvel Studios TV shows to their ranks, and LEGO® Icons Everyone is Awesome (40516) made minifigures into colorful, affirming art!

LEGO HARRY POTTER

Seven of this year's sets came with gold-colored minifigures, marking 20 years since the launch of LEGO Harry Potter. Fans could display the full line-up on a brick-built stand that came with special anniversary set, Hogwarts Icons: Collectors' Edition (76391). Elsewhere, new Hogwarts Moments sets were built to look like life-size books and opened to reveal a minifigure-scale school scene.

- Same face print as Bellatrix Lestrange
- Unique torso print

Madam Rosmerta The owner of the Three Broomsticks Inn makes her minifigure debut serving Butterbeer in Hogsmeade Village Visit (76388).

- Cat head fits over standard minifigure head
- Long fur resembles Hermione's usual hair

Cat Hermione Hogwarts: Polyjuice Potion Mistake (76386) comes with a unique cat head piece for giving Hermione a magical kitty makeover!

- Sweet-wrapper pattern on shawl
- Same face print as Molly Weasley

DID YOU KNOW? A glow-in-the-dark variant of Nearly Headless Nick haunted one of this year's Hogwarts sets.

Mrs. Flume This sweet-natured shopkeeper runs the Honeydukes candy shop with her husband, Ambrosius Flume, in Hogsmeade Village Visit (76388).

- New witch's hat piece
- Unique face print
- Gold-colored arms

Aurora Sinistra This Hogwarts professor isn't one of the year's anniversary minifigures—she just likes to feel good in gold!

Black Chess Rook Hogwarts Wizard's Chess (76392) is a life-size chess set with 32 brick-built pieces, including this well-defended rook.

- Rare white knight's helmet
- Crozier top is a minifigure whip
- Classic LEGO® Castle helmet
- LEGO® NEXO KNIGHTS™ shield

White Chess Bishop The Wizard Chess scene from *Harry Potter and the Sorcerer's Stone* inspired these minifigure-sized playing pieces.

LEGO MINIFIGURES

New faces with new pieces for LEGO Minifigures Series 21 included a Beekeeper with a protective veil, an Airplane Girl with wearable wings, a Violin Kid with his instrument, and a Shipwreck Survivor with a friendly crab companion. Was that all, folks? No, it was not! This year's line-up included a Looney Tunes Series, packed with classic cartoon icons.

Flying jacket with aviator patches

Short, nonposable legs

Spinning propeller

Airplane Girl Like 2018's Race Car Guy, this Minifigure wears a new toy vehicle element between her torso and legs.

OH NO— A PLANE-CLOTHES DETECTIVE!

Unique head is one part made using two colors

Printed glint in eye

Breathing tubes print continues on back

Visor subtly obscures face

Alternative expression is licking lips!

Honey blob

Double-sided head: both with tongues out!

Open-mouthed mask fits over standard head

Medium-length legs

Beekeeper A unique hat with a transparent visor recreates the mesh veil that keeps this beekeeper safe from his bees.

Pug Costume Guy The latest in a long line of animal-imitating Minifigures is a good little boy. Yes, he is! Yes, he is!

SERIES 21

The dozen delightful characters in this series also included a Space Police Guy to chase the Alien crook and a Centaur Warrior. The latter's four-legged lower body piece was first seen in LEGO Harry Potter.

Alien This cosmic crook wears futuristic prison fatigues but relies on a good old-fashioned crowbar for breaking out of jail!

LOONEY TUNES SERIES

Twelve of the world's most famous cartoon characters starred in this series, each boasting an all-new head mold and exclusive printing. Porky Pig, Road Runner, Lola Bunny, and Marvin the Martian numbered among the icons.

RABBIT SEASON

Distinctive white ring around neck

Legs molded in black and orange

Tail piece attaches between legs and torso

Daffy Duck Daffy's decades-long rivalry with Bugs Bunny is clear from his printed sign accessory, declaring rabbit-hunting season!

Skirt piece created for 2016's Disney Series

Printed petticoat

Petunia Pig She may not hog the limelight, but this little piggy has been a *Looney Tunes* regular since 1937.

Printed pink ears

One of the tallest-ever LEGO heads!

Head molded in gray and white

DID YOU KNOW?
Orange carrot and green stalk pieces first appeared in LEGO® BELVILLE™ and LEGO® SCALA™ sets in 1999.

Bushy tail piece

Unique bulbous head

Bright yellow torso

Flame yellowish orange legs

Head piece extends down length of torso

Bugs Bunny First seen on screen in 1940, this instantly recognizable rabbit is still as fresh as his trademark carrot.

Tweety Feathers may fly when Sylvester the Cat finds out that Minifigure Tweety is almost as big as he is!

Printed spinner base

Tasmanian Devil Uniquely, Tas comes with a two-piece round base for sending him into a whirlwindlike spin!

WHY WEAR LEATHER WHEN YOU CAN WEAR FEATHERS?

Chicken helmet can be swapped for hair piece

Confident look on other side of head

Clemmens This plucky racer is no chicken—his scared look is just "fowl" play to make his shows more "egg-citing"!

Citrus the Clown This tumbler plunges into a piranha tank as part of a stunt show with black-clad biker Incognitro.

Fictional Vita Rush drink sponsors Stuntz shows

Brick-built clown shoes

STUNTZ

A diverse range of daredevils sped into action in the first year of Stuntz sets. Each rode a flywheel-powered motorcycle that used friction to send the bikes flying over, through, and into obstacles when released.

Choice of hair or rose-red helmet

Denim jacket over torn T-shirt

Rose Speedway Biker Rose speeds through a ring of fire in a thrilling Stunt Competition (60299) against Duke DeTain.

LEGO CITY

Relaxation was not on the menu for City minifigures in 2021! First, an intrepid team of wildlife rescuers gave up their creature comforts to save lions, crocodiles, and elephants in the wilderness. Then the Stuntz motorcycle team set pulses racing with their flywheel-motor-powered displays. Other city dwellers could also get active at a dojo for martial arts training!

New hair piece with long, braided ponytail

Headband first seen on Jessica's 2020 Ocean Explorers variant

New torso print with tasseled scarf detail

Jessica Sharpe Wildlife Rescue Off-Roader (60301) sees this animal-loving adventurer reunite a lion with its wayward cub.

New torso print found in two Wildlife Rescue sets

WILDLIFE RESCUE

Five Wildlife Rescue sets mixed fresh minifigures with all-new elephant, monkey, lion, and lion cub figures. The rescue team was led by LEGO City *Adventures* character Jessica Sharpe and included vets, pilots, and documentary filmmakers.

Veterinarian Light blue scrubs and a stethoscope mark out this member of the Wildlife Rescue team as a vet.

Black brim built into helmet

Visor is detachable

New torso print updates a 2013 design

Sarah Feldman This LEGO *City Adventures* firefighter is one of just four minifigures to wear this new helmet in white.

Guide dog trained to assist people with visual impairment

Harness fits onto knob on dog's back

CITY FOLK

One of this year's largest City sets was Town Center (60292), which included nine minifigures, four vehicles, a carwash, a recycling drop-off, a pizzeria, a dojo, and a small park. Several other sets focused on firefighting.

New face print

Man with Assistance Dog This Town Center visitor and his guide dog are the first to use a new animal harness piece.

Kendo Instructor This Town Center (60292) minifigure wears the same armor as Maddy. He knows its proper name is *bōgu*.

Torso protector is called a *dō*

Leg protectors are called *tare*

Maddy This LEGO *City Adventures* character wears protective gear for her kendo class at the Town Center (60292) Dragon Dojo.

Helmet can be swapped for bunched hair

Second variant Maddy minifigure since 2020

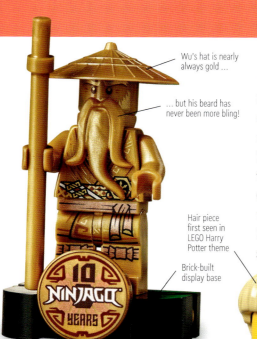

LEGO NINJAGO

In their tenth year of adventures, the ninja explored the Endless Sea. First, they met the mysterious Keepers on a storm-enshrouded island, then they plunged beneath the waves to find the underwater city of Merlopia. Gold-colored minifigures in seven sets marked the theme's anniversary, as did the epic Ninjago City Gardens (71741), a 5,685-piece modular set with 18 exclusive minifigures.

Wu's hat is nearly always gold …

… but his beard has never been more bling!

Hair piece first seen in LEGO Harry Potter theme

Brick-built display base

Anniversary Wu All six ninja got golden outfits this year, but only Master Wu is made entirely from gold-colored parts!

NINJAGO CITY GARDENS

The third in a series of large-scale Ninjago City scenes boasted more minifigures than any other NINJAGO set to date. As well as an Anniversary Wu, it included new versions of Lloyd, Cole, Jay, and Nya.

Faces painted with lightning-bolt design

All Lloyd minifigures since 2018 have green eyes

Young Lloyd The only other minifigures of young Lloyd show him as a wannabe villain before he joined the ninja.

Bark-based armor worn by other Keepers

PoulErik The Keepers' second-in-command is the only minifigure to have one head piece stacked on top of another!

Unique transparent hair piece

Unique head with fishlike fins

Vortex effect built onto neck bracket

Standard legs fit into swirling base

Nya NRG Nya's True Potential form has a leg extender and other add-ons, showing her merged with the Endless Sea.

Five squidlike tentacles instead of legs

Prince Kalmaar This deep-sea despot isn't content to rule one underwater world. He wants to flood Ninjago City as well!

THE ISLAND/SEABOUND

This year's linked storylines took Nya the Water Ninja to new and dangerous places. It wasn't smooth sailing for the other ninja, either, when they faced the weather-controlling Keepers and the sea monster-summoning Merlopians.

LEGO® MONKIE KID™

This year's Monkie Kid sets saw MK continue his battles with Red Son and the Spider Queen while also starting a new one with the big, bad Bone Demon. Besides the regular sets, the 1,949-piece Legendary Flower Fruit Mountain (80024) told the story of the original Monkey King with four minifigure variants of the character, plus his brother and sister.

Six-eyed visor for spider vision

Same hair and ears as Monkey King, but in brown

Red top distinguishes Sister Monkey from Brother Monkey

Sister Monkey A baby version of Monkey King plays with his sister and brother in the Flower Fruit Mountain set.

New scary skull design

Extra arms fit onto neck bracket

Detailed print shows ribcage on front and spine on back

Bone Spirit The Bone Demon's spectral servants "float" into action on parts first molded for LEGO NINJAGO ghosts.

Lab pass around neck

Syntax The Spider Queen's chief scientist might share some DNA with Spyclops from LEGO® Ultra Agents!

MOVIES

Sets based on brand-new Marvel Studios movies let fans recreate scenes from *Eternals*, *Shang-Chi and the Legend of the Ten Rings*, and *Spider-Man: No Way Home*. Others were inspired by earlier Spidey films and the Infinity Saga.

Hairstyle first worn by Ms. Marvel in 2017

Sersi The Prime Eternal has been on Earth for thousands of years, but her Celestial Armor still looks brand new.

Printed armor

Each Eternal wears a different color

Kingo The Eternals don't age, so Kingo has spent centuries pretending to be different generations of his own family!

Alternative face print is a quizzical smirk

Choice of neutral and determined expressions

Powerful dragon scale armor

Shang-Chi This brave martial artist quit the Ten Rings crime gang, but the gang wasn't ready to quit him.

LEGO® MARVEL SUPER HEROES

More LEGO Marvel sets were released in 2021 than in any year before or since. They included 18 sets based on nine different movies; two sets based on the *What If...?* TV series; and 10 sets based on various Spider-Man comics. On top of that, there was also a series of 12 collectible Minifigures inspired by Marvel Studios productions.

Spider-Man Peter wears his costume inside out in one of three 2021 sets based on the "Home" trilogy of Spidey films.

Spider design matches right-way-out variant of this costume from 2017

Detailed internal wiring prints on all parts

Same face print as Sersi

Ta Lo outfit pattern inspired by dragon scales

Katy Shang-Chi's best friend just wanted to drive cars until she drove one into the magical world of Ta Lo!

WHAT IF...?

Animated Marvel TV series *What If...?* imagines how the Marvel Cinematic Universe might look if key events had happened differently. Two sets dipped into its alternative realities, like the alien Watcher, who sees them all.

Alternative face has gritted teeth

Union flag on armor

Captain Carter In a universe with no Captain America, it is British agent Peggy Carter who becomes the first Avenger.

Blank but all-seeing eyes

Extravagant Watcher uniform

The Watcher This powerful being lives beyond the Multiverse and observes its infinite variety. Not a bad gig for a minifigure!

Stylish wraparound sunglasses

Body armor under coat

Tactical belt holds anti-vampire gear

Blade Half-human, half-vampire, this black-clad Super Hero gets his name from his incredible swordfighting skills.

DID YOU KNOW?
Gwen Stacy (a.k.a. Ghost-Spider) gets her first plain-clothes minifigure in *Daily Bugle* (76178).

Horns also used for Black Panther's cat ears

Face printed on red head piece

Classic costume with "DD" motif

Daredevil A respected lawyer by day, Matt Murdock fights crime as Daredevil at night.

DAILY BUGLE

This year's largest Marvel set was the 3,772-piece *Daily Bugle* (76178), as seen in Spider-Man comics. Peter Parker's New York newspaper workplace came with 25 minifigures, including several characters never seen before in LEGO sets.

Captain America Sam Wilson learns what it means to be the new Cap in *The Falcon and The Winter Soldier*.

New hair piece is exclusive to Sam in 2021

Unique wing piece with printing on both sides

New hair piece is exclusive to Monica in 2021

Alternative face is smiling

Uniform of S.W.O.R.D. (Sentient Weapon Observation and Response Division)

Monica Rambeau Before becoming a Super Hero in *The Marvels*, Monica gained her powers by traveling between realities in *WandaVision*.

Shield inherited from Steve Rogers

Combined hair and crown—with one broken horn

Sylvie Parallel universes collide as this female version of Loki comes with the alligator version of both of them!

Blue eyes are a hint that this is no ordinary alligator!

Unmasked face

New combined hair-and-mask piece

Same quadblasters used by Peter Quill

T'Challa Star-Lord In one episode of *What If ...?*, T'Challa takes Peter Quill's place in space instead of becoming Black Panther!

Printed rocket boosters

COLLECTIBLE MINIFIGURES

The LEGO® Minifigures Marvel Studios Series featured characters from small-screen favorites *WandaVision*, *Loki*, *The Falcon and The Winter Soldier*, and *What If ...?*. Loki himself made three appearances: twice in humanoid form and once as an alligator!

LEGO® *DISNEY* MICKEY AND FRIENDS™

The first Mickey and Minnie Mouse minifigures made their debut in 2016, following on from larger LEGO figures of the pair and their pals. But it was not until 2021 that LEGO *Disney* Mickey and Friends became a dedicated play theme. Its first five sets for younger builders also featured Donald Duck, Daisy Duck, and Goofy minifigures, plus a Pluto figure.

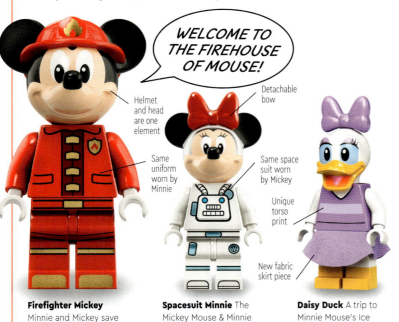

WELCOME TO THE FIREHOUSE OF MOUSE!

Helmet and head are one element

Detachable bow

Same uniform worn by Minnie

Same space suit worn by Mickey

Unique torso print

New fabric skirt piece

Firefighter Mickey Minnie and Mickey save hot dog Goofy from a barbecue blaze in Fire Truck & Station (10776).

Spacesuit Minnie The Mickey Mouse & Minnie Mouse's Space Rocket set (10774) also includes a space station and an alien!

Daisy Duck A trip to Minnie Mouse's Ice Cream Shop (10773) gives Daisy an excuse to wear her sundae best.

LEGO® *DISNEY* ENCANTO™

A year after micro dolls debuted in LEGO *Disney* storybook sets, they returned as small children in some mini doll sets. These included The Madrigal House (43202), based on the Disney movie *Encanto*.

Brand-new hair piece

Body also used in an *Encanto* storybook set

Antonio When Mirabel's 5-year-old cousin talks to animals, they understand him and talk back!

Brand-new hair piece

Hair piece originally designed for Padmé Amidala minifigure

Butterfly brooch used to secure house keys

Family name written on colorful skirt

Mirabel In *Encanto*, Mirabel tries to save the magic of her village, despite having no magic of her own.

Abuela Alma Mirabel's grandmother uses her magical house to protect her family and her village.

Dark Trooper These bulky baddies are droids, not clones, so there's a robot face print under that new helmet.

Eye holes in helmet show red on head beneath

Printing on armor repeated on torso beneath

Plain black head piece under unique helmet

The Armorer Mando wouldn't be Mando without his beskar armor, as forged by this mysterious member of his original clan.

Fur cape detail continues on back

Skirt print starts on torso and continues on legs

THE MANDALORIAN

New *Mandalorian* sets for 2021 included the first minifigures of key characters Moff Gideon, Fennec Shand, Paz Vizsla, and the Armorer. Minifigure army builders could also collect all-new artillery stormtroopers and extra-scary Dark Troopers.

THE SKYWALKER SAGA

More than 20 years after LEGO *Star Wars* launched, could there still be original trilogy characters that hadn't been made into minifigures? Yes, cried General Jan Dodonna, as he strode into his first ever set!

General Dodonna This legendary leader ran the rebel base on Yavin 4 and planned the attack on the original Death Star.

Receding hairline

Choice of open- and closed-mouth expressions

Five pips on rank insignia

Goggles printed on head piece

Bad Batch symbol

Clone Commando Tech The most unusual-looking member of the Bad Batch wears a helmet unlike any other clone trooper's.

Brick-built backpack

LEGO® STAR WARS™

This year's LEGO *Star Wars* range was anything but a bad batch, but it did include the first set based on new animated series *Star Wars: The Bad Batch*! Five sets explored the worlds of *The Mandalorian* (the most in one year since the show began), two returned to *The Clone Wars*, and many more celebrated the original movie saga.

Same helmet mold as the Armorer, but very different printing

Gar Saxon This Mandalorian Super Commando pledged his loyalty to the rogue Sith Lord Maul during the Clone Wars.

Hair can be swapped for Mandalorian helmets

Armor has been in the Kryze family for three generations

Black-and-red armor inspired by Maul's tattooed Zabrak skin

ANIMATED ADVENTURES

Star Wars: The Bad Batch tells the tale of six renegade clones. One set contained five members of the team, with the sixth following in 2022. Meanwhile, this year's *Clone Wars* sets included more Mandalorians!

Bo-Katan Kryze Fans may know Kryze from *Star Wars Rebels* and *The Mandalorian*, but she debuted in *The Clone Wars*.

LEGO SEASONAL

By 2021, minifigure sets inspired by traditional Chinese festivals had become something of a tradition themselves! With seven exclusive minifigures, Story of Nian (80106) told the tale of a monster that is scared away by Lunar New Year celebrations. Then Spring Lantern Festival (80107) depicted the event that brings those celebrations to a close, with help from eight new minifigures.

Unique headdress with detachable horns

HAPPY MOOOO YEAR!

Red and gold are traditional Lunar New Year colors

Transparent head is a lantern

"2021" design includes an ox head and tail

Printed hood on back of torso has ox horns!

Torso has lantern and sticky rice balls design on back

Purple is a lucky color in China

Year of the Ox Guy This smiling Story of Nian (80106) minifigure is dressed as 2021's Chinese Zodiac animal.

Festival Statue The Chinese characters on the statue mention the Spring Lantern festival on the 15th day of the first month.

2021 Woman Two happy minifigures wear matching hoodies and snap New Year selfies in Spring Lantern Festival (80107).

LEGO ICONS

The LEGO® Creator Expert range became LEGO Icons in 2020. In 2021, the theme lived up to its new name, depicting a famous soccer stadium in microscale, an all-star shoe at life-size, and the *shamazing* Queer Eye crew in minifigure scale. The iconic minifigure form was also the star of Everyone is Awesome (40516), which celebrated a rainbow of diversity.

Everyone Is Awesome
The display of 11 minifigures in set 40516 reminds us that we are all the same, and all different!

The colorful design is inspired by Pride flags

The classic minifigure shape was always meant to represent everyone

Adidas Superstar Part beatboxer, part shoebox, this unique minifigure was a tie-in with replica sneaker set Adidas Originals Superstar (10282).

Box front is a sticker on a 2×3 tile

AS A RAPPER IN A BOX, I'M THE COMPLETE PACKAGE!

Same torso as 2018's Brick Suit Girl collectible Minifigure

FC Barcelona Celebration Early purchasers of stadium set Camp Nou—FC Barcelona (10284) from LEGO.com also received this celebration scene (40485).

Font de Canaletes is a famous meeting place for Barca fans

All four minifigures share the same exclusive torso

QUEER EYE

Hit makeover show *Queer Eye* got its own LEGO set in The Fab 5 Loft (10291). Its seven minifigures included the star stylists themselves, plus "before and after" variants of one of their makeover heroes.

Hairstyle also seen in Everyone Is Awesome (40516)

Alternative face shows an even bigger smile!

Tailored jacket details continue on back

Legs molded in two colors to create metallic skirt look

Tan France Fashion and styling expert Tan looks both *zaddy* and *zhuzh* in this sand green suit and spotted shirt ensemble.

Jonathan Van Ness *Gorg* hair and makeup guru JVN is instantly recognizable with his dark, flowing hair and immaculate mustache!

LEGO® SPEED CHAMPIONS

The new marques on this year's Speed Champions starting grid were Koenigsegg and Toyota. Koenigsegg Jesko (76900) depicted the Swedish supercar in stunning detail, while Toyota GR Supra (76901) did the same for one of Japan's most popular sports models. Both cars featured new, even more realistic wheel and wheel trim elements and came, as ever, with unique minifigure drivers.

Helmet can be swapped for dark orange hair piece

Larger Koenigsegg logo on back of torso

Koenigsegg Jesko Driver
Five other Speed Champions minifigures share this driver's smiling face, along with 43 inhabitants of LEGO City!

Swap for a face with a big grin

"GR" on front of torso; Toyota name and logo on back

Toyota GR Supra Driver
The "GR" design on this driver's outfit is the logo of Toyota's motorsport division, Gazoo Racing.

> IN MY DAY, WE ALL HAD THE SAME FACE AND LIKED IT!

LEGO® IDEAS

The fan-led LEGO theme featured more minifigure-scale sets than ever before in 2021. First, there was the Medieval Blacksmith (21325), inspired by Classic LEGO® Castle sets. Then Winnie the Pooh (21326) brought minifigures to the Hundred Acre Wood for the first time. Seinfeld (21328) recreated the classic TV sitcom in miniature, while Home Alone (21330) brimmed with big-screen Christmas charm.

SEINFELD

For a show about nothing, the LEGO version of Seinfeld (21328) sure packs in a lot! Stars Jerry, Elaine, George, Kramer, and Newman all feature as minifigures in a set packed full of fan-pleasing details.

Same hair as LEGO City police chief Wheeler

Shoulder armor from LEGO NINJAGO

Male Black Falcon This knight is proud of his age and remembers the 1984 LEGO Castle range like it was yesterday!

Black Falcon emblem first used in 1984

MEDIEVAL BLACKSMITH

At the time of its release, Medieval Blacksmith (21325) was the largest-ever LEGO Castle-style set—towering over some actual LEGO castles! Its four minifigures included the blacksmith himself, an archer, and two Black Falcon knights.

Poleax made from three parts

Hair can be swapped for helmet

Shoulder armor from LEGO *Star Wars*

Female Black Falcon The first specifically female Black Falcon knight was soon followed by another in a 2021 LEGO® Creator set.

Double-sided head: happy or annoyed expressions

Trademark red jacket with hood print on back

Stylish 1990s suit

George Costanza The only minifigure in the Seinfeld set not to have two face prints packs plenty of expression into one!

Elaine Benes Elaine shares a hair piece with another New York screen icon: Dana Barrett from 2016's LEGO® Ghostbusters range.

WINNIE THE POOH

LEGO® DUPLO® Winnie the Pooh figures debuted in 1999, but the honey-loving bear didn't become a minifigure until 2021. Winnie the Pooh (21326) also included Piglet, Rabbit, and Tigger minifigures, plus an Eeyore figure.

Winnie the Pooh With an all-new head mold, Pooh has room for more brain than he is usually credited with.

All four body parts have printed stripes

Arms molded in two colors

Rotund belly printed on red torso

Fully posable, unlike 1999's Pooh figures

Tigger Pooh's bounciest pal has an exclusive head, but shares his tail mold with several other minifigure animal characters.

HOME ALONE

The biggest LEGO Ideas set so far, Home Alone (21330) is a 3,955-piece recreation of the McCallister family home from the 1990 festive film. Minifigures included two McCallisters, neighbor Marley, and crooks Harry and Marv.

Shocked face can be swapped for a smile

Kevin McCallister Young Kevin's alarmed look isn't because he's been left alone at Christmas—it's because he's just tried aftershave!

Posable, medium-length legs

Hair piece designed for Qi'ra in LEGO *Star Wars*

Happy face for safe reunion with Kevin

Kate McCallister Kevin's mom also comes with a panicked face option, for when she realizes that Kevin is home alone!

LEGO® EXCLUSIVE

In 1928, Amelia Earhart became the first woman to fly solo across the Atlantic Ocean, blazing a trail for women in aviation. To coincide with International Women's Day 2021, Amelia Earhart Tribute (40450) celebrated her achievements with a brick-built model of her plane and a minifigure of the pilot herself. The set was available exclusively with certain purchases from LEGO.com.

Classic LEGO® Adventurers aviator cap

Unique torso with neckerchief print

Map is a sticker on a 2×2 tile

Amelia Earhart This pioneering pilot carries a map showing her transatlantic route from Newfoundland to Northern Ireland.

LEGO® JURASSIC WORLD™

All four of this year's LEGO Jurassic World sets were based on animated TV series, *Jurassic World: Camp Cretaceous*. No DNA was needed to bring the show's new heroes to life in minifigure form, as Darius and Yaz took a boat with a Baryonyx; Sammy and Kenji cornered a Carnotaurus; and Brooklynn and Ben set their sights on a Stygimoloch!

Choice of confident and scared faces

Darius Young dino expert Darius is the only new minifigure to appear in more than one *Jurassic World: Camp Cretaceous* set.

Dino tooth necklace

Unique face print

Colorful, mud-free top

First minifigure to wear this hair piece in pink

Face first seen on Fleur Delacour in LEGO Harry Potter

Sammy Exclusive to Carnotaurus Dinosaur Chase (76941), this happy camper is not to be confused with her mud-spattered 2024 variant.

Brooklynn This social media star needs all her influencing skills to save the day in Stygimoloch Dinosaur Escape (76939)!

LEGO® MINIONS

Five new sets expanded the world of LEGO Minions in 2021. All were minifigure-scale, but only one featured actual minifigures. Minions Bob, Stuart, and Kevin all returned with updated looks, and were joined by Minion Otto. The one new minifigure was Belle Bottom, leader of super-villain gang the Vicious 6!

Hair piece is new for 2021

Mini disco ball on end of belt chain

Belle Bottom Illumination's *Minions: The Rise of Gru*'s disco-loving villain shares her hair with the similarly groovy Jacob from LEGO NINJAGO.

Otto No other Minion shares Otto's unique head and body parts, which measure three LEGO knobs wide instead of two.

New hair piece, since used as plants and sea anemones!

Same arms as other Minion figures

Eyes are printed 1×1 round tiles

Click-hinge pieces can hold any pose

Bob with Robot Arms It takes a total of 20 pieces to build this Bob variant with massive mechanical arms!

LEGO® MINECRAFT®

Piglin mobs were the big new threat in this year's LEGO Minecraft sets (unless you were wearing golden armor, of course, in which case they were no threat at all). Builders hoping to battle them or barter with them could do so in all-new minifigure player skins, ranging from panda and ocelot animal costumes to winged beekeeper and pilot outfits.

New Piglin head piece

Unique pixelated face print

Piglin A brave Huntress minifigure faced two variant Piglins, a brick-built Hoglin, and more in The Warped Forest (21168).

Variant in same set has golden legs

Panda Player minifigures in animal costumes made their home in this year's largest LEGO Minecraft set, The Modern Treehouse (21174).

Plain black legs—a favorite since 1978!

Grocery Shopper Five minifigures frequented the City's first Grocery Store (60347), including this shopper with a new prosthetic leg piece.

Smiling face found in more than 50 sets

Cart element first seen in LEGO® Friends sets

Upper leg and lower prosthesis are all one part

Same wheels as minifigure skateboards

2022

THE LEGO GROUP celebrated 90 Years of Play in 2022, revisiting some fan-favorite themes, including LEGO® Vikings and LEGO® Castle. It reached back even further to make minifigures of Vincent van Gogh and Gustave Eiffel, but stayed current with characters from the latest films and video games. At times, it seemed like everyone wanted to be a minifigure, as James Bond, the Muppets, and real-life scientist Jane Goodall were all honored with LEGO likenesses!

Outfit also available in medium azure and bright purple

Ice Cream Vendor Three City minifigures dressed as ice cream vendors in 2022, but two of them were really crooks. Chilling!

LEGO® CITY

There were lots of ways to play in this year's LEGO City sets. As well as new buildings for all three emergency services, the city got its first-ever grocery store and school and its second-ever farm. There were all-new trains, buses, trucks, and cars, and more Stuntz bikes with friction motors. City minifigures even reached the moon in NASA-inspired sets!

DID YOU KNOW?
This year's space-themed City sets are all based on NASA's plans to build a real-life moon base.

MIND IF I CHANGE INTO SOMETHING MORE BREATHABLE?

Same face and hair as School Bus Driver

New uniform print shared with Train Driver

Mustache fits onto torso "neck"

Train Manager This minifigure is always on the move! In another 2022 set, she wears high-vis gear and drives a school bus.

Two face prints show goggle shades worn down and flipped up

Minifigure skull medallion print

Lone Wolf Biker This walrus-mustachioed maverick was among the disassembly-defying riders in a second year of Stuntz sets.

Goggles also worn by City swimmers and helicopter pilots

Outfit based on real NASA flight suits

Lunar Explorer In Lunar Research Base (60350), two astronauts swap bulky space suits for these casual coveralls.

Bulky costume hides beads of sweat on seller's face

Epaulettes originally designed for LEGO® Pirates

Practical, collarless undershirt

Outfit also seen in LEGO® City *Adventures* TV series

City Farmer Six farm workers wear these green overalls in 2022—three with white shirts and three with orange ones.

Tippy Doorman All advent calendars have doors, but only the 2022 LEGO City Advent Calendar (60352) came with a Doorman!

LEGO® AVATAR

After the first film's record-breaking success, LEGO Avatar sets based on the original film by James Cameron were released just as excitement was building for the next installment. Four sets depicted the alien flora and fauna of Pandora, with special figures as the native Na'vi. These featured extra-long arms and legs (last used in LEGO® Toy Story™ sets), plus all-new heads and tail pieces.

Elongated head piece has ears and a distinct jawline

Torso with long arms

Leg piece is one standard brick taller than most minifigure legs

Jake Sully Four Jake figures in 2022 include one in human form in his wheelchair and three variations on his Na'vi avatar.

Same torso print as banshee rider variant

Hair fits on to a LEGO knob in the usual way

Tail piece fitted between torso and legs

Neytiri This year's Neytiri variants include one in her warrior costume, one in her banshee rider costume, and this one in her classic Avatar look.

DID YOU KNOW?
Six-legged direhorse figures in two Avatar sets have their kuru that can connect to Na'vi riders.

LEGO® IDEAS

Before 2022, there had never been more than eight minifigures in a LEGO Ideas set. That all changed with The Office (21336), featuring 15 characters from the hit US sitcom, and Table Football (21337) with its whopping 22 players! At the other end of the scale, Vincent van Gogh and Sonic the Hedgehog were the only minifigures in their respective sets.

Sonic head mold first used in a 2016 LEGO® DIMENSIONS set

Arms are tan colored on 2016 variant

Buckles printed on sides of feet

Sonic the Hedgehog This gaming icon is the centerpiece of display set Sonic the Hedgehog—Green Hill Zone (21331).

Face print based on an 1889 self-portrait

Palette piece printed with "The Starry Night" colors

Brush strokes on legs and torso echo van Gogh's painting style

Vincent van Gogh This great painter accompanies a brick-built tribute to his art in Vincent van Gogh—The Starry Night (21333).

Hair piece is new this year

Hairstyle also found in Table Football set

Distinctive sideburns are printed

Mustard-colored shirt is short-sleeved for "attack readiness"

Lucky pink cardigan

Legs molded in blue and white, with light nougat printing

Pam Beesly The welcoming face of Dunder Mifflin's reception desk can be set to a wicked smile or a grimace!

TABLE FOOTBALL

The working Table Football set (21337) comes with 44 minifigure heads in six skin tones and 43 hair pieces in 11 colors, to make a total of 22 custom minifigures at any one time!

First minifigure to have this hair in dark brown

Blue Player One of 22 male heads and a new hair piece top this custom blue team player.

First minifigure head to depict vitiligo (a loss of pigment on parts of the skin)

LEGO brick badge shows red team allegiance

Only the goalies wear gloves

Alternative face has a wide grin

No other player wears this color

Face prints show nonplussed or underwhelmed looks

Plain shirt and tie combo

Ten blue pairs of legs and torsos are included

Ten players wear this red uniform design

Dwight Schrute Michael Scott's right-hand man wears a pen in his belt and a choice of smug or disgruntled expressions.

THE OFFICE

Based on the much-loved "mockumentary" of the same name, The Office (21336) is a detailed recreation of the Dunder Mifflin Paper Company HQ. Minifigures included regional manager Michael Scott and 14 members of his staff.

Jim Halpert Salesperson Jim loves playing pranks on Dwight, often with a helping hand from his soulmate Pam!

Red Player This soccer star is made using one of the set's 22 female heads, 18 of which are new for 2022.

Goalie This orange-clad keeper plays for the red team. Lavender-colored gear is included for the blue team's goalie.

Printed top features LEGO snake, LEGO lightning bolt, and minifigure hand designs

Torso has star on the back

Same medium legs seen in *Spidey and His Amazing Friends* sets

America Chavez This Multiverse-hopping hero travels with one version of Doctor Strange before teaming up with his Sacred Timeline self.

Eerie, possessed eyes

Zombielike skin

Outfit torn in a fight with a demon

Dead Strange Doctor Strange reanimates this grisly, lifeless version of himself using magic to help fight The Scarlet Witch.

DOCTOR STRANGE IN THE MULTIVERSE OF MADNESS

With 2,708 pieces, Sanctum Sanctorum (76218) was the largest *Multiverse of Madness* set, depicting Doctor Strange's home in incredible, LEGO® Icons style detail. The smaller Gargantos Showdown (76205), meanwhile, boasted an exclusive America Chavez minifigure.

Baron Mordo A 2016 set featured the Sacred Timeline version of Karl Mordo. This one is a villain from Earth-838!

New long, braided hair piece

Option to have smiling or stern expression

Portal-conjuring Sling Ring on belt

Only Mordo wears this cape piece in sand green

THOR: LOVE AND THUNDER

Both sets based on the latest Asgardian adventure featured Thor, the Mighty Thor, and the gruesome gray villain Gorr. But only The Goat Boat (76208) came with Thor's returning allies, Valkyrie and Korg, as well.

Unique hair-and-helmet piece

Classic Asgardian armor

The Mighty Thor Astrophysicist Jane Foster wields the enchanted hammer of Mjölnir in Marvel Studios' *Love and Thunder*, becoming the Mighty Thor.

Same fabric cape as Thor minifigure

Craggy head extender

Collar piece first worn by Spider-Man villain Kraven the Hunter

Ram's head belt buckle

Korg This Kronan gladiator appeared in two Marvel Studios' *Avengers: Endgame* sets, but gets a bold new look for *Love and Thunder*.

LEGO® MARVEL SUPER HEROES

Three new Marvel Studios movies lit up theaters in 2022, each with their own LEGO sets. For younger fans, a new range based on the animated TV series *Spidey and His Amazing Friends* depicted a world where Spider-Man, his allies, and his enemies are all super-powered kids. These were among the first Marvel sets to feature minifigures with medium-length legs.

New hair piece

Unique face print

Exclusive printing

Shuri T'Challa's sister becomes Black Panther in *Wakanda Forever*, and both of her 2022 minifigures wear new Super Hero costumes.

BLACK PANTHER: WAKANDA FOREVER

The 30th film in the Marvel Cinematic Universe inspired three LEGO sets in 2022. They included new minifigure variants of Wakandans Shuri, Okoye, and Nakia, and the first minifigures of King Namor, Attuma, and Ironheart.

Hair piece created for Monica Rambeau Minifigure in 2021

Ironheart Mk 1 Inventor Riri Williams features in two *Wakanda Forever* sets, wearing different versions of her Super Hero armor.

Choice of faces, both with goggles

Jetpack made from 14 pieces

Unique shark's head helmet

Alternative face print shows bared teeth

Molded ears have printed turquoise tips

Stern look can be swapped for a smile

Sharks' teeth worn around knees!

King Namor The ruler of Talokan is entirely unique, from the points on his ears to the wings on his legs.

Printed wings on sides of legs

Attuma Namor's closest advisor in the underwater realm of Talokan wears a hammerhead shark skull as a helmet!

Mask print with extra-large eyes

Simple but iconic torso print

Medium-length legs

Spidey The webbed wonder battles Rhino, Doc Ock, and the Green Goblin in this year's *Spidey and His Amazing Friends* sets.

Unique side-swept hairstyle

Extra arms clip onto neck bracket piece

Doc Ock The *Spidey and His Amazing Friends* version of this familiar villain is elementary school science whiz Olivia Octavius.

SPIDEY AND HIS AMAZING FRIENDS

School-aged versions of Peter Parker, Miles Morales, and Gwen Stacy battle similarly youthful villains in Disney Jr.'s animated kids' series Marvel's *Spidey and His Amazing Friends*. Four sets based on the hit show were released in 2022.

LEGO® STAR WARS™

Star Wars turned 45 in 2022, and this year's May the 4th set featured the first minifigure version of a character who was there in the very beginning: Luke Skywalker's Aunt Beru. For the most part, however, the LEGO theme looked forward, taking its minifigure inspirations from Disney+ shows such as *Andor* and *The Book of Boba Fett*.

> **THIS IS GREAT WITH WOOKIEE COOKIES!**

Face first seen on Helga Hufflepuff from LEGO® Harry Potter™

Blue milk "mustache"

Torso print inspired by *A New Hope*

Aunt Beru Luke's aunt was exclusive to Lars Family Homestead Kitchen (40531), free with qualifying LEGO.com purchases on May the 4th.

Unique printed milk carton brick with bantha design

Luke Skywalker with Blue Milk This minifigure came with the LEGO *Star Wars: The Skywalker Saga Deluxe Edition* video game.

Head and neck are one piece

THE SKYWALKER SAGA

Special minifigures of Luke Skywalker and his Aunt Beru were available only as free gifts this year. The first minifigure of a Kaminoan was more widely available, however, in one *Attack of the Clones* set.

DID YOU KNOW?
This year's LEGO *Star Wars* Advent Calendar (75340) included a beach-ready Darth Vader wearing flippers!

Torso and skirt are printed on both sides

Taun We Obi-Wan's memorable visit to Kamino in *Attack of the Clones* is brought to life by this unique minifigure.

TV ADVENTURES

Live-action series *Andor*, *Obi-Wan Kenobi*, *The Mandalorian*, and *The Book of Boba Fett* were all represented in this year's LEGO *Star Wars* line-up, alongside animated series *The Bad Batch* and *The Clone Wars*.

Medium tan skin color is new for 2022

Neutral expression can be swapped for gritted teeth

Torso has hood print on back

Cassian Andor This minifigure bears little resemblance to his *Rogue One* variants, but perfectly captures the rebel's younger *Andor* look.

Goggles pushed up onto forehead

Neck bracket for brick-built backpack

Short legs slot into blurrg build

Scarf print continues on back

Both 2022 variants have the same hair and head

Ben Kenobi Two *Obi-Wan Kenobi* sets depict the eponymous Jedi Master in the years between the prequel and original trilogies.

Tattered fabric poncho is a new piece

First Kenobi minifigure to wear blue

Head, shoulders, and chest are one piece

Brick-built powerpack

Arms are part of standard torso, hidden under chest

NED-B This loader droid doesn't speak, but he makes his loyalties known by helping Ben and Leia in *Obi-Wan Kenobi*.

Exclusive head with two expressions

Belt piece first worn by LEGO® Batman

Comlink attached to jacket

Peli Motto This starship engineer works on The Mandalorian's N-1 Starfighter (75325), as seen in *The Book of Boba Fett*.

Same hairstyle as LEGO Harry Potter

Smile can be swapped for fierce expression

Short legs

Omega The sixth member of the *Bad Batch* team is also the clone "sister" of famous bounty hunter Boba Fett!

Kuiil This Ugnaught ally of the Mandalorian rides a brick-built blurrg in the Ultimate Collector Series version of The *Razor Crest* (75331).

SERIES 22

The 12 diverse characters in the class of 22 included a high-speed Wheelchair Racer; a heavy-duty Repair Robot; an intrepid Birdwatcher; a fairy-tale Forest Elf; and a big-mouthed, bug-eyed Space Creature.

New helmet piece

Rear wheels attach at an angle

Detachable medal

Front wheel also used for minifigure bicycles

Neatly crossed bootlaces

Wheelchair Racer This medal-winning athlete makes use of a new racing chair frame with attachment points for three wheels.

Face shared with a 2022 Lion Knight

Exclusive toucan piece

Birdwatcher Time is on this ornithologist's side—she is the first Minifigure to have a wristwatch printed on her arm.

Rosy cheeks and choice of two smiles

Smiling mushroom pal

Forest Elf This enchanting and enchanted Minifigure might just be life-sized, given his acorn hat and oak tree leaf cape.

Medium-length legs

LEGO® MINIFIGURES

This was the first time since 2016 that two waves of the main LEGO Minifigures line were released in the same year. Series 22 boasted athletes, aliens, elves, and more, while Series 23 included a dragon, a ship's captain, and several seasonal Minifigures. In between the two came The Muppets Series, featuring Kermit, Miss Piggy, and 10 of their showbiz pals.

SERIES 23

Several characters in this series had a festive feel, including a Snowman, a Christmas Elf, and a decorative Nutcracker soldier. Others had year-round appeal, such as the Ferry Captain and the Green Dragon Costume Girl.

Standard minifigure top hat

Carrot nose is part of mask piece

Ferry Captain Just like last year's Airplane Girl, this smartly dressed sailor wears his vehicle between his legs and torso.

Unique nautical face print

Gleaming rank bands on wrists

Minifigures can grasp these detachable funnels

Detachable horn pieces

Smiling and roaring face options

Snowman Is this Minifigure hot or cold? Lifting off his snowman mask reveals a standard head with a sweating face.

Minifigure broom has seen no sweeping change since the 1970s

Tail attached between torso and legs

Green Dragon Costume Girl The companion Minifigure to 2018's Red Dragon Guy shares all of his molds and his fiery attitude.

Wings fit onto collar element

Head and hair can be swapped for a suited-up look

Hair can be swapped for a helmet

Shoulder armor piece developed for LEGO *Star Wars*

Choice of open- or closed-mouth smiles

More detailed printing than *Toy Story* variants

Buzz Lightyear Buzz wears his Space Ranger uniform in two *Lightyear* sets, but pairs it with wings in just one.

Izzy Hawthorne New hero Izzy wears this Junior Zap Patrol uniform in one set and Space Ranger gear in another.

LEGO® LIGHTYEAR

In 2010, the fictional action figure Buzz Lightyear was turned into a real LEGO minifigure. In 2022, the fictional hero that supposedly inspired the original, fictional action figure was also turned into a real minifigure! Confused? Don't worry— it all makes sense when you watch Disney and Pixar's *Lightyear* or play with the three sets based on the film!

Unique head mold

Printed frill

Medium-length legs

Kermit The most famous Muppet of all comes with a new silver banjo piece and an exclusive rainbow-patterned tile.

Flowing hair is part of head piece

Arms molded in two colors to make long gloves

Standard-length legs

Miss Piggy Did someone say Kermit was the most famous Muppet? Don't let this movie-star Minifigure read that caption.

THE MUPPETS SERIES

The most sensational, inspirational, celebrational, Muppetational series of Minifigures so far starred a dozen Muppet icons. Dr. Bunsen Honeydew, Beaker, Fozzie Bear, Rowlf the Dog, the Swedish Chef, and Animal completed the line-up shown here.

Gonzo The Great Gonzo isn't just a stunt performer. He's also a fashion icon, as this awesome outfit shows.

Chili pepper shirt and spotted tie combo

Pants and shoe print continues on sides of legs

Janice This musical Muppet plays lead guitar in house band The Electric Mayhem, alongside Animal on drums!

Head molded in three colors to make face, hair, and hat

Boho belt print on hips and leg

WHAT DO YOU THINK OF THE BOOK SO FAR?

TERRIBLE!

Unimpressed, narrowed eyes

ZZZ

Plain brown three-piece suit

Medium legs

Waldorf Statler and Waldorf are The Muppets' most ardent followers. They never miss a show, despite loathing every one.

Incredulous look

Buttoned-up style

Standard legs

Statler The taller of The Muppets' two in-house hecklers has a strong jaw that never threatens to crack a smile.

Horned helmet last seen in 2011

Two minifigures in the set have this same torso

Face print shared with several LEGO City crooks

Beard covers a firmly set jaw print

Red Beard Viking This is the first LEGO Viking to wear a beard piece. His predecessors made do with hairy face prints.

Long hair and winged crown are one piece

New armored torso print

Blonde Braid Viking Female minifigures played no part in the original LEGO Vikings range, but made up half the crew in 2022.

LEGO® CREATOR

Not to be confused with the LEGO® Creator Expert theme that became LEGO Icons in 2020, the LEGO Creator range spans everything from realistic animal builds to minifigure dream houses. This year, the theme's largest set was Viking Ship and the Midgard Serpent (31132). It updated a popular LEGO Vikings set from 2005, complete with all-new marauding minifigures.

NINETEEN YEARS LATER ...

Five minifigures in Hogwarts Express—Collectors' Edition (76405) are inspired by the epilogue to *Harry Potter and the Deathly Hallows*. In this final scene, the grown-up Harry and Ginny see their own children off to Hogwarts.

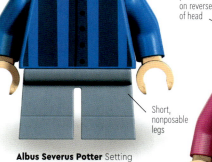

Scar no longer aches since Voldemort's defeat

Same old glasses but new stubble

Grown-up Harry Now aged 37, Harry has three children with Ginny Weasley and works at the reformed Ministry of Magic.

Exclusive head with two expressions

First Ginny minifigure to wear this hair piece

Smart-casual jacket and jeans look

Grown-up Ginny After Hogwarts, Ginny married Harry, became a star Quidditch player, and wrote columns for the *Daily Prophet*.

Hairstyle created for Cole in THE LEGO® NINJAGO® MOVIE™

Medium-length legs

James Sirius Potter In the *Deathly Hallows* epilogue, Harry and Ginny's eldest is returning to Hogwarts for his third year.

Smile can be swapped for a nervous frown

Short, nonposable legs

Albus Severus Potter Setting off for his first year at Hogwarts, young Albus is worried about being sorted into Slytherin.

Same hairstyle as most Ginny minifigures

Sad face printed on reverse of head

Lily Luna Potter Lily is not yet old enough for Hogwarts, so she waves her brothers off alongside her parents.

LEGO HARRY POTTER

This year's largest Harry Potter sets stepped away from Hogwarts to explore locations such as The Ministry of Magic (76403), the Shrieking Shack & Whomping Willow (76407), and 12 Grimmauld Place (76408). The largest set of all was the 5,129-piece Hogwarts Express—Collectors' Edition (76405), which came with 20 minifigures, all but four of which feature in no other set.

I'M THE CHAIR OF MY FACULTY, YOU KNOW!

Head is Slughorn's only standard minifigure part

Armchair "body" made from 14 pieces

Professor Slughorn Well-upholstered Horace adopts his go-to armchair disguise in this year's LEGO Harry Potter Advent Calendar (76404).

Unique nurse's cap with hair

Sand timer brooch

Patient's chart can be attached to brick bed

Madam Pomfrey The first brick depiction of the Hogwarts Hospital Wing (76398) is staffed by the first Poppy Pomfrey minifigure.

Standard plume in new hat-and-hair piece

Choice of expressions: stern or sterner

Robe printed on torso and skirt

Madam Pince Hogwarts: Dumbledore's Office (76402) is the only set so far to feature this prickly witch and librarian.

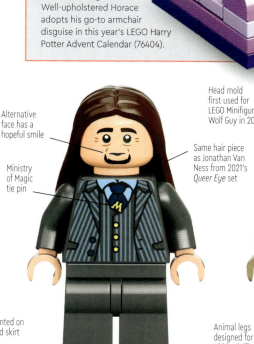

Alternative face has a hopeful smile

Ministry of Magic tie pin

Pius Thicknesse This Minister for Magic and the Death Eater that controls him both make their minifigure debuts in 2022.

Head mold first used for LEGO Minifigures Wolf Guy in 2015

Same hair piece as Jonathan Van Ness from 2021's *Queer Eye* set

Lupin has same eyebrow scar in human form

Animal legs designed for LEGO Minifigures Faun in 2016

Professor Lupin Remus Lupin's werewolf form was last depicted in 2004. This new update looks very different indeed.

LEGO ICONS

It was an epic year for LEGO Icons, with some unexpected minifigures! Replica games console Atari 2600 (10306) had a hidden gamer inside it, while the enormous Eiffel Tower (10307) launched alongside a much smaller Gustave Eiffel tribute. Lion Knights' Castle (10305) updated some classic LEGO Castle characters, while Horizon Forbidden West: Tallneck (76989) brought gaming minifigures up to date.

Hairstyle first worn by Lloyd in THE LEGO NINJAGO MOVIE

Exclusive Atari torso print

Atari Gamer Opening a panel in the life-size Atari 2600 (10306) reveals this gamer playing Asteroids on his own tiny console.

Suit first seen in a LEGO Harry Potter set

Minifigure made from four pieces— 9,997 fewer than Eiffel Tower set

Gustave Eiffel France's most famous civil engineer came free with LEGO.com purchases of Eiffel Tower (10307) on Black Friday 2022.

LION KNIGHTS' CASTLE

The largest LEGO castle of all time celebrated 90 years of LEGO play. It came with nine Lion Knights; their queen; three Black Falcons; three Foresters; a wizard; and five other residents, including a skeleton.

Crown slots into hair piece

Unique torso print under armor

Fabric cape has Lion Knights' emblem on back

Lion Knight Queen When not wearing her crown, the queen favors a gold-and-silver helmet with a striking white plume.

Tousled hair first worn by Luke Skywalker in LEGO Star Wars

Alternative face shows a nervous smile

All nine of the set's Lion Knights have the same torso and leg prints

Hair tied in braids at back

Tousled Lion Knight The set's only Lion Knight with a scared expression might be wishing that he had a helmet!

Printed wear and tear

Same torso print as the set's adult Foresters

Forest Girl This young Forester and her friends live in a base beneath the castle, reached through a secret passage.

DID YOU KNOW?
Lion Knights' Castle (10305) also includes a Majisto minifigure, first seen in sets in 1993.

HORIZON FORBIDDEN WEST

Video game *Horizon Forbidden West* was released to acclaim in February 2022. Three months later came Horizon Forbidden West: Tallneck (76989) which recreated the game's unique aesthetic, complete with its lead character in minifigure form.

Ring of light surrounds over-ear Focus device

Archer's bracers (arm guards) printed on both arms

Aloy The *Horizon* series' playable protagonist has a unique hair piece with a built-in "ring of light" on one side.

Shoe stitching printed on feet

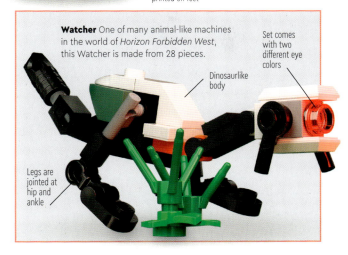

Watcher One of many animal-like machines in the world of *Horizon Forbidden West*, this Watcher is made from 28 pieces.

Set comes with two different eye colors

Dinosaurlike body

Legs are jointed at hip and ankle

LEGO EXCLUSIVE

The popularity of 2021's Amelia Earhart Tribute (40450) ensured another International Women's Day set for 2022. Jane Goodall Tribute (40530) depicted the famous ethologist studying a group of chimpanzees in their natural habitat— as she did for almost 30 years before devoting her life to conservation and activism. The exclusive 275-piece set was available free from LEGO.com with qualifying purchases.

No other minifigure wears this hair piece in white

Exclusive face print

Jane Goodall As an ethologist, Dr. Goodall studies animal behavior. As a conservationist, she works to protect chimps and other creatures.

Unique torso print

DID YOU KNOW?
Chimpanzee figures swung into sets in 2011 and 2012, accompanying collectible LEGO Minifigures.

LEGO® MONKIE KID™

MK and his pals took a journey to the West this year, as well as traveling to the moon and The Heavenly Realms (80039). The latter was the largest Monkie Kid set of the year and—like 2021's Legendary Flower Fruit Mountain (80024)—stepped back from the modern-day storyline to tell another tale from the literary Monkey King's past.

Alternative face has no visor

First MK with shoulder armor

Chinese symbol for sky or heavens

Monkie Kid in Battle Armor MK's looks in 2022 included a space suit, swimming gear, a tourist outfit, and this striking armor.

Crescent moon hair piece

Winking face can be swapped for a stern look

Rabbit-head belt clasp

Chang'e Monkie Kid meets this TV chef and lunar deity when he takes a rocket to her cake-making moon base!

Rabbit ears piece fits over standard minifigure head

Alternative face has angry red eyes

Lunar Rabbit Robot The Chang'e Moon Cake Factory (80032) is run by lovable robo-rabbits with a scary security-bot mode.

Unique hair, horns, and beard piece

Spiky shoulder armor first seen in LEGO® Teenage Mutant Ninja Turtle™ sets

2023 variant has legs instead of skirt

Dragon of the East The leader of the powerful Dragon Clan is also the original owner of MK's golden staff.

Crown is part of long hair piece

Alternative face lacks jewel-like third eye

Howling Celestial Dog design on armor

Erlang Shen This celestial warrior battles one of the three Monkey King variants featured in The Heavenly Realms (80039).

LEGO® DC SUPER HEROES

All but one of this year's DC sets were based around new film *The Batman*. The hit movie starred Robert Pattinson as the Caped Crusader and Zoë Kravitz as Catwoman—a role she first perfected in 2017's THE LEGO® BATMAN MOVIE. Both characters appeared in the new sets, alongside fresh takes on the Riddler, Penguin, Alfred, and Jim Gordon.

Outfit is all gray— even the Utility Belt!

Batarang-style bat symbol

More belt gadgets printed on back

Batman This year's largest DC set, Batcave: The Riddler Face-Off (76183), features a plain-clothes Bruce Wayne alongside this new Batsuit.

Prescription glasses worn over mask

Homemade symbol on jacket

Riddler *The Batman*'s Riddler is the creepiest yet, hiding his entire face behind a military surplus cold-weather mask.

Unique head with option of two faces

Realistic costume— no cat's ears here!

Selina Kyle This new Catwoman can be hero or villain in sets such as Batman & Selina Kyle Motorcycle Pursuit (76179).

Dragon's head helmet

Huge new wing pieces fit onto shoulder armor

Transparent red arms and legs

Dragon Form Kai This year, Kai, Cole, Zane, and Jay didn't have to summon dragons—they could actually turn into them!

Mask flips up like a visor, revealing a gruesome face

Purple crystals embedded in armor

Crystal King This rebranded version of the villainous Overlord has formed a fearsome Crystal Council from the ninja's greatest foes.

New head piece resembles a dragon's skull

Transparent pink shoulder armor and arms

Crystal Army emblem

Vengestone Guard The foot soldiers of the Crystal Army do the Overlord's bidding in three sets, alongside similar Vengestone Warriors.

LEGO® NINJAGO®

The LEGO NINJAGO TV series came to a dramatic end in 2022, making way for *Ninjago: Dragons Rising* in 2023. The final storyline was called "Crystallized" and saw the ninja unlocking their Dragon Forms in order to defeat their oldest enemy, the Overlord. Eight sets tied in with the animated action, reassuring fans that LEGO NINJAGO was far from over.

LEGO® SPEED CHAMPIONS

The replica racers theme flew the (checkered) flag for Great Britain in 2022, with the Lotus Evija (76907) and Aston Martin Valkyrie AMR Pro and Aston Martin Vantage GT3 (76910) joining its illustrious line-up. As film-famous cars with fictional drivers joined the range for the first time, there was also room for another British icon—James Bond 007.

Hair can be swapped for black helmet

Lotus Driver The theme's first Lotus driver wears British racing green, perfectly matching his car and the traditional Lotus logo.

Realistic stitching printed on torso and legs

Choice of helmet or bob-style hair piece

Aston Martin Racing logo

Aston Martin Valkyrie Driver This minifigure forms a pair with a Vanquish driver, who wears the same colors, but reversed.

Vanquish driver wears green with gray details

First Speed Champions driver to have a hair piece but no helmet

I'LL TRY TO BRING IT BACK WITH ALL ITS PIECES!

Unique tuxedo print continues on legs

James Bond The driver of 007 Aston Martin DB5 (76911) is based on Daniel Craig's depiction of super-spy James Bond.

LEGO® MINECRAFT®

This year's largest LEGO Minecraft sets were The Llama Village (21188) and The Red Barn (21187). Both introduced new villager figures and player skin minifigures, but only the latter featured a Baby Zombie as part of a Chicken Jockey build! Elsewhere, The Ice Castle (21186) gave fans chills with its exclusive Yeti and Royal Warrior player skin minifigures.

Pixelated shovel accessory

Poncho print suited to savanna biomes

Llama Herder In The Llama Village (21188), this minifigure tends to brick-built llamas and lives inside a giant one.

Single-pixel teeth at mouth corners

Minecraft crossbow introduced in 2020

Yeti LEGO Minecraft's first trip to the ice spikes biome since 2017 is worth it for this player skin alone.

Chicken Jockey It takes two pieces to make a Baby Zombie and another seven to complete this rare hostile mob.

New unprinted Minecraft baby body piece

Pixelated chicken head found in two other sets

LEGO® JURASSIC WORLD™

Dinosaurs roamed the world in this year's big-screen blockbuster, *Jurassic World Dominion*! Ten sets brought the mayhem down to minifigure size, starring brand-new dinosaurs and characters alongside updated old favorites. Elsewhere, even older favorites were revisited in T. rex Breakout (76956), a display set recreating a classic, car-flipping moment from *Jurassic Park*—the 1993 movie that started it all.

Dr. Ian Malcolm This fan favorite was there at the dawn of Jurassic Park and barely looks a day older in *Jurassic World Dominion*.

Confident look is easily swapped for fear

Chest hair still on show after 30 years

Subtle smile can be swapped for a gritted teeth expression

Hat-and-hair combo designed for LEGO® Hidden Side

Two 2022 Maisie variants share this torso

Maisie Lockwood Shown as a child in a 2018 set, Maisie's *Jurassic World Dominion* minifigure is a determined teenage dinosaur protector.

Both kids have mud-colored hair in 2022

Same outfit as 2018 variant

Lex Murphy The granddaughter of Jurassic Park creator John Hammond is muddied but unbowed in T. rex Breakout (76956).

One arm entirely caked in mud

Tim Murphy Just like his sister, Lex, Tim looks much cleaner in 2018's Jurassic Park Velociraptor Chase (75932).

Unmuddied 2018 variant has blue legs

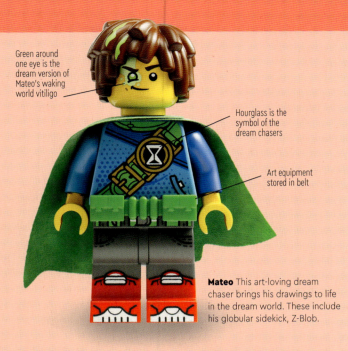

Green around one eye is the dream version of Mateo's waking world vitiligo

Hourglass is the symbol of the dream chasers

Art equipment stored in belt

Mateo This art-loving dream chaser brings his drawings to life in the dream world. These include his globular sidekick, Z-Blob.

2023

THIS YEAR'S BIGGEST theme was the stuff of dreams—literally! LEGO® DREAMZzz™ was inspired by research into the way kids dream and how dreaming helps us understand the world around us. Other new themes included LEGO® Sonic the Hedgehog™ and LEGO® Gabby's Dollhouse, while LEGO® *The Lord of the Rings*™ and LEGO® *Indiana Jones*™ made triumphant returns. The LEGO® *Disney* range celebrated 100 years of movie magic, and LEGO® Friends welcomed all-new main characters.

LEGO® DREAMZzz™

Twelve LEGO sets and an animated TV series told the story of Mateo, Izzie, Cooper, Logan, and Zoey in 2023. Seemingly ordinary school friends in their waking hours, they come together again in sleep as the dream chasers. Using the power of their imaginations, they thwart the schemes of the Nightmare King and keep the dream world safe for everyone.

Standard-size minifigure head and hair

New dream creature body piece

Logan In the dream realms, this gung-ho gamer can shrink down to become Lo-Lo, the smallest of all dream chasers.

Iridescent blue-and-pink hair piece

Double-sided face prints both have hearts and stars on cheeks

Face can be swapped for a sleeping one

Dream world variant wears racing gear based on this jacket

New hair piece with detailed twists

Cooper Of the five dream chasers, Cooper is the first to get a minifigure depicting his waking world appearance.

Izzie Mateo's sister is the youngest member of the LEGO DREAMZzz team. In the dream world, her hair glows pink.

Zoey This reluctant dream chaser likes to go solo and styles herself as the Dream Bandit in an outlaw cape.

LEGO® SPORTS

Following in the fancy footwork of the LEGO Sports theme (though not branded as such), LEGO® Icons of Play (40634) was a playable minifigure soccer game. Four real-world soccer stars featured as minifigures, alongside a goalie, a coach, a referee, and eight spectators. Two of the same set could be combined to make a perfect game of two halves.

Iconic pink hair

Smile can be swapped for a cheer

Front torso print also seen in 2022's Table Football set

Unique name-and-number print on back

Sam Kerr The Australia women's national team captain is considered one of the world's best and fastest soccer strikers.

Megan Rapinoe This Olympic gold medalist and former US women's national team co-captain is also famous for her activism.

Mr. Oz The team's science teacher was once a young dream chaser himself. Now, he mentors the next generation.

Combined hair-and-beard piece

Tweed jacket under dream world space suit

Crown has one ever-wakeful eye

Jayden A second face print with closed eyes sends this minifigure to sleep and into a world of unicorn dreams.

Orthodontic headgear print

Unicorn-print pajamas

DON'T LOSE ANY SLEEP OVER ME— SERIOUSLY!

Night Hunter The Nightmare King's scary second-in-command has a closer connection to the dream chasers than they realize.

True identity hidden by hat and scarf

Scarf reaches out like a clawed hand

Standard minifigure head mold

Unique body with built-in backpack

Arms also used for LEGO® Super Mario™ figures

Mrs. Castillo This wise old woman's waking world food truck turns into a giant turtle in the dream world.

Cape looks like a mass of shadowy monsters

Same head as Night Hunter under helmet

Grimspawn Six named members of the Nightmare King's minions haunt this year's sets, along with this all-purpose imp.

Same body as Logan, but in black

Nightmare King The villainous ruler of the Grim Realm wants to turn the dream realms into one big nighttime terror.

LEGO SONIC THE HEDGEHOG

First, there was a Sonic the Hedgehog minifigure in 2016's LEGO® DIMENSIONS line. Then LEGO® Ideas launched a full minifigure-scale Sonic set in 2022. Finally, in 2023, the Blue Blur got his own theme, complete with pals Amy and Tails and arch-villain Dr. Eggman. Three sets also came with a new pod assembly and launcher to send minifigure Sonic spinning.

Unique double-tail piece

Short legs molded in two colors with white printing

Tails This twin-tailed fox is as fast as Sonic. His real name is Miles Prower (as in "miles per hour").

Hair and hairband are part of head

Molded skirt fits between legs and torso

Amy Sonic's hammer-wielding sidekick uses her trademark accessory to activate functions in three of this year's sets.

Head and torso are one unique piece

New, chunky arm pieces

Long legs also used in LEGO® Avatar sets

Dr. Eggman Also known as Dr. Robotnik, Sonic's archenemy was brick-built when last seen in the LEGO® Ideas theme.

2023

DISNEY 100

Anniversary sets included the first minifigure versions of characters from *Up*, *Moana*, and *The Princess and the Frog*. There were also new Mickey and Minnie Mouse variants, plus a minifigure depiction of Walt Disney himself.

Walt Disney The world's most famous animator stands beside Mickey, Minnie, Dumbo, and Bambi in Walt Disney Tribute Camera (43230).

Can be swapped for close-mouthed smile

Sketch of Mickey Mouse in 1928's *Steamboat Willie*

Same hair piece as Moana mini doll

Unique smart suit print

LEGO *DISNEY*

The Walt Disney Company began life as the Disney Brothers Cartoon Studio, as founded by Walt and Roy Disney on October 16, 1923. In 2023, the much-loved entertainment brand marked its first century in the movie-making business with a series of Disney 100 celebrations. These included several commemorative LEGO sets and a bumper series of 18 collectible LEGO® Minifigures.

Pinstripe pattern continues on back

Pocket watch ready for the next 100 years

Mickey Mouse This unique Mickey variant drives the engine and keeps things running to time in Disney Celebration Train (43212).

Heart of Te Fiti necklace

Polynesian skirt print

Moana This Disney Princess became a mini doll in 2017, but Disney Celebration Train (43212) marks her debut as a minifigure.

Tiara slots into unique hair piece

Water lily dress design

Tiana *The Princess and the Frog*'s female lead has been a mini doll, a micro doll, and a minifigure.

Grin can be swapped for ... a different grin

Flower and leaf details match Tiana's dress

Naveen *The Princess and the Frog*'s male lead comes in human and frog forms in Disney Castle (43222).

Binoculars and bugle on backpack

Grimace or kindly smile on double-sided head

Walking cane with minifigure roller skate base

Treasured grape soda badge

Carl The older star of *Up* shares his home with Wilderness Explorer Russell and talking dog Dug, in "Up" House (43217).

Wilderness Explorer badges

Choice of smiles

Russell The younger star of *Up* wears a new hat-and-hair piece, a brick-built backpack, and an awful lot of badges!

COLLECTIBLE MINIFIGURES

Besides the characters shown here, the Disney 100 Series of LEGO Minifigures also included Aurora from *Sleeping Beauty*, the Queen of Hearts from *Alice in Wonderland*, Cruella De Vil from *101 Dalmatians*, and many other icons.

Face is a forerunner of Mickey Mouse's look

Waistband printed on torso

Clapperboard accessory

Oswald This Lucky Rabbit featured in some of the earliest Disney shorts, including 1927's *Trolley Troubles* and *All Wet*.

Mulan The first Mulan minifigure shares her mini doll's hair and carries a lantern with a printed Cri-Kee piece.

Nervous smile can be swapped for a mean one!

Ribs visible under jacket

Face can be shown smiling or scowling

Emperor's crest, worn as a medallion

"Lucky" cricket, Cri-Kee, printed on round brick

Hat and hair are one piece, molded in two colors

Ernesto de la Cruz This skeletal musician is one of two *Coco* characters in this collectible series, alongside Miguel Rivera.

Unique guitar with golden details

Wide smile can be swapped for a more neutral look

New windswept hair piece

Sacred turquoise necklace

Pocahontas This Disney Princess comes with three colorful leaf pieces and a printed tile representing explorer John Smith's compass.

LEGO *DISNEY WISH*

Three mini doll sets tied in with magical Disney movie *Wish*. All featured the film's lead character—would-be sorcerer's apprentice, Asha. Just one, King Magnifico's Castle (43224), came with the shady sorcerer himself.

Box braid hairstyle

Printed embroidery detailing

King Magnifico The man who can grant his people's wishes chooses instead to hoard their desires in his private observatory.

Clothes fit for a sorcerer and a king

Asha In a land where wishes can be granted through magic, Asha wants to see her grandfather's dream come true.

Cape is starry on the inside and metallic silver on the outside

New hat-and-hair piece

First Indy with two faces—smiling and frowning

INDIANA JONES! I ALWAYS KNEW SOME DAY YOU'D COME BACK.

Steely look can be swapped for a scream

No other Indy variant wears gloves

Indiana Jones This year's three new Indy minifigures depicted him in a tie, in gloves, and with a cobweb-covered face.

Marion Ravenwood The 2023 take on Indy's fellow adventurer has a more determined look than her 2008–2009 variants.

Earlier Marion variants all have plain legs

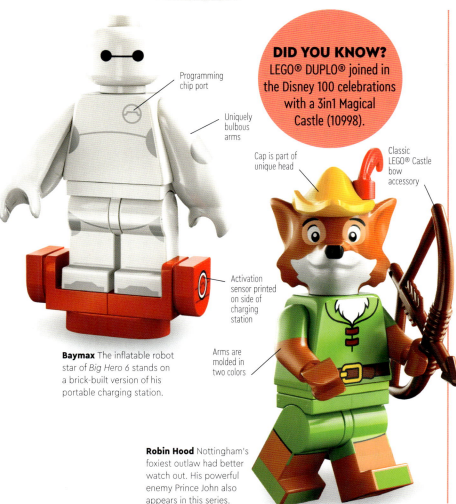

Programming chip port

Uniquely bulbous arms

DID YOU KNOW?
LEGO® DUPLO® joined in the Disney 100 celebrations with a 3in1 Magical Castle (10998).

Cap is part of unique head

Classic LEGO® Castle bow accessory

Activation sensor printed on side of charging station

Baymax The inflatable robot star of *Big Hero 6* stands on a brick-built version of his portable charging station.

Arms are molded in two colors

Robin Hood Nottingham's foxiest outlaw had better watch out. His powerful enemy Prince John also appears in this series.

LEGO *INDIANA JONES*

For 14 years, LEGO *Indiana Jones* had been locked away in a top-secret vault, like something that belonged in a museum. But in 2023, the man in the hat was back: on the big screen in *Indiana Jones and the Dial of Destiny*, and in three new LEGO sets inspired by *Raiders of the Lost Ark* and *The Last Crusade*.

Turban also worn by Dengar in LEGO® *Star Wars™* sets

Mummy Indy isn't scared by this mummy in Escape from the Lost Tomb (77013). He's more bothered by the snakes!

Hint of nerves behind confident smile

Bandages decayed over thousands of years

Even more visible ribs printed on back

Sallah Indy's exuberant Egyptian pal makes his minifigure debut in this year's Escape from the Lost Tomb (77013).

New flexible head-tails piece

Smiling face can be turned fierce

Wear and tear printed on feet

Ahsoka Tano Anakin Skywalker's former apprentice has come a long way since *The Clone Wars*—and goes even further in *Ahsoka*!

Magnifying eyeglass

Unique head piece

Professor Huyang This wise old droid was first seen in *The Clone Wars* in 2012, but his minifigure is all-new.

Helmet can be swapped for hair piece

Alternative face lacks visor and chinstrap

Same torso print and legs as Lt. Beyta

Captain Porter The first minifigure New Republic pilots were this human hero and his Mon Calamari colleague, Lieutenant Beyta.

Lightsaber clips onto back of armor

Plain black head under unique helmet

Rust speckles printed all over

Marrok Once an Inquisitor for the Empire, Marrok is now the sinister right-hand man of main *Ahsoka* villain Morgan Elsbeth.

AHSOKA

Three *Ahsoka* sets featured 12 minifigures and two astromech droids. All-new characters such as Marrok, Morgan Elsbeth, and Captain Porter rubbed shoulders with updated versions of fan favorites Hera Syndulla, Sabine Wren, and Ahsoka Tano herself.

DID YOU KNOW?
Six different minifigures of Ahsoka have been created since the first Padawan version in 2008.

LEGO *STAR WARS*

Two new and very different shows inspired LEGO *Star Wars* sets in 2023. Live-action adventure *Ahsoka* revisited favorite characters from *The Clone Wars* and *Star Wars Rebels* and took place in the same post-Empire era as *The Mandalorian*. Animated preschool series *Young Jedi Adventures*, meanwhile, was set hundreds of years earlier and focused on a whole new cast of Younglings.

Earlier Jedi Knight Lukes all have classic 1970s LEGO hair

Glove covers damaged robotic hand

Luke Skywalker Love the hair, Luke! This new piece was designed especially to match his *Return of the Jedi* look.

THE SKYWALKER SAGA

From *A New Hope*'s Yavin 4 Rebel Base (75365) to the sequel trilogy's *Millennium Falcon* Holiday Diorama (40658), 2023's sets spanned the entire Skywalker Saga. Several sets also marked *Return of the Jedi*'s 40th anniversary.

Hairstyle shared with 2019 Padmé variant

Gritted teeth appear on the reverse side

Hairstyle shared with 2023 Padmé variant

Earlier variant has more stylized facial features

Unique torso with vice admiral's rank badge

Senatorial rank badge

Padmé Amidala This is the second minifigure to be based on Padmé's "action costume" in *The Clone Wars* animated series.

Vice Admiral Sloane *Star Wars* novels established this Imperial officer's role in *Return of the Jedi*, though she is not seen on screen.

Half smile can be swapped for a frown

Knitted sweater print shows the *Millennium Falcon*

Holiday Rey This festive minifigure uses her lightsaber to carve the turkey in *Millennium Falcon* Holiday Diorama (40658)!

Choice of smile or scared look

Resistance symbol surrounded by snow

Holiday Finn Finn also wields a lightsaber in the diorama based on *The LEGO Star Wars Holiday Special*.

Dress details printed on front and back

Princess Leia The latest variant of Leia in her Yavin 4 medal-giving garb is the first to have a skirt piece.

YOUNG JEDI ADVENTURES

This animated series sees lovable Younglings Kai Brightstar and Lys Solay learning the ways of the Jedi from Master Yoda. All three featured in the first set based on the show, Tenoo Jedi Temple (75358).

DID YOU KNOW?
Yoda is lime green for the first time for his *Young Jedi Adventures* minifigure.

Grin gets bigger on reverse of head

Unique hair piece echoes Leia's iconic buns

High Republic symbol on lightsaber sheath

Lys Solay Kai's best friend is the first member of the blue-skinned Pantoran people to be made into a minifigure.

Alternative face looks startled

Unique High Republic hairstyle

Kai Brightstar Youngling Kai wears gleaming High Republic–era robes and wields Yoda's old training lightsaber (after losing his own).

Medium-length legs

272

LEGO® MARVEL SUPER HEROES

Avengers Tower (76269) became the biggest LEGO Marvel Super Heroes set of all time in 2023, with 5,201 pieces; 28 Marvel Cinematic Universe minifigures; and a bonus Kevin Feige minifigure. There were sets inspired by new movies *Guardians of the Galaxy Vol. 3* and *The Marvels*, plus a second series of collectible Minifigures based on Marvel Studios TV shows.

Hair is only piece shared with 2017 variant

Two different smiles on double-sided head

Suit made by Kamala's mom, Muneeba

Ms. Marvel The MCU minifigure of Kamala Khan is very different from her long-armed variant of 2017.

Hairstyle originally worn by LEGO Minifigures Banshee in 2015

Purple dark magic accessory

Winking face Agatha's winking face is printed on the reverse of the head.

Agatha Harkness This *WandaVision* villain is notoriously two-faced, and her twin expressions in Minifigure form include her infamous wink.

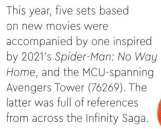

Mystery gem in forehead

Adam Warlock The golden boy of *Guardians of the Galaxy Vol. 3* can be friend or foe in The New Guardians' Ship (76255).

Raccoonlike skull on collar

COLLECTIBLE MINIFIGURES

The 12 characters featured in LEGO® Minifigures Marvel Studios Series 2 were drawn from streaming shows *WandaVision*, *What If ...?*, *Hawkeye*, *Moon Knight*, *She-Hulk: Attorney at Law*, and *X-Men '97*, plus streaming special *Werewolf by Night*.

Larger eyes than other movie Spideys

Supernatural mummy-style costume

Printed Scarab of Ammit tile

Unique crescent dart accessory

Moon Knight Turning Moon Knight's head reveals his alter Marc Spector. His alters Mr. Knight/Steven Grant also feature in this series.

MOVIES

This year, five sets based on new movies were accompanied by one inspired by 2021's *Spider-Man: No Way Home*, and the MCU-spanning Avengers Tower (76269). The latter was full of references from across the Infinity Saga.

Printing based on suit worn by actor Andrew Garfield as Spider-Man

Amazing Spider-Man Spideys from three realities team up in *No Way Home* set Spider-Man Final Battle (76261).

Same hair as 2017 She-Hulk minifigure

She-Hulk Jennifer Walters doesn't get angry—she gets justice in her day job as a lawyer for other Super Heroes!

Case file for client Emil Blonsky

Wong calling on smartphone

Smaller spider motif than Amazing Spider-Man

Silver suit webbing is unique to Maguire's Spidey

Friendly Neighborhood Spider-Man This is the first Spidey minifigure based on Tobey Maguire's depiction of the character since 2004.

Unique face print

Exclusive Avengers cap

Kevin Feige The real-life president of Marvel Studios watches the action as a minifigure bystander in Avengers Tower (76269).

Ears built into unique hair piece

Alternative face is snarling and lacks glasses

X-Men branded mug

Beast The first minifigure version of mutant Hank McCoy is one of three based on animated series *X-Men '97*.

LEGO® CITY

City life looked more modern than ever in 2023. Colorful minifigures lived colorful lives in the likes of Custom Car Garage (60389); Gaming Tournament Truck (60388); and largest LEGO City set ever, Downtown (60380). Police sets focused on new-recruit training for the first time, while Arctic Explorer sets took City tech and minifigures on a mission to the North Pole.

Welder This custom car mechanic has a mask to match her hair and a chair to match her classic yellow skin tone.

City minifigures get violet hair for the first time in 2023

Flaming tire T-shirt print

Yellow wheelchair first seen in LEGO Avatar theme

Welding mask can be worn instead of hair piece

Arms created for Cactus Girl Minifigure in 2018

Helmet can be swapped for supplied hair piece

Afro-textured hair piece is new in this color

USB stick attached to bodywarmer

Badge helps dogs recognize police officers

Arctic Explorer This research scientist travels by ship, helicopter, and mobile lab in this year's Arctic Explorer sets.

Police Dog Trainer Nips from new-recruit police dogs are not a problem for this trainer in his padded suit!

> MY HOUSE SETLIST IS ALL MODULAR BUILDINGS!

First City minifigure to have bright green hair

Headphones from LEGO® Monkie Kid theme

DJ The 14 minifigures in Downtown (60380) can enjoy music from a street violinist or courtesy of this rooftop DJ.

> GIMME ANOTHER BIG HAND!

Giant fist merch matches top

Winning smile can be swapped for a losing look

Pink Gamer This colorful eSports enthusiast goes up against a similarly striking blue opponent in Gaming Tournament Truck (60388).

LEGO MINIFIGURES

Series 24 of the main collectible Minifigures range looked to the LEGO past with Classic Castle characters and retro astronauts; to the wider past with a Rococo Aristocrat and a T-rex Costume Fan; and to the far future with a robot warrior. Elsewhere, a Conservationist, a Soccer Referee, and a farmers' market Carrot Mascot flew the flag for the present day.

Unique ragged cape

Printed baby monitor tile on classic walkie-talkie piece

Standard head fits in to jaw-and-ears piece

No other minifigure wears this helmet in brown

Spacebaby is all one piece

Troll emblem first seen in 2008

Orc This monster Minifigure is straight out of LEGO Castle Fantasy Era and wears the emblem of its Troll faction.

Brown Astronaut and Spacebaby The latest additions to the Classic Space family were this proud parent and their adorable offspring.

Exclusive powdered wig piece

Rococo Aristocrat This 18th-century scenester wants everyone to know that her wide dress element was designed for Series 15's Queen.

Both face prints are heavily made up

Stylized flower design on printed bodice

DID YOU KNOW?
Classic-style LEGO astronauts have been made in red, white, yellow, blue, black, green, orange, pink, and brown.

Mic for talking to assistant referees

Alternative face is much less calm!

Watches printed on both wrists

Soccer Referee With two watches, a pen, a whistle, and red and yellow cards, this ref is ready for anything.

Angelina Johnson This Quidditch captain shares the Gryffindor common room with Harry and Neville Longbottom in Gryffindor House Banner (76409).

- Gryffindor Quidditch sweater
- Half smile can be swapped for wide grin

- Printing represents carved details on statue
- New braided beard piece
- Model of Hogwarts Great Hall made mostly from upside-down pieces

- Alternative face has dragon-fire scorches and broken glasses
- Suit print shared with one LEGO Marvel Super Heroes minifigure

Bogrod This goblin bank teller is one of 11 exclusive minifigures in the 4,803-piece Gringotts Wizarding Bank—Collectors' Edition (76417).

- Neutral face can be swapped for scary scowl
- Lost Diadem of Ravenclaw

Gray Lady One of Hogwarts' many ghosts, Helena Ravenclaw haunts Harry, Hermione, and co. in Hogwarts: Room of Requirement (76413).

LEGO® HARRY POTTER™

This year, House Banner sets turned from pennants into minifigure common rooms. They were the perfect place to introduce some Hogwarts students that had never made it into sets before, such as Angelina Johnson, Blaise Zabini, and Pansy Parkinson. Also making their minifigure debuts in 2023 were goblins Bogrod and Ricbert, the ghostly Gray Lady, and the Architect of Hogwarts himself!

- Rolled-up architectural plans

The Architect The only minifigure in microscale set Hogwarts Castle and Grounds (76419) is based on a statue in the school.

LEGO® MINECRAFT®

The deep dark was the new biome on the block in 2023's LEGO Minecraft range, as explored by two new knight player minifigures. Knights also starred in The Iron Golem Fortress (21250), with one winning their spurs in an online vote. Elsewhere, the theme's most frequently seen minifigure, Steve, got an intriguing new look, courtesy of some strange green armor!

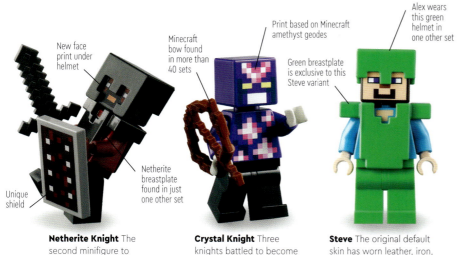

- New face print under helmet
- Unique shield
- Netherite breastplate found in just one other set

Netherite Knight The second minifigure to wear full netherite armor (after Steve) stars in The Deep Dark Battle (21246).

- Minecraft bow found in more than 40 sets
- Print based on Minecraft amethyst geodes

Crystal Knight Three knights battled to become minifigures in a LEGO online poll. The eventual winner was crystal clear!

- Alex wears this green helmet in one other set
- Green breastplate is exclusive to this Steve variant

Steve The original default skin has worn leather, iron, golden, diamond, and netherite armor. Now he's moved on to purest ... green!

LEGO FRIENDS

The original mini doll theme got a major refresh in 2023, with sets and storylines based around eight new main characters. The original five Friends were not forgotten, however, and still made guest appearances.

- Unique hair piece
- Argyle pattern cardigan
- New hair piece has a loose braid at the back
- Same hairstyle as Rex from THE LEGO® MOVIE 2™
- Autumnal print on top
- First mini doll depicted with a limb difference
- Foodie Leo even wears watermelons on his shirt!

Autumn The daughter of original LEGO Friends character Mia loves adventure, animals, and the wilderness surrounding Heartlake City.

Leo When he isn't on the soccer field, Leo explores his Mexican heritage by cooking with his grandmother.

Aliya Head girl Aliya is a born leader with far too much to do. If only she'd let her friends help out!

Ears, trunk, and tusks are one piece, worn like a minifigure beard

Ink General Whoever holds the cursed Scroll of Memory can control the Ink Demons and Ink Generals held within it.

Same face and torso printing as standard Ink Demons

Golden details from tusks to toes!

Yellowtusk the Wise This mighty elephant demon unloads a trunkful of trouble in jumbo mech set Yellow Tusk Elephant (80043).

Unique torso print with dragon details

Ink Demons have legs; only Generals have wispy tails

LEGO® MONKIE KID™

The demons kept on coming in this year's Monkie Kid assortment. First, the team tackled Ink Demons conjured from a cursed scroll. Then they took on Monkey King's demon brothers: Azure Lion, Yellowtusk, and Peng the Golden Winged Eagle. Luckily, the Monkie Kids now had power-up armors and potential underwater pals in the shape of Crab Generals and Shrimp Soldiers.

Mei Power-Up MK, Me , Pigsy, Sandy, and Mr. Tang all get matching but not quite identical power-up armors this year.

Same legs as other power-up minifigures

Crab General The upper crustaceans in the Dragon of the East's underwater army have no problem snapping to attention.

Segmented body print

Shrimp head includes a long tail

Same torso print as Crab General

Unique crab head piece

Shrimp Soldier These brawny shrimp can be friend or foe, depending on the orders of their crab superiors.

LEGO® NINJAGO®

The world of the ninja changed forever in 2023. New TV series *Ninjago: Dragons Rising* saw the original heroes disappear and new ones emerge to take their place. Eventually, ninja old and new came together and formed a greatly enhanced team. In sets, the original ninja didn't disappear at all, but their new friends and enemies were central to the action.

Unique upper head wrap with horns

Lower head wrap piece used by most of this year's ninja

Dragon design continues on back

Arin The youngest ninja is a lifelong fan of the original team and followed their example to teach himself Spinjitzu.

Same shoulder pads as Beatrix

Reverse side shows pouting face

Face markings indicate social status

Shoulder pads are all the rage in Imperium

Empress Beatrix The ruler of ultramodern Imperium has a shameful secret. Her empire gets its energy by draining captured dragons.

Sora The first ninja team member not to use Spinjitzu relies instead on her Elemental Power to transform technology.

Cat keychain print on torso

Unique bearded tiger head piece

Tiger stripes and armor details on arms

Lord Ras Beatrix's fellow baddie helped her take the Imperian throne. But is he really just out to help himself?

Hair and cat-ears hood are one piece

Same lower head wrap as Arin

DRAGONS RISING

The first wave of *Dragons Rising* sets pitted the expanded ninja team against the dragon-hunting forces of Imperium. All six classic heroes got updated looks, while the newcomers redefined just what a ninja could be.

No head wrap for this ninja!

Same hairstyle as LEGO Monkie Kid's Chang'e

Flame details on robe print

Wyldfyre The Elemental Master of Heat was raised by dragons. Her untamable spirit is like nothing else on the team.

NINJAGO CITY MARKETS

With its 6,163 pieces, Ninjago City Markets (71799) became the largest LEGO NINJAGO set ever. It continued the Modular Buildings series begun with 2017's Ninjago City (70620) and came with 21 mostly exclusive minifigures.

First gray fedora piece

Exclusive face print with ice-white smile

Ninja *gi* visible under trenchcoat

Detective Zane The Ice Ninja loves a cold case and investigates Ninjago City Markets (71799) in his best sleuthing gear.

Black turtleneck sweater print

Cyborg arm

First dark gray wheelchair piece

Cyrus Borg This inventor is a friendly face in Ninjago City Markets (71799), unlike his scary cyborg variant from 2014.

LEGO ICONS

Ten years after the end of the LEGO *The Lord of the Rings* theme, LEGO Icons went on an unexpected journey back to Middle-earth. The result was *The Lord of the Rings*: Rivendell (10316): an epic, 6,167-piece set that dwarfed (and Hobbited) its similarly themed predecessors. Also returning after an extended absence were the Bluecoat defenders of Eldorado Fortress (10320).

Hat style worn by LEGO wizards since 1993

Gandalf the Gray This is the first Gandalf minifigure to have a printed skirt piece instead of plain legs.

Same beard worn by all Gandalf the Gray variants

Robe folds printed on both sides of skirt piece

Smile can be swapped for a Ring-influenced face

The One Ring—as found in more than 30 sets!

Frodo Baggins This year's Hobbits are the first to have their legs and feet molded in two different colors.

Dual-molded short legs

THE LORD OF THE RINGS: RIVENDELL

The biggest LEGO set of the year came with 21 Middle-earth minifigures. These included five brave Hobbits, two gallant Men, five noble Elves, two determined Dwarves, one gray Wizard, and six stony-faced statues!

Belt detail visible below shorter beard

Same hair-and-ears piece as Lord of Rivendell, Elrond

Helmet fits around separate beard piece

Middle-earth's first medium-length legs

Gimli With a shorter, redder beard and slightly longer legs, the latest Gimli variant is the most movie-accurate so far!

Option of smiling or serious look

Printed Evenstar pendant

Arwen The Lady of Rivendell is shown here wearing her Evenstar pendant, just before she gives it to Aragorn.

ELDORADO FORTRESS

With five times more pieces than the 1989 LEGO® Pirates set that inspired it, this Bluecoat stronghold stood taller than ever in 2023. This time around, its eight minifigures all had unique looks as well.

Plume pieces have been around since 1984

Broad grin can become a tight-lipped smile

Bluecoat with Ponytail Don't tell her, but this Bluecoat's hair-and-hat combo was first worn by a LEGO Minifigure pirate.

Hair tied in ponytail at back

Subtle update of 1989 Bluecoat torso print

Epaulettes created for the very first LEGO Pirates sets

Bluecoat with Mustache Three of this year's Bluecoats wear shako hats and backpacks, but only one has a stylish mustache!

LEGO GABBY'S DOLLHOUSE

Mini dolls and new cat figures came together in a new play theme based on the hit Netflix series DreamWorks *Gabby's Dollhouse*. Four cat-eriffic sets featured Gabby and her friends, Cakey, MerCat, Pandy Paws, and Kitty Fairy.

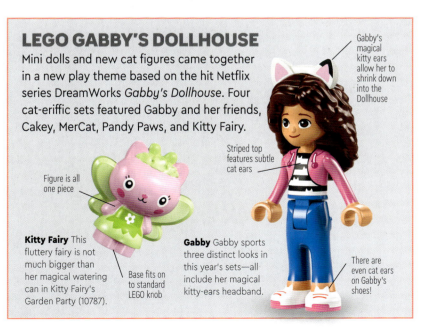

Figure is all one piece

Kitty Fairy This fluttery fairy is not much bigger than her magical watering can in Kitty Fairy's Garden Party (10787).

Base fits on to standard LEGO knob

Gabby's magical kitty ears allow her to shrink down into the Dollhouse

Striped top features subtle cat ears

Gabby Gabby sports three distinct looks in this year's sets—all include her magical kitty-ears headband.

There are even cat ears on Gabby's shoes!

LEGO® DC SUPER HEROES

There had never been a set like this year's Batcave—Shadow Box (76252) before! A literal showcase for the 1992 movie *Batman Returns*, it was the biggest LEGO DC set to date, but also minifigure scale. The 3,981-piece display scene could be viewed through a bat-shaped window or opened up to reveal every detail of an intricate Batcave build.

Stern Batman face on other side of head

Torso print also found in LEGO Ideas Home Alone set (21330)

Cup of tea poured by butler Alfred

Whip can be used for daring escapes

Bruce Wayne As well as two Batman minifigures, Shadow Box included this entirely unrelated billionaire, based on actor Michael Keaton.

Metallic gray patches suggest reflective material

Catwoman This Selina Kyle may have been hanging out with the Joker, given that she seems to be in stitches!

Hand-sewn details, as seen in *Batman Returns*

DID YOU KNOW?
Out of 3,981 pieces in the Shadow Box set, 1,719 are Batman's favorite color—black!

Lightning bolts are new in transparent green

Unique pouf hair piece

Angry face can be swapped for a smile

Winifred Sanderson
This 17th-century witch is one of six minifigures in Disney Hocus Pocus: The Sanderson Sisters' Cottage (21341).

Hairstyle first seen in LEGO Ideas Doctor Who set (21304)

Same face as this year's Gandalf minifigure

Galileo Galilei This Renaissance polymath studies a working model of Earth orbiting the sun in Tribute to Galileo Galilei (40595).

NEEDS MORE HORNS!

Hairstyle shared with Autumn from LEGO Friends

Helmet also found on the seabed by LEGO City Arctic Explorers

Viking Blacksmith Four Norse warriors populate the Viking Village (21343), which includes a fiery forge for this metalworker.

LEGO IDEAS

Minifigures in this year's fan-designed sets included all seven members of BTS, the three Sanderson sisters from Disney's *Hocus Pocus*, and the one-and-only Galileo Galilei! The Orient Express Train (21344) took minifigures back to the golden age of train travel, while Viking Village (21343) offered landfall for the ones from 2022's LEGO® Creator Viking Ship and the Midgard Serpent (31132).

RM's hair piece is new in blue

Only V has this hair in sand yellow

Each head has two expressions

Torso prints all exclusive to this set

BTS K-pop sensations RM, Jimin, Jungkook, V, J-Hope, Suga, and Jin bring the fire and set the night alight in BTS Dynamite (21399).

BTS DYNAMITE

"Dynamite" is one of BTS's best-loved songs, with well over a billion views on YouTube. BTS Dynamite (21399) lets fans recreate the video in minifigure form, complete with disco, donut shop, and record store backdrop.

Facial features shared with a LEGO City Arctic Explorer

Station Manager He may not get to ride the Orient Express, but this staff member loves to see it pulling in to his platform.

Same outfit as 2022's LEGO Ideas Lighthouse Keeper

Writer Despite traveling incognito, fellow Orient Express passengers will surely recognize LEGO® Adventurers hero Pippin Reed.

Hair is part of cloche hat piece

Alternative expression is a look of alarm

THE ORIENT EXPRESS TRAIN

This year's largest LEGO Ideas set came with eight minifigures in 1930s garb. Four worked on the world's most famous railway, while a writer, a duchess, a scientist, and a film director came aboard as passengers.

LEGO® JURASSIC WORLD™

All five of this year's dinosaur sets featured brand-new minifigures in classic scenes from 1993's *Jurassic Park*. The largest was Visitor Center: T. rex & Raptor Attack (76961), inspired by the movie's climax, while the tallest was Brachiosaurus Discovery (76960). The dinosaur figure in this latter set stood as tall as six minifigures and fed from an even larger tree.

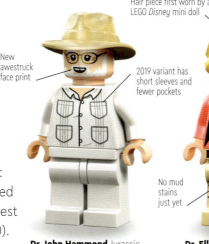

New awestruck face print

Hair piece first worn by a LEGO *Disney* mini doll

2019 variant has short sleeves and fewer pockets

No mud stains just yet

Dr. John Hammond Jurassic Park's creator made his minifigure debut in a 2019 display set. This year, he's here to play!

Alternative face is scared but unsprayed

Smiling or shocked expression

Dr. Ellie Sattler Two 2023 variants of this paleobotanist are newly arrived at Jurassic Park, and two more are covered in mud.

Park-issue raincoat

Dennis Nedry This two-faced techie shows his most unpleasant side in Dilophosaurus Ambush (76958), then gets sprayed with Dilophosaurus venom.

Uncertain smile can become a definite grimace

2019 variant has knotted tie and lab coat print

Ray Arnold When Jurassic Park's defenses start to come undone, so do its chief engineer's top button and tie.

Ronal This respected shaman and her warrior husband, Tonowari, are the most important Na'vi in the Metkayina Reef Home (75578).

Tattoos for the Metkayina clan are symbolic and tell stories of their lives

Shell necklace serves a ceremonial purpose

Recom team badge

Flak jacket with equipment pouches

Skirt made from shells and seagrass

RDA Quaritch This year's human/Na'vi Recom version of Quaritch is just as unlikable as his fully human 2022 variant!

Spider Spider was an orphan raised by the remaining humans on Pandora after the RDA were expelled. He is the Sully family's best human friend.

Exo-mask allows Spider to breathe on Pandora

Body paint mimics Na'vi stripes

LEGO AVATAR

The second year of LEGO Avatar sets focused on sequel movie *Avatar: The Way of Water*. Large brick-built versions of the film's fabulous oceangoing creatures included a skimwing, an ilu, and Payakan the tulkun. Meanwhile, new RDA tech builds included a Mako submarine and an RDA Crab suit. Diving in to explore this beautiful, aquatic biome were 14 all-new minifigures and figures.

Messier hairstyle than most Na'vi

Lightweight top decorated with marine algae

Kiri Like the other young Na'vi in this year's sets, Kiri's minifigure has standard-length arms and legs.

LEGO SEASONAL

Just one Lunar New Year set came with minifigures in 2023, but it came with more than any previous seasonal set! The 18 merrymakers in Lunar New Year Parade (80111) comprised two masked flagbearers, five musicians, four costumed LEGO fans, a Year of the Rabbit mascot, and six spectators in everyday dress. All traveled on or flocked around three magnificent floats.

Masked Performers This flag-waving pair come with standard minifigure heads, as well as oversized ones representing traditional *dai tou fut* masks.

Matching Year of the Rabbit *tangzhuang* jackets

Large head mold first used for a LEGO Marvel Thanos figure in 2021

Flags offer a springtime blessing

First ever purple air tanks

Purple Astronaut Parader Four performers ride a LEGO themed float in costumes reflecting the Space, Castle, Pirates, and NINJAGO play themes.

LEGO brick emblem on jacket

Printed sweat suggests a hot helmet!

Alternative face wears ordinary glasses

Scarf and cable-knit sweater ideal for New Year

Spectacled Spectator As well as watching the parade, this bystander is looking to the future in his rabbit-ear glasses!

Same hair piece as Jin from BTS Dynamite

I'M FAST, BUT I'M NOT AT ALL FURIOUS!

Fine stitching continues on back

Pagani Utopia Driver With detailed printing, including an authentic Pagani logo, this driver can turn heads even without his car!

DID YOU KNOW?
Two minifigure ice skates are included in the Pagani Utopia set to create some of the intricate bodywork.

First Speed Champions minifigure with arms molded in two colors

Face print based on actor Paul Walker

Brian O'Conner There's no mistaking the minifigure behind the wheel of the *2 Fast 2 Furious* Nissan Skyline GT-R (R34) (76917).

LEGO® SPEED CHAMPIONS

Alongside theme stalwarts Ferrari, Porsche, and McLaren, 2023's Speed Champions sets added hypercar manufacturer Pagani to the mix. Several new parts and unusual building techniques were used to create the unique Pagani Utopia (76915), and a suitably distinctive minifigure was provided to drive it! The theme also gained another movie-star car and driver, this time from *2 Fast 2 Furious*.

LEGO Minifigure The first brick-built minifigure (3723), released in 2000, was also the first supersized LEGO display set of any kind. Made from 1,850 pieces, it stood 18 in (45 cm) tall, with arms and hands that could move like a real minifigure's.

LEGO® Originals Wooden Minifigure Back in the 1930s, master craftsman Ole Kirk Kristiansen crafted the first LEGO toys from wood. In 2019, this 8-in (20-cm) statue (853967) was created to honor that tradition, combining sustainably sourced oak with a selection of brick-built accessories.

Harry Potter & Hermione Granger The first model minifigures (76393) to be fully posable launched in 2021. They use hidden LEGO® Technic parts for their joints. Both stand 10 in (26 cm) tall and wield brick-built wands. Harry's look is completed by a fabric cape.

A Minifigure Tribute This impressive LEGO® Pirate (40504) stands 2.5 in (6 cm) taller than Harry and Hermione, thanks to his hat, epaulettes, and display stand. He was designed especially for sale at the LEGO® House visitor attraction in Billund, Denmark, in 2023.

Scaled-up LEGO Minifigure Released in 2023, the fourth supersized minifigure (40649) to be built in the same way as Harry, Hermione, and A Minifigure Tribute comes with a hidden surprise. Lift the classic LEGO cap and you'll find a matching minifigure running a tiny control room!

MEGA MINIFIGURES

Once, all LEGO® figures were built from bricks. Then came the LEGO minifigure. Now, those little characters have become so iconic, you can build big ones from bricks as well! Since the year 2000, four large-scale sets have celebrated the unique appeal of minifigures in brick sculpture form, while a fifth achieved the same thing using wood. No two are quite the same, but all share the classic proportions and timeless charm that made the originals such a success. Mini may well be beautiful, but for these adorable display pieces, mega is the only way to go!

Adventure Peely Fortnite's famous yellow fellow looks more a-peeling than ever in minifigure form, with a unique banana head piece.

Large head piece covers front and back of standard torso

"NANA" belt buckle print

2024

FEW CORNERS OF POPULAR culture went without a minifigure or mini doll in 2024, as the LEGO Group joined forces with *Fortnite*, *Animal Crossing*, *Wicked*, *Wednesday*, *Dungeons & Dragons*, and more. Big-screen characters from *Dune* and *Jaws* became minifigures, while superstar Pharrell Williams put himself on the big screen as a minifigure! Amid all these new collabs, there was also time to celebrate the one that started it all, as LEGO® *Star Wars*™ turned 25.

LEGO® FORTNITE®

The online world of LEGO Fortnite launched in late 2023, putting a new, cooperative spin on the global gaming phenomenon. Just like the original game, LEGO Fortnite offered vast worlds of adventure, only this time you played as a minifigure and had access to a bottomless box of bricks! Four real-world sets based on the game followed in 2024.

Head molded in three colors, with black printing

Fur and tattoo printing on one arm

Meowscles A small head gives this pumped-up pussycat an extra beefy look, despite a standard-sized torso.

Tail piece attaches between legs and torso

Unmasked face A hair piece can replace the mask.

Helmet shape created for 2019's Galactic Bounty Hunter collectible Minifigure

Shoulder armor first seen in LEGO® NINJAGO® sets

Changing style Removing the helmet creates the alternative "Trespasser Cubed" look.

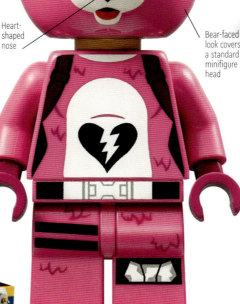

Heart-shaped nose

Bear-faced look covers a standard minifigure head

Trespasser Elite Some LEGO Fortnite characters are more serious-looking than others, such as this imposing alien android.

Cuddle Team Leader Unlike Peely and Meowscles, this teddy bear's head is actually a mask, covering a friendly human face.

Battle Bus All nine of this year's Fortnite minifigures are exclusive to this set (77073). The other sets in the initial range were all larger than minifigure scale.

LEGO® DUPLO®

Preschool favorite Peppa Pig joined the LEGO DUPLO range this year. She was accompanied by four family members (Daddy Pig, Mummy Pig, Grandpa Pig, and brother George) and friends Pedro Pony and Suzy Sheep.

New head piece

LEGO DUPLO body parts are not detachable

Swappable fabric skirt

Peppa Pig Across four sets, Peppa wears this spotted dress, one plain one, one flowery one, and a swimming costume.

LEGO® ANIMAL CROSSING™

A charming village where friendly animals run shops, drive cars, and fly planes? No, it's not the return of LEGO® FABULAND™—it's LEGO Animal Crossing! Based on the gentle video game of the same name, this new play theme captured all the magic of the online original. Eight sets with 14 unique minifigures were released in this first year.

Town hall variant wears a hoodie and pants

Isabelle This civic-minded Shih Tzu works at the town hall and visits a friend's house in a pair of 2024 sets.

Smart outfit for visiting Fauna the deer

Molded skirt worn over short legs

Rosie One of two friendly felines in this year's range, Rosie is named after her cheeks, which glow through her fur!

Headwear accessory slot

Same head mold as fellow feline Tangy

Tail piece sandwiched between legs and torso

All Animal Crossing heads are new this year

Posable medium-length legs

Bunnie Clad in plaid for a camping trip, this apple-red rabbit gets back to nature in Bunnie's Outdoor Activities (77047).

Plaid print continues on back

Julian This haughty horse is the only minifigure in Julian's Birthday Party (77046). The other guests must be running late!

Detachable party hat

Out-of-this-world hoodie

Standard-length legs

LEGO® WICKED

Highly anticipated movie *Wicked* flew into theaters in 2024, with key characters magicked into mini dolls for three LEGO sets. Glinda and Elphaba appeared in them all, alongside Nessarose, Fiyero, Madame Morrible, and the Wizard.

Detachable bow in new hair piece

Glinda Three variants of Elphaba's best friend chart her journey from popular student to glamorous gal.

Glinda arrives at Shiz University in this outfit

Exclusive witch's-hat-and-hair piece

Classic LEGO FABULAND broom

Elphaba Differently dressed variants of this misunderstood witch make her the first-ever (and second, and third) green-skinned mini doll!

Long, fabric cape

LEGO® THE LEGEND OF ZELDA™

Inspired by the long-running video game series, LEGO *The Legend of Zelda* launched with just one set—but what a set! Standing up to 13 in (33 cm) tall, with 2,500 pieces, Great Deku Tree 2-in-1 (77092) let fans recreate the saga's friendly forest guardian in two distinct but equally impressive forms. Four minifigures completed the unique display piece.

Alternative face is sleeping

Unique hair-and-ears piece

Hair-hat-and-ears piece shared with Young Link variant

Choice of stern and shouting faces

Exclusive ocarina accessory

Link Three variants of the series' hero, Link, include this one based on 1998's groundbreaking *Ocarina of Time* game.

Zelda The wise princess of Hyrule is depicted in her adventuring gear from 2017's acclaimed *Breath of the Wild*.

Printed Sheikah Slate tile

LEGO® WEDNESDAY

Hit TV show *Wednesday* was the subject of three sets in 2024. Two featured large, brick-built characters, while a third starred mini doll versions of Wednesday Addams and Enid Sinclair, plus a special Thing figure.

New hair piece with two long braids

Wednesday The youngest member of the Addams family wears her Nevermore Academy uniform in Wednesday & Enid's Dorm Room (76781).

Nevermore Academy badge

Wrist can be gripped by a mini doll

Piece grips onto a LEGO knob

Thing Whenever Wednesday needs a hand, she turns to this Addams family friend. The special piece is larger than a minifigure hand.

25 GLORIOUS YEARS

None of this year's anniversary minifigures had been depicted in LEGO form before, despite being fan-favorite characters. Each one came with a brick-built plinth, printed with a "25 Years of LEGO Star Wars" logo.

Exclusive Sullustan head piece

Same flying suit also worn in the sequel trilogy

Nien Nunb This Sullustan co-piloted the *Millennium Falcon* in the Battle of Endor, so fully deserves his long-awaited minifigure!

LEGO *STAR WARS*

Now officially longer-lasting than the Galactic Empire, LEGO *Star Wars* celebrated its quarter-century in 2024. To mark the occasion, six sets came with special anniversary minifigures, while a seventh included an anniversary astromech droid. Elsewhere, it was business as usual with sets based on all the latest streaming shows, and business very much *not* as usual in *Rebuild the Galaxy* sets!

Unique head with smiling and frowning faces

Young Leia Okay, this isn't the first ever Leia minifigure, but it is the first of her young self from *Obi-Wan Kenobi*.

Leia's droid, Lola, is a single printed piece

Unique jaw piece covers printed vocabulator

Same narrow cape shape as the Mandalorian

Darth Malak This Sith Lord is the main villain in much-loved video game *Star Wars: Knights of the Old Republic*.

Hair piece first worn by Luke Skywalker, in a dark tan color

Neutral look can be swapped for gritted teeth

Lamellar armor undershirt print

DID YOU KNOW?
Other 25th anniversary minifigures included clone trooper Fives and video game hero Cal Kestis.

Ezra Bridger Last seen as a teen in *Star Wars Rebels*, Ezra returns as an adult Jedi in one *Ahsoka* set.

Hair piece first worn in LEGO® Disney *Encanto* sets

Alternative expression looks alarmed

At-Attin middle school uniform jacket

Cybernetic visor is raised on other face print

Gadgets stored in top pocket

Medium-length legs

KB A cybernetic link-up between KB and starship The *Onyx Cinder* (75374) opens the door to a galaxy of trouble.

Wim This adventure-prone schoolboy is one of four lost kids trying to find their way home in *Skeleton Crew*.

No other character wears this braided bun

Powerful Blade of Talzin

Annoyed expression can be swapped for an enraged one

2023 variant has a skirt instead of legs

Morgan Elspeth This *Ahsoka* villain debuted in a 2023 set, but her scary Nightsister tattoos are new for 2024.

LIVE-ACTION TV

New live-action show *Star Wars: Skeleton Crew* premiered in December 2024, but LEGO fans could build its lead ship, The *Onyx Cinder* (75374), from August. Other summer sets focused on *Ahsoka* and *The Mandalorian*.

Similar features to Ortolan species

Unique head mold

Jetpack piece designed for 2019's First Order Jet Trooper

Neel Wim's bestie looks a bit like musician Max Rebo, but is actually the first minifigure member of his species.

Short, nonposable legs

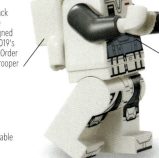

Mandalorian-style T-shaped visor

Blaster-proof beskar alloy armor

Imperial Commando Just like the Praetorian Guard, these Imperial holdouts are tougher than stormtroopers, with Mandalorian-influenced armor.

Helmets reminiscent of the Emperor's Royal Guard

Armor akin to standard stormtrooper gear

Brick-built energy weapon

Praetorian Guard The Empire has fallen by the time of *The Mandalorian*, but these red remnants are out to revive it.

REBUILD THE GALAXY

When a Force-sensitive nerf herder rewrites reality, rebels turn into bounty hunters, Jedi become Sith, and stormtroopers end up as fish! That's the premise for the animated miniseries LEGO *Star Wars: Rebuild the Galaxy* and its three tie-in sets.

> MESA BERRY, BERRY, BERRY BAD BINKS!

Gungan booma bomb

Double-bladed lightsaber

No need for a cape with these ears

Jedi Vader This is not snow Vader from an advent calendar set. This is *Rebuild the Galaxy*'s Lord of Lightness.

Mask covers a kindly, smiling face

Blue and green details echo Jedi lightsaber colors

Darth Jar Jar Everyone's favorite Gungan shows his Sith side in *Rebuild the Galaxy*—in a double act with Darth Rey.

YOUNG JEDI ADVENTURES

The second set based on animated series *Star Wars: Young Jedi Adventures* completed the line-up of main characters begun in 2023. Nash Durango flew The *Crimson Firehawk* (75384), while Nubs traveled on a speeder bike.

One-of-a-kind Pooba head piece

Leaf design on lightsaber sheath

Neck bracket for carrying droid pal RJ-83

First minifigure to wear this hair piece

Nubs Much like his teacher, Yoda, this Jedi Youngling should not be judged by his size or super-cute appearance.

Nash Durango Whenever Nubs and his Youngling friends need non-Jedi advice, they turn to this tweenage mechanic and pilot.

LEGO *DISNEY*

Following on from 2023's Disney 100 celebrations, Snow White and the Seven Dwarfs' Cottage (43242) continued the trend for minifigures in larger, more complex Disney sets. This time, Snow White, the Prince, and the Evil Queen all returned from last year's range, while the Seven themselves were all brand new. The 2,208-piece build also came with six adorable animal figures.

New short beard piece shared with Happy and Sneezy

Six of the Seven wear this new hat piece

Kiss from Snow White on forehead

Hat-with-ears mold first used for 2013's Holiday Elf Minifigure

Doc The self-appointed leader of the Seven is a welcoming soul, and his minifigure has two equally friendly smiles.

All seven friends have short minifigure legs

Same hat as Doc, but worn the other way around

Choice of drowsy face or full-on yawn!

Each dwarf has his own jewel-mining tool

New long beard piece shared with Bashful and Grumpy

Sleepy It's hard work digging for diamonds every day, and Sleepy doesn't hide the effect it has on him!

Dopey The only one of the Seven not to wear a beard is also the only one to keep his ears outside his hat.

LEGO *INSIDE OUT 2*

New mini dolls in this year's LEGO *Disney* sets included characters from *Ariel* and Joy from *Inside Out 2*. The latter came with brick-built and micro doll companions in *Inside Out 2* Mood Cubes (43248).

First mini doll to wear this hairstyle

Shiny sparks of joy printed on dress

Unique head with pained expression

Neon yellow helmet first seen in LEGO® City in 2022

Round body piece also used to make snow figures and lanterns

Standard micro doll body with unique printing

Joy The first Emotion ever felt by Riley in the *Inside Out* movies is also the first to become a mini doll.

Anxiety Riley's teenage years are full of strange new feelings, including this little bundle of doom and doubt!

Margie The set comes with two brick-built Mind Workers to carry out repairs and upgrades on the Emotions' control console.

Botanical Garden Visitor
Face print used to represent a blind or visually impaired person

This minifigure follows in the footsteps of LEGO® Friends mini doll Savannah, who first used a white cane in 2021.

Cane is a LEGO® Harry Potter™ wand piece

LEGO® IDEAS

More LEGO Ideas sets hit the shelves in 2024 than in any previous year. Of the 10 fan-designed releases, six came with minifigures. The largest was The Botanical Garden (21353), with 3,792 pieces. Its 12 minifigures included one who got around with help from a white cane.

Hair can be swapped for hood in villain mode

Male and female Merry/Ervan heads supplied

Merry Rumwell/Ervan Soulfallen A double-sided head lets you switch this character from seemingly innocent innkeeper to villainous wizard.

DUNGEONS & DRAGONS

Marking 50 years of the tabletop role-playing game Dungeons & Dragons: Red Dragon's Tale (21348) was an epic 3,745-piece depiction of Cinderhowl the Red Dragon and various other beasts menacing a minifigure-scale fortress.

Detachable horns

Dragon's head mold first used in 2021

Female head can be shown smiling or frowning

Coin bags hang from belt

Alax Jadescales This member of the Dragonborn species is the set's true innkeeper, imprisoned by pesky Ervan Soulfallen.

Torso print follows line of shoulder pads

Alternative, green-eyed face shows Bruno seeing the future

Alternative face is blowing a raspberry!

Same hair as 2023 Pocahontas minifigure

Lilo Eight years after Stitch became a minifigure, the other star of *Lilo & Stitch* surfed into her first LEGO set.

Bruno's visions turn into emerald slabs

Traditional *ruana* garment print

Bruno The first minifigure to be based on 2021's *Encanto* depicts the future-foretelling uncle of main character Mirabel Madrigal.

MAGIC OF DISNEY

Conjuring memories of seven classic movies, Magic of Disney (21352) centered on a large, brick-built Mickey Mouse. The surrounding vignettes included minifigures, animal figures, and brick-built broom figures.

New hair piece with pointed ears

JAWS

Film's most famous shark got a bite of the LEGO action in Jaws (21350). The 1,497-piece display set showed the greatest of great whites rising up from the waves to attack the fishing boat *Orca*.

Simple, plain clothes for shark hunting

Worried face can be swapped for a relieved one

Authentic 1970s sideburns

Brody In Steven Spielberg's *Jaws*, this police chief is the first to take the threat of a giant shark seriously.

Quint The captain of the *Orca* is an experienced shark hunter, but this time he might need a bigger boat!

Easily detachable legs

Elf Wizard Like Merry Rumwell/Ervan Soulfallen, this adventurer comes with two head pieces, so the character can be male or female.

LEGO® MINIFIGURES

If the 25th series of collectible Minifigures had a theme, it would be animals. Besides a Pet Groomer and a Goatherd, there were characters in dinosaur- and bat-themed costumes, plus a detective with a red herring. Series 26 was definitively themed around outer space, while the Dungeons & Dragons Series was all about swords, sorcery, and scary brain-eating monsters.

Unique eaglelike head

New wings piece

Anima legs first used for Faun in 2016

Aarakocra Ranger Also known as bird folk, the Aarakocra are mostly peaceful, but slow to trust anyone who can't fly.

Flexible mask fits over plain black head piece

Exclusive cape, cut into ribbons

DUNGEONS & DRAGONS SERIES

The 12 characters in this series were technically 17, as five came with male and female heads. Together, they expanded the world that began with the single LEGO Ideas Dungeons & Dragons set earlier in the year.

New lightning and dragon accessories

Exclusive hair-and-horns piece

Option to have smiling or stern face

Tiefling Sorcerer Part human, part infernal being, tieflings can see in the dark and cloak themselves in darkness at will.

Male head

Scary, squidlike tentacles

Armor printed on arms and torso

Mind Flayer These cunning creatures are drawn to big brains. They acquire all the knowledge of each one they eat!

Lady of Pain The all-powerful ruler of the city of Sigil answers to no one, so don't even try to ask.

Transparent brick for "levitation"

LEGO® MONKIE KID™

Five Color Stones were spread across this year's Monkie Kid sets. Collecting them all gave MK the power to save the universe. Of course, the quest was not an easy one, and MK met many new demons along the way. Fans who followed the adventure in Asia could also collect a special Monkey King minifigure, marking the theme's fifth birthday.

Crown is part of hair piece

100-Eyed Demon This centipede demon sees all and can make his enemies relive the memories they would rather forget.

Eyes printed all over torso and legs

Helmet also worn by LEGO® City Stuntz bikers

Digital display visor printed on head

Glittery DJ suit with shoulder pads

Halolike ring built onto shoulder armor

Gold Horn Demon This year's largest set, Megapolis City (80054), is full of reformed villains—including this demon-turned-DJ.

Unique printed hair piece

Nüwa The Goddess of Destiny is surrounded by the five powerful Color Stones she created in Celestial Pagoda (80058).

Lower body style first seen in LEGO NINJAGO sets

Turning the head reveals a "blowing out candles" face

Detachable party hat

Printed novelty sunglasses

Unique snake "hair" piece

Party Monkey King This minifigure topped the limited-edition gift-with-purchase set, Monkie Kid 5th Anniversary Cake (6476261).

Same ragged cloak shape as Orc collectible Minifigure

Nine-headed Demon The Tenth King of the Underworld has one standard minifigure head and eight tiny snake heads for hair.

Printed armor plating looks like snake scales

SERIES 25

As well as the Minifigures shown here, series 25 also featured a Mushroom Sprite with a butterfly friend; an E-Sports Gamer with a retro LEGO® Castle vibe; and a Train Kid with a colorful eyepatch.

Exclusive Afghan hound figure

New ponytail-and-cochlear-implant piece

Pet Groomer This dog lover is one of two 2024 minifigures to mitigate hearing loss with a cochlear implant.

Dog hairs all over apron

Unique fedora piece with pulled-down brim

Film Noir Detective Straight out of a 1940s crime drama, this grayscale gumshoe is on the trail of something fishy!

"Red herring" is a term for a misleading clue

Turned-up collar is a unique fabric piece

Unique prosthetic legs piece

Double-sided head: smiling or sweating

Sprinter This athlete is the first minifigure to have two realistic leg prosthetics. He comes with a winner's podium accessory.

SERIES 26

This space-themed series included a realistic astronaut, several unusual robots and aliens, and characters inspired by 1990s LEGO® Space factions Blacktron II, M:Tron, and Ice Planet 2002. There was even a Minifigure version of a constellation!

Dome fits over standard head shape

Gold-colored hands

Legs and feet are one unique piece

Robot Butler This house-of-the-future helper will whip up your breakfast, then vacuum the floor with its feet!

New helmet can be swapped for a red hair piece

Energy saw for cutting through ice

Ice Planet Explorer Classic LEGO Space fans will get chills from this update to 1993's Ice Planet Woman.

Robo-penguin pal with Ice Planet 2002 logo

Hairstyle first seen on series 25's Sprinter

Starlike glitter molded into head, legs, and arms

Constellation of Orion printed on shield

Orion The constellation of Orion is named after a character from Ancient Greek myth. This Minifigure combines the two!

New helmet piece with fixed-position visor

New suit piece with classic LEGO Space logo

Orange City Astronaut Five of this year's astronauts wear light orange space suits with knobs on the back for mission-specific builds.

Adjustable solar panels built onto backpack

Helmet style first worn by LEGO® NEXO KNIGHTS™

Unique eyepiece print

A LITTLE GREEN MAN? WHERE?

Green City Astronaut Six green-clad Space Explorers wear a style of backpack first used by the LEGO City Sky Police.

SPACE EXPLORERS

This year's City space sets had more of a sci-fi edge than earlier Mars Exploration and Spaceport subthemes. They included a Modular Space Station (60433), an Interstellar Spaceship (60429), and a Space Construction Mech (60428).

Standard minifigure head element

Legs are an upside-down crown piece

Printed dome brick also found in one LEGO Friends space set

This piece is most often used to make leaves and flower petals

Six-legged Alien This friendly-looking extraterrestrial is able to keep one eye on all three sets in which it appears.

Four-legged Alien What this alien lacks in legs compared to its friend, it more than makes up for with cuteness.

LEGO CITY

It was a year of big discoveries for LEGO City minifigures as the Jungle Exploration team encountered all-new LEGO animals and Space Explorers met their first aliens! Back home, City firefighters got a striking new station and upgraded gear, burger-loving minifigures found a new favorite food truck, and the Robot World amusement park got down with a digital DJ.

Winking face on other side of head

Coat off, but gloves still on

Suspenders hold up protective pants

Firefighter in Suspenders Fire crews don't wear full uniform all day, and this one is dressed down in between jobs.

Alternative face is wide awake

Same hair as Cole from LEGO NINJAGO

Flame-patterned pajamas

Firefighter in Pajamas He may look drowsy, but this hero sleeps in the station so he can leap into action at any time.

Jungle Explorer This year's jungle-themed sets included new gorilla and red panda figures, as well as this adventurous fellow.

There's no time to shave on a jungle adventure!

Timeless outfit, as worn by many other explorers

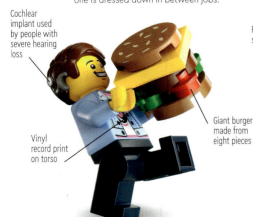

Cochlear implant used by people with severe hearing loss

Vinyl record print on torso

Giant burger made from eight pieces

Burger Truck Customer This hungry minifigure is very happy with his burger order and with his new hair-and-cochlear-implant piece.

Pixelated smiley face

Hood piece first worn by Spider-Heroes in LEGO® Marvel sets

Hoodie has scary minifigure face on the back

Robot World DJ Is it a robot DJ or is it a DJ dressed as a robot? Who cares, so long as the tunes are good!

DID YOU KNOW?
The giant mech suit in Robot World (60421) is based on a 2006 LEGO® EXO-FORCE™ set.

LEGO HARRY POTTER

The magic word in this year's Harry Potter range was *Engorgio*, with large-scale sets including a buildable Buckbeak, a life-size Mandrake, and a spectacular Sorting Hat that really talked! Things were no less impressive at minifigure scale, with a towering new Durmstrang ship and the largest standalone version of Hogwarts Great Hall so far—complete with mighty Mountain Troll!

Face molded into folds of Sorting Hat

This relieved smile can be swapped for a concentrating face

Harry in Sorting Hat The Talking Sorting Hat (76429) came with a sound brick with 31 phrases and this unique Harry.

Bowler hat first worn by 2012's Businessman collectible Minifigure

Pinstripe suit helps Crouch pass as a Muggle

Barty Crouch Sr. This long-awaited minifigure welcomes the Durmstrang and Beauxbatons delegations to Hogwarts in Triwizard Tournament: The Arrival (76440).

Smile can be swapped for a ghostly snarl

Fat Friar Hufflepuff's house ghost materializes as a one-of-a-kind minifigure in Hogwarts Castle: The Great Hall (76435).

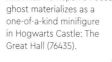

Hairstyle originally designed for Ron Weasley

Exclusive face print

Hufflepuff house colors

Rigid skirt piece fits over legs

Leanne This smiling student is one of three to debut in this year's Great Hall, along with Daphne Greengrass and Terry Boot.

More muscular arms than 2002 variant

Head, body, and clothes are all one piece

Mountain Troll Hogwarts' resident troll has clearly been working out since his last set appearance in 2002!

Each foot is as wide as two minifigure legs

LEGO® DREAMZzz™

The future of dreaming hung by a thread in the second year, as the vengeful Never Witch began stealing memories. She set out to undo the dream world, and only the dream chasers could stop her hypnotic rise. For our heroes, that meant facing their own twisted reflections, coming to grips with the stealthy Sandman, and dreaming bigger than ever before.

Unique hair-and-crown component

One of two villainous faces

Big boots, for stomping on people's dreams

Never Witch This nightmare creature doesn't like change! She's out to extinguish creativity and growth in the dream world.

Jeweler's loupe (magnifying glass) for detailed repair work

Sandy speckles all over body

Sandman Don't let this dream creature slip through your fingers—he can mend your broken hourglass and remember your forgotten dreams.

Same hairstyle as Izzie, but dark

Spiky shoulder armor instead of soft, flowing cape

Hypnotic swirl replaces Izzie's hourglass belt buckle

Dizzy This creepy copy of dream chaser Izzie is one of several dark doppelgangers created by the Never Witch.

Exclusive beanie-hat-and-hair piece

New vest piece also worn by Mateo and his doppelganger

Robot Cooper In "dreamgineer" mode, Cooper conjures up a robotic look for himself along with a cool new puffer vest.

New hair-and-ears piece

Standard minifigure head

Unique animal body

Sneak This catlike Grimspawn found a new home with the dream chasers after the defeat of the Nightmare King.

BARAD-DÛR

The glowing Eye of Sauron tops this terrifying tower, casting a baleful gaze over nine exclusive minifigures and one new Gollum figure. The finished build stands 33 in (83 cm) tall and features 5,471 pieces.

Sauron The actual Lord of the Rings was last seen in a 2013 set, in his "Necromancer of Dol Guldur" guise.

Fiery face print visible through eye holes

Combined helmet-and-shoulder-armor piece

Bare head has wisps of white hair printed on the back

Armor plate printing continues on legs

Gothmog This Orc general was absent from the original LEGO® *The Lord of the Rings™* range and seems none too happy about it!

Helmeted Orc This grisly gladiator is one of five Orcs in *The Lord of the Rings*: Barad-dûr (10333).

Unique gladiator-style helmet

Stern expression can be swapped for neutral look

Distinctive *Uruk-hai* sword

SHACKLETON'S LIFEBOAT

Two of this year's sets celebrated early Antarctic explorer Sir Ernest Shackleton. The 3,011-piece *Endurance* (10335) recreated his famous ship at 1:55 scale, while Shackleton's Lifeboat (40729) was a much smaller set in minifigure scale.

Hat first worn by LEGO® *Indiana Jones*

Face also seen in LEGO® Icons *The Lord of the Rings*: Rivendell (10316)

Torso print shared with a LEGO Harry Potter wizard

Ernest Shackleton Minifigures of this real-life expedition leader and his photographer Frank Hurley are found only in Shackleton's Lifeboat (40729).

OVER THE MOON

In documentary movie *Piece by Piece*, music megastar Pharrell Williams tells his life story through LEGO animation. This tie-in set put Pharrell at the controls of his own space shuttle, leaving a rainbow trail behind him!

Hat can be swapped for black-and-gold space helmet

Exclusive Pharrell face print

Golden shuttle emblem

Pharrell Williams Minifigure versions of Pharrell and his wife Helen Lasichanh wear matching space suits in the Over the Moon set.

PHARRELL'S PHRIENDS

Over the Moon (10391) comes with 49 extra minifigure heads in seven different skin tones for making custom astronauts. Pharrell's "Phriends" can also be displayed in their own brick-built frame.

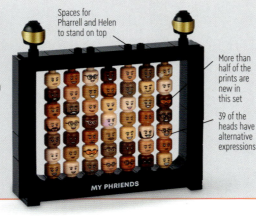

Spaces for Pharrell and Helen to stand on top

More than half of the prints are new in this set

39 of the heads have alternative expressions

MY PHRIENDS

LEGO® ICONS

By far the largest of the year's LEGO Icons sets was *The Lord of the Rings*: Barad-dûr (10333). *Dune* Atreides Royal Ornithopter (10327) explored another epic fantasy world, while Shackleton's Lifeboat (40729) celebrated real-life adventure. Another set blurred the lines between fantasy and reality, going Over the Moon with Pharrell Williams (10391).

Robe covers plain black torso and legs

Unique face print

ATREIDES ROYAL ORNITHOPTER

The insectlike flying machine from the *Dune* film series is recreated in this 1,369-piece build, complete with folding and flapping wings. Eight characters in minifigure form added further spice to the set.

Stillsuit printing shared with two other minifigures

Side-on hawk symbols on collar

Front-facing hawk symbol on chest

Alternative face wears a stillsuit mask

"Floating" effect achieved with transparent elements

Paul Atreides This young member of noble House Atreides looks every inch the royal heir in his green dress uniform.

Chani Kynes Like the rest of her Fremen tribe, Chani has piercing blue eyes and wears a desert-survival stillsuit.

Baron Harkonnen *Dune*'s anti-grav antagonist floats above his foes in a robe three times as long as he is!

LEGO® EXCLUSIVE

One of the greats of 19th-century French literature was celebrated in Tribute to Jules Verne's Books (40690). Given away free with certain purchases at LEGO.com, the 351-piece set was shaped like a pop-up book, with vehicles from Verne's adventure stories bursting out of the pages. Verne himself was included in minifigure form.

Face print shared with Obi-Wan Kenobi from LEGO *Star Wars*

Suit print shared with LEGO® Batman butler, Alfred

Jules Verne The *Around the World in Eighty Days* author is shown here as an older gentleman of letters, circa 1880.

LEGO MARVEL SUPER HEROES

Everyone's favorite mutants returned this year, first in X-Men X-Jet (76281), then in the 3,093-piece X-Men: The X-Mansion (76294), aimed at adult fans. *Spidey and His Amazing Friends* sets continued to delight younger builders, while everybody enjoyed a sneak peek of 2025 movie Marvel Studios' *Captain America: Brave New World*.

X-MEN

The 10 mutant minifigures in this year's sets take their inspiration from *X-Men: The Animated Series* and Marvel Animation's *X-Men '97*. The line-up includes the first LEGO versions of Professor X, Gambit, and Iceman.

Exclusive hair-and-mask piece

Lightning-bolt mask also printed on head

One-of-a-kind head-and-shoulders piece

TV-screen face print

Rare arms designed for 2012's LEGO® Monster Fighters theme

Zola This robot wrongdoer is made from just three pieces.

Electro The *Spidey and His Amazing Friends* version of this classic villain is a tech-tampering tearaway called Francine Frye.

Medium-length legs

Ghost-Spider The fifth *Spidey and His Amazing Friends* variant of Gwen Stacy is the first to have web-wings.

SPIDEY AND HIS AMAZING FRIENDS
Made for kids aged 4 and over, these sets combine large "starter bricks" and simple building steps with bold and iconic minifigures.

Hairband is printed on head

White streak printed on hair piece

Short jacket worn over bodysuit

Rogue Appearing in both of this year's X-Men sets, Rogue can absorb other people's memories, talents, and super-powers.

Alternative face is smiling

Body armor worn under trenchcoat

Gambit Former crook Remy LeBeau can make objects move with explosive force. His eyes are pink with pent-up energy!

Scuffed metal knee pads

Wings made from 12 pieces, including neck bracket

Falcon Pilot Joaquin Torres is the latest Falcon, wearing an updated version of Sam Wilson's old EXO-7 wing-suit.

More colorful costume than previous Marvel Cinematic Universe Falcons

MARVEL STUDIOS' CAPTAIN AMERICA: BRAVE NEW WORLD
In Captain America vs. Red Hulk Battle (76292), the Sam Wilson incarnation of Cap takes on a raging Red Hulk with help from a new-look Falcon and former Black Widow agent Ruth Bat-Seraph.

Red Hulk The latest Red Hulk figure has a turning head, making him more posable than his 2017 counterpart.

Head fits on like a minifigure's

Large hair piece shared with green Hulk figures

Mr. Pale Like Tox, the Elemental Master of Light looks back to LEGO® Ultra Agents—specifically the see-through Invizable.

Sunglasses printed on transparent head piece

Same hat as 2015's Invizable minifigure

Energy claws are built out from a neck bracket

Dollar signs on shirt echo Invizable's dollar-bill design

Hair first seen in a LEGO Friends set

Skull symbol often seen on poison bottles

Torn pants print

Tox The Elemental Master of Poison is inspired by Toxikita, a venomous villain from 2015's LEGO Ultra Agents range.

DID YOU KNOW?
The Wolf Mask Warrior's energy claw piece is also wielded by X-Men minifigure Gambit.

Mask hides similarly scary face prints

Smaller claws fit into hands

LEGO NINJAGO

The second year of *Ninjago: Dragons Rising* proved even more explosive than the first. The expanded ninja team made new dragon friends, battled Wolf Mask Warriors, and sparred with other Elemental Masters in an all-or-nothing tournament. Each ninja team member got at least one new look, with the most surprising being the dark blue Evil Jay.

Wolf Mask Warrior The scariest of six Wolf Mask Warrior variants has huge red energy claws coming out of its back!

Choice of sly smile or gleeful grin

Harley Quinn Harley was created for *Batman: The Animated Series*, so naturally appears in both this year's tribute sets.

One red leg with black printing, one black leg with red printing

Molded cape flares out behind

New legs molded in black and gray

Batman Despite crusading in a brand-new rubber cape, Batman still fits comfortably inside the cockpit of his Batmobile.

WHEN DO I GET A CATMOBILE?

First LEGO Catwoman to wear gray

Catwoman In *Batman: The Animated Series*, Catwoman commits some crimes for ethical reasons and others purely for kicks!

Gold disc chain belt— probably stolen!

LEGO® DC SUPER HEROES

LEGO Batman went back to the '90s this year in two sets inspired by *Batman: The Animated Series*. The first was a huge, Art Deco display piece: a microscale Gotham City skyline measuring 30 in (76 cm) across, with a separate stand for four minifigures. The second was *The Animated Series'* Batmobile, built in minifigure scale for play or display.

LEGO® DESPICABLE ME 4

First seen in a pair of 2020 sets, Gru and his Minions returned this year in builds based on Illumination's new movie *Despicable Me 4*. The largest set in the new range was Minions and Gru's Family Mansion (75583), which included five minifigures, three Mega Minion figures, and Gru Jr. Four more sets included another nine unique Minion characters.

Scarf piece made in gray for the first time

"G" for "Gru" on zipper

Gru Jr. made from two pieces

Alternative face wears stylish sunglasses

Lucy and Gru Jr. Lucy and Gru Jr. live in a Minion-assisted life in the Family Mansion set.

Gru Even without his famous nose, Gru is instantly recognizable by his deep-set eyes and sly smile.

Mega Minion Jerry Mega Minions in this year's sets include this bigger, boulder version of Jerry.

New rock-textured head and body parts

Printed mouth

Printed "M" on overalls

LEGO® SPEED CHAMPIONS

Though its MINI brand raced into the range in 2019, BMW waited until 2024 to put its famous initials on a Speed Champions set. The result was BMW M4 GT3 & BMW M Hybrid V8 (76922), a two-car set showcasing the range of its motorsport division. This year also saw the first NASCAR-branded Speed Champions racer, a Chevrolet Camaro ZL1.

BMW M4 GT3 Driver Both BMW racers wear the same design of overalls, but the Hybrid V8 driver's are red.

Hair echoes the flame decorations on his car

NASCAR stands for National Association for Stock Car Auto Racing

Stylized Chevrolet symbol

BMW M Motorsport logo

First Speed Champions team to have different-colored legs

NASCAR Driver This racer's bold colors are a perfect match for his NASCAR Next Gen Chevrolet Camaro ZL1 (76935).

LEGO® MINECRAFT®

The original *Minecraft* video game celebrated its 15th anniversary in 2024, while LEGO Minecraft minifigures turned 10. Marking the first of those milestones was The Crafting Table (21265), a 1,195-piece, cube-shaped display set that returned to the LEGO theme's microscale roots. Meanwhile, the minifigure-scale range reached its 100th release—one of 14 unveiled in this landmark year.

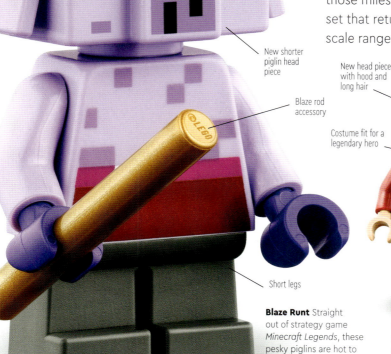

New shorter piglin head piece

Blaze rod accessory

Short legs

Blaze Runt Straight out of strategy game *Minecraft Legends*, these pesky piglins are hot to trot with their fiery rods.

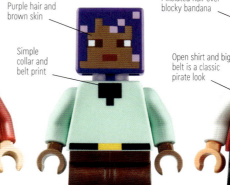

New head piece with hood and long hair

Costume fit for a legendary hero

Ranger Hero This minifigure is based on one of five looks available to players at the start of *Minecraft Legends*.

Purple hair and brown skin

Simple collar and belt print

Efe Default player skin minifigures got more diverse this year as Steve and Alex were joined by Efe and Sunny.

Pixelated hair over blocky bandana

Open shirt and big belt is a classic pirate look

Swashbuckler The first pirate player skin minifigure set sail in a 2019 set. This year, he finally got some shipmates!

LEGO® SONIC THE HEDGEHOG

Seven LEGO Sonic the Hedgehog sets were released in 2024, but Sonic himself appeared in just two. In the other five, the Blue Blur made way for a wealth of friends and foes, most of whom were making their LEGO debuts. As well as minifigure versions of Knuckles, Rouge, and Shadow, there were plenty of brick-built Badniks to battle.

Mouth set firmly shut

Air Shoes are the source of Shadow's speed

Shadow the Hedgehog The prickly antihero with a troubled past wears his trademark Air Shoes in two of this year's sets.

Knuckles This emerald-guarding echidna gets his name from his supersized fists, represented by an all-new LEGO element.

Fists clip onto standard minifigure hands

New bat-eared head piece

Wings also worn by Gargoyle and Dragon collectible Minifigures

Left and right fists are the same interchangeable part

Rouge This jewel-loving bat-burglar has her eye on the Master Emerald in Knuckles' Guardian Mech (76996).

LEGO® JURASSIC WORLD™

The Jurassic World theme explored different dinosaur scales in 2024, with a buildable baby Ankylosaurus and a showpiece Tyrannosaurus skull. But there was still room in the range for minifigure-sized sets. One continued the *Jurassic World: Camp Cretaceous* story, while two focused on its sequel, *Jurassic World: Chaos Theory*. These introduced new Stegosaurus and Allosaurus figures, alongside updates of familiar minifigures.

New head with choice of smile or look of alarm

Same hair as 2021 *Camp Cretaceous* variant

Kenji The self-proclaimed VIP of *Jurassic World: Camp Cretaceous* is older, wiser, and generally much more likable in *Jurassic World: Chaos Theory!*

Hair was worn up in 2021

Same head as *Camp Cretaceous* variant

Yaz This member of the Camp fam teams up with old friends Kenji and Darius in Dinosaur Missions: Allosaurus Transport Truck (76966).

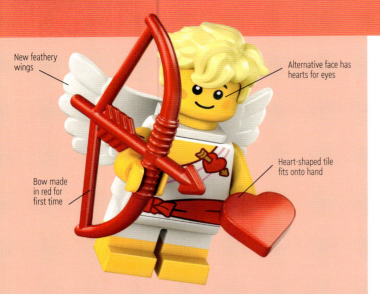

New feathery wings

Alternative face has hearts for eyes

Bow made in red for first time

Heart-shaped tile fits onto hand

Cupid What's not to love about this little angel? He's been setting hearts aflutter for more than 2,000 years!

2025

AMAZINGLY, THIS YEAR marked half a century since the first proto-minifigures appeared in LEGO® sets. These simple figures had no faces, arms, or posable legs, but hinted at whole new worlds of expressive role-play. In 2025, these worlds included ninja, Jedi, Super Heroes, wizards, dream chasers, gaming icons, and the return of a classic astronaut. It was also a bumper year for motorsport fans, as F1 minifigures raced through several themes.

LEGO® MINIFIGURES

Who could blame series 27's Astronomer Kid for looking up, when her fellow Minifigures included two characters with wings, a Jetpack Racer, and a pirate with a beautifully plumaged parrot! Keeping their feet on the ground, meanwhile, were a Bogeyman, a Cat Lover, a Hamster Costume Fan, a Plush Toy Collector, and a classic LEGO® Castle Wolfpack renegade.

Detachable horns first seen on LEGO cows

Unique monster head piece

Exclusive book cover print

Bogeyman He may look scary, but this mild thing loves nothing more than curling up with a good boo(k)!

One eye closed to see better through scope

Brick-built telescope made from nine small pieces

New prosthetic hand piece

Medium-length legs are rare in this theme

Astronomer Kid This little star always has one eye on the skies—or two if you turn her double-sided head around.

One-of-a-kind Pterodactyl helmet

Wings are part of unique arms

Talons printed on feet

Pterodactyl Costume Fan Costume party? What costume party? This prehistory lover is just going to the store!

Alternative face is a wide-eyed smile

Same hairstyle as Sora from LEGO® NINJAGO®

Hole for bows and other accessories

Snuggly lilac onesie print

Plush Toy Collector Cousins of this character's kawaii cuddly toys can also be found in this year's LEGO® DREAMZzz™ sets.

Steampunk Inventor This top-hatted tinkerer has just invented a brilliant new gadget. Now, he needs to work out what it does.

Ice cream element makes a puff of steam

Face print with monocle, sideburns, and mustache

Essential tools in pants pocket

Classic smiling face belies this baddie's reputation

Yellow Blacktron logo first used in 1987

First classic Blacktron minifigure with printed legs

I HAVE FINALLY BEEN BOOKED!

Blacktron logo on helmet

Blacktron Monochrome no more, the latest classic Blacktron minifigure adds a dash of yellow to his torso, legs, and helmet!

LEGO® EXCLUSIVE

LEGO® Space changed forever in 1987, when it got its first rival factions: Futuron and Blacktron. In 2023, the first Blacktron Astronaut to have a printed back featured in a LEGO® Icons set, and this year, their classic look was updated once again. The new Blacktron minifigure was exclusively designed for DK's LEGO *Minifigure: A Visual History*.

Bow slots into unique head piece

Detachable hat accessory

Wrists printed with feather details

Garden shop flower logo on apron

Hole for a headwear accessory

Squirrel tail piece attaches between torso and legs

Unique gingham apron print

Poppy This stylish squirrel prefers nuts, but today she's on a mission to buy seeds from Leif's garden shop.

Round brick makes a yarn bobbin

Short, nonposable legs

Leif Nature-loving Leif sells plants and seeds at his garden shop and enjoys taking his caravan into the great outdoors.

Printed coin tile

Celeste This nightbird comes with a telescope build, an astronomy book accessory, and tea things for a moonlit picnic.

Medium-length legs

Alpine dress bought from Able Sisters' clothing shop

Mabel The least prickly hedgehog you could ever hope to meet runs a clothes shop with her sister, Sable Able.

Rigid skirt element forms lower part of apron

LEGO® ANIMAL CROSSING™

Five new minifigure faces launched the second year of this cozy social gaming theme. Celeste the owl shared her favorite hobby in Stargazing with Celeste (77053); Leif the sloth welcomed Poppy the squirrel to his store in Leif's Caravan and Garden Shop (77054); and Mabel the hedgehog helped Sasha the rabbit update his wardrobe in Able Sisters Clothing Shop (77055).

Hat can be swapped for pushed-up glasses

Sasha This fashion lover can mix and match looks with a choice of three tops plus hat and sunglasses accessories.

Jazzy top selected from Able Sisters' window

Sasha's other outfit options

Hooded top has hood printing on back

"K" jacket is Sasha's default game outfit

Mask hides a pair of pointy fangs

Robes adorned with arcane symbols

Nokt The first member of the Forbidden Five to escape from Nether-Space has centuries of villainy to catch up on.

Roningasa traditionally worn by exiled samurai

Chains cannot contain Zarkt's villainy!

Zarkt The most mysterious member of the Forbidden Five hides everything but his eyes behind a unique *roningasa* hat.

New spiky shoulder armor ...

... matches new spiky torso print

Drix The Forbidden Five all wield corrupted Elemental Powers. The demonic-looking Drix is the Elemental Master of Swarm.

LEGO NINJAGO

Corrupted Elemental Masters the Forbidden Five were the ninja's main enemies in 2025. Drawing their powers from a Chaos Dragon called ThunderFang, the Five set out to free the ancient beast from its prison beneath a Dragonian village. In pursuit of this goal, they turned the peaceful Dragonian villagers into their feral followers and set them against the ninja team.

Dragon brow fits over standard minifigure head

Dragon jaw fits between head and armor

New *sandogasa* hat piece

Alternative face wears a ninja mask

Lightning print hints at true identity

Samurai X emblem on torso

Tail and wings built onto shoulder armor

Sword slots into single-shoulder armor piece

Dragonian Warrior Corrupted by the Forbidden Five, the once-noble Dragonians are now the sworn enemies of the ninja.

Rogue A blue-clad master swordsman with lightning flashes on his *gi*? Could this really be the ninja's long-lost member, Jay?

P.I.X.A.L. Whoever Rogue may be, this is definitely the ninja's other long-lost ally, appearing in her first Dragons Rising set.

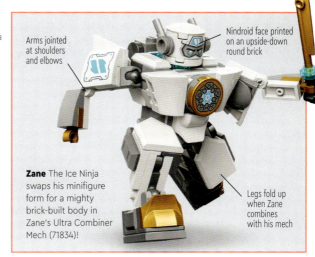

Arms jointed at shoulders and elbows

Nindroid face printed on an upside-down round brick

Zane The Ice Ninja swaps his minifigure form for a mighty brick-built body in Zane's Ultra Combiner Mech (71834)!

Legs fold up when Zane combines with his mech

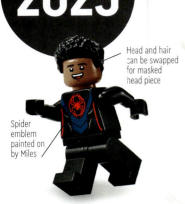

Head and hair can be swapped for masked head piece

Spider emblem painted on by Miles

Miles Morales The first Miles minifigure with an unmasked head is inspired by the movie *Spider-Man: Across the Spider-Verse*.

LEGO® MARVEL SUPER HEROES

Minifigures based on the animated *Spider-Verse* movies swung into sets for the first time this year. Classic comics were represented by the likes of Red Hulk, Anti-Venom, and Spider-Woman, while *Spidey and His Amazing Friends* sets introduced fun new dinosaur figures. The Marvel Cinematic Universe (MCU), meanwhile, was celebrated with a buildable Marvel Logo (76313), complete with five built-in Avengers.

New flexible web accessory can ensnare villains

No hair piece or accessories

The Spot This blotchy baddie makes his getaways by jumping through holes he makes in the fabric of reality.

Spots on body are dimensional portals

Same hair as 2016 Spider-Girl minifigure

Resemblance to Venom is not coincidental

Spider-Woman Julia Carpenter is the second Spider-Woman, and the second to be made into a minifigure after Jessica Drew.

Same hairstyle as 2021 civilian Gwen minifigure

Gwen Stacy Like Miles, this *Across the Spider-Verse* Gwen comes with a choice of masked and unmasked head pieces.

Updated Ghost-Spider costume with purple hands

Accessory makes a swirling alien tentacle

Similar look to Venom, but with colors reversed

Anti-Venom This shape-shifting alien repels his "brother," Venom—and Spider-Man doesn't like him much, either!

Alternative face is full Hulk without shades or facial hair

Muscular torso print includes pectoral veins

Red Hulk The minifigure version of Thaddeus Ross shows him half transformed from mustachioed man to monster.

Growl can be swapped for a rage-free smile

Torso print is similar to Red Hulk's, but hairier

Hulk Press a button on this year's buildable Marvel Logo (76313), and this MCU minifigure smashes out of one side.

Printed pilot's goggles

Trapster This *Spidey and His Amazing Friends* villain battles Ghost-Spider and a dinosaur version of Spidey in one 2025 set.

Printed utility belt

Posable, medium-length legs

Unique dinosaur figure with moving jaw

Claws can grasp minifigure accessories

Spidey-rex Team Spidey, Green Goblin, and Rhino are all turned into dinosaurs in this year's *Spidey and His Amazing Friends* sets.

LEGO® *DISNEY* LILO & STITCH

The animated stars of 2002 Disney film *Lilo & Stitch* first became minifigures in 2024 and 2016 respectively. This year, the pair returned in Lilo and Stitch Beach House (43268), updated to reflect their looks in a brand-new live-action movie. They were joined in the 834-piece set by familiar characters from both films: Nani Pelekai, David Kawena, and Cobra Bubbles.

Same hair piece as 2024 Lilo, but with printed highlights

Shorts and open-toed sandals print on blue legs

Nani Pelekai Lilo's older sister and guardian is a much-needed voice of reason in the ever-hectic Pelekai household.

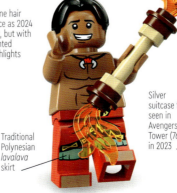

Stern face belies a good heart

Skilled performer's fire knife

Traditional Polynesian *lavalava* skirt

David Kawena When he isn't surfing or studying, Nani's laid-back boyfriend loves to show off his fire-knife dancing skills.

Silver suitcase first seen in Avengers Tower (76269) in 2023

Cobra Bubbles This secret agent-turned-social worker is surprisingly unsurprised when he learns that Stitch is an alien.

LEGO® FRIENDS

The Hidden Disabilities Sunflower lanyard was introduced across three LEGO sets. They included a resident of LEGO Icons Tudor Corner (10350), a young traveler in LEGO® DUPLO® First Time at the Airport (10443), and Ryan in LEGO Friends.

Headphones are part of head piece

Sunflower lanyard used in more than 90 countries

Ryan This mini doll wears his Hidden Disabilities Sunflower lanyard and noise-canceling headphones in Heartlake City Airport and Airplane (42656).

LEGO® STAR WARS™

Revenge of the Sith celebrated its 20th anniversary in 2025, and a new ARC-170 Starfighter (75402) marked the occasion in style. The set featured the first Phase II clone pilots since 2015 and the first R4-P44 astromech droid since 2010. It was joined in battle by the first LEGO version of Ahsoka's Jedi Interceptor (75401), from the *Clone Wars* TV series.

Unique helmet markings

Phase II clone pilot flight suit

Clone Pilot Jag This ARC-170 starfighter pilot was loyal to Jedi General Plo Koon until the Emperor issued Order 66.

Ahsoka Tano The first Ahsoka minifigure to have medium-length legs depicts the character at the start of her Jedi journey.

Confident smile can be swapped for gritted teeth

Update of outfit last worn by 2013 variant

Anakin Skywalker The latest variant of this ill-fated Jedi Knight accompanies his Padawan in Ahsoka's Jedi Interceptor (75401).

Choice of stern or scowling expressions

Black robe hints at dark side future

Identical face to fellow clone pilots

Life-support unit worn over armor

Clone Pilot Odd Ball Clone CC-2237 flew an ARC-170 in the Battle of Coruscant, alongside Anakin Skywalker and Obi-Wan Kenobi.

LEGO DREAMZzz

In the third year of this fantasy theme, Mateo and the team face the techno threat of Cyber Brain. With its army of imagination-sucking Cyber Brain Spiders, the misguided supercomputer is on a mission to remake the dream world as a colorless land of conformity. Naturally, it falls to Mateo, Izzie, Cooper, and the other dream chasers to save the day (and night).

Z-Blob badge worn on new jacket

Alternative face has a determined look

New-look red boots with zigzag trim

Mateo Our hero's familiar blue top and red boots get a subtle update in Mateo and the Z-Blob Action Race (71491).

Skull and circuitry printing on head

Open jacket reveals cyber skeleton

D-Shock Cyber Brain's most colorful crony flies into action against Mateo and Z-Blob in just one 2025 set.

Helmet style also worn by Cyberlings

Double zeroes on jacket

Zero This Cyber Brain general leads a squad of Cyberlings in Cooper's Tiger Mech & Zero's Hot Rod Car (71497).

Hat-and-hair piece worn over printed visor

Alternative face has visible eyes and a scowl

Cooper This dream chaser's latest look follows this year's trend of outfits with big, bold writing on them.

LEGO® CITY

Vehicle racing took LEGO City by storm this year. As well as a range of Formula 1 cars (aimed at younger builders than LEGO® Speed Champions sets), there were also six soapbox derby vehicles, racing for victory across three eye-catching sets. These included karts shaped like a bed, a hot dog, and a lavatory, all driven by minifigures in suitably themed attire.

Plunger accessory introduced in 2013

Hard hats worn by minifigures since 1978

Toilet logo on overalls

RACE YOU TO THE U-BEND!

Fast-food franchise uniform with smiley badge and name tag

Helmet makes clear this is no ordinary restaurant worker

Toilet Racer Win or lose? Take a spin around the block(age) with this super-speedy plumber, and you'll find out in a flush.

Hot Dog Racer This driver is literally on a roll as she redefines fast food in a hot-dog-shaped racing kart.

Alternative face has glasses and no swelling

Clothes show signs of rough handling by captors

Alternative face is wide awake and smiling

Torso print shared with another unnamed witch from 2024

Captured Harry Quick-thinking Hermione uses a Stinging Hex to give Harry this swollen-faced disguise in Malfoy Manor (76453).

Sleeping Witch This snoozing sorcerer rides the triple-decker Knight Bus (76446) alongside Harry and Padfoot (Sirius Black in dog form).

LEGO® HARRY POTTER™

The LEGO Wizarding World continued to surprise in 2025, and not just in minifigure scale. All of Diagon Alley was recreated in magical microscale, while a brick-built Hagrid model stood as tall as four minifigures, despite being comfortably seated! More traditional sets saw minifigure Harry visit Malfoy Manor (76453) and meet new passengers on board the iconic Knight Bus (76446).

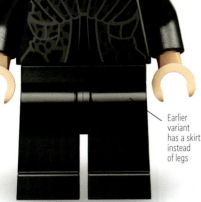

Neutral face can be swapped for a snarl

Earlier variant has a skirt instead of legs

Narcissa Malfoy The first Narcissa minifigure since 2011 shares Malfoy Manor with her husband, Lucius; son, Draco; and sister Bellatrix Lestrange.

DIAGON ALLEY

Twelve microfigures populated this year's Diagon Alley Wizarding Shops (76444). The detailed build could be displayed as one long row of stores or folded to make an enclosed alleyway with Gringotts Bank at its far end.

Golden printing on necktie and lapels

Each microfigure is a single, printed piece

Tailor's pinking shears

Tape measure also worn by minifigure version

Decorative charm worn as a necklace

Same zip-up cardigan as 2023 minifigure

Garrick Ollivander The wand shop owner is just as elegantly dressed in microfigure form as any of his four minifigures.

Madam Malkin This purveyor of Robes For All Occasions wears a tape measure around her neck and dressmakers scissors on her belt.

Lavender Brown This Hogwarts student visited Diagon Alley in a 2023 minifigure set, and now her microfigure can do the same.

LEGO® MONKIE KID™

More myths and legends got a modern twist in the sixth year of LEGO Monkie Kid. In Mythical Creature Qilin (80066), Monkie Kid, Mei, and Sandy rode a giant, brick-built dragon-horse into battle against a Celestial Warrior. Then, in Erlang's Celestial Mech (80065), MK, Monkey King, and Mr. Tang faced off against lead warrior the Celestial General—and a Celestial Dog!

New helmet with decorative eyes and nose

Red plume denotes rank

Same helmet as Celestial Warrior, but in gold

Same torso print as Celestial General

Celestial Warrior The white-clad Guards of the Celestial Court may help or hinder mortals, depending on their heavenly orders.

Celestial General When she isn't giving orders, this high-ranking warrior takes them directly from truth-seeing Celestial, Erlang Shen.

LEGO® SONIC THE HEDGEHOG™

There was no let-up for LEGO Sonic in the third year of this fast-paced theme. In Sonic's Campfire Clash (77001), a laid-back camping scene was interrupted by robots, while in Super Shadow vs. Biolizard (77003), our hero helped his arch-rival battle a mighty monster. In Cyclone vs. Metal Sonic (77002), the Blue Blur even got a Badnik minifigure doppelganger!

Fusion engine print on torso

Same head mold as standard Shadow, but in yellow

Screws molded into cheeks

Silver screw detail on arms

Gold rings on wrists and ankles sustain Super state

Metal Sonic This blue-steel Badnik was built by Dr. Eggman to match the real Sonic in strength, speed, and agility.

Super Shadow Both Sonic and Shadow the Hedgehog got yellow, powered-up Super variants in Super Shadow vs. Biolizard (77003).

Cactus Knight This prickly player is well-dressed to defend their home against Illagers, even without their diamond armor.

T-shaped visor print on "helmet" head piece

Torso print is hidden when diamond armor is worn

Classic LEGO Minecraft helmet

Pixelated pockets

Safari Ranger Why is this LEGO Minecraft minifigure smiling? Because they've just made friends with the theme's first armadillo mobs.

Bangs and face printed on red Minecraft head piece

Arm molded in two colors to make a gauntlet

Parrot Handler This bird-lover's hair is the perfect match for one of two macaw-shaped sanctuaries in The Parrot Houses (21282).

LEGO® MINECRAFT®

The crafting world was bigger than ever in 2025, thanks to the release of *A Minecraft Movie*. And as the LEGO Minecraft world expanded alongside the film, there were builds for long-time fans and newcomers alike. As ever, the sets included eye-catching new player skin minifigures, characterful brick-built animal mobs, and remarkable buildings that captured the game's diverse biome environments.

LEGO SPEED CHAMPIONS

Lots of this year's LEGO sets had a Formula 1 flavor, with LEGO City, LEGO Icons, LEGO DUPLO, and LEGO® Technic all featuring branded motor-racing builds. Leading the pack was LEGO Speed Champions, which dedicated its entire 2025 range to F1 cars. Every team was represented, for a total of 10 cars, all driven by minifigures in new racing helmets.

New helmet has aerodynamic fin at rear

Torso also worn by a 2025 LEGO City driver

BWT Alpine F1 Driver This racer's garb perfectly matches the colors of her BWT Alpine F1 Team A524 Race Car (77248).

Williams F1 Driver The woman at the wheel of the Williams Racing FW46 F1 Race Car (77249) wears classic white racing overalls.

New visors come in a range of colors

Williams logo printed on torso and helmet

LEGO® DC SUPER HEROES

Some of DC's most iconic pairings returned in 2025, as Superman tackled Lex Luthor, Batman took on the Joker, and Two-Face wrestled with ... himself! Superman Mech vs. Lex Luthor (76302) was inspired by decades of comics starring the Man of Steel, while Batman Tumbler vs. Two-Face & The Joker (76303) harked back to the 2005–2012 *Dark Knight* trilogy of movies.

Same smirking face as 2021 variant

Exclusive half-hair piece

Smart suit print is an update of 2014 variant

Unique torso with one black arm

The Joker The *Dark Knight* Joker first appeared in a 2014 set, but his 2025 variant is the most menacing yet.

Two-Face The sixth Two-Face minifigure is the first to be based on the character's look in the *Dark Knight* series.

LEGO ICONS

The theme for advanced builders entered its sixth year in typically diverse style. Leonardo da Vinci's Flying Machine (10363) was based on the Renaissance master's 15th-century plans for an ornithopter and came with an exclusive Leonardo minifigure. Tudor Corner (10350), meanwhile, was the 20th entry in the Modular Buildings collection and included eight minifigures in a typically English street scene.

Printed tile based on Leonardo's drawings and mirrored writing

Unique head has printed beard behind molded one

Classic top hat piece on plain white head

Tuxedo first worn by LEGO® Batman's butler, Alfred

Knee-length coat print on legs and torso

Leonardo da Vinci This polymath takes pride of place at the front of the display stand for his visionary flying machine.

Shop Window Dummy This minifigure is a mannequin in the Tudor Corner haberdasher's, but could also be its resident ghost.

Index

A

actors 87, 91, 95, 171
Admirals 52, 61, 142, 195, 219
  Vice Admirals 219, 272
Advanced Models 127, 153, 163
advent calendars 73, 114, 115, 132, 145, 150, 153, 162, 192, 234, 258, 261, 264, 275, 285
Adventure Time 208
Adventurers 70, 79, 83, 87, 91, 103, 158
Agents 133, 144
Airport 35, 51, 55, 100, 115
  DUPLO Airport 55
Alice in Wonderland 204
Alien Conquest 160
Alien Defense Unit 160
aliens 9, 14, 37, 67, 71, 78, 90, 112, 113, 126, 143, 151, 155, 159, 160, 180, 190, 200, 204, 208, 233, 235, 249, 252, 282, 288, 296
Alpha Team 92, 98, 106, 133
androids 60, 67, 106, 160, 175, 193, 282
The Angry Birds Movie 208
Animal Crossing 15, 282, 283, 295
anniversaries, LEGO 14, 58, 94, 126, 130, 132, 137, 142, 155, 223, 232, 234, 241, 245, 248, 251, 270, 271, 272, 284, 287, 293, 297
Ant-Man 200, 207
  Ant-Man and The Wasp 227
AppBricks 195
Aqua Raiders 126
Aquaman 182, 217
  Aquaman: Rage of Atlantis 225
Aquanauts 58, 66
Aquaraiders 66
Aquasharks 58, 66
Aquazone 58, 66, 71
Arctic 85, 182, 191, 222, 274

Arctic Action 37
artists 175, 230
astronauts 19, 20, 33, 34, 37, 40, 48, 51, 58, 67, 76, 105, 126, 135, 137, 143, 153, 163, 190, 199, 205, 229, 230, 245, 274, 279, 288, 294
Atlantis 15, 140, 148, 151, 161, 171, 182
Augmented Reality 228, 242
Avatar 15, 259, 279
Avatar: The Last Airbender 122
Avengers 168, 169, 193, 218, 245, 273, 297
  Avengers: Age of Ultron 200
  Avengers Assemble (TV) 193, 207
  Avengers: Endgame 233, 260
  Avengers: Infinity War 227

B

babies 15, 21, 68, 138, 175, 203, 218, 222, 240, 244, 251, 267, 274
  DUPLO 79
Baby 59
bandits 53, 61, 72, 78
bank workers 62, 68, 96, 275
baseball players 77
Basic 27, 37
basketball players 102
Batman 120–21, 127, 139, 157, 166, 182, 190, 198, 208, 217, 225, 277, 299
  Batman 234
  Batman Returns 277
  Batman: The Animated Series 292
  Batman v Superman: Dawn of Justice 208
  DIMENSIONS 194
  The Batman 266
  The Dark Knight 139, 299
  THE LEGO BATMAN MOVIE 212–13, 215, 224
The Beatles 204
Beetlejuice 215
BELVILLE 13, 57, 85
The Big Bang Theory 199
BIONICLE 88, 118, 127
Black Panther 207

Black Panther 227
  Black Panther: Wakanda Forever 260
blacksmiths 33, 98, 256, 278
Blacktron 40, 45, 235, 294
  Blacktron II 51, 52, 287
Blizzard Entertainment 231
Bluecoats 195, 277
boat crew 29, 41, 69, 77, 101, 131, 135, 169
bounty hunters 86, 95, 104, 124, 155, 173, 184, 235, 261, 282
boxers 139, 171, 205
Brand Store minifigures 163, 183
brides 153, 158
BTS 278
Bugatti 217
Building Figures 7, 12

C

camera operators 68, 87, 91, 95, 125
Captain America 169, 253
  Captain America: Civil War 207
  Captain America: Brave New World 291
Captain Marvel 207, 233
Cargo 28, 30, 33, 41, 135
  cargo workers 19, 41, 58, 59, 73, 222
carol singers 145
Castle 49, 51, 53, 54, 59, 61, 66, 72, 84, 98, 109, 118, 123, 129, 132, 145, 150, 163, 265
Castle (LEGOLAND) 19, 20, 31, 32–33, 34, 37, 41, 43, 45
cavalry 19, 38, 62, 129
cave people 148, 159
  DUPLO 69, 79
cheerleaders 148, 197
chefs 21, 31, 48, 115, 195, 203, 228, 242, 266
chess sets and pieces 89, 118, 121, 129, 132, 141, 195, 248
Chinese New Year 231, 247
A Christmas Carol 247
circus 65, 148
  DUPLO 43
City 114–15, 122, 131, 135, 144, 145, 153, 169, 175, 185, 191, 199, 203, 219, 222, 230, 239, 250, 258, 274, 288, 297
City Adventures 230, 239, 250
City Center 76, 77, 85
CLIKITS 115
clone troopers 94, 116, 130, 138, 139, 284, 297
clowns 148, 242, 250
  DUPLO 43
Coast Guard 58, 76, 77, 101, 135, 219
coast guards 18, 45, 48, 51
Comic-Con 121, 157, 166, 168, 173, 190, 193, 198
community workers 35
commuters 51, 101, 239
conquistadors 61, 171
Construction 100, 115, 199
construction workers 21, 25, 56, 122, 131, 163, 187
  DUPLO 79
cowboys 30, 62
crane operators 59, 115, 222
Creator 263

Creator Expert 189, 223, 255
crooks 9, 55, 72, 99, 100, 114, 135, 174, 185, 199, 222, 249
  DUPLO 51
CUUSOO 173, 190
Cyber Strikers 72
CyberSlam 70
cyclists 85, 235

D

Dark Forest 61
DC Super Hero Girls 217
DC Super Heroes 190, 198, 208, 217, 225, 234, 241, 266, 277, 292, 299
DesignByMe 137
Despicable Me 292
DFB Series (Deutsche Fussball-Bund) 205
Digital Designer 137
DIMENSIONS 194, 208, 215, 220, 221, 269
DINO 167, 196
  DUPLO 69
Dino Attack 117
Dino Island 83
disco fans 149, 197, 212, 257
Discovery 105
Disney 62, 148, 155
  collectible Minifigures 204, 233
  Disney 100 anniversary 270, 271
  Disney Pixar 155, 218, 262
Disney (theme) 185, 244, 253, 268, 270, 271, 285, 286, 296
Disney Princess 193
divers (minifigures) 98, 115, 126, 133, 199, 239
  DUPLO 33
Divers (subtheme) 68, 69
Doctor Octopus 168
Doctor Strange 207
Doctor Who 194, 199
doctors 24, 27, 29, 90, 115, 122, 222, 234
  DUPLO 57
Dodge 235
dogs 105, 203, 224, 228, 229, 250, 287
Dragon Kingdom 150
Dragon Masters 54, 61
DreamWorks 243, 277
DREAMZzz 15, 268, 289, 294, 297
drivers 21, 24, 25, 28, 35, 36, 41, 42, 45, 53, 57, 58, 63, 68, 77, 100, 105, 125, 130, 135, 136, 137, 144, 154, 196, 209, 217, 223, 235, 238, 245, 247, 255, 267, 279, 292, 297, 299
  DUPLO 107
droids 56, 60, 113, 137
  Star Wars 75, 95, 116, 124, 130, 137, 138, 162, 173, 192, 200, 206, 232, 261, 272, 284, 297
Drome Racers 99
Dune 282, 290
Dungeons & Dragons 15, 282, 286
DUPLO 13, 19, 20, 29, 31, 33, 37, 43, 45, 49, 51, 53, 55, 57, 63, 69, 74, 79, 107, 144, 256, 271, 282, 297, 299
Duracell 102
dwarves 15, 121, 132, 159, 180, 277, 285

WHY IS AN INDEX LIKE A TELESCOPE?

E

Education sets 48, 121, 153, 163
Egyptians 64, 113, 159, 231, 271
  Pharaoh's Quest 156, 158, 206
elves (minifigures) 38, 96, 97, 159, 164, 180, 181, 189, 191, 194, 216, 262, 286
Elves (theme) 15, 196, 216
Encanto 253
engineers 217, 261, 265
  DUPLO 63
E.T. 202, 208
Euro 2016 soccer 205
Ewoks 86, 142
exclusive sets 164, 245, 256, 265, 290
EXO-FORCE 14, 64, 65, 120, 125, 126, 128, 139
Explore 105
explorers
  Antarctic 290
  Arctic 38, 85, 186, 222, 274
  DUPLO 57
  jungle 167, 219, 288
  ocean 33, 69, 199, 239
  space 40, 48, 52, 76, 90, 126, 143, 145, 153, 160
Extreme Team 73
Exxon workers 21, 25

F

FABULAND 12, 20, 21, 27, 29, 186
Factory 114, 127, 137
fan builders 190, 204
Fan Weekends 158
Fantastic Beasts and Where to Find Them 220–21
Fantastic Beasts: The Crimes of Grindelwald 220–21
Fantasy Era 129, 150, 274
Farm 144
  DUPLO 20, 31
farmers 8, 144, 160, 258
Ferrari 106, 107, 125, 128, 196, 217, 223, 279
FIFA World Cup 98
film crews 87
finger puppets 27
Fire 51, 55, 56, 68, 77, 114, 185
firefighters 7, 8, 18, 27, 30, 38, 41, 48, 51, 57, 76, 114, 131, 135, 169, 185, 203, 223, 250, 253, 288
  DUPLO 29, 37
fishermen 228
  DUPLO 33
flight attendants 57
the Flintstones 231
Ford 209, 217, 220, 223
Forest Police 169
Foresters 38, 40, 41, 43, 45, 48, 49, 61, 145, 265
Formula 1 15, 107, 217, 297, 299
Fortnite 282
4+ Spider-Man 111
Freemakers 206
Friends (theme) 14, 15, 170, 181, 275, 297
Friends (TV) 228, 231
Fright Knights 66
Frozen 233
Futuron 38, 40, 42, 45, 48, 294

G

Gabby's Dollhouse 277
Galaxy Squad 176, 180, 188
Games (theme) 15, 140, 145,
  HEROICA 158
games
  board games 15, 67, 103, 161
  chess 89, 118, 121, 129, 132, 141, 195, 248
  DIMENSIONS 194, 208, 215, 269
  Minifigures Online 189
  Tic Tac Toe 129
  video games 12, 15, 68, 73, 99, 192, 206, 232, 245, 265, 284
gear 174–75
Ghostbusters 209
ghosts 13, 49, 67, 89, 91, 201, 207, 209, 220, 224, 228, 242, 275, 289, 299
gingerbread people 113, 231
gladiators 8, 260, 290
glow-in-the-dark 13, 67, 89, 108, 126, 133, 142, 172, 191, 248,
goblins 96, 158, 216, 275
gold minifigures 14, 126, 131, 161, 178, 183, 248, 251, 275
The Goonies 215
Gravity Games 99, 102, 111
grooms 153, 158
ground crew 35, 73, 76
Guardians of the Galaxy 193, 218, 227, 273
  Guardians of the Galaxy 193
  Guardians of the Galaxy Vol. 2 218
  Guardians of the Galaxy Vol. 3 273
guards 25, 32, 33, 34, 39, 43, 68, 93, 124, 180, 226, 266, 284

H

hair 64–65
harbor workers 175
Harry Potter 13, 14, 88–89, 96–97, 108, 126, 215, 220–21, 234, 240, 248, 264, 275, 280, 289, 298
  Harry Potter and the Chamber of Secrets 94, 96
  Harry Potter and the Deathly Hallows 161, 264
  Harry Potter and the Goblet of Fire 114, 119
  Harry Potter and the Half-Blood Prince 152
  Harry Potter and the Order of the Phoenix 128
  Harry Potter and the Prisoner of Azkaban 108, 240
  Harry Potter and the Sorcerer's Stone 88, 89, 96, 248
  Wizarding World 220–21, 234, 240, 298
hats 9, 19, 38–39
heads 112–13
helicopter pilots 27, 33, 35, 37, 48, 69, 73, 85, 92, 100, 135, 239
Hero Factory 188, 190
HEROICA 158
Hidden Side 14, 38, 113, 228, 242
The Hobbit 164, 165, 180, 191
  An Unexpected Journey 180
  The Battle of the Five Armies 191
Hobbits 164, 180, 181, 277

Hockey (subtheme) 111
hockey players 111, 159, 175
Home Alone 256
Homemaker 21
Horizon Forbidden West video game 265
horse riders 36, 38, 65, 171
horses 19, 20, 32, 34, 144, 187, 283
Hospital 115
  DUPLO 57
Hydronauts 70, 71

I

Ice Planet 2002 55, 287
ice skaters 65, 159
Icons 15, 248, 255, 260, 265, 277, 290, 297, 299
Ideas 173, 188, 190, 209, 217, 231, 247, 256, 259, 269, 278, 286
Illumination 242, 257, 292
Imperial Armada 52, 61
Imperial Guard 52, 141
Imperial Soldiers 52
The Incredibles 2 218, 253
Indiana Jones 132, 134, 142, 268, 271
  Indiana Jones and the Dial of Destiny 271
  Indiana Jones and the Kingdom of the Crystal Skull 134
  Indiana Jones and the Last Crusade 134, 271
  Indiana Jones and the Raiders of the Lost Ark 134, 271
  Indiana Jones and the Temple of Doom 134, 142
Insectoids 70
Inside Out 2 285
Iron Man 169, 177, 218, 233
Islanders 56, 61
Island Xtreme Stunts 94, 99

J

Jack Stone 73, 88, 90
Jaguar 247

Jaws 282, 286
Jedi 74, 75, 94, 116, 124, 130, 138, 155, 184, 185, 192, 200, 219, 226, 244, 261, 272, 284, 285, 297
jesters 38, 132, 139, 150, 157, 163, 167, 202, 216
Journey to the West 238
Jungle 74, 79
Jungle Explorers 219, 288
Jurassic Park 223, 267
  The Lost World: Jurassic Park 87
Jurassic World 196, 234, 257, 267, 278, 293
  Jurassic Park III 91, 196
  Jurassic World: Camp Cretaceous 257, 293
  Jurassic World: Chaos Theory 293
  Jurassic World Dominion 267
  Jurassic World: Fallen Kingdom 223
  Jurassic World: Legend of Isla Nublar 234
Justice League 190, 198, 212, 217, 224, 225

K

K-pop 278
kickboxers 205
Kingdoms 145, 148, 150, 163
kings 39, 59, 65, 84, 109, 117, 118, 121, 123, 129, 145, 150, 161, 164, 171, 176, 177, 181, 191, 195, 243, 260, 268, 269, 271
knights 9, 19, 20, 31, 32, 38, 39, 49, 53, 54, 59, 84, 89, 145, 153
  Black Falcons 32, 34, 36, 41, 256
  Black Knights 43, 49
  Crown Knights 112, 129
  Dragon Knights 150, 163
  Fright Knights 66
  Lion Knights 32, 33, 34, 36, 41, 51, 150, 163, 265
  Knights' Kingdom 84, 109, 118, 123
  Minecraft knights 246, 275
  NEXO Knights 15, 202–203, 216, 225, 246
  Shadow Knights 109
Knudsen, Jens Nygård 6

THEY'RE BOTH GOOD FOR LOOKING UP!

L

Lamborghini 105, 247
large-scale buildable minifigures 280
Launch Command 58, 76
lawmen 62
The Legend of Zelda 283
Legends of Chima 14, 113, 176–77, 186, 190, 201
LEGO *Batman: The Visual Dictionary* 166
THE LEGO BATMAN MOVIE 15, 205, 212–13, 215, 224
LEGO Championship Challenge 83, 98
LEGO Club 40
LEGO.com 60, 98, 173, 190, 224, 247, 255, 256, 261, 265, 290
The LEGO Group 24, 74, 114, 126, 131, 156, 173, 184, 185, 204, 206, 219, 220, 232, 258, 282
LEGO *Harry Potter: Building the Magical World* 161
LEGO House 219
LEGO *Idea Book* 24
LEGO *Island* video game 12, 68, 99
  LEGO *Island 2* video game 99
LEGO *Loco* video game 73
LEGO *Minifigures Character Encyclopedia* 178
LEGO *Minifigure: A Visual History* 245, 294
THE LEGO MOVIE 14, 186–87, 189
THE LEGO MOVIE 2 14, 229
THE LEGO NINJAGO MOVIE 214–15
LEGO offices 10
LEGO *Star Wars Character Encyclopedia* 162
LEGO *Star Wars Visual Dictionary* 142
LEGOLAND (theme) 13, 18–21, 24–37, 42
LEGOLAND (theme parks) 74, 83, 115
life guards 73, 131, 149, 189
Life on Mars 88, 90, 126
Light and Sound 36
Lightyear 262
Lilo & Stitch 286, 296
Lion Kingdom 150
Lion Knights 32, 33, 34, 37, 41, 43, 51, 163, 265
The Little Mermaid 193, 204
Little Robots 105
Looney Tunes 249
The Lone Ranger 62, 176
The Lord of the Rings 14, 15, 164–65, 180, 181, 194, 277, 290
Lucasfilm 185, 232

M

M:Tron 48, 51, 214, 287
Mærsk workers 25, 58, 163
maidens 37, 216
Mars Mission 14, 117, 126
martial artists 103, 149, 188, 205, 252
Martians 90
Marvel's Avengers video game 245
Marvel Studios 248, 252, 253, 273
Marvel Super Heroes 110–11, 164, 168–69, 177, 193, 200, 207, 218, 227, 233, 245, 252, 260, 273, 291, 296
McDonald's workers 77
McLaren 196, 217, 279
mechanics 21, 33, 35, 42, 73, 77, 78, 92, 106, 143, 230, 235, 239, 274

DUPLO 107
medics 24, 27, 29, 57, 85, 90, 115, 122, 140, 222
Mercedes-Benz 217
mermaids and mermen 14, 171, 193, 204
Mickey Mouse 204, 253, 270, 286
microfigures 15, 161, 200, 221, 298
  Mighty Micros 207, 208, 217, 218, 225, 227
"midfigs" 90
Mime 38, 149
Minecraft 14, 186, 188, 201, 209, 230, 246, 257, 267, 275, 293, 299
  A Minecraft Movie 299
miners 58, 71, 78, 140
mini dolls 9, 14, 15, 170, 181, 193, 196, 216, 217, 229, 277, 283, 285, 297
minifigures
  based on real people 14, 83, 107, 125, 128, 187, 204, 205, 217, 256, 259, 265, 270, 273, 278, 290, 299
  characteristics 8–9
  collectible 10, 15, 148–49, 159, 167, 170–71, 178–79, 186, 187, 189, 197, 204, 205, 210–11, 213, 215, 216, 224, 225, 229, 233, 235, 240, 241, 249, 253, 262, 270, 273, 274, 286, 287, 294
  creation of 10–11
  origins 6–7
  promotional 25, 45, 68, 69, 73, 77, 85, 87, 91, 96, 99, 102, 107, 127, 131, 154, 155, 157, 162, 168, 190, 223
  seasonal 39, 73, 145, 153, 231, 247, 254, 279
  Vintage Minifigure Collection 73, 84, 132, 135, 141, 143, 145
Minifigures Online game 189
Minions 238, 242, 257, 292
  Minions: The Rise of Gru 242, 257
Mission Deep Freeze 106
Mission Deep Sea 71, 94, 98
Moana 270
Modular Buildings 126, 127, 153, 163, 223, 276, 299
Monkie Kid 14, 238, 251, 266, 276, 287, 298
Monster Fighters 14, 148, 164, 172, 190, 291
monsters 9, 78, 95, 113, 140, 172, 195, 197, 198, 215, 216, 228, 229, 254, 274, 294
  HEROICA 158
motorcycle riders 30, 33, 35, 36, 42, 114, 131, 222, 227, 250, 258
  DUPLO 49
Mountain Police 222
mummies 70, 95, 172, 235, 271, 273
The Muppets 263
mythological minifigures 14, 189, 190, 205, 287

N

NASA 14, 48, 99, 105, 217, 258
NBA Basketball 102
Never-Realm 235
NEXO Knights 15, 202–203, 216, 225, 246
Nickelodeon 122, 179, 191
The Nightmare Before Christmas 233
Ninja (subtheme) 70, 72, 84, 145
Ninjago 14, 38, 64, 84, 112, 113, 140, 156–57, 165, 176, 183, 193, 194, 201, 209, 214, 215, 227, 235, 238, 243, 251, 266, 276

THE LEGO NINJAGO MOVIE 15, 214–15
  Minecraft 246
  Ninjago: Dragons Rising 266, 276, 291, 295
nonminifigures 9
nurses 18

O

Ocean Explorers 239
Octan workers 115, 135
office workers 115
Outback 66, 68
outlaws 43, 49, 53, 61, 62, 143, 268, 271
Overwatch 231

P

Paradisa 52, 53, 59, 63, 69, 113
paramedics 57, 113, 115
passengers 18, 30, 37, 63, 101, 109, 174, 183
peasants 32, 43
Peppa Pig 282
pharaohs 70
  Pharaoh's Quest 156, 158, 206
Phoenix Tribe 190
photographers 29, 103, 125, 167, 205, 222, 290
pilots 35, 37, 63, 68, 69, 70, 76, 85, 90, 91, 101, 109, 115, 124, 131, 230, 239, 256
  boat 91, 101, 169, 219
  DUPLO 29, 55
  helicopter 27, 33, 35, 37, 48, 69, 73, 85, 92, 100, 135, 239
  Star Wars 75, 93, 116, 124, 155, 184, 219, 232, 285, 297
  stunt 55, 203
pirates (minifigures) 44, 50, 52, 56, 61, 141, 195, 247, 277, 281
  Minecraft 230, 293
Pirates (theme) 12, 44, 50, 52, 56, 59, 61, 84, 112, 140, 141, 194, 195, 247
Pirates of the Caribbean 163, 212, 218
  The Curse of the Black Pearl 163
  Dead Man's Chest 163
  Dead Men Tell No Tales 212, 218
  On Stranger Tides 163
Playhouse 20
podracers 75
Police 56, 100, 114, 185, 239, 274
police officers 18, 21, 25, 26, 55, 68, 100, 101, 114, 131, 175, 187, 203, 225, 230, 239
  DUPLO 51
  Forest Police 169
  Mountain Police 222
  Sky Police 230, 288
  Space Police 15, 44, 45, 52, 56, 140, 143
  Swamp Police 199
pop stars 149, 204, 223, 278, 282, 290
Porsche 196, 209, 223, 279
Post Office 28, 135
post office workers 28, 135, 239
power core 125
Power Miners 140
Power Racers 114
The Powerpuff Girls 215, 221

PRIMO 59
Prince of Persia 148, 180
princes 20, 122, 150, 251
The Princess and the Frog 270
princesses 20, 64, 84, 86, 107, 129, 131, 150, 193, 202, 208, 226, 227, 232, 238, 243, 270, 272
prisoners 55
  DUPLO 51

Q

queens 9, 38, 64, 71, 74, 84, 89, 113, 118, 121, 129, 145, 150, 159, 163, 173, 195, 205, 239, 243, 265, 285
Queer Eye 255
Quicky the bunny 91

R

Race 55, 57, 68, 85, 99
  DUPLO 49
racecar drivers 15, 24, 63, 77, 107, 125, 128, 299
Racers 85, 99, 105, 107, 125, 128, 136
railway workers 30, 50, 56, 63, 175, 183, 222
reporters 70, 103, 160
Res-Q 73, 90
Rescue 55, 57, 73
Roboforce 66, 67
robots 14, 34, 37, 40, 45, 56, 60, 67, 71, 92, 99, 105, 106, 112, 113, 137, 170, 171, 180, 187, 188, 242, 262, 266, 271, 287, 288, 289, 291
Rock Monsters 140
Rock Raiders 74, 78, 87, 140
roller skaters 178, 179, 197
Romans 38, 64, 170, 178, 216
Royal Guard 39, 93

S

Safari 57
sailors 33, 39, 41, 79, 159, 191, 262
  DUPLO 19
Salvage Crew 151
samurai 72, 165, 209, 215, 235, 295
Santa Claus 38, 73, 145, 153, 162, 171, 189, 192
SCALA 12, 20, 68, 78, 249
scientists 58, 76, 135, 140, 151, 160, 190, 195, 199, 203, 251, 274
Scooby-Doo 198
security guards 76, 86, 95, 124, 196
Seinfeld 256
Serpentine tribes 165, 235
service station staff and patrons 18, 27, 29, 31, 115, 131
Sesame Street 247
Shang-Chi and the Legend of the Ten Rings 252
Shark Army 214
Shell employee 77
SHIELD 200
shoretroopers 206
The Simpsons 14, 189, 194, 197
Sith 74, 75, 86, 116, 130, 138, 139, 173, 185, 192, 244, 284, 285
skateboarders 99, 102, 183, 239
Skeleton Army 98, 129, 157

skeletons 9, 12, 14, 59, 67, 92, 106, 118, 119, 129, 157, 163, 181, 192, 197, 265
 Minecraft 188, 230
skiers 37, 149, 171
Sky Pirates 91, 209
Sky Police 230, 288
Sleeping Beauty 204, 270
snowboarders 102, 159
Soccer 73, 82–83, 93, 98, 102, 205
Sonic the Hedgehog 208, 259, 269, 293, 298
Space 48, 50, 51, 52, 55, 56, 58, 60, 66, 67, 70, 71, 76, 90, 99, 113, 126, 135, 143, 160, 180, 186, 245, 274, 279, 287, 294
 (LEGOLAND) 13, 19, 20, 26, 28, 30, 33, 34, 36, 37, 38, 40, 45
Space Explorers 288
Space Police 15, 44, 45
 Space Police II 52, 56
 Space Police III 140, 143
Space Port 76, 85, 199
Spartan warriors 149
Speech Bubbles Minifigure 158
Speed Champions 15, 194, 196, 209, 217, 223, 235, 247, 255, 267, 279, 292, 299
speedboat driver 36, 53, 91, 101, 135
Spider-Man 13, 94, 95, 105, 110–11, 168, 200, 207, 227, 233, 245, 260, 273
 Spider-Man 105
 Spider-Man 2 106, 110
 Spider-Man: Across the Spider-Verse 296
 Spider-Man: Far From Home 233
 Spider-Man: Homecoming 218
 Spider-Man: No Way Home 252, 273
 Spidey and his Amazing Friends 260, 291, 296
 Ultimate Spider-Man 168, 200
Spider-Man 4+ 111
Spielberg, Steven 87, 91, 286
spies 56, 92, 133
SpongeBob SquarePants 123, 156
Sports 82, 100, 102, 111, 120, 268
Spyrius 55, 56, 113
stable hands 36, 53
Star Wars 9, 13, 14, 74–75, 82, 86, 88, 93, 94, 100, 104, 106, 107, 114, 116, 124, 126, 130–31, 132, 138–39, 140, 142, 155, 162, 173, 184, 192, 194, 200, 206, 212, 226, 232, 244, 254, 261, 272, 282, 284–85, 297
 Ahsoka 272
 Andor 261
 The Book of Boba Fett 261
 The Clone Wars 132, 138, 140, 254, 261, 272, 297
 LEGO *Star Wars: The Freemaker Adventures* 206
 LEGO *Star Wars: The Yoda Chronicles* 184–85
 The Mandalorian 232, 244, 254, 261, 272
 Obi-Wan Kenobi 261
 Rogue One: A Star Wars Story 206
 Solo: A Star Wars Story 226
 Star Wars: The Bad Batch 254, 261
 Star Wars Battlefront video game 206, 232
 Star Wars: Episode I *The Phantom Menace* 74, 93, 130
 Star Wars: Episode II *Attack of the Clones* 94, 261

Star Wars: Episode III *Revenge of the Sith* 114, 116, 297
 Star Wars: Episode IV *A New Hope* 93, 142, 272
 Star Wars: Episode V *The Empire Strikes Back* 93, 107, 130, 155
 Star Wars: Episode VI *Return of the Jedi* 93, 130, 232, 272
 Star Wars: Episode VII *The Force Awakens* 194, 200, 219, 232
 Star Wars: Episode VIII *The Last Jedi* 212, 219, 226
 Star Wars: Episode IX *The Rise of Skywalker* 228, 232, 244
 Star Wars: Knights of the Old Republic video game 192, 284
 Star Wars: The Padawan Menace 162
 Star Wars Rebels 192, 219, 254, 272
 Star Wars Resistance 232
 Star Wars: Skeleton Crew 284
 Star Wars: Young Jedi Adventures 272, 285
statues 24, 25, 89, 143, 153, 161, 170, 254, 275, 280
Steamboat Willie 231, 270
Stone Army 176, 183, 216
stormtroopers 75, 93, 130, 138, 142, 173, 200
Stranger Things 228, 229
Studios 73, 78, 87, 88, 91, 95, 102, 105, 196
stunt performers 56, 87, 91, 99, 188, 203, 233, 250, 263
stunt sticks 99, 102
Stuntz 248, 250, 258
Supergirl 198, 217, 225, 241
 Supergirl 241
Super Heroes *see* Batman; DC Super Heroes; Marvel Super Heroes; Spider-Man, etc.
Super Mario 14, 246
Superman 157, 166, 182, 208, 217
 Batman v Superman: Dawn of Justice 208
 Man of Steel 182, 208
surgeons 27, 170
Swamp Police 199
swimmers 45, 53
System 21, 34, 45, 58, 88, 107, 144
Szeto, Kevin 204

T
Table Football 15, 259
taxi driver 21
teachers 89, 108, 161, 181, 228, 269
Team GB 171
Team X-Treme 154
Tech Monsters 225
Technic 12, 36, 37, 70, 72, 86, 107, 121, 280, 299
Teen Titans 215, 241
Teenage Mutant Ninja Turtles 14, 176, 179, 191
tennis players 159
Thor: Ragnarok 218
tigers 219
Time Cruisers 60, 66, 67
time teaching clock 91
Time Twisters 66, 67
Tiny Turbos 114
Town 48, 51, 53, 55, 57, 58, 63, 68–69, 73, 76–77, 85, 91, 100, 114

Town (LEGOLAND) 18–19, 21, 24–25, 26–27, 28–29, 30–31, 33, 35, 36, 41, 42, 45
Town Jr. 68, 77
Toy Story 15, 148, 155, 204
 Toy Story 4 233
Train 30, 50, 56, 63, 122, 245
train workers 19, 30, 50, 56, 63, 73, 122, 183, 245, 258, 278
 DUPLO 31, 63
treasure hunters 69
trolls 15, 96, 132, 145, 238, 274, 289
Trolls World Tour 243

U
UFO 66, 67
Ultra Agents 186, 188, 195, 291
Unikitty 186
Unitron 55, 56, 58, 67
Up 270

V
vampires 65, 95, 149, 172, 252
Vermillion Warriors 215
Vestas workers 137
Vikings 117, 121, 263, 278
Vintage Minifigure Collection 73, 84, 132, 135, 141, 143, 145

W
waiters and waitresses 48, 179
WandaVision 253, 273
Wednesday 282, 283
werewolves 95, 108, 152, 158, 172, 264, 273

Western 60, 62
What If…? 252, 253, 273
Wicked 283
Williams racing team 105, 299
Winnie the Pooh (DUPLO) 74, 256
Winter Village 145, 189, 223, 231
Wish 271
witches 39, 66, 88, 132, 149, 152, 191, 194, 197, 204, 220, 264, 278, 283, 289, 298
The Wizard of Oz 194, 229
Wizarding World 15, 220–21, 234, 240, 298
wizards 39, 54, 88, 96, 129, 132, 150, 181, 194, 202, 203, 220, 248, 277, 283, 286
Wolfpack 45, 53, 294
wooden minifigures 280
Wookiees 86
World City 100–101, 109, 114
World Racers 148, 154
wrestlers 148, 167

X
X-Men 168, 193, 218
 X-Men: The Animated Series 291
 X-Men '97 273, 291
Xtreme Daredevils 154
Xtreme Stunts 94, 99

Z
zombies 148, 172, 197
 Minecraft 188, 201, 267
zookeepers 9
 DUPLO 49
Zotaxians 71

YOU STILL HAVE MUCH TO LEARN

ACKNOWLEDGMENTS

DK would like to thank the following people
and companies for their help in producing this book:

Editors of the previous editions: Ruth Amos, Pamela Afram, Tori Kosara, Julia March, Rosie Peet, and Nicole Reynolds; designers of the previous editions: Owen Bennett, Anna Formanek, and Lisa Sodeau; Julia March for proofreading and indexing; Randi K. Sørensen, Kristian Reimer Hauge, Martin Leighton Lindhardt, Jette Orduna, Anders Ditlev Pedersen, and Mimi Thi Tran at the LEGO Group; Ferrari S.p.A. for inclusion of their minifigures; MINI for inclusion of their minifigures; James Camplin, Giles Kemp, and Lucy Boughton for additional consultancy help; Joseph Pellegrino for additional photography; Huw Millington and the brickset.com community; and, lastly, all the wonderful LEGO® fans and collectors from across the world who lent us their minifigures to be photographed: Ann and Andy at minifigforlife.com, Jeremy Allen, Suzanne Allen, Carl Olof Andersson, Bozó Balázs, Daniel Cooley, Prentice Donnelly, Helen Floodgate, Lluís Gibert, Tim Goddard, Doug Harefeld, Ben Johnson, Wesley Keen, Giles Kemp, David Kirkham at minifigsandbricks.co.uk, Simon La Thangue, Richard Lawson, Mark Lee, Brandon Liu, Stefano Maini, David McClatchey, Neal McClatchey, Huw Millington, Jon Roke, Caroline Savage, Harry Sinclair, Joseph Venutolo, Sophie Walker, Adam White, and Mark Willis.